People, Care and Work in the Home

Introducing novel theoretical, empirical, and practical investigations with case studies from the UK, Europe, South America, and South East Asia, the book offers a novel global outlook on how contemporary homes are facing genuine challenges from operational, economic, spatial, social, and wellbeing perspectives.

The changing demographics of our modern society have inevitably impacted the dynamics and relationships within the home from being personal and private to that of multiple work relationships; domestic work, care for older people, or supporting people with special needs. Whilst the home is a concept universally experienced, permeating every aspect of our lives, it remains an entity whose influence on health and wellbeing is poorly understood.

This book brings together 17 different contributions from scholars, researchers, and practitioners from different disciplinary and professional backgrounds including three feature articles by leading figures, such as Lord Best and Baroness Hollins. The chapters are organised within three parts that look at the triangle of people + work + care in the home. At a time when homes are increasingly becoming local hubs for care and wellbeing, this volume is a critical and useful addition to current literature in the social sciences, humanities, economics, culture, care, and wellbeing in the domestic sphere.

Mohamed Gamal Abdelmonem is Professor of Architecture and Director of the Centre for Architecture, Urbanism and Global Heritage (CAUGH) at Nottingham Trent University. He is the 2014 recipient of the IASTE's Jeffrey Cook Award and author to numerous publications and books on the home's socio-spatial domains.

Antonio Argandoña is Emeritus Professor of Economics and Business Ethics, IESE Business School. He has taught in the Universities of Barcelona, Málaga, and Navarre. He has published numerous books and articles on macroeconomics, monetary economics, and the home and family issues, including, *The Home: Multidisciplinary Reflections* (2018).

Routledge Advances in Sociology

Magical Realist Sociologies of Belonging and Becoming
The Explorer
Rodanthi Tzanelli

Queer Campus Climate
An Ethnographic Fantasia
Benjamin Arnberg

Children in Social Movements
Rethinking Agency, Mobilization and Rights
Diane M. Rodgers

The Global Citizenship Nexus
Critical Studies
Edited by Debra D. Chapman, Tania Ruiz-Chapman and Peter Eglin

Europe In Love
Binational Couples and Cosmopolitan Society
Juan Díez Medrano

Neurodiversity Studies
A New Critical Paradigm
Edited by Hanna Bertilsdotter Rosqvist, Nick Chown and Anna Stenning

The Class Structure of Capitalist Societies
Volume 1: A Space of Bounded Variety
Will Atkinson

People, Care and Work in the Home
Edited by Mohamed Gamal Abdelmonem and Antonio Argandoña

For more information about this series, please visit: www.routledge.com/Routledge-Advances-in-Sociology/book-series/SE0511

People, Care and Work in the Home

Edited by
Mohamed Gamal Abdelmonem
and Antonio Argandoña

Routledge
Taylor & Francis Group
LONDON AND NEW YORK

First published 2020
by Routledge
2 Park Square, Milton Park, Abingdon, Oxon OX14 4RN

and by Routledge
52 Vanderbilt Avenue, New York, NY 10017

Routledge is an imprint of the Taylor & Francis Group, an informa business

British Library Cataloguing-in-Publication Data
A catalogue record for this book is available from the British Library

Library of Congress Cataloging-in-Publication Data
Names: Abdelmonem, M. Gamal, editor. | Argandoña Rámiz, Antonio, editor.
Title: People, care and work in the home / edited by Mohamed Gamal Abdelmonem and Antonio Argandoña.
Description: Milton Park, Abingdon, Oxon ; New York, NY : Routledge, 2020. | Series: Routledge advances in sociology | Includes bibliographical references and index.
Identifiers: LCCN 2020002513 (print) | LCCN 2020002514 (ebook) | ISBN 9780367422998 (hardback) | ISBN 9780367495022 (paperback) | ISBN 9780367823351 (ebook)
Subjects: LCSH: Housing—Social aspects—Case studies. | Housing—Economic aspects—Case studies. | Home care services—Case studies.
Classification: LCC HD7287 .P455 2020 (print) | LCC HD7287 (ebook) | DDC 640—dc23
LC record available at https://lccn.loc.gov/2020002513
LC ebook record available at https://lccn.loc.gov/2020002514

ISBN: 978-0-367-42299-8 (hbk)
ISBN: 978-0-367-82335-1 (ebk)

Typeset in Times New Roman
by Apex CoVantage, LLC

Contents

Figures

Tables

Contributors

Teresita Abay-Krueger is a former IBM Corporation program manager, scientist and engineer, capping off a 25-year career. She specialised in the areas of research, strategy, operations, and consulting on emerging technologies. Teresita earned several corporate awards, and had an extraordinary career beginning in advanced semiconductor laboratories, developing technology proof of concepts, and ultimately designing and executing public sector information technology solutions for defence and intelligence. Consequently, while at IBM, she presented to C-level executives from the notable IBM Watson Industry Solutions Labs on how to pursue innovation. Teresita now leads her own consulting practice in New York City for the New American Workforce of the National Immigration Forum, a Washington, DC policy organization, and is a senior fellow with the Fordham University, Center for Digital Transformation New York, working on selected projects addressing the role of technology in successful business transformation. Other key passions of Teresita's are mentoring professional women from the Murray Hill Institute program, where she is "happy to share useful wisdom, rather than dole out advice." In addition, she is currently engaged in research regarding the home as a workplace and creative disruptor in the economic arena. Teresita obtained a BS in biology and chemistry from the Marymount College of Fordham University, New York, and a graduate certificate in project management.

Stefania Abbondanza, after graduating from socio-psycho-pedagogical high school in 2008 and graduating in piano at the "Niccolò Piccinni" Conservatory of Bari (Italy) in 2012, continued to dedicate herself to her true vocation in a more systematic way by volunteering at the Italian National Union for the Transport of the Sick at Lourdes and International Sanctuaries (UNITALSI). In particular, she assisted an autistic student during primary school hours from 2012 to 2014. This awakened in her an interest in and passion for the nursing sciences, so from 2015 to today she has been enrolled in the degree course in nursing sciences at the Campus Bio-Medico University of Rome and is now in her third year. Her field of study mainly concerns welfare activities and qualitative studies. During the last year of her studies, her attention has turned to the assistance of frail elderly people and their socio-health context.

Mohamed Gamal Abdelmonem is Professor and Chair in Architecture and the Director of the Centre for Architecture, Urbanism and Global Heritage (CAUGH) at Nottingham Trent University. He is the co-founder and lead of the university's research theme "Global Heritage: Science, Management and Development." A Fellow of the Royal Society of Arts and the 2014 recipient of the Jeffrey Cook Award of the International Association for the Study of Traditional Environments (IASTE), Gamal was a visiting professor at the Royal Academy of Arts in London and the University of California at Berkeley. His research focuses on the architectural heritage of urban centres, medieval culture, the architecture of home, and the smart preservation of urban heritage in the Digital Era. His recent books include *Peripheries: Edge Conditions in Architecture* (Routledge 2012), *The Architecture of Home in Cairo: Social-spatial practice of the Hawari's everyday life* (Routledge, 2015), and the forthcoming *Architecture, Space and Memory of Resurrection in Northern Ireland* (Routledge, 2019). Most recently, he guest-edited a special issue of the *International Journal of Architectural Research* (IJAR, 2017) on "Architectural and Urban Heritage in the Digital Era."

Remei Agulles is an assistant professor of the faculty of humanities and a researcher at the Institute of Advanced Family Studies at the Universitat Internacional de Catalunya (UIC Barcelona, Spain). She holds a degree in philosophy (University of Navarra, Spain) and a PhD in social sciences (Universitat Internacional de Catalunya, Spain). She has coordinated a study on "The Value of Care in the Home. The Care of Children in the Family Environment" (2015), supported by The Family Watch and the Foundation Barcelona i Família. She has also co-authored the report of the Global Home Index, Spain section (2017), which has involved a worldwide survey about time allocation and satisfaction related to homemaking and care in the home. She is also a member of the IsFamily Santander Chair and of the SARX Research Group on the Anthropology of Corporality (GRC). She was previously a researcher in the Department of Entrepreneurship at IESE Business School (2006–2013). Her current research interests involve family relationships and care, human beings as dependent beings, and corporality.

Antonio Argandoña is Emeritus Professor of Economics and Business Ethics, IESE Business School. He has taught in the Universities of Barcelona, Málaga, and Navarre. He is a member of the Real Academia de Ciencias Económicas y Financieras de España (Royal Academy of Economics and Finance), Chairman of the Comité de Normativa y Ética Profesional (Committee of Standards and Professional Ethics) of the Association of Economists of Catalonia, member of the Commission on Corporate Social Responsibility and Anti-Corruption of the International Chamber of Commerce of Paris, and of the Commission on Control and Transparency of the FC Barcelona. He has published numerous books and articles on macroeconomics, monetary economics, Spanish and international economics, the home and family issues, business ethics, economic ethics, corporate social responsibility, and related topics. He has been the editor or co-editor and co-author of "The Home," *Multidisciplinary Reflections*, Cheltenham, UK: Edward Elgar, 2017; "The Social Dimensions of Employment," *Institutional Reforms in Labour Markets*, Cheltenham, UK: Edward Elgar, 2002 (with J. Gual); and *The Ethical Dimension of Financial Institutions and Market*, Heidelberg: Springer Verlag, 1995.

Lord Richard Best co-chairs the APPG on Housing and Care for Older People and chaired its recent inquiry, "Rural Housing for an Ageing Population: Preserving Independence" (R-HAPPI). He is Vice President at the Town and Country Planning Association and Vice President (formerly President) of the Local Government Association. Until May 2017, he was the chair of The Property Ombudsman Council and the House of Lords Select Committee on Communications. Previously, Lord Best was the chair of the Hanover Housing Association, chief executive of the Joseph Rowntree Foundation, and, before that, the National Housing Federation. He has piloted four Private Members Bills on housing successfully through the House of Lords, most recently the "Homelessness Reduction Act 2017."

Maria Rosaria Brizi is a licensed lawyer who has earned a PhD in international relations at the University of the Witwatersrand, Johannesburg. Currently, she is a co-lecturer in human ecology and sustainability at Università Campus Biomedico (Faculty of Engineering), Rome, as well as a fellow in energy and environmental policies at Luiss–Guido Carli (Faculty of Political Sciences), Rome. In addition, she is a research and communication affiliate with Home Renaissance Foundation, London. Previously, she was a course lecturer (international negotiation/international disputes settlement) in Estonia at the Tallinn University of Technology (School of Economics), as well as a course lecturer (international arbitration) in Armenia at the European Regional Academy of Yerevan (Faculty of Law). In addition, she has been working as a legal officer in the Italian civil service (Ministry of Infrastructures and Transports, Rome). Her current research interests pertain to home and society, global justice and sustainable development, environmental politics and law, and international disputes settlement.

Marco Clari earned a PhD in nursing sciences jointly supervised by Campus Bio-Medico University of Rome and the University of Rome Tor Vergata (Italy). He specialises in the care of people affected by COPD and their carers, and he has researched on this topic for the last five years. He is also interested in mixed-methods research and multilevel and dyadic analyses. His research has focused on nursing issues of the elderly, people suffering from oncological diseases, and orthopaedic patients. Since 2015, he has held the position of adjunct professor for the bachelor's and master's degrees in nursing at the University of Eastern Piedmont (Italy) and the University of Turin (Italy). He also works as a registered nurse at the Department of Quality and Safety of Care at the Città della Salute e della Scienza University Hospital of Turin (Italy). He is a member of the European Academy of Nursing Science and the Italian Society of Nursing Science, as well as of the European Respiratory Society.

Cristina Costa holds a degree in business administration and a MBA from ESADE Business School (Barcelona). She worked as a professional consultant in business strategy, product innovation, and product service for more than ten years. She has been involved in business projects with social impact. After giving birth to her son, Cristina made a career change and focused on her real passion: promoting a more conscious way of inhabiting the planet and developing the local economy and responsible consumption. She decided to merge her interest in interior and furniture design with her business consulting experience, and she founded her entrepreneurial project, "The Home Therapy," in 2015. At The Home Therapy she works as Home Consultant and designs spaces to live or work that promote wellbeing and health. She has been trained in design thinking and applies a human- and planet-centred approach in the creation of spaces for clients. She is currently building a platform to promote local, sustainable, and handmade furniture and home decor. She also teaches creativity and design thinking at ESADE Business School and at the Instituto Europeo di Design. She has attended courses on sustainability at the Blekinge Institute of Tecnology (Sweden) and courses on furniture design at the Istituto Europeo di Design in Barcelona.

Maria Grazia De Marinis is Professor and Director of the Research Unit in Nursing Science, President of the Nursing Degree at the Medical School of the Campus Bio-Medico University of Rome, and Professor of General and Clinical Nursing at the same university. She also teaches general nursing in the Specialization School of Surgery of the Digestive System at the Campus Bio-Medico Faculty of Medicine. Since 2003 she has been director of the master's degree in oncology and palliative treatment at the same university. She has taught in the master's degrees programs of clinical tutoring, geriatric nursing, and management of coordination. She teaches the PhD course of nursing and public health at the University of Rome Tor Vergata, and the PhD course of bioethics at the Campus Bio-Medico University of Rome. She has been scientific director of the journal *International Nursing Perspectives*, published by Società Editrice Universo. She has worked as consultant of the IPASVI Federation for the study and development of guidelines for the nursing degree and specialisation. She is the author of about 200 publications.

Asunción Esteve is Associate Professor at the Law School of the University of Barcelona where she teaches law of obligations, family, and contract law. Her research interests are intellectual property and privacy protection. She has published different books and articles on embryo protection, fault and breach of contract, copyright, and personal data protection. She is currently involved in research projects related to contract law and open access to academic journals. She has been a visiting researcher at the Max-Planck Institute for Innovation and Competition (Munich), the Columbia Law School (New York), and at the Law School of the university. She has lectured as an Erasmus professor at the Law School of the Humboldt University (Berlin). She is generally interested in legal problems related to family protection by public institutions.

Gabriella Facchinetti is a PhD candidate who earned her bachelor's degree in nursing at the Campus Bio-Medico University of Rome in 2013, after having completed a period of extracurricular clinical experience at the Universidad de Navarra Hospital in Pamplona (Spain). In 2015 she gained a master's degree from the Catholic University of the Sacred Heart in Rome and started a PhD programme in nursing and public health at the University of Rome Tor Vergata. Since 2014 she has worked as a nurse in the home hospitalization service, providing assistance to chronic patients. Since 2015 she has been a teaching assistant in the degree course in nursing at the Campus Bio-Medico University of Rome. In 2016, she began attending the prestigious Summer School organised by the European Academy of Nursing Science (EANS) for three years, where she had the opportunity to meet and work with nurse researchers from all over Europe. She developed a particular interest in applied research on older people with chronic diseases and continuity of patient care.

Sandra Idrovo Carlier, PhD is a Professor of Organizational Behavior and Communication at INALDE Business School – Universidad de La Sabana, in Colombia, where she is the Director of the Research Center: Culture, Work, Care. She served as Research Director of INALDE from 2006–2019; and as member of the executive board of the school from 2011–2016. Her research interests and publications deal with harmonizing work and personal life, women in management, care of the home and human resources. She has published in Colombian and International peer-reviewed journals and books. She got her PhD (1992) from Universidad de Navarra (Spain) and worked as Director of Graduate Studies at Universidad Casa Grande (2001–2004) and as Dean of the School of Communications (1998–2000) at Universidad Espíritu Santo, both Ecuadorian institutions. Among her latest publications: With Bosch, M. (2019), "The impact of different forms of organisational support and work–life balance in Chile and Colombia; with Costamagna, R. and Mendi, P. (2019), "Initial informality as an obstacle to intellectual capital acquisitions"; with Mesurado, B., Crespo, R.F., Rodríguez, O., Debeljuh, P. (2018). The development and initial validation of a multidimensional flourishing scale, among others.

Patricia Debeljuh gained her PhD in Philosophy, University of Navarra, Spain (2002) and attended the Program Focused on Human Resource Management at

IESE in Barcelona and the Senior Management Program at the IAE Business School. She graduated with a Diploma of Honour as a Licentiate in Industrial Relations at the Universidad Argentina de la Empresa. She is the Director of the Centre for Work Family Balance of the IAE Business School, Austral University; Professor in Management Practices and the Doctoral Program at the IAE and Visiting Professor at several business schools in the region. Dr Debeljuh has published several books: "Male + Woman = Complementarity" (LID Editorial, 2013); "Business Ethics" (Cengage, 2009); "Ethics: learning to live" (Focus Publishers Ltd., Nairobi, 2006) and in collaboration with other authors: "Towards a new work-family pact" (IAE 2015); "The feminine side of power" (LID 2015); "Towards Corporate Family Responsibility" (IAE 2013); "Towards a family-friendly business" (IAE 2011), "Women and Leadership: building from complementarity" (LID Editorial, 2010), among others. She has been invited to participate as a lecturer and exhibitor at international events in the United States, Australia, Spain, Italy, Mexico, Costa Rica, Panama, El Salvador, Guatemala and in all Latin American countries.

Belén Mesurado, earned her PhD in Psychology at the National University of San Luis, Argentina (2010), with top marks. She currently serves as Vice-Director of the Interdisciplinary Centre for Research in Mathematical and Experimental Psychology (CIIPME). She is also an Associate Researcher at the National Council for Scientific and Technical Research (CONICET) - The Philosophy Institute of Universidad Austral. Dr Mesurado has been the recipient of several Doctorate and Post-doctoral Scholarships from CONICET, as well as Scholarships from international organizations such as the Carolina Foundation, the Society for Research on Adolescence (SRA), the Society for Research in Child Development (SRCD) and the International Union of Psychological Science (IUPSyS). She has conducted research stays at the University of Valencia, Spain on different occasions: 2012, 2014 and 2016, as well as at De La Salle University, Philippines and University of Nottingham, Malaysia in 2013. She has published several articles and book chapters on her specialty in subjects of positive psychology, family and pro-social behaviours.

Kathleen Farrell works as a lecturer in Food Entrepreneurship and Management in the School of Culinary Arts and Food Technology at the Technological University of Dublin. She has also worked for some years in the hospitality industry in both managerial and training roles. She holds a Masters in Business Studies and a PhD from Smurfit Business School, University College Dublin. Her research interests include work/home harmony, work/life balance, the female entrepreneur and entrepreneurship education. She has some publications in the aforementioned areas of research. In 2017 she worked on a joint project with representatives from Dublin City University (DCU), Cork Institute of Technology, Dun Laoghaire Institute of Art, Design and Technology, and Dundalk Institute of Technology the purpose of which was to design a digital badge for entrepreneurship education. Recently she visited Kaohsiung

University of Hospitality and Tourism in Taiwan in order to foster educational relations and cooperation between Dublin Institute of Technology and Kaohsiung University. She has delivered a module in Strategic management in Hainan University China.

Horacio Joffre Galibert is a lawyer who graduated from the Argentine Catholic University. Dr. Galibert founded the Argentine Association of Parents of People with Autism (APAdeA) in 1994 and the Argentine Federation of Autism (FAdeA) in 1999. He has been working for over 30 years promoting public legislation for people with autism and other disabilities, informing parents in different organisations about the rights of their children. Dr. Galibert is a university professor and delivers lectures in his country and abroad. He is the author and publisher of several works on NGOs (non-governmental organisations), autism, and legislation on disability. In 2000, Dr. Galibert founded a respite care home for adults with autism. His son, Ignacio, who is 35 years old, lives there, together with 15 other adult people with ASD (Autism Spectrum Disorder). A leader in innovation and social inclusion, Dr. Galibert offers, through APAdeA, treatment for autistic people, parental support, and employment positions for people with ASD. In 2012, Dr. Galibert received the "Solidarity Entrepreneur Award" from the Social Ecumenical Forum, and he is the "godfather" of the therapeutic centre called "Rayito de Sol" (a beam of sunshine) in his native town of Villa Guillermina in Santa Fe province.

Nahieli Greaves-Fernández is a researcher at ESDAI, Universidad Panamericana, where she teaches food biochemistry to undergraduates. She is a pharmaceutical chemist and has an MS degree in biochemistry and a diploma in public communication of science, both from the National Autonomous University of Mexico, as well as a PhD in science education from the University of York in the UK. Dr. Greaves has more than 15 years' worth of experience teaching at different universities and designing science-based resources for different educational levels. She has published several textbooks, as well as online resources, for science education. She has also designed and taught courses for the professional development of science teachers. Her current research involves the study of different aspects of food culture, from the safe handling of food to the eating practices of people suffering from diabetes. The main aim of her research is to understand how to empower others to make healthy lifestyle choices relating to food.

Sheila the Baroness Hollins is an independent crossbench life peer in the House of Lords, and emeritus professor of psychiatry of disability at St. George's University of London. She has been a clinical specialist, researcher, and policy maker in mental health and published both scientific and professional papers and books. In 1989, she founded the long-running Books Beyond Words series of picture books for young people and adults with developmental intellectual disabilities, which includes stories about everyday life such as moving home, as well as physical and mental health, and criminal justice. Baroness Hollins was president of the Royal College of Psychiatrists (2005–2008), president of the British Medical Association (2012–2013) and chair of the Board of Science of the British Medical Association (2013–2016). She has completed a four-year term as a member of the Pontifical Commission for the Protection of Minors and Vulnerable Adults in 2017, and is currently the president of the Royal College of Occupational Therapists.

Usochi Ilozumba obtained her bachelor's degree in pure and industrial chemistry at the University of Nigeria, Nsukka, Enugu State, Nigeria. She has worked as an industrial chemist at Juhel Nigeria Limited, a NAFDAC and ISO-certified private pharmaceutical company in the southeast of Nigeria. She has also worked as a facility manager, and later as administrative officer for Atlantika Cultural Centre in Lagos, a private non-profit organisation providing multifaceted personal, cultural, and professional development for young girls. From October 2013 to June 2018, she held and completed a five-year study scholarship at the Pontifical University of the Holy Cross in Rome, Italy, specialising in philosophical ethics and anthropology. She is currently a full-time lecturer at the Institute of Humanities, Pan Atlantic University, Lagos, Nigeria. Usochi has interests in international relations, anthropological studies, social and political ethics, education and development of women and girls, as well as human dignity and rights awareness projects.

Aleksandra Kroll is a researcher, practicing psychologist and speech therapist with the Independent Clinical Psychology Unit, Department of Psychiatry, Pomeranian Medical University, Szczecin, Poland. She earned an MA in clinical psychology and Polish language and literature from Adam Mickiewicz University, and then postgraduate in cognitive neuroscience. She earned her PhD at the Pomeranian Medical University. Her research interests include developmental and clinical neuropsychology, especially in the context of neurorehabilitation of language and cognition.

Consuelo León holds a degree in journalism (University of Navarre, Spain) and a PhD in business administration (Universitat Politècnica de Catalunya, Spain). She is currently the director of the Observatory of Public Policies in the Institute of Advanced Family Studies (Universitat Internacional de Catalunya, Spain), where she is also the academic coordinator and professor of the postgraduate degree in family policies. As a specialist in the area of work-life balance, she is a member of the IsFamily Santander Chair. She is the author of several articles about gender, women in the job market, and the new patterns of flexible work, stress and technology, and work-family balance, among which, the co-authored books *Female Ambition* (2005), *Aprender con juegos digitales* (2012), and *Aquí hay empleo* (2017). She was previously a researcher in the ICWF (International Centre of Work and Family) in IESE Business School, Spain (2000–2010).

Michela Piredda is Assistant Professor in Nursing Science at the Campus Bio-Medico University of Rome. She gained extensive clinical experience as a registered nurse there for a number of years, developing an interest in clinical nursing research, specialising in the field of oncology. She went on to complete a master's in nursing research at King's College London. Dr. Piredda gained a PhD in nursing science on nursing care dependence and has researched and published extensively about nursing topics, in particular, cancer nursing. She was made a research fellow at the Centre of Excellence of Nursing Culture and Research in 2011.

Maria del Carmen Rabiela-Sotelo is a pharmaceutical chemistry biologist from Universidad LaSalle and has a masters of education from Universidad Interamericana para el Desarrollo. She is a professor of microbiology and food safety, and a researcher at Escuela de Administración de Instituciones, Universidad Panamericana. She has a Hazard Analysis and Critical Control Points (HACCP) certificate by Alliance International. This certificate allows specialisation in safe food handling by identifying the hazards associated with all aspects of food preparation. In addition, Professor Rabiela has a certificate in Competencies EC0081 in hygienic food handling, which allows to serve as a reference for the evaluation and certification of food handlers. She is currently researching the best hygienic food-handling practices, as well as the proper way to preserve food for its best use. The main aim of her research is to identify sources of food's contamination in the food preparation process in the hospitality industry.

José Víctor Orón Semper is a Piarist priest. After 15 years of educational practice with high school students in various schools in Spain, he opened a new period of his life dedicated to research for educational improvement. His basic education is very varied, including civil engineering, philosophy and theology, a master's degree in cognitive neuroscience and another one in bioethics. He obtained his doctorate in education from the University of Navarra where he currently works as a researcher in the Mind-Brain Group. Its central field of research is emotional education, but it complements it with other related topics such as educational neuroscience and human development psychology. So, his approach is always interdisciplinary, uniting philosophy, psychology, and neuroscience. His work as a researcher is centralised through the Mind-Brain Group, but he works towards agreements with other universities such as Reading University (UK) for research in psychological development and with UPAEP (Mexico) for research in education. He created an educational program, UpToYou, which he directs. This program develops formation courses in emotional education and implements educational programs in the world of school, family, and business. The program has been developed in several cities and colleges in Spain, Cameroon, Mexico, and Brazil.

Audrey Tan is the head of Home Management at Kenvale College, Sydney, and comes from a background in medicine from the University of Sydney and has a fellowship in ophthalmology from the Australian New Zealand College of Ophthalmology. She had lived in Singapore for 15 years, and during that time became involved in family enrichment activities for a decade before becoming interested in developing a home management course, which she saw as an extension of family enrichment. She has a postgraduate diploma in marriage and family education from the International University of Catalunya.

Belén Zárate teaches philosophy of law at the Universitat Internacional de Catalunya, Spain. She holds a degree in philosophy and law (University of Navarre, Spain) and a PhD in law (Universidad Complutense de Madrid). She is a researcher in the Institute of Advanced Family Studies (Universitat Internacional de Catalunya) and the author of several books, which include *La familia en la ley de dependencia, El tratamiento de la dependencia como derecho social*, and *La tutela de la dependencia en el ordenamiento jurídico español*. Her research is focused on family and dependency, which has also been the topic of the articles and conference papers she has authored. As a specialist in this area, she is a member of the Is Family Santander Chair. She was formerly the assistant director of the Institute of Advanced Family Studies (2004–2008) and a member of the Commission for the Rights of the Elderly in the Barcelona Bar Association (2001–2012). Since 2008 she has been the vice-rector for the University Community at the Universitat Internacional de Catalunya.

Foreword: A place called home

The home is a concept universally experienced, permeating every aspect of our lives, yet at the same time it is an entity whose influence on health and wellbeing is poorly understood. This book addresses the influence of that place called home as the place where later-life changes, including physical and mental health, and personal and social relationships, have their beginnings. These early experiences are ones that last a lifetime and impact not only the individual but his or her family, community, and society at large.

This opportunity to draw attention to the role the home plays in lifelong health and wellbeing is one of great significance to the Home Renaissance Foundation (HRF). As co-founder and chair, I am delighted to see the engagement and expertise represented in this volume. At HRF we speak of renewing the culture and restoring the value of the home for everyone. Since our beginnings in 2006 we have commissioned and encouraged research based on recognition of the contribution of the home to individuals and to wider society. This begins by raising the status of the home as both a subject for serious academic examination and as a vital, yet often unrecognised, key to human thriving. This lack of recognition does not only mean that it has missed academic scrutiny, but also that the home's vital role of nurturer has been overlooked—at a cost to all of us.

HRF has overseen the development of multidisciplinary approaches to this subject. This has included the contribution made by understanding the work of the home as having a professional dimension; studying how home environments impact child development, care of the elderly, and wider family wellbeing; exploring how economic paradigms might better recognise and record the value of work taking place in the home; and contributing to broader ontological and epistemological questions concerning the nature of home.

In this volume, we see the further development of this valuable multidisciplinary approach as contributors from a range of academic fields have addressed the role of the home in providing lifelong care, as well as further investigation into the changing understanding of home in a fast-moving world.

The authors whose work has been gathered together in this book have brought the emphases of their own disciplines to shed light on the themes of care, work, and people. Through these different approaches, from the theoretical to the practical, emerges not only an in-depth study of the role of the home in care and health, but a platform for greater multidisciplinary engagement in its vital contribution to human wellbeing and societal thriving.

I am grateful to Professors Abdelmonem and Argandoña for their work in bringing to publication such an important milestone in this increasingly recognised and valued area of study, and indeed, life.

Bryan K. Sanderson, CBE
President, Home Renaissance Foundation, London

Preface: The home, a place for families to grow

From the outside, a home is simply a building. It's inside that the magic happens. If a home is a place where children feel safe and happy, they will learn they are loved and respected and, as a result, they are likely to grow up to love and respect others. They will grow in health and wellbeing and develop a sense of purpose, allowing them to make decisions as to the future direction of their lives. Children who experience a nurturing, safe upbringing are likely, as adults, to create a positive home environment for their own children and so, positive outcomes for families are handed on to the next generation. However, children who do not have a positive experience of family life are more likely to experience difficulties and fail in adult life. They as less likely, as parents, to provide safe and secure nurturing for their own children. There is now robust scientific evidence which explains much about how the experiences children have in the home can influence their behaviour as adults, and the probability that they will have successful, productive lives.

The impact of home life on health and wellbeing

In 1948, the World Health Organisation defined health as "a state of complete physical, mental and social wellbeing and not merely the absence of disease or infirmity" (World Health Organisation, 2006). More recently, others have added the concept that "health also involves the ability to adapt and self-manage in the face of social, physical, and emotional challenges" (Huber et al., 2011). The science is very clear. The physical and social environment in which a child is born and grows shapes that child's health, wellbeing, and ability to manage themselves successfully in society. Failed home life is strongly associated with failure in other aspects of life.

Several studies have followed cohorts of children into adulthood. Those children who have been brought up in difficult home circumstances are more likely to experience a range of difficulties in adulthood. In 1972, in the city of Dunedin in New Zealand, 1,000 children were recruited into one of the most successful of these cohort studies (Poulton et al., 2015). Over 90% of these children have been followed up to the present day. Risk factors measured in childhood that predicted poor adult outcomes included low family socioeconomic status and, particularly, a history of maltreatment in the home.

Children experiencing neglect and abuse had low levels of self-control and lower IQs. These children were significantly more likely to have poor health and social outcomes in adulthood. They were more likely to fail at school and become unemployed. They have a significantly increased risk of criminal convictions. The study provided information that allowed researchers to predict with a high degree of accuracy, by age three, those cohort members who would go on to become high users of public services such as health care, social care, and criminal justice services.

In California, the Adverse Childhood Experiences Study gathered information from over 9,000 adults on their experience of psychological, physical, or sexual abuse; domestic violence; or living with household members who were substance abusers, mentally ill or suicidal, or ever imprisoned (Felitti et al 1998). Compared to those adults who had no adverse experiences, those adults who had four of more adverse experiences had a four- to 12-fold increased health risks for alcoholism, drug abuse, depression, and suicide attempt, and a two- to four-fold increase in smoking and poor self-rated health. The greater the exposure to childhood adversity, the more likely they were to have multiple health risk factors later in life. These observations have been confirmed by studies in the UK (Hughes et al., 2017).

The association between the quality of childhood experiences and subsequent adult outcomes is consistent across many studies. In studies of the origins of disease, however, it is important to recognise that it does not necessarily confirm causation. Mechanisms linking cause and effect should be identified. The mechanisms which link adversity in childhood with failure in adulthood have been extensively studied, and the causality of the relationship confirmed. A comprehensive description of the biological pathways involved begins with the work of American sociologist Aaron Antonovsky.

The biological consequences of adverse home life

Antonovsky studied the health of adults who, as children, had been in concentration camps. He found that 70% of those children had significant problems. They had, he suggested, failed to develop a "sense of coherence." He defined this as the ability to see the world as structured, predictable, and, therefore, manageable. Without a sense of coherence, Antonovsky suggested these children would experience a state of chronic stress (Antonovsky, 1979).

The relationship between social and economic status and elevated levels of stress hormones has been extensively documented (McDermott et al., 2018). Development of such stress involves the process of epigenetics. Adverse home circumstances such as maltreatment affect the genes that produce the proteins that detect high levels of the hormone cortisol (McGowan et al., 2009). The epigenetic modification of the genes involved in control of the stress response prevents maltreated children from exerting normal levels of control over stress hormones. What has also been demonstrated is that it is the chronically elevated stress levels – what has been described as "toxic stress" – that affects the developing brain (Shonkoff et al., 2012).

Exposure to prolonged stress modifies brain development in ways that increase emotional liability and reduces ability to control impulsive behaviour (McEwen, 2011). This adaptation makes sense in evolutionary terms. If a child experiences uncertainty and danger, he must be prepared to react quickly to threats. The elevated stress hormones allow him to quickly generate energy as part of the "flight or fight" response. Unfortunately, in modern society, impulsive and occasionally violent behaviour is often inappropriate and results in the individual being excluded from normal relationships. The consequences of adverse childhood experiences to society are profound. The Californian study suggested in 2012 that the lifetime cost of neglect to a cohort of children born in any one year in the US was $124 billion dollars (Fang et al., 2012). This figure comprised extra health care costs, costs of special education, and costs associated with criminal justice issues. There were also costs associated with the fact that few of these adults were employed and paying taxes.

More recent calculations that take into account the costs of fatalities amongst neglected children have revised the estimated lifetime economic burden of each year's cohort of neglected children in the US upwards to $2 trillion ((Peterson et al., 2018). A literature review of the health care costs attributable to individuals with adverse childhood experiences suggested that the annual cost to health systems in Europe is $581 billion (Bellis et al., 2019).

We have, therefore, well-documented social and biological drivers of strong, causally associated links between chaotic and troubled lives of children in the home and failure in adult life. In addition, we have evidence of the significant social and economic consequences of such failure. It is a matter of social justice that we take action to tackle poor care in the home and ensure that babies and children receive the kind of nurture and love that their dignity as defenceless human beings warrants. For those individuals who do not see this as a human rights issue, the cost to society of failure to address the issue must surely make them take action.

Making the home a nurturing environment

When child neglect is discovered, there is a tendency to focus on the failings of the responsible adult. However, that adult might, themselves, have experienced neglect and abuse. Their decision-making capacity might be impaired. Their neglect of their own children might, in fact, be learned behaviour. Although adverse experiences occur in families across the economic spectrum, it is more common in low-income families, but it is not restricted to them.

However, poor parents are more likely to encounter stressful situations. If they have low levels of resilience, the stresses associated with poverty are more likely to overwhelm them, making them more likely to take out their anger and frustration on their children. If we are to make the home a successful institution, we need to consider the impact of social chaos on families and support policies and action to tackle the social and economic factors which influence the stresses we encounter in daily life. Poverty which limits a family's ability to feed itself, or prevents the children from participating in normal day-to-day activities, is stigmatising and damaging to family relationships. If a parent who may, because of their own upbringing, be stressed and emotionally labile, is violent towards their children, society usually criminalises them, making the child's life even more chaotic. A public health analysis of the problem defines the issue of family neglect and violence not as a problem of the individual, but as an issue of the circumstances in which they find themselves.

Public policy on income, social security, affordable housing, and the overall costs of living are all relevant to the issue of safe, nurturing homes. In 2018, the Scottish government published a child poverty action plan called "Every child, every chance: tackling child poverty delivery plan" (2018), which outlines a cross-government approach to alleviating the stresses of poverty in families. If effectively implemented, such policies can help improve family life.

The policies outlined in the Scottish document include support to improve employment opportunities for poor families. There is also support for after-school childcare for working parents. Help with the costs of living are featured in the policy. There is a provision for providing clothing and food for children, and help with fuel bills. Investment in communities and enhancement of education opportunities is also a feature of the policy. Other countries have implemented similar approaches to support poor families.

However, the other preventive approach to child neglect is more direct and involves teaching parents the skills they need to support their children's social and intellectual development. Several reviews of these approaches have been published (Moran and Ghate, 2005). More recently, the European commission has published a review entitled "Positive Parenting Interventions: Empowering parents with positive parenting techniques for lifelong health and well-being" (2019). The critical features of a nurturing environment seem to be: (a) promoting and reinforcing pro-social behaviour; (b) minimising coercion, aggression, and conflict behaviours; (c) reducing opportunities for problem behaviour; and (d) promoting mindful, flexible pro-social values (Biglan, 2015).

Identification of families who are struggling to deliver a nurturing environment for their children and supporting them to develop a positive approach to parenting is a critical element in turning the home into the kind of institution described in this book. Together with public policies which support disadvantaged families in delivering a safe environment for their children, society can deliver transformative change. Positive parenting in such environments will enhance health and wellbeing, improve educational achievement, and create adults who are productive and nurturing of their own children.

Professor Sir Harry Burns
University of Strathclyde

References

Antonovsky, A. (1979) *Health, stress, and coping*. San Francisco: Jossey-Bass Inc.

Bellis, M.A., Hughes, K., Ford, K., Ramos Rodriguez, G., Sethi, G., Passmore, J. (2019) Life course health consequences and associated annual costs of adverse childhood experiences across Europe and North America: a systematic review and meta-analysis. *Lancet Public Health*, 4: e517–528.

Biglan, A. (2015) *The nurture effect: How the science of human behavior can improve our lives and our world*. Oakland, CA: New Harbinger.

Every child, every chance: tackling child poverty delivery plan 2018–2022. (2018) www.gov.scot. ISBN: 978-1-78851-731-7.

Fang, X., Brown, D.S., Florence, C.S., Mercy, J.A. (2012) The economic burden of child maltreatment in the United States and implications for prevention. *Child Abuse and Neglect*, 36: 156–165.

Felitti, Vincent J. et al. (1998) Relationship of childhood abuse and household dysfunction to many of the leading causes of death in adults. *American Journal of Preventive Medicine*, 14(4): 245–258.

Huber, M. et al. (2011) How should we define health? *BMJ*, 343, 4163. doi:10.1136/bmj.d4163.

Hughes, K., Bellis, M.A., Hardcastle, K.A., Sethi, D., Butchart, A., Mikton, C. (2017) The effect of multiple adverse childhood experiences on health: a systematic review and meta-analysis. *Lancet Public Health*, 2(8): e356–366.

McDermott, C.L. et al. (2018) Longitudinally mapping childhood socioeconomic status associations with cortical and subcortical morphology. *Journal of Neuroscience*, 39(8): 1365–1373.

McEwen, B.S. (2011) Effects of stress on the developing brain. *Cerebrum*, 2011–2014.

McGowan, P.O. et al. (2009) Epigenetic regulation of the glucocorticoid receptor in human brain associates with childhood abuse. Nature Neuroscience, 12: 342–348.

Moran, P., Ghate, D. (2005) The effectiveness of parenting support. *Children Society*, 19: 329–336.

Peterson, C., Florence, C., Klevens, J. (2018) The economic burden of child maltreatment in the United States, 2015. *Child Abuse & Neglect*, 86: 178–183.

Positive Parenting Interventions. (2019) European Commission (PDF ISBN: 978-92-79-99865-2 doi: 10.2767/784009 Catalogue number: KE-02–19–122-EN-N).

Poulton, R., Moffat, T.E., Silva, P.A. (2015) The dunedin multidisciplinary health and development study: overview of the first 40 years, with an eye to the future. *Social Psychiatry Psichiatric Epidemiology*, 50(5): 679–693.

Shonkoff, J.P., Garner, A.S. (2012) The lifelong effects of early childhood adversity and toxic stress. *Pediatrics*, 129(1): 232–246.

World Health Organization. (2006, October). Constitution of the world health organization. Forty-fifth edition, Supplement, www.who.int/governance/eb/who_constitution_en.pdf.

Acknowledgements

We would like to acknowledge the substantial contribution and support made by the Home Renaissance Foundation; by its Chairman, Bryan K Sanderson CBE, the Board of Directors and the management, including Mercedes Jaureguibeitia, Susan Peatfield, Angela de Miguel, and Maria Rosaria Brizi, amongst others. We are grateful to the support and contribution of all authors and contributors, especially with the many revisions and reviews they had to make. Particular thanks are due to Sir Harry Burns for his very informative Preface, and Richard Lord Best, Baroness Hollins and Professor Orón Semper for their feature articles. We also appreciate support provided by the Routledge Editorial Team. Without all this help and support, this volume would not have been possible.

This book and its chapters were written and edited long before the spread of the Coronavirus Pandemic, which forced billions of individuals and families to stay at home for several weeks during March and April 2020, and yet it is published at a time when the COVID-19 Virus impact has been felt across the globe. Whilst there are no aspects of this book which have considered the pandemic and its impact, the topics of its chapters are very relevant to our understanding of the critical importance of the home and family in modern society; especially care at work and at home. This is something that has been long forgotten, yet this pandemic has brought it back to the centre of public debate on the socio-political and wellbeing of modern societies. Home now emerges yet again as the safe haven in a fast-changing world.

Chapter 1

Home and care in a changing society

Mohamed Gamal Abdelmonem and Antonio Argandoña

Introduction

Modern society has elevated family and household matters from their formerly private position to that of concerns of political institutions. The emergence of society, seen by Hanna Arendt in the rise of housekeeping, its activities, problems, and organisational devices, has moved the home from the shadowy interior of the household into the light of the public sphere. It has not only blurred the old borderlines between private and political, but has also changed almost beyond recognition the meaning of the two terms and their significance for the life of the individual and the citizen (Arendt, 1958: 28). Housing policies, management of households, and professional rules of home workers are a few discrete examples of how the institution of the society interferes in the matters and system of the home.

A quick look at the housing layout of most European cities shows clear signs of accelerating displacement of the family from their urban centres towards the peripheries. There is increasing segregation and distance between places of work and living spaces, with lengthier daily journeys between work and home. In the search for good careers, young people live in shared accommodations near their workplaces in the centre. People with families have to live at greater distances from work and provide alternative means of caring for their house, children, and elderly. Such spatial segregation between where people work and live has resulted in a decline of support from within the family and has increased the demand on outside care services, be it domestic workers, childminders, or care for elderly people. Hence, other forms of professional relationships were brought into the home at a time when homeowners are experiencing a greater distance between work and home.

However, we need to be clear about what we mean by home. Home is an everyday notion that carries subjective clarity as well as collective ambiguity. Are we talking about the home of the family or the home of the collective group of individuals? We are living in an ever more dynamic and mobile environment where our activities overlap and the traditional boundaries of privacy have become blurred regarding where a certain activity stops and another starts. In our contemporary society, we have a multiplicity of homes, of which some domains are not as private as they used to be. Homes could host professional and work activities, or provide medical care. Hence, here we can introduce a common understanding of what we mean by home and our understanding of its complex and multi-layered nature.

Home is that contested environment where several processes, interactions, and engagement are at work on a constant basis. Over time, the challenges to home as an institution emerged from changing socioeconomic and cultural landscapes that offer new problems and opportunities based on the various elements that make up the home (family, marriage, motherhood, fatherhood, children, home production and consumption, housing, work, health, upbringing and education, family policies, etc.). These challengers are tackled in this book from the diverse viewpoints of science and humanities research fields. Most of the current endeavours, however, are quite specialised, although there are also a limited number of studies that deal with such topics in a more interdisciplinary way.

While books on home relations and environments are mostly defined by specific discipline or research area, such as social psychology, environmental psychology, sociology, humanistic geography, ethnology, and sociology, this book offers a unique interdisciplinary approach that engages a multitude of research domains based on shared enquiries on home as place of care, of people, and of work. This book aims to develop an enquiry on the function and practices of the contemporary home. It adopts the broader conception of the home, including people (the family), place (the housing), environment (neighbourhood, city, town), and society, taking it as the unit of analysis and considering its multifaceted dimensions: anthropological, ethical, economic, political, social, psychological, and spatial. It looks to: a) identify and sensitise different experiences, situations, and challenges of the home; b) offer a series of diagnostic investigations that cover a number of issues from the perspectives of health, care, work, and engagement; c) instigate a number of creative perspectives towards new evolutions of the way home works and operates for modern families and stakeholders; d) evaluate the resultant impact on the home and on the people, on the nearby community, and on society; e) analyse and contribute to the design and execution of public policies on home and care; f) interrogate different impacts on people (knowledge, skills, values, virtues, etc.) and environments (family, business, social entities, public bodies, etc.).

This volume is a collaborative and multidisciplinary endeavour with contributions from the point of view of different disciplines and from practice. There are descriptive, theoretical, empirical, and practical chapters. The thread of the book is the triangle of people + work + care. Many people participate in the home, with different degrees of involvement, not only the family members, but also the extended family, those who help from outside, those around, the most distant, and the institutional collaborators (schools, universities, medical centres, homes for the elderly and disabled, etc.)

We look at the home as a multipurpose organisation whose tasks include reproduction; nutrition, learning and socialisation of children; production of goods and services; care for the sick and elderly; provision of physical, psychological and ontological security; and a means for the acquisition of a social identity. It is a place where virtues are learned, a door to enter society, a place from which one leaves every day, but to which one returns, and to which we all hope to return in the final stages of our life. This multipurpose organisation implies that people must perform a set of functions, much more extensive and varied over time than those of other organisations, however complex they may be, such as a hospital. Everyone at home has to be willing to perform very different tasks.

A home encompasses people, community, and space or environment in a society, in which the home performs a function.[1] The number of people is not the most important factor. The home can be single-person, or it can take on more complex forms, such as the nuclear family, the extended family, the single-parent family, separated parents, compound family, same-sex parents, or people who live in a home for the elderly or the disabled. However, its relational nature is important because it determines its social function within its immediate (village, neighbourhood, city) and general environment (society at large). This book is about the home, its nature and its functions, its importance, difficulties, and hopes. It is the fruit of the work of 27 authors from different disciplines and countries, with different approaches – some of them theoretical, others empirical, and yet others whose outlook is eminently practical. We have grouped them in three parts, focused on care, people, and work, because these are three basic aspects of the home that account for its social function. In the following pages, we will explain very briefly the book's underlying conception of the home: first, its social function; next, the three themes around which the three parts of the book revolve: care, people, and work, led by three key feature articles that drives the agenda for our discussions.

This book offers a rare insight into the multiplicity of challenges from theoretical, practical, policy perspectives of the home in the twenty-first century, and how professionals and researchers alike tried to address them. Above all, it highlights the commonality of these challenges and how ordinary people relate them to their own daily lives. But, before we delve into the detailed arguments introduced in the book chapters, here we introduce a basic and shared theoretical framework of the home and its meanings as used throughout this book.

Making sense of the home

We have inherited this subtle notion of the home as a haven and refuge that transcends different conditions and relations of living within the house. Homes are socially constructed and have continually changed their forms, uses, and meanings.[2] While houses are built with the capacity to serve a wide range of social activities that differ through generations and vary according to material means, homes are constructed out of continuities of social traffic, activity, and conduct (Abdelmonem, 2016). Hence, we seem to have a conceptual contradiction in the attributes of the home. How can it be private while it associates its form, organisation, and meaning largely within the commonality of a group, culture, or society (Abdelmonem, 2011)? As a social-spatial system of living, the home is integral to circles of selective socialising that overlap public and private life with obligation and trust beyond the family to the expansive formation of the city and society at large. In the second half of the twentieth century, we have sought better understanding of the home as a multidimensional concept,[3] hence multidisciplinary understanding of its formation and evolution as human practice is needed (ibid). Since the mid-1980s, the home has been subject to a well-documented and long-established history of architecture and the built environment from various points of view and research areas: sociologists, environmental psychologists, architects, and historians. From Nietzsche to Martin Heidegger and Hannah Arendt, the act of building and inhabiting space is a process of mediation with nature and contextual condition.

Home emerges as a stronghold territory, in which certain security measures, control, and defence are continuously at work. Home is an intermediate territory that lies between the personal spaces, in which people maintain certain distance from others, and public spaces, in which individual requirements are superseded by the superior shared interest of society. Homes fit the definition of human territoriality as "the relationship between an individual/group of people and particular physical settings that is characterised by a feeling of possessiveness, attempts to control the appearance and the use of space" (Bower, 1980: 179). Homes, thus, could be realised through a network of spaces (indoor and outdoor) that a person uses routinely as a haven with a high degree of comfort and intimacy. They envisage specific codes of human behaviour learned through cultural training that require adjustment every time people cross their boundaries. Spatial configurations of homes are not limited to the physical boundaries; rather, people construct their home domain beyond what appear to be physical boundaries. The immediate front of a house is part of the home's territory. With the emergence of new technology and telecare, on the other hand, some of the most private spaces in the home have become accessible to medical and social care professionals, as experienced by many elderly people. Home has again become a place of work, with many self-employed and young professionals working from home. Such changing dynamics at home require continual investigations to what a home means at certain times and to certain generations.

The home

Home is an ambiguous term that retains different meaning within different contexts and disciplinary approaches. Its inclusive meaning reflects the physical parameters of a residential space (house, dwelling), place (neighbourhood, town), environment (domestic life), as well as the social determination of a particular community. *Home* is defined by Oxford English Dictionary as:

> A dwelling-place, house, abode; the fixed residence of a family or household; the seat of domestic life and interests; the dwelling in which one habitually lives, or which one regards as one's proper abode. Sometimes including the members of a family collectively; the home-circle or household.[4]

This inclusive definition encompasses a number of meanings that share similar references, but different meanings, about domestic environments for individual members of the household or for the social makeup of the family. However, the contemporary literature of domestic architecture alienates itself with the use of three basic terminologies: home, house, and household. Home is used for the analysis of the environment; house for the characteristics of physical space and its economic aspects of production; and household refers to the economic unit that occupies the house, its affordability, and ecology.[5] Home, as we acknowledge it in this book, not only refers to the spatial settings that accommodate the personal and family socio-cultural and psychological needs, and enables certain sets of functions – like social space and a place for work and care – but we refer to the home as the environment and social conditions that enable and facilitate these functions. Its boundaries are constructed based on conditions of functions, relationships, and economies of contemporary society.

Different analytical approaches tend to deal with the house as a unit of accommodation with a number of objective physical attributes, such as size, amenities, and form. Some reduce the house to its materialistic nature, that is, "the bricks and mortar or other building materials that comprise the constructions within which people live" (Kemeny, 1992). The house is used as a unit of planning and target of governmental policies (housing policies). As a physical product, it is determined; it could be counted, improved, and measured in terms of housing stock and future requirements according to population growth. In this sense, housing becomes a consumable product that is bought, used, and disposed of based on the changing needs and conditions of its occupants (Abdelmonem, 2016). According to the well-known view of Le Corbusier, the house/dwelling is "a machine for living" (Harris, 1997). At the basic level, homes provide the space which defines many activities that constitute primary relationships in the home and for those living within it – those who care, work, and support each other.

The social function of the home

An institution's social function is what justifies its existence and its role in society, and confers its legitimacy in the public sphere. This legitimacy is determined in turn by recognition, not in a law (legality), nor even by public opinion, which can be volatile, but by individual citizens. "Human development and the advancement of society will only be possible if it is based on societies made up of stable families organised in a personalised home environment; this is what will lead to a stable and personalising society" (d'Entremont, 2018: 164). Here, we can identify three levels in the explanation of this social function: "why" the home exists as an institution, "for what" it exists, and what is its "purpose."

The "why" looks towards the past and seeks to give an explanation. We need food, physical protection, shelter when we are tired or sick, and something that allows us to remember who we are. These needs can be met in many ways, with better or worse results, but, as a general rule, they are best met when we have a home.[6] The "what for" looks towards the future. In the home, someone (family members or external collaborators) prepares our food, protects us, and offers us an identity. This may be one person, or several people, or everyone, with cooperation from people outside of the home and material resources: the house, the furniture, the household appliances, and everything that makes "our" home special. The "what for" invokes a function, first for its members, but later on for others outside of the home, and eventually reaching society as a whole (Argandoña, 2018).

A home without a "what for" can function for quite some time; it simply has to satisfy the motivations of the people who are its members – the "why": in other words, perform the functions of a restaurant, hotel, social club, cinema, and sometimes hospital. But it will be lacking a "purpose," which is the "what for" as defined, shared, and accepted by that particular community's members. This "purpose" is not usually stated explicitly (families do not usually write a mission statement, agreed and implemented by all, as is the practice of many firms), but this does not mean that they do not have an implicit "purpose" or "project." The lack of a "project," or the existence of several unshared "projects," implies a lack of unity, and this is a threat for the home's continued existence.

The key is the development of knowledge, skills, attitudes, values, and virtues. The works done in the home, mentioned before, are focused, directly or indirectly, to that learning and formation, including the task of "replicating" the organisation in future new homes, which will be very different, but which will be rooted in the homes existing now. The home has many dimensions: temporal, spatial, economic, ethical, legal, cultural, communicative, political, psychological, sociological, religious, and others (Argandoña, 2018). Here, we refer to three aspects of the home's "purpose" which provide the rationale for how this book is organised: care, people, and work. Each of these sections are fronted by a key feature article that drives the research agenda in its field, led by Lord Richard Best, Professor Sheila the Baroness Hollins, and Professor José Víctor Orón Semper. That is why the three dimensions of people, work, and care developed in the book are important.

PART ONE: ON CARE. Because what people do at home is to take care (of the people, of the home, of the future, of society). The different chapters of the first part develop various aspects of care: with everyone, with the vulnerable (children, the elderly, the sick), and in preparing for ageing in all aspects, such as food, health, and sustainable housing.

PART TWO: ON PEOPLE. The home is for people, and they contribute in many ways (in addition to those who apparently cannot contribute, such as babies), with special consideration of children, the elderly, disabled, and caregivers.

PART THREE: ON WORK. Work, in a very broad sense, from the material tasks of the home, performed by family members or external collaborators, to tasks that we do not usually call work, such as resting together, chatting, listening to others, etc. Including social perceptions of work at home in different environments, and some special types of work, such as the on-demand economy and working from home.

In the following sections we discuss the makeup of those parts and their theoretical underpinnings from different interdisciplinary and multidisciplinary perspectives.

On care

There is a growing understanding of the challenges facing health services and providers to offer care at formal health care institutions. With public spending on health and social care in decline, the culture of care is shifting towards providing care at home, and wherever possible by the family with local community support. Hence, the relationship between the home and care is getting very crucial in the make-up of twenty-first-century homes. The home exists because it satisfies needs. The first need that appears in people's lives is linked to their vulnerability: we are born biologically destitute, unprotected, and unable to survive without other people's help. That is why we need an institution[7] that gives shelter, food, protection, and that teaches us and helps us learn (sometimes, the lessons can be very hard) how to be human beings (Marcos, 2016, Marcos and Bertolaso, 2018). And here is where care appears as one of the home's basic components. Care requires a safe, pleasant physical environment, which is the home's spatial dimension; a community of people who perform these functions, which is the family, in its different forms; and an extensive range of goods and services provided by the neighbourhood, the village, the city, and, ultimately, by society in general. All of these elements of the home are embraced in the concept of care.[8]

While the specific needs related with care change over time, the need for care persists: we are vulnerable and dependent, even when we are at the peak of our strength and physical and mental capacities. The home is a place where we can take shelter from inclement weather, an opportunity to enter and retire into our private space, a place for mental repose, and a means for recouping strength. This is obvious at times of illness or disability, or in the infirmity of old age, but the home is always a place – albeit not the only one – where everyone can find care.

And it is also a place where we learn to care for others, whether driven by biological forces or sentiment, whether for self-interest, selfishness, or love. Caring is giving of oneself, and this is learned in the home – not just in the home, but it is the first place where this learning takes place. The first thing that a baby usually sees when it opens its eyes is the face of its mother or father while they are caring for him. It is true that the home is intended, first and foremost, to foster individual autonomy, particularly of children and young people. However, autonomy is the counterpart of dependency: the autonomous person chooses how he or she will put him or herself at the service of those who are vulnerable and dependent – and that is care (cfr. Marcos and Bertolaso, 2018).

The literature on the ethics of care has grown considerably, particularly since the works of Carol Gilligan (1982) and Nel Noddings (1984). Although opinion is not unanimous regarding the foundations of this ethics, there are certain qualities which seem to be particularly useful in an appraisal of care in the home.[9] A number of definitions of care can be found in the literature on ethics: as a counterpoint to the concept of justice, as a type of work, as a special relationship, as a practice, a value, a disposition, or a virtue.[10] Whatever the definition used, care is a unique relationship that involves two parties, the one "caring" and the "cared-for," both with obligations (Noddings, 1984).[11] In the home, this relationship is always personal and direct (Bubeck, 1995; cfr. Zárate et al., Chapter 2), but it can never be considered a commercial exchange (Bahr and Bahr, 2001),[12] nor even as fulfilment of a contract (Held, 1993), and is much less driven by selfish motives alone.[13] Neither can care relationships in the home be reduced to the mere performance of deontological duties. On the contrary, they will include other qualities such as gentleness, agreeability, compassion, sympathy, and good temperedness (Baier, 1987), which align with virtue ethics (Halwani, 2003, McLaren, 2001, Ruddick, 1989).

Tronto (1994: 126–136) argues that care is a practice which has four stages or virtuous dispositions: a) attentiveness, the predisposition to understand that a particular person has a need; b) responsibility, the attitude of responding and taking responsibility for the provision of care; c) competence, the skill in offering effective care; and d) responsiveness by the person receiving the care, which does not mean reciprocity, as this is not always possible in situations of vulnerability and inequality, but the effort to understand what those who are in this vulnerable position have expressed.

These reflections on the nature of care, although they are usually directed towards other activities, such as medicine, nursing, or education, are particularly important for the home. When Hamington (2004; 3) says that "care is committed to flourishing and growth of individuals," he seems to be thinking of the home's social function, particularly with respect to children.[14] But, in fact, it applies to everyone, so he adds that care "acknowledges our interconnectedness and interdependence" (Ibid., 3; Mayeroff, 1971). Since its inception, the ethics of care has been associated with female ethics, because its roots were found in motherhood. However, care is not something that is exclusively female. The experience of many homes shows that care relationships exist between parents and children (although, logically, with distinctive features in each case), and also between siblings, between other relatives and with people who, while not members of the family community, contribute to the performance of the home's tasks.

Care has a dimension that goes far beyond the boundaries of the home.

> The home is a place where one "learns to live" during a long and changeable process. It is here that children receive knowledge and develop abilities; they internalize rights, autonomy, participation, mutual respect and freedom. It is a place where the other is acknowledged, where one participates and also learns how to manage disputes and diversity . . . and this is learnt precisely in coexistence with the rest of the family members, and is therefore joint and shared learning.
>
> (Argandoña, Chapter 10)

It is logical that the home should be the place where one learns to care for others, projecting this responsibility towards other spheres outside of the home, for example, care for the environment (Brizi, Chapter 5).

To frame this section, a feature article is written by Lord Richard Best. Under the title of "A Home for Later Life," Lord Best urges us to critique our decisions today with a view of the impact on our later life. He discusses the inability of the market to provide the homes needed for an ageing society and proposes key steps to achieving the homes we will need. The argument of the multidisciplinary approaches to care is developed over four chapters. In Chapter 2, Belén Zárate, Remei Agulles, and Consuelo León discuss the transformation of other care environments in homes, looking at the characteristics of care within the family and how both health care and residential care in Spain have developed new means of a collaborative, patient-centred approach. In Chapter 3, Costa and Esteve, on the other hand, investigate the healthy home during early years, looking at guidelines to build healthy home interior environments with particular attention to child development at an early stage. They make the case for building a healthy home with solid structures and materials to make healthy indoor environments. In Chapter 4, Greaves-Fernández and Rabiela-Sotelo discuss the high-risk practices that occur in the homes of families suffering from food poverty. They look at how care could be affected by everyday practices and the implications on healthy living at home, and how education is central to building awareness for such a growing segment of society in an attempt to safeguard both the health and the wellbeing in these homes. Responsible citizenship and our common home is the key focus of Maria Rosaria Brizi in Chapter 5, where she addresses a sense of responsibility and commitment towards the natural environments from within the household. She explores embracing the principle of sustainability in everyday living and making homes sustainable practices.

On people

The person is the core of the home because he has dignity, "the inalienable value of worth every human being has for the fact of being human" (Zárate et al., Chapter 2). The home is a means, not an end; it exists for people. The restaurant, the hotel, the social club, the cinema, and the hospital that are part of the home, as we said earlier, are also focused on the person, but the home has a "purpose" which is not the sum of different services, no matter how important they may be, but the development and flourishing of the person – of all persons – from the moment of their birth and during the rest of their lives.[15]

> The person's place in the home can be analyzed primarily from two viewpoints: privacy and relationality. The home is the place for the person's privacy, to which one retires to keep one's life in order and regain control over it: it is "the place to which one always returns,"
>
> (Alvira, 2010)

> that most recondite, private, secure and comfortable place for the self, where it takes shelter from the natural world, to where it belongs as its innermost shelter, and where it addresses the world and the other, opening itself to transcendence.
>
> (Patrão Neves, 2018: 73)

In the home, we can be as we are, because we are accepted for what we are, not for what we have, give or do. "It is in the home where we find the true expression of the interiority of the human being, a natural base that is necessary in order to carry out the tasks demanded by society" (d'Entremont, 2018: 170) (Argandoña, 2018: 13). In short, the home is the "space open for the quiet flourishing of what is human" (Marcos and Bertolaso, 2018: 35). This is probably what best defines each home's project, and its function in society.

The other way of understanding people in the home is their relationality: not because the person is his relationships, but because he understands himself in his relationships, and because "home is that site where relation originally occurs and within which individuals are constituted" (Patrão Neves, 2018: 73). These relationships determine people's expectations in the home, what they give and receive (and what they themselves receive when they give), at the physical, mental, emotional, cognitive, or ethical level.

> This entails rights and responsibilities, work, formal organization (rules, judgment, hierarchy, authority) and informal organization (trust, implicit understanding, putting aside personal criteria to favour the needs of other members), material possessions, human and social capital and many other elements, all of them focused on achieving certain material and spiritual results for the people and the internal community.
>
> (Argandoña, 2018: 14; Allan and Crow, 1989).

However, people's relationships are not limited to the narrow confines of the home, but are open to the outside world: the home is "within but open" (Marcos and Bertolaso, 2018: 53). Society in general, and individual social communities (neighbourhood, village, city, companies, educational institutions, social organisations, and many more) receive the "gift" of strong homes that efficiently fulfil their purpose, namely, the human and social development of its members. In turn, the home is supported on the legal, cultural, social, and economic framework of society and its individual communities, policies, and services. Ideally, these are win-win relationships, although they can also be destructive.[16]

To look at a human-centred approach, the second section of this book, People, encompasses a number of studies that look at the experience of people with special needs, like ageing parents, children with disabilities, caregiving challenges, as well as how the home environment impacts of our cognitive and sensation development. The section opens the argument with a feature article by prominent scholar and campaigner Professor Sheila The Baroness Hollins, under the title "My home, my life: Aspirations of people with intellectual disability for an ordinary home and an ordinary life." In this article, Baroness Hollins looks at the barriers and challenges to living an ordinary life at home as opposed to living in institutional care, where individuals with intellectual disabilities can find themselves in a locked ward. The section follows with four chapters that tackle theoretical and empirical investigations. In Chapter 6, Usochi Ilozumba investigates the anthropological construct of the home and its impact on the our cognitive, sensation, and intellectual knowledge in light of Sarti's scientific-experimental thesis of response-transmission interaction, Piaget's cognitive development stages, and Sanguineti's metaphysical approach to the study of human cognition.

The complexity and challenges of ageing parents living with adult persons with disability was the focus of Horacio Joffre's chapter, which is found in Chapter 7. He discusses the chronic, sustained, and systematic stress that faces ageing parents looking after a disabled person and the need for public policies, education, recreation, and health services that support such complex needs and environments. Along a similar line, Aleksandra Kroll looks, in Chapter 8, at the special care needed for disabled children at home, especially when family members become caregivers to both mentally and physically disabled children at home. In Chapter 9, Gabriella Facchinetti et al, focus on the expectations elderly people experience and needs for their residential care facilities. The chapter explores what contributes to the feeling of a "sense of home" and what the housing needs of elderly are through a qualitative study of 14 older adults in Rome.

On work

The people who make up the home, and those who collaborate with them, whether regularly or occasionally, are continuously performing actions.[17] We could call some of these actions work because of their productive or operational qualities, or because they entail effort or fulfil a duty or obligation, with or without an explicit remuneration. However, in the home, the concept of work becomes broader and goes beyond being a task-performing activity (Witzel and Warner, 2015). There may be one or more motives in any human action: extrinsic (because of the consequences received from the environment or other people: goods and services, approval or reprobation, etc.), intrinsic (the consequences that the action has directly on the agent: satisfaction, learning), and transcendent or prosocial (the consequences on other people which, in turn, generate consequences – moral learning – in the agent) (Pérez López, 1993; Argandoña, 2008).

These actions can be individual or shared; in the case of the latter, there is cooperation between several people, each one with their own motives, but who are all interested in a shared result or purpose (the "what for"). For example, if they are working together on preparing a meal, everyone wishes to satisfy their hunger (extrinsic motivation), they are doing something that gives them pleasure (intrinsic), and they also want the other participants to satisfy their hunger and have a good time (transcendent). However, everyone has a shared purpose in this joint action, which may simply be to prepare a lunch together in a coordinated manner, or perhaps something more ambitious, such as a party or a celebration for one of the people there.

The important thing in this action, which has some of the qualities of work (effort, dedication, order, discipline), is the shared purpose, which does not necessarily need to align with the agents' motives, and can be something as simple, but as important, as wanting to do something together. Sometimes, one person's action is independent from another person's action; other times, there are strategic interdependencies, so that the results of one person's action depend on the results of another person's action. In these cases, social motivation is needed, which will be part of each individual's intrinsic and transcendent motives. These actions require coordination and commitment, generating a learning that strengthens the home's purpose, and they are often part of the care we talked about earlier.

On this basis, we can now identify what characterises work in the home: awareness of human vulnerability and dependence and, consequently, responsibility for the service. The social value of the work done in the home is not confined to the economic value of certain goods and services that are produced; it also contributes to the welfare of society and people's development (MacIntyre, 1999; cfr. Frezza et al., 2017).

When one talks of work in the home, it can encompass a variety of situations. We usually highlight the work done by the mother, and rightly so, because historically it has been the mother who has performed most of these tasks. However, we must increasingly take into account the work done by the father which, while having different qualities from the work done by the mother, is no less important. And the work done by the children; often the first school for work, the work done in the home leaves a lifelong mark and includes when they give back to their parents the services they received when they were children. And, lastly, the work of external agents, from shopping, cooking, cleaning, and tidying up to looking after children, disabled people, and the elderly. Such carers often adopt the home of the people they care for as their own, because this care is more than just time spent on a particular activity. Work is always care.

Part Three on Work, starts with feature article addressing the educational approach for children's growth at home. The article, written by José Víctor Orón, focuses on how the UpToYou educational program focuses on how the emotional education of young children should be understood in the family environment during the first years of life, from the theory of attachment and social reference, to the emotional development and complexity perspectives. This part is made up of an additional four chapters that look at the economics of working at home from theoretical and practical points of view. In Chapter 10, Antonio Argandoña investigates the theoretical approach to work at home as a shared human action that takes place in a special community. He looks at personal and collective motives, common purposes, coordination, and the trust collective work generates. In Chapter 11, Teresita Abay Krueger discusses the alignment of the on-demand economy with the home as a workplace, as future work agendas focus on the home. In Chapter 12, Sandra Idrovo Carlier et al. discuss a cross-country comparison for caregiving in the home in Latin America. They look at how housework is perceived and how it helps develop skills in ten Latin American countries and Spain. They report results that show certain general homogeneity in their perception, but with some statistically significant differences among some of them and when considering gender. In Chapter 13, Kathleen Farrell studies the impact of the evolution of technology as key to teleworking from home and its impact on domestic life. She looks at how such changing dynamics at home provide women more opportunities for flexible working conditions, and how that has an impact on work/life balance and deprives the family its physical independence from work without a managed balance through set barriers of time and space. Finally, Audrey Tan introduces a novel structured programme on developing life skills from Kenvale College, Sydney, to address the true value of the work in the home in Singapore. Through the programme, participants are challenged to develop professionalism in the work they do at home as a fundamental role in developing character strengths and value systems in children

Notes

1 Concerning the home's spatial or physical dimension, Karjalainen (1993), Fox O'Mahony (2013), Graham et al. (2015), and Abdelmonem (2011, 2016). These authors underscore that this dimension is not just physical but also psychological and spiritual (Argandoña, 2018).
2 Ibid.
3 Mallett, "Understanding Home."
4 Oxford English Dictionary. Online edition, as it appears on 25 June 2013.
5 On the other hand, dwellings are used to denote the primitive, non-professional and mainly vernacular production of housing, while residence, shelter, and family are associated with the functions which humans require within their living space.
6 The reader may perhaps think that this way of explaining the home is too traditionalist or even idealistic. This does not mean that we are not aware of the difficulties that arise in the home, or the criticisms that have been levelled at the different models. However,

our purpose here is simply to explain this book's content and its three sections: care, people, and work.

7 The use of the word "institution" here does not have an academic intention; it is understood simply as a way of organising coexistence in certain specific circumstances, created not by human design but by society's self-organization (Hayek, 1967) Argandoña (2004).

8 The literature on care is usually focused from the perspective of the care professions; González and Iffland (2014).

9 In this Introduction, we will not discuss issues such as transferring the responsibility for care from the family and the immediate environment to external professionals (who often become integrated as members of the needy person's home), or the reasons why care is mostly a woman's job, or why many care activities are poorly paid, etc.

10 For some of these conceptions, see Held (2006), Ruddick (1998), and Tronto (1994).

11 It is true that a baby or an old person with dementia cannot be considered as having obligations towards the person who cares for them, at least not at that particular time. However, they can "pay" for this care in other ways: when a hungry baby cries, it is a call to the carer to give the best of herself, and the baby's smile after it has been fed can be the best payment.

12 This is one of the reasons why the neoclassical economics of the family cannot be considered a complete theory of the home Zamagni (2018).

13 We say "solely" by selfish motives because although they may be present, they cannot be the dominant motives: the father who cares for a sick child may do so hoping that in the future the child will look after him, but this extrinsic motivation cannot be the sole motivation. There must be, above all, an intrinsic, transcendent (Pérez López, 1993), or prosocial motivation (Grant, 2013).

14 Held (1993) puts this more directly: viewed from political and social ethics, he sees the application of the ethics of care as the opportunity to create a culture that conceives as "its most important task the flourishing of children and the creation of human relationships."

15 Obviously, the identity of the person or persons who are the centre of attention in the home changes as time goes by; the important point is that the actions performed within the home always target people, even when they apparently target an object: leaking roofs are repaired because the house, which is a means, must always be in the best possible state of repair for its people, who are the end.

16 On the relationships between the home and society, Argandoña (2018: 15–17).

17 For a development of these ideas, see Argandoña (chap. 10).

References

Abdelmonem, M.G., 2011, Understanding everyday homes of urban communities: the case of local streets (Hawari) of old cairo, *Journal of Civil Engineering and Architecture*, 5(11), 996–1010.

Abdelmonem, M.G., 2016, *The Architecture of Home in Cairo: Socio-spatial Practice of the Hawari's Everyday Life*. London: Routledge

Allan, G. and G. Crow, eds., 1989, *Home and Family: Creating the Domestic Sphere*. London, UK: Macmillan.

Alvira, R., 2010, *El lugar al que se vuelve: Reflexiones sobre la familia*. Pamplona, Spain: Eunsa.

Arendt, H., 1958, *The Human Condition*. Chicago: The University of Chicago Press.

Argandoña, A., 2004, Economic ethics and institutional change, *Journal of Business Ethics*, 53(1–2), 191–201.

Argandoña, A., 2008, Integrating ethics into action theory and organizational theory, *Journal of Business Ethics*, 78(3), 435–446.

Argandoña, A., 2018, The home: multidisciplinary reflections, in A. Argandoña, ed., *The Home: Multidisciplinary Reflections*. Cheltenham, UK: Edward Elgar, 1–31.

Bahr, H.M. and K.S. Bahr, 2001, Families and self-sacrifice: alternative models and meanings for family theory, *Social Forces*, 79(4), 1231–1258.

Baier, A., 1987, Hume: the woman's moral theorist? in E.F. Kittay and D. Meyers, eds., *Women and Moral Theory*. Lanham, MD: Rowman & Littlefield.

Bower, S.N., 1980, Territory in urban settings, in I. Altman, et al. eds., *Environment and Culture; Human Behaviour and Environment*, Vol. 4. New York: Plenum Press, 179–193.

Bubeck, D., 1995, *Care, Gender and Justice*. Oxford, UK: Clarendon Press.

d'Entremont, A., 2018, Spatial relationality and domesticity: reality and functions of the home from a human geography perspective, in A. Argandoña, ed., *The Home: Multidisciplinary Reflections*. Cheltenham, UK: Edward Elgar, 163–175.

Fox O'Mahony, L., 2013, The meaning of home: from theory to practice, *International Journal of Law and Built Environment*, 5(2), 156–171.

Frezza, G., H. Keefe and M. Bertolaso, 2017, Work of the home and social relationships as a guide to domestic care for the elderly, in F. Cavallo, V. Marletta, A. Monteriù and P. Siciliano, eds., *Ambient Assisted Living*. New York, NY: Springer.

Gilligan, C., 1982, *In a Different Voice*. Cambridge, MA: Harvard University Press.

González, A.M. and C. Iffland, eds., 2014, *Care Professions and Globalization: Theoretical and Practical Perspectives*. New York, NY: Palgrave Macmillan.

Graham, L.T., S.D. Gosling and C.K. Travis, 2015, The psychology of home environments: a call for research on residential space, *Perspectives on Psychological Science*, 10(3), 346–356.

Grant, A., 2013, *Give and Take: A Revolutionary Approach to Success. Why Helping Others Drives Our Success*. London, UK: Weidenfeld & Nicolson.

Halwani, R., 2003, *Virtuous Liaisons: Care, Love, Sex, and Virtue Ethics*. Peru, IL: Open Court.

Hamington, M., 2004, *Embodied Care: Jane Addams, Maurice Merleau-Ponty and Feminist Ethics*. Chicago, IL: University of Illinois Press.

Harris, S., 1997, Everyday architecture. In D. Berke and S. Harris, eds., *Architecture of the Everyday*. Princeton: Princeton University Press.

Hayek, F.A., 1967, *Studies in Philosophy, Politics and Economics*. Chicago, IL: University of Chicago Press.

Held, V., 1993, *Feminist Morality: Transforming Culture, Society, and Politics*. Chicago, IL: University of Chicago Press.

Held, V., 2006, *The Ethics of Care*. New York, NY: Oxford University Press.

Karjalainen, P.T., 1993, House, home and the place of dwelling, *Scandinavian Housing and Planning Research*, 10, 65–74.

Kemeny, J., 1992, *Housing and Social Theory*. London: Routledge.

MacIntyre, A., 1999, *Dependent Rational Animals*. Chicago: Carus Publishing Company.

Marcos, A., 2016, Vulnerability as a part of human nature, in A. Masferrer and E. García, eds., *Human Dignity of the Vulnerable in the Age of Rights: Interdisciplinary Perspectives*. Dordrecht, the Netherlands: Springer, 29–44.

Marcos, A. and M. Bertolaso, 2018, What is a home? On the intrinsic nature of a home, in A. Argandoña, ed., *The Home: Multidisciplinary Reflections*. Cheltenham, UK: Edward Elgar, 35–56.

Mayeroff, M., 1971. *On Caring*. New York, NY: Harper & Row.
McLaren, M., 2001, Feminist ethics: care as a virtue, in P. Desaultes and J Waugh, eds., *Feminists Doing Ethics (Feminists Constructions)*. Lanham, MD: Rowman and Littlefield, 111–127.
Noddings, N., 1984, *Caring: A Feminine Approach to Ethics and Moral Education*. Berkeley, CA: University of California Press.
Patrão Neves, M., 2018, Self and others: home as a cradle of a non-violent relationship, in A. Argandoña, ed., *The Home: Multidisciplinary Reflections*. Cheltenham, UK: Edward Elgar, 57–76.
Pérez López, J.A., 1993, *Fundamentos de dirección de empresas*. Madrid, Spain: Rialp.
Ruddick, S., 1989, *Maternal Thinking: Toward a Politics of Peace*. New York, NY: Ballentine Books.
Ruddick, S., 1998, Care as labor and relationship, in M.S. Haflon and J.C. Haber, eds., *Norms and Values: Essays on the Work of Virginia Held*. Lanham, MD: Rowman & Littlefield.
Tronto, J., 1994, *Moral Boundaries: A Political Argument for an Ethic of Care*. New York, NY: Routledge.
Witzel, M. and M. Warner, 2015, Taylorism revisited: culture, management theory and paradigm-shift, *Journal of General Management*, 40(3), 55–70.
Zamagni, S., 2018, The family and economic theorizing, in A. Argandoña, ed., *The Home: Multidisciplinary Reflections*. Cheltenham, UK: Edward Elgar, 123–143.
Zárate, B., R. Agulles and C. León, 2019, From care in the home to the transformation of other care environments in homes, chapter 2 in this volume.

Part 1

Home and care

Feature ARTICLE one

A home for later life

Lord Richard Best

Introduction

In "The Hundred Year Life," Andrew Scott and Lynda Gratton urge all of us to think ahead. They suggest that we should imagine a conversation with our older self, our avatar aged 90+. No doubt that older self will rebuke us for failing to put enough into our pension scheme, failing to take enough exercise, and not choosing a better diet! But will our avatar also ask why – when we were fit and able – we did not find the home that would suit us for our later years? Will we regret that we did nothing to "rightsize" while we had the energy and good sense to sort out our comfort and care in older age?

This chapter considers the importance of the home for our later years. It discusses the inability of the market to provide the homes needed for an ageing society, and it proposes key steps to achieving the homes we will need.

The importance of the right home for later life

For each of us, the place we call home is of acute importance to our health and wellbeing for our older age. Bad housing impoverishes, isolates, and imprisons us. It requires us to pay more than we can afford to maintain a house and garden that is no longer suited to our needs. It confines us to a place where we cannot readily find companionship and where it is difficult for any care needs to be met. It causes us to have accidents and the hazards of negotiating steps, stairs, and the bathroom. It makes it difficult for us to leave the hospital when we should. It denies us independence.

The right home protects us from harm, including from the scourge of loneliness. It prevents and postpones the need for admission to a hospital and to a residential home care and it provides the secure base from which we can enjoy retirement. It is a place we can share with family and friends.

For society, ensuring the older generation is in accommodations that meet their needs for space and light, warmth, accessibility, and manageability means less need for social care and less pressure on health services. At a time when local authority care budgets are in crisis and the NHS is desperately short of funds – and hospital beds – the importance of housing for senior citizens makes sense at every level.

The homes we need

We know what kind of housing an ageing population requires: the standards established by the HAPPI initiative (Housing for an Ageing Population: Panel for Innovation) in 2009 spell out the attributes of decent homes for retirement living. We need enough space – including storage space not necessarily inside our apartment – and a balcony if we're not at ground level. We need plenty of light, preferably with a dual-aspect so that we are not stuck in a home that faces just one way and so that we can get proper ventilation through our home. We need level access through the front door, around the home, and into a shower. These and other features, like good insulation and a highly efficient heating system, will make our lives easier and sustain our independence.

Importantly, we need opportunities to be as sociable, or as private, as we wish. Purpose-built "retirement housing" is a mixture of the physical – the bricks and mortar – and the social – the chance to mix, to help, and to be helped. At a minimum, there is extra social value from some communal space outside, where we can sit in the sun and a "Club Room" inside, where we can meet together, sometimes eat together, and sometimes celebrate together. In the larger-scale developments where costs can be spread over many households, more extensive common facilities can be expected – a coffee house, restaurant, gym, even a pool. And in the "Assisted Living" or "Extra Care" schemes, there will be care services on hand for emergencies and for daily help, if required.

The inability of the market to provide suitable homes for an ageing society

But where are all these homes for older "right-sizers"? DEMOS research suggests over 3.5m older people would be interested in moving if something suitable was available not far away. And the research shows a market for at least 30,000 new homes a year – 10% of the government's overall target of 300,000. Yet the actual number of tailor-made homes for retirement living is around 7,000 per annum (with the bulk of these being built by just two specialist house builders).

Why are the major house builders – who account for over two-thirds of all new homes – shunning this market? And why are the non-profit housing associations not stepping into the breach?

The answer is that the house builders are doing very well without having to bother with older purchasers who are likely to be more discerning and more trouble. The builders can secure substantial profits producing very ordinary new accommodation for younger households, with low space standards compared with other European countries. Because of the severe shortages of new homes, these house builders have been able to sell to families who have no option but to pay what is demanded of them. These developments attract huge subsidies from the government under the Help to Buy scheme, further assisted by relief from Stamp Duty for first-time buyers. Such incentives are not available for any homes built for the older generation.

Moreover, new homes for older people will often require a location near shops, surgery centres, and local facilities. This means acquiring brown field sites, often in competition from supermarkets or car showrooms, or for other commercial uses. Such sites may well need remedial work. By contrast, the business model for the major house builders involves securing large, greenfield sites which are much easier, and more profitable, to develop.

It seems unlikely that, without incentives or obligations, anything approaching a sufficient number of new homes for our ageing population will be built in the years ahead.

Ways to achieve enough new homes

As always, government can either help or hinder. HM Treasury could level the playing field between older and younger by announcing Stamp Duty relief for people over pension age who acquire a new home. And, to help those whose existing property is worth a bit less than the retirement home they want to buy, support equivalent to Help to Buy could be made available. After all, supporting the older generation to rightsize brings much needed family homes onto the market – achieving "two-for-one." It is worth noting that whenever we decide to move, in preparation for a healthier, more amenable later life, we create a chain of property sales: this means that the Exchequer receives Stamp Duty, on average, for three transactions in return for forfeiting the receipt from one!

The government's agency, Homes England, needs to encourage the nation's housing associations to recognise and provide for the older generation. Its grant funding needs to target affordable homes, to at least enable those renting from councils and housing associations themselves to release a family home to those on the waiting list. Local government also has a crucial role to play. The government's National Planning Policy Framework encourages local authorities to recognise and respond to the housing needs of the senior citizens in their area. To begin with, councils need to assess those needs and incorporate measures in their local plan/strategic plan to satisfy this demand. It may well be sensible for the authority to allocate specific sites to be developed exclusively for housing for older people, removing the competition from other uses that drives up the price of land.

In many places, local authorities have land that is suitable for new homes for the older age group. For example, the redundant garages on the council estate can make way for some high-quality bungalows to accommodate older people under-occupying adjacent family houses. In some areas, a revival of council housebuilding is emerging and the local authority will seize the development opportunity itself. In other cases, a partnership with a housing association can do the job.

In all areas, the power of the planning system should enable councils to require private-sector house builders, as a condition of planning consent, to incorporate some affordable homes into their larger schemes. Although it is true that some of the major house builders have reneged on their commitments and used a loophole in the system – the "viability test" – to avoid their planning obligations, with firm resolve local authorities can and should continue to use this route to securing much-needed affordable homes, not least for older citizens.

Councils are also the key players in supporting local Home Improvement Agencies. These "care and repair" organisations can enable people to stay put for longer in properties that, with some upgrading and/or adaptation, can meet accessibility and even energy-saving requirements that are almost comparable to the advantages of moving to purpose-built accommodation.

With backing and encouragement, both the for-profit and the not-for-profit sectors in the UK could emulate the model prevalent in so many other countries where good, quality homes attract those from their 60s onwards. And, in doing so, the housing providers repay society by enhancing health and wellbeing, and saving taxpayers' money by reducing falls and other accidents in the home, enabling earlier and more successful discharge from hospital, allowing home care to be more effectively delivered, and postponing or preventing unwanted moves to residential care.

"Tech" to the rescue for our care needs?

Meeting the care needs of an ageing population is becoming one of the highest national priorities. Costs are rising, public resources are severely constrained, and the numbers of older people in need of extra help is set to increase relentlessly. We can no longer rely on the younger generation, living nearby, to supply the care we need on an informal basis.

In looking at ways of solving the problems of scarce human and financial resources, some are hoping that technical solutions will come to the rescue. It will not be easy to recruit and retain enough paid carers to take the place of the army of family and friends who currently do so much. Some observers predict a future of robots fetching and carrying – even of robot pets to keep us company. These ideas seem fanciful, but so did driverless cars until a few years ago. The government's Industrial Strategy points to potential opportunities for technology helping out. In theory, "smart" homes can use automation to help us with daily chores. And "telemonitoring" can keep an eye on our health needs, summoning help if necessary. But in reality, successful projects – beyond introducing older residents to the communication support which tablets and mobile phones can provide – have done little to harness the advances of the digital age to support our later years.

Undoubtedly, there are applications and equipment that could improve the quality of life for all of us, including those with long-term conditions. But funding from health and social care budgets is hard to direct to this new market. And a lack of coordination between small companies doing imaginative work that needs rigorous evaluation confines "tech" solutions to the margins.

And then there's the human element

When we talk to our 90-year-old self, our avatar from the future, we will want to know – perhaps above all else – whether we are going to be lonely in old age. Loneliness and isolation are the hidden horrors of living alone or living as a carer with a partner who – perhaps because of dementia – can no longer fulfil our social needs. The house in the pretty village, for example, was great when we were 60 and able to drive to see family, visit the doctor, shop, and meet friends. It is another story when we have had to give up the car and the bus service is wholly inadequate. It is not much fun to be isolated and home alone, worried about security as well as the problems of keeping up the house and garden.

If we are over 90, its very likely we will have some ailments or some health conditions that are troublesome. But most older people can learn to live with imperfect health – and indeed can stave it off – if they can enjoy an engaging social life.

As social animals, while we need our private space, we also need contact with others. Tailor-made new housing for our later years brings opportunities to do things with neighbours, whether in the all-singing, all-dancing context of full-blown retirement communities, or the more intimate settings of small retirement developments.

In conclusion

Ultimately, how we fare as septuagenarians, octogenarians, and nonagenarians will depend on the actions of all of us while we are younger. We have the power to act, both as citizens – as voters – and as consumers. To secure more and better homes to suit our later life, we need to persuade the government to give as much priority to their housing policies for older people as for younger people. To get the private sector to create the homes that will persuade us to rightsize, we need to wield our consumer power, to be prepared to pay for quality, to demonstrate the demand which the market should fulfil, and to even consider reinventing some of the equity stored in our home to achieve a better lifestyle for our later years.

Sometimes we can come together to create "senior co-housing" in a development of apartments that can be co-designed and co-managed by a like-minded group (maybe under the wing of a housing association). More generally, if we move to accommodations that protect us from loneliness by affording opportunities for neighbourliness and companionship, we can benefit ourselves and those around us. At the end of the day, it will be the human, personal, and social interactions that make the most difference.

Chapter 2

From care in the home to the transformation of other care environments in homes

Belén Zárate, Remei Agulles, and Consuelo León

Introduction

The world's population is ageing globally (UN, n.d.). The pace of this phenomenon is faster in developed countries, and this has generated diverse focuses of concern and study. Among them, and mutually intertwined, we can find the economic impact of the decrease of active population, and the need to adapt the provision of care to these demographic changes. The latter thread admits a micro perspective, i.e., care from the point of view of carer and receiver, which is the approach we have chosen without forgetting the larger picture, which, in our case, will be Spain, a country with 25% of its population over 60 years old.[1]

When an old person is in a situation of vulnerability, he or she seeks the support of closer and more solid interpersonal relations. Studies taking either the caregiver's or the care receiver's perspective show that the latter's home and family becomes the first choice.[2] Body and mind, we are told, need rest and repair[3] in an atmosphere that is comforting and allows us to recognise ourselves. But when being cared for at home becomes impossible or undesirable, either because of a lack of resources or because of the state of the dependent person, how do we make up for the shortcomings that the alternative solution – residential care – shows in terms of closeness, affection, and personalisation? The answer to this question is articulated. To address it, we have divided this chapter into two theoretical sections and two practical sections: we discuss, first, the main concepts involved; second, we analyse the characteristics of care within the family; and third, we present different initiatives that have been implemented in the health care and residential care sectors in Spain that show some of the traits described in the previous section. Finally, we sketch out a strategy to provide these and similar actions with a stronger basis for them to develop.

Care, vulnerability, and personal dignity

The person: vulnerability and dignity

Human beings go through diverse stages of life, and in all of them, the person loses and acquires something. This susceptibility of change includes a typically human characteristic: **vulnerability**. We understand vulnerability or fragility as the characteristic of the human condition that makes us "susceptible to receive or suffer evil or pain, such as sickness, and also the possibility to be physically or emotionally harmed" (Feito, 2007).[4] "We human beings are vulnerable to many kinds of affliction and most of us are at some time afflicted by serious ills" (MacIntyre, 1999: 1). Vulnerability, or fragility, is particularly obvious at the beginning and end of life, and, in any case, we cope with it mostly thanks to the help of others.[5] Situations of vulnerability bring us back to the reality of what we are: brilliant but limited, dependent beings. Our limitation is a consequence of our being corporeal, spatially and temporally located. These situations take us closer to others, to ask for assistance and to also be more heedful to what others may need from us. In the midst of weakness emerges the need for others – our need to be completed along with *those who are like us* – who can give us what we do not have.

As Chirinos (2007b) notes, in ancient Greek hospitality, the recognition of the other as a peer, as *another like me*, is the first step to perform the care of hospitality.[6] We could add that it is the condition for any type of care action. And this is how the notion of vulnerability is linked to that of human **dignity**.

The concept of human dignity is a particularly evanescent one. Although it is the basis of many declarations and legal systems, it is rarely defined in any of these fields (Riley and Bos, n.d.). We will not enter a discussion regarding this term, and will take the most usual definition, which some authors deem to be Kantian (see, for example, Dillon, 2018), but we argue that it traces back to the roots of Western philosophical tradition: human dignity is the inalienable value or worth every human being has for the fact of being human. That means, for example, that during the stages of progressive impairment, one's personal dignity does not decrease and it can even become more obvious to us.

> Every human existence on the Earth – applauded or reviled, triumphant or defeated, happy or unhappy, generous or mean – represents the irruption in history of a radical novelty, the presence of an excellence superior to that of any other observable entity.
>
> (Del Barco, 1993: 129)

If we go back to Chirinos (2007b), as a second condition for taking care of the stranger, she marks the knowledge of him or her as a person – a peer – *in need*, someone vulnerable. It is precisely this fragility that makes the practice of hospitality – and any other practice of care – become disinterested, because in this situation of inequality, no reciprocation is expected. The assistance of the ailing and vulnerable covers the distance between them and the rest of peers and makes it possible for them to grow in spite of their disadvantaged situation. From this point of view, ages are not degrees of growth and subsequent decline, like in an inverted-U shape, but always of growth. We will go back to this notion later.

Personal dignity is especially acknowledged in the family, where relationships are not based on one's potential contribution and everyone is accepted as he or she is. Everyone is loved *because he or she is*, regardless of merits or qualities. Each one is acknowledged as exceptional and unique in traits and potentialities, despite their fragility.

The concept of care

If the other's vulnerability is a call for us, then **to care** is *to feel appealed by and provide for the needs of the other*. The nature of this appeal, who is the one to supply care, and what the outcome of care will be are still objects of discussion. An interesting account is that of Weicht (2015). Although we do not fully share his thesis that care is an entirely socially constructed notion, he reviews the different, and often colliding, approaches to it. For example, focusing on the needs of the care receiver by the caregiver – emphasised by virtue ethics – can be a source of internal and relational conflicts. Feminist literature highlights that care is often a gendered activity – women are expected to provide it – whose consequences are often the abuse, self-defeat, and isolation of the caregiver (Gilligan, 1982). Some authors view this approach as permeated by a rational, calculating mind-set – the trade-off costs-benefits[7] – and insist on the positive effects of care for both the giver and receiver (Bahr and Bahr, 2001).[8] In any case, this critique does not address the core of the gender perspective, which questions why only a part of the population (i.e., women) should be carrying out the tasks of care – be they rewarding or degrading – while the other part does not take responsibility for them. In fact, several studies about the use of time show empirically that this unequal distribution generates a double burden on working women (Durán, 2010), especially for those taking care of dependent relatives (Zárate, 2016).

Although co-responsibility of men and women in care within the home is one of the most supported solutions, Weicht (2015) explains how some authors propose generalised externalisation of services and institutionalisation as the solutions to lift the burden of care from families, and specifically women, or at least to bring unpaid care provided within the home to the public sphere with some type of economic retribution (Durán, 2018a, 2018b). This relates to the dichotomy of private-public, and it has relevant implications outside the economic sphere. Are the virtues of care to be cultivated only in the private sphere (the home) or, rather, they are part of good citizenship? And if so, how do you make the perfect, individualist citizen really *care* for the other? Is care to be first addressed by those close to us, or is it something so "universal" and abstract that it must be equally distributed among all our peers (Bahr and Bahr, 2001)? Each of these different proposals is a subsequent attempt to solve the paradoxes previously developed. With Bahr and Bahr (2001), we agree that sacrifice always entails risks and that the question is not whether to give oneself or not, but if the recipient *is worth it*. On the other hand, if virtues of care and sacrifice are only attached to women, then this is bad ethics.[9] This said, we also think that proper support by society, institutions and the state is necessary to provide care. And by *proper* here we mean that which takes into account the needs of the vulnerable ones and their carers.

If human dignity is the basis of social ethics, then the duty to care for the others – and the right to be looked after – is a natural one that starts from the very first social sphere, which is the family, to expand to the rest of human beings.

> To care for another person, in the most significant sense, is to help him grow and actualise himself . . . The meaning of caring I want to suggest is not to be confused with meanings such as wishing well, liking, comforting, and maintaining, or simply having an interest in what happens to another (Mayeroff, 1972: 1).

MacIntyre (1999) uses the term "flourish" to indicate what happens to a (dependent) person who is cared for properly. In the professional field, for example, that of nursing, there is the distinction between restorative care and care to make life thrive (Domínguez Alcón, 1986).

In addition, caregiving is enriching for those who undertake it, either men or women. It produces in the carer a whole collection of virtues, social habits, and also skills and knowledge that are important for the development of their personality (Bahr and Bahr, 2001; Chirinos, 2011; Chirinos et al., 2012). In summary, we need to acknowledge our dependency on care, our right to receive care, our duty to provide care, and our personal development in doing it (Chirinos, 2007b).

Characteristics of care within the family

The caring family: An attentive and spontaneous carer

> Even though it is obvious that there are also other actors involved in the provision of care, the family still remains the main association. This occurs through an emphasis on values and virtues linked to the family so that family care always becomes the point of comparison . . . People's homes have a particularly important meaning in this context as the nexus of intimate relationships (Weicht, 2015: 31).

Polo (1996) puts it in different words: if we observe, he suggests, those kinds of interpersonal relations that are fuller and more "saturated," we can discover the key for understanding the characteristics that must appear in the task of taking care of each other, regardless of the place or institution where this care is implemented. This is how care at home becomes the paradigm of human caring relations. We will see here the particular elements of care within the family that can and must be applied to any other situation of caring to build a model of interpersonal care.

Care takes place spontaneously within the family because the family itself is the source of the different generations. Small children are taken care of by their parents, but also – currently, more and more – by grandparents. The care of grandparents directly involves their adult children, but grandchildren also play this role. This is the main and most valuable intergenerational transference. In any society seeking to develop strong community values, care must be an activity performed by all – men and women; elderly, adults and young – and towards all those who are in need. This activity ranges from the environment closest to the person (the family), to the neighbourhood, the community, and independent organisations. It is a network of relationships that look for each other. This contrasts with the typically rationalistic ethics of autonomy (Gregory, 2012), which advocates for a society that seeks the maximisation of the individual's independence at the minimum cost.[10]

Traits of care within the family environment

We have mentioned the home as the most appropriate *place* for care. We could say that time and space coordinates shape the first relevant traits of care: synchronisation and recognition.

Coordinates of time and space in care shape the first traits: synchronisation and recognition

The home as space of relationships includes **temporality** (Argandoña, 2018). The passage of time imposes some characteristics to our task of care. First, we need to accept the age of the person: his or her developmental stage gives us another perspective of human coexistence. They modulate the specific type of attention, be it, for instance, continuous and affectionate instructing or just unobtrusive accompaniment. Second, the subjective perception of the time by the cared for person is very different from the perception of the carer. Third, to coexist means to *synchronise*, to adjust our own time to that of the others. The others are *other times* (Innerarity, 2001). Respect has much to do with spatial categories: boundaries, thresholds and so on, but also with temporal categories such as patience, rhythm, synchronisation, punctuality, coordination, and delay. Without all these categories we cannot correctly talk about the care of dependent persons.

In this sense, Innerarity (2001) alerts us of the current model of temporality: the temporality of rush, of haste. The time devoted to others is never a wasted, futile time, but *a time in construction*, a time that contributes to all, givers and receivers. Therefore, it is not a question of running more but of "opening our time to that of the others and so gain time in an intersubjective way" (p. 169).

The time of the family home is a daily time, made of habits and meetings, of flexible order, adapted to all those who coexist within it. It is a humanised order that helps the care processes, with adapted routines that facilitate an orderly, rush-free pace of life.

Caring also requires a suitable **space** or environment (Argandoña, 2018). When feeling vulnerable, a person's universe seems to collapse, giving way to a feeling of being uprooted. The vulnerable one perceives himself as an outlier. As the family home is a place of meeting and interpersonal communication, it is easier to understand the other as a whole being and not as an ailing body, and the other can recognise oneself in those – persons and objects – close to him or her.

These coordinates of care refer to something that is very important to not forget: we are corporeal beings – dependent, rational animals – so care always involves a physical aspect, in which manual work and physical contact play an essential role. Once again, the rationalistic approach (and, we could add, current constructivism) tends to ignore the body and all its demands as something apart from the *true* human being (Chirinos, 2007a; MacIntyre, 1999).

Family care is personalised

Care cannot be performed en masse or in general, because every person is unique, with their own biology and biography, circumstances, freedom, and life project. That means that caregiving requires face-to-face interaction. Again, our corporeal condition determines a characteristic of care, but it is a presence that does not mean just *staying by* the person but *being* – coexisting – with him.

To care:

> consists in contributing to the fulfilment of this person's life project. Hence the need to understand in order to care: an approach of sympathy, of shared *pathos*, is required . . . To understand is to be aware, i.e., to share the other's burden. This requires attention to qualitative aspects (Innerarity, 2001: 169).[11]

Therefore, the person's *psycho-biological, social,* and *spiritual* circumstances must be considered (Marcos and Bertolaso, 2018). The psycho-biological level includes the eventual appearance of pain and other limitations, and the person's emotional trajectory and current situation. The social level encompasses the relationships this person is in and how dependency affects them.[12] As per the spiritual level, we find the person's transcendent views and motivations to carry on.

Family care is integral

Those close to and taking care of a person in a situation of vulnerability do not see a sickness or a disability to be cared for, but an ailing person. "This requires a fundamental knowledge of the patient as a person who must be treated with what the classics call *aidos* (decorum and respect)" (Innerarity, 2001: 164). The particular aspects of the person that have been previously mentioned need to be addressed, not in a compartmental way, but unitarily, within one and the same action, because they all take part in the subjective experience of vulnerability.[13]

The need to understand the different aspects of the patient makes *respect for privacy* essential. *Familiarity* – the close intimacy that is proper to family relationships – and *confidentiality* – the quality of a relationship based on trust that binds a person to keep privacy or secrecy regarding certain facts or situations – are basic categories that must go along. In fact, care creates

> an emotional bond, usually mutual, between the caregiver and the cared-for – a bond in which the caregiver feels responsible for other's wellbeing and does mental, emotional, and physical work in the course of fulfilling that responsibility (Hochschild, 2003: 214).

Thus, the relationship of care giver and care receiver cannot be understood from only a merely contractual point of view.

Family care is a life accompaniment

This is the most valuable element of care. Care situations generate an *us* full of shared experiences, which particularly helps them endure the moments of loneliness that may appear. In addition, it makes technology more human and effective. Discovering a peer capable of sympathising, understanding, and offering help is a great relief. The vulnerable person needs to know that even though he or she spends some time physically alone, there is somebody thinking of him or her, and who looks after the individual's day-to-day needs. The feeling of not being alone in the world is essential for the subject's balance and development. This accompaniment is the main builder of the dwelling – the home – the dependent person needs, where he or she feels welcomed, belonging and self-recognised. It also lessens the feeling of being uprooted that fragility causes.

Virtues of care within the family

In this way of practicing care, we could detail several virtues and attitudes that are present and could be transferred to institutionalised modalities of care or to those performed by formal carers, thus enhancing the perception of quality care by the care receiver.

Understanding/empathy: To partake in the burden the other is carrying. To place oneself in the other's shoes in all its complexity.

Compassion: It is the regard that grasps the other's fragility and invites him or her to transfer his or her anxiety to us. It includes assistance that gives autonomy back to the person. It is being aware of the other's difficulties because we ourselves are vulnerable.

Trust must be generated for the vulnerable person to put his or her life and worries in the carer's hands.

Serenity: Constant and patient attention. It requires resting and reflecting, promptness and self-control in adverse circumstances.

Commitment: There has been a conscious choice of taking care of the other as something good for the carer.

A note on the concept of quality of life

One of the fuzziest concepts related to our real expectations from a care relationship is that of *quality of life*. Any concept of quality of life must always include acknowledging the unconditional *dignity of life* itself. Being a living person is a fact with an *essential quality* in itself, so there are no human lives worthy of being lived and others that are not.[14] The specific dignity of the person does not fade when the body weakens, falls ill, or ages. Therefore, we understand by quality of life, not the mere wellbeing, but the set of physical, psychological, social, and spiritual conditions that facilitate the flourishment of a person given their unconditional dignity and with their current circumstances.

Dignity is a title that claims a proportionate response by every man. Thus, we can distinguish the types of action to help those in need from those that are harmful. "Help, the action with which we assist life in need, is the clearest practical manifestation of moral dignity" (Ballesteros and Aparisi, 2004: 40). As we have said before, when we take care of another like us, it entails, first of all, our recognition of the other, and on the other hand, it shows the human greatness of the actions of care and dedication to others. Only a human being can discover the true value of those around him or her and know their reality and their need. Only a human being can dispense a truly human help to others.

The assistance we provide a person has a clear basis on the person's nature, on what happens to him or her, and on what the person needs in particular. Not only do we do what the person's nature and situation indicate to us: the point is *how* we do it. Virtue – that is where quality of life lies. Being an object of virtuous treatment is a factor that increases everyone's quality of life (MacIntyre, 1999). Definitely, being treated as a person, being taken care of by a kind and intimate face, being welcomed: this is quality of life. And this treatment also includes the application of the tools of medicine, technology, or psychology (to cite some examples) to provide us with the ability to facilitate the flourishing of the care receiver.

How familial solidarity strengthens society

We have mentioned before that one of the threads of discussion around the concept of care has been the private-public dichotomy. We have focused on the person's home and family. What does this approach have to offer with regards to society? Is the care a person gives and receives at home a social good? This has relevant implications for the person of the carer and the social consideration and acknowledgement of his or her task.[15] The family as a community assists its members from the first moment of their life and on, even when they are emancipated. We will now see that when it works this way, society works, too.

Real solidarity generates cohesion of the social fabric. But solidarity requires using parameters other than exchange or benefit, otherwise we would be playing the game of measuring the contributions of each generation to society and the advantage we can obtain from them, and that makes social cohesion unviable in the long run. Therefore, we need parameters that strengthen intergenerational relationships, because they leave space for gratuitousness, especially with the weakest or more disadvantaged. This is what makes a community flourish. If the small and weak flourish, it is a symptom of the flourishing of the whole community (MacIntyre, 1999).

It could be argued that care, as it is provided in the home, remains in the private sphere and that the public sphere has a different logic. However, the family is the first locus of development of intergenerational relationships and assistance to the vulnerable. We have all been children and can recognise ourselves in them; we all have been ill and can be ill again, and we will all probably become elderly; therefore, these fundamental goods apply to us all. This ongoing reciprocity between generations appeals to us all. It is virtually impossible to educate citizens in solidarity without the regular practice of solidarity within the family (Bernal, 2005).

As younger members grow in autonomy, they need to learn how to exercise their duties and rights, and how to practice respect and tolerance. They also learn to take responsibility for the most vulnerable. Therefore, a basic criterion for the public authorities would be to ensure that the care of the weakest is performed in the best environment – the family – providing it with the required support to be able to perform its function. In summary, family care in the home environment has first-rate social functions, and it can be proposed as the model of care everywhere, but especially for the institutions that replace the family on some occasions. These qualities could be considered quality indicators in the care relationship.

Some initiatives looking at family care as their model

Persons in need want to be cared for in their own environment and, at the same time, those who love them would like to meet this request. In Spain, preliminary studies of different regulations regarding dependency, protection of elderly people, and care of children highlight this arrangement as the most advisable.[16] But this is constantly challenged by difficulties typical of our society: lack of time, massive presence of women – traditionally, the main caregivers at home – in the workplace, reduced family nuclei, and so on. These difficulties are at the root of the feelings of ambivalence[17] and frustration families often experience towards what is, paradoxically, one of the most enriching tasks a person can undertake. Such circumstances often make it necessary for the families, in order to care for elderly people, for example, to resort to residences in which several services and health care are guaranteed and where an atmosphere similar to that of a home is also sought. However, the families and residents' wishes often clash with the reality of institutionalisation,[18] which is a highly regulated field. The Spanish legislation does not always facilitate personalised attention, and this has given rise to several initiatives seeking to provide residents with attention tailored to their needs and likings.

The big challenge in public policies is to reach a balance between guaranteeing the users' safety and reducing potential abuse risks, and a type of care that favours the persons' flourishment and freedom in all those aspects that are especially cherished by them. This often involves promoting their participation and the actual presence of families in the activities of these organisations.

We will now show some initiatives of different sectors that are transferring these principles, ingredients, and attitudes that work in care within the family to their residential activities in the health and social sphere, with the intention of achieving a more satisfying and suiting system of attention. This way, the humanisation of the tasks appropriate for formal carers is being attained.

In Spain, more and more endeavours can be found that have the intention to work within an integrated and interdisciplinary framework of social and health care, and in which the different public departments and private organisations work together (Iglesias, 2016). Previously, the formal provision of care was so fragmented that the results have been far from satisfactory for the care receivers (for example, they received excellent health care but no social attention or vice versa), and that does not seem the best way to face chronicity and the massive ageing of society in the coming years.

If coordinating the public and private sectors is difficult, it seems even more complicated to promote synergies between carers and families, and between social and health services, and also to clearly detail the needs of those who remain in the home environment, which is where they are usually better assisted.

For the last ten years, often because of the economic crisis, some best practices have been implemented in Spain that aim to ensure an appropriate and personalised response. That has promoted a new mentality: the acknowledgement that persons need to be the agents of change and the protagonists of their own life, even in situations of high dependence in which social and family support are indispensable.

It seems that the future in our individualistic societies, with a diminished community culture, will impose an interdisciplinary perspective that encompasses health care, assistance, and civil action, all intertwined and coordinated.

Integrated social and health attention is becoming a core issue in the agenda of social and health services in Spain. This new model of attention requires a deep transformation of the whole health care system and that of social services, as well as a clear change in the professionals' and citizens' role with regards to health and welfare. At the very end, it is about guaranteeing a new model of support based on community-focused attention in which the person's preferences and values are the axis.

One of these initiatives belongs to **the hospitals sector**. It is the HU-CI[19] Project. It emerged from the need to humanise the attention in Intensive Care Units (ICUs), but especially because of the impact of human loss in the patient's family and their subsequent need of attention and accompaniment during the farewell and bereavement period. The family joins the care process as one more carer who in turn needs to be cared for. Visiting times become longer and more flexible, waiting rooms become warmer and welcoming. There is participation in information and decision-making. Going back to normal and being taken care of by their families is the priority for these units' patients. This project develops broad training in order to humanise the day-to-day professionals' practice and also offers detailed information to the patient's relatives about what an ICU is and how they can participate in the care of their relative.

Another positive experience regards the ways of **living and being cared for at home**. The Cuidador Experto Catalunya (n.d.) [Expert Carer Catalunya] Programme, integrated in the Health Plan 2011–2015, has among its goals the attention of persons with chronic and/or degenerative conditions and the development of a training and support network for their carers. Typically, a family carer who has already gone through an experience of care in all its stages, receives training, and then accompanies other carers that are in similar situations. This person passes on not only the best practices of a complex type of care, but also hope. The aim is to empower families, to show them that there is always a way out for every situation, that they are not alone, and that they have the support of the community. Therefore, the scope of the meetings is fundamentally instructional, and the expected outcomes are the improvement of the quality of care, and the attitude and expertise of the carer, the development of a sense of support and exchange with other carers, the acquisition of strategies promoting the management of emotions, especially in difficult situations, and, finally, the development of a sense of humour and affection towards the patient.

In the **residential health care** field, we could highlight three innovative initiatives.

The first is the RESICS Project (n.d.). The pilot plan has been recently implemented in the neighbourhood of Bellvitge[20] through a public residence and an adult day-care centre which coordinates the work in diverse nursing care residences, primary care centres, and families. It has reduced the number of referrals to emergency rooms by 75%. In practice, this initiative means that residents – usually with chronical conditions, complex situations, fragility, or loss of physical and mental functions – are always attended to by the same team of primary care professionals and they always work in coordination with the professionals of the residence where they live.

In addition, a smaller number of admissions in the emergency departments means an optimisation of resources in terms of ambulances and hospitalisations, and an increase in the patients' comfort because they are assisted in their own residence. The administration of medical prescriptions also improves. A final outcome is a decrease in the occurrence one of the most common consequences of the admission of an elderly patient in a hospital: the development of acute confusion syndrome or delirium, which is correlated with high mortality rates.[21]

The second example is how a professional organisation called UPIMIR[22] is promoting a new philosophy towards an authentic sense of care (UPIMIR, n.d.). The associate (private) residences are small and reproduce a family environment, where residents can take their own personal objects, and which aim at promoting the residents' decision-making capabilities. Therefore, they disagree with either hospital-like or high-standing hotel-based models, with disproportionate fees and little personal attention. They understand these centres as places to live that must be peaceful, devoid of tension, and with care and advantages such as those that make the life of these people more comfortable, allowing them to live intensely in those years.

Likewise, another initiative seeking a more humanised care is called SUMAR (n.d.). Among its diverse projects[23] we can find "You Decide,"[24] which is based on the interests and preferences of the residents to avoid additional disruptions in addition to moving from their own home. Residents are considered in their right to keep their habits and thus, they can choose their getting up hour, they hold weekly meetings to decide aspects of their life in the residence, the professionals working there do not wear uniforms, and every user has a person to refer to who attends to him or her in a personalised way. Families can take part in many of the activities offered to the residents because the idea is that the resident lives in an environment as similar to his or her home as possible.

These are some samples of the way the social and health care sectors are building bridges to the family environment and the way the family carries out its care role to improve the way the needs of people in a situation of vulnerability are met, and also to improve their perception about the care they receive.

Conclusion with a further research proposal

We have described a current model of residential health care that in some of its mechanisms shows the paradox of elderly people with little social visibility and influence in a world that is globally ageing. Therefore, as a first conclusion, society needs to undergo a change of paradigm that includes the consideration that tomorrow the person assisted may be any of us.

As we have seen, we have been exploring a care ethics that relies on the fact that every person expects to be treated integrally, and that both the principle of personal autonomy and the human being's need of interdependency must be respected (Schalock and Verdugo, 2002; Gómez et al., 2008). If we apply this to residential care in an ageing society, first, professionals in this area – caregivers, health workers, educators, trainers, therapists, nurses, psychologists, and so on – must be well aware of the type of person they are taking care of. That means a specific training, first, to improve their work and speech so they better fit the concept of quality of life that has emerged in the most recent studies. Second, they need to develop and follow a health care model that focuses less on the professionals as on the care receivers. Whenever possible, the health care scheme should be designed along with them and tailored to their needs and characteristics, as well as their ability to contribute to society (Gómez et al., 2008).

A practical way to start this change of perspective is to ask and assess. How do residents perceive the treatment they receive in their dwellings? Do they feel underestimated or belittled? Where are the areas where they see their agency constrained and their privacy violated? What types of changes do they more often suggest for their residences? What are the things they feel comfortable with?

Hence, we think that a good contribution by the academia to this task could be to provide professionals in residential care units with a standard, validated tool, not only to periodically assess their task in terms of resident satisfaction – an index – but also to implement a quality care certificate for residences. White books and handbooks have been issued, but we argue that professionals are left alone with the task of interpreting and implementing them, and they need a support to work along with. The results of this research could be also useful for the improvement of the professionals' training and also to influence the government policies and regulations in the sector, which, as previously said, are perceived as an obstacle to provide the care the residents and their families expect.

Notes

1 This is exactly the same figure of Europe considered as a whole, which is the oldest continent (UN, 2017). See also INE (2017), where the projection for 2031 for this segment of population, all things being equal, is 33%, i.e., one third of the population.
2 For example, in the last IsFamily Santander Chair Report, Cavallotti and Marcaletti (2018) show how 65–74 year-old Spaniards living alone report a much lower level of overall life satisfaction and score negatively in other indicators such as health condition, economic and emotional support network, life expectations, and so on.
3 D'Avenia makes an interesting reflection about *repair* as a way of negotiating with the limits in our life (Chirinos et al., 2012).
4 This is what Feito calls the anthropological definition. She adds a socio-political one, related to certain conditions that may make a person vulnerable.
5 Chirinos (2011) mentions how authors with diverse philosophical approaches, such as Kass or Nussbaum, insist on vulnerability as a typically human trait.
6 There the author examines the etymology of the word *hospitality*, understood as the ancient tradition of welcoming the stranger in one's own house and honouring his/her dignity as an equal. Contemporary phenomenology has developed the concept of *alterity* in-depth and how this acknowledgement stays at the root of our responsibility towards the *other* (Patrão Neves, 2018).
7 The social exchange theory states that all human relationships obey a cost-benefit analysis from each of the parties involved. There is, therefore, no space for altruism, disinterest, or gratuity. On the contrary, our position is that the family is a network of relationships primarily dominated by these attitudes.
8 These authors note how little "love" appears in family studies. It often appears under "the poorer, sanitized guise of 'attachment,' 'bonding' or 'affect'" (Bahr and Bahr, 2001: 1234) – and even less "sacrifice" – which they equate to "care" – unless in a negative light, although it is considered "natural" in other areas of life – "callings, careers, and most human enterprises" (p. 1247).
9 They sharply point out how literature systematically ignores sacrifices performed by men and children, as if sacrifice were a private feminine dominion.
10 It is against this approach that MacIntyre (1999) addressed his work.
11 Chirinos (2011) also insists on the need to develop *empathy*.
12 For example, the caring family often focalises on the suffering person. At other times, this person needs to be replaced in his or her previous roles. Those are situations in which family support allows the person to gauge the real texture of his or her personal relationships.
13 For example, patients under hospice care are typically treated by an interdisciplinary team and the family is included as a part of the team, to take a holistic perspective.
14 In any case, there may be human behaviours that are according to the person's dignity and others that are beneath it.
15 "Carers do not get political and economic support, which could be associated with their role as people doing important and moral social tasks" (Weicht, 2015: 15).
16 See, for example, Ministerio de Trabajo y Asuntos Sociales-IMSERSO (2005: 11-ff).
17 There is a whole literature regarding the concept of *ambivalence*, which is understood as the tension felt by an individual with a certain social role that is the contending place of conflicting normative expectations. See, for example, Merton and Barber (1963) and Luscher and Pillemer (1998).

18 Elderly residents often report being treated as children instead of adults, being talked about as if they were not present, feeling that they have no voice about day-to-day aspects of their life such as their schedule or their place in common spaces, invaded in their privacy or rooms, or meddled in their conversations. They mention being labelled or publicly censored, and certain criteria imposed on behalf of an alleged "professional authority" (Mañós and Castillo, 2011). These and other attitudes reflect an organization of care which is efficiency-oriented and authority-based, rather than dialogue-focused (Mansell et al., 2007).
19 HU-CI: Human (HU) + Intensive Care Unit (UCI in Spain). This initiative has been promoted by Gabi Heras, MD, specialist in Intensive Care and creator and blogger of Proyecto HU-CI. (Proyecto HU-CI, n.d.)
20 Bellvitge is a neighbourhood of the city of L'Hospitalet del Llobregat, which is integrated in the Metropolitan Area of Barcelona.
21 See, for example, Formiga et al. (2005), Espino et al. (1998), and Jiménez-Vilchez Roure et al. (2004).
22 Unió de Petites i Mitjanes Residències [Union of Small- and Medium-Size Residences].
23 For example, they have another project for temporary homes for women at risk of abuse and their children.
24 The complete name is "You Decide How You Want to Age."

References

Argandoña, A. (2018) The Home. Multidisciplinary Reflections. In A. Argandoña, ed., *The Home. Multidisciplinary Reflections*. Cheltenham, UK: Edward Elgar, pp. 8–31.

Bahr, H.M. and Bahr, K.S. (2001) Families and Self-Sacrifice: Alternative Models and Meanings for Family theory. *Social Forces*, 79(4), pp. 1231–1258.

Ballesteros, J. and Aparisi, A. (2004) *Biotecnología, dignidad y derecho: bases para un diálogo*. Pamplona: EUNSA.

Bernal, A. (2005) *La familia como ámbito educativo*. Madrid: Rialp.

Cavallotti, R. and Marcaletti, F. (2018) *Older Parents, Generations and Family Solidarity. A Multilevel Analysis of the Spanish Context. Report*. Barcelona: IESF-Universitat Internacional de Catalunya. Available at: <www.uic.es/sites/default/files/en_older_parents_generations_and_family_solidarity.pdf>

Chirinos, M.P. (2007a) Antropologia della dipendenza: Il lavoro e la costituzione dell'essere umano. *Acta Philosophica*, 16(2), pp. 195–212.

Chirinos, M.P. (2007b) Hospitalidad y amistad en la cosmovisión griega. In M. D'Avenia and A. Acerbi, eds., *Philia: riflessioni sull'amicizia*. Rome: Edusc, pp. 43–48.

Chirinos, M.P. (2011) *Care ethics*: la revalorización del cuidado cotidiano en el ámbito familiar. In M. Miranda and D. López, eds., *Ideología de género; perspectivas filosófica, antropológica, social y jurídica*, I. San José de Costa Rica-Pamplona: Promesa-Universidad de Navarra, pp. 329–345.

Chirinos, M.P., Crawford, M. and D'Avenia, M. (2012) The Value of Manual Work. *Acta Philosophica*, 21(1), pp. 171–184.

Del Barco, J.L. (1993) *El poder de la sinrazón*. Pamplona: EUNSA.

Dillon, R.S. (2018) Respect. In E.N. Zalta, ed., *The Stanford Encyclopedia of Philosophy*, Spring 2018 edition. Stanford, CA: Stanford University. Available at: <https://plato.stanford.edu/archives/spr2018/entries/respect/>, accessed July 18, 2018.

Domínguez Alcón, C. (1986) *Los cuidados y la profesión enfermera en España*. Madrid: Pirámide.

Durán, M.A. (2010) La doble jornada en la economía global. In A. Ferrer, S.M. Ruesga and C. Resa, eds., *Anuario de relaciones laborales en España: Objetivo el trabajo*, I. Madrid: Union General de Trabajadores, pp. 242–243

Durán, M.A. (2018a) *La riqueza invisible del cuidado*. Valencia: Publicacions Universitat de València.

Durán, M.A. (2018b) Las cuentas del cuidado. *Revista Española de Control Externo*, 20(58), pp. 57–89.

Espino, D.V., Jules-Bradley, A.C., Johnston, C.L. and Mouton, C.P. (1998) Texas Diagnostic Approach to the Confused Elderly Patient. *American Family Physician*, 57(6), pp. 1358–1366.

Feito, L. (2007) Vulnerabilidad. *Anales del Sistema Sanitario de Navarra*, 30(Suppl. 3), pp. 7–22.

Formiga, F., Marcos, E., Sole, A., Valencia, E., Lora-Tamayo, J. and Pujol, R. (2005) Síndrome confusional agudo en pacientes ancianos ingresados por patología médica. *Revista Clínica Española*, 205(10), pp. 484–488.

Gilligan, C. (1982) *In a Different Voice: Psychological Theory and Women's Development*. Cambridge, MA: Harvard University Press.

Gómez, L., Verdugo, M.A, Arias, B. and Navas, P. (2008) Evaluación de la calidad de vida en personas mayores y con discapacidad: la Escala Fumat. *Intervención Psicosocial*, 17(2), pp. 189–199.

Gregory, B.S. (2012) *The Unintended Reformation*. Cambridge, MA: The Belknap Press of Harvard University Press.

Hochschild, A.R. (2003) *The Commercialization of Intimate Life: Notes from Home and Work*. Berkeley, CA: University of California Press.

Iglesias, F. (2016, June 1) *Secretary of Social Affairs and Families (Generalitat de Catalunya), Speech, I Seminario sobre Familia y Dependencia*. Barcelona: UIC Barcelona.

INE [Instituto Nacional de Estadística de España] (2017) accessed July 17, 2018, <www.ine.es>

Innerarity, D. (2001) *Ética de la hospitalidad*. Barcelona: Península.

Jiménez-Vilchez, A., Roure-Murillo, R. and Viñas-Salas, J. (2004) Study of Confusion Syndrome in Patients Admitted to a Trauma Unit: Why do Elderly Patients Get Disorientated? *Journal of Orthopaedic Nursing*, 8(1), pp. 4–10.

Luscher, K. and Pillemer, K. (1998) Intergenerational Ambivalence: A New Approach to the Study of Parent-Child Relations in Later Life. *Journal of Marriage and Family*, 60(2), pp. 413–425.

MacIntyre, A. (1999) *Dependent Rational Animals. Why Humans Need the Virtues*. Chicago, IL: Open Court.

Mañós, F. and Castillo, M., eds. (2011) *Modelo de calidad de vida aplicado a la atención residencial de personas con necesidades complejas de apoyo. Technical document 21020*. Madrid: IMSERSO.

Mansell, J., Knapp, M., Beadle-Brown, J. and Beecham, J. (2007) *Deinstitutionalization and Community Living–Outcomes and Costs: Report of a European Study. Volume 2: Main Report*. Canterbury, UK: Tizard Centre, University of Kent. Available at: <www.kent.ac.uk/tizard/research/DECL_network/documents/DECLOC_Volume_2_Report_for_Web.pdf>

Marcos, A. and Bertolaso, M. (2018) What Is a Home? On the Intrinsic Nature of a Home. In A. Argandoña, ed., *The Home. Multidisciplinary Reflections*. Cheltenham, UK: Edward Elgar, pp. 35–56.

Mayeroff, M. (1972) *On Caring*. New York, NY: HarperCollins.

Merton, R.K. and Barber, E. (1963) Sociological Ambivalence. In E.A. Tiryakian, ed., *Sociological Theory, Values and Sociocultural Change: Essays in Honor of Pitirim A. Sorokin*. London: Free Press of Glencoe, pp. 91–120.

Ministerio de Trabajo y Asuntos Sociales-IMSERSO. (2005) *Libro blanco de la dependencia*. Madrid: IMSERSO. Available at: <www.dependencia.imserso.es/InterPresent1/groups/imserso/documents/binario/libroblanco.pdf>

Patrão Neves, M.C. (2018) Self and Others: Home as a Cradle of a Non-Violent Relationship. In A. Argandoña, ed., *The Home. Multidisciplinary Reflections*. Cheltenham, UK: Edward Elgar, pp. 57–78.

Polo, L. (1996) *Ética, hacia una versión moderna de los temas clásicos*. Madrid: AEDOS.

Programa Cuidador Expert Catalunya (n.d.) accessed August 21, 2017, <http://salutweb.gencat.cat/web/.content/home/ambits_tematics/linies_dactuacio/model_assistencial/atencio_al_malalt_cronic/documents/arxius/programa_cuidador_expert.pdf>

Proyecto HU-CI (n.d.) accessed August 31, 2017, <www.proyectohuci.com>

Proyecto RESICS (n.d.) accessed August 31, 2017, <http://omis.newhealthfoundation.org/proyecto-resics-hospitalet-del-llobregat/>

Riley, S. and Bos, G. (n.d.) Human Dignity. In *The Internet Encyclopedia of Philosophy*. Martin, TN: University of Tennessee at Martin. <www.iep.utm.edu/> accessed July 9, 2018.

Schalock, R.L. and Verdugo, M.A. (2002) *Handbook of Quality of Life for Human Service Practitioners*. Washington, DC: American Association on Mental Retardation. [Translated by Verdugo, M.A. and Jenaro, C. (2003) *Calidad de Vida. Manual para Profesionales de la Educación, salud y Servicios Sociales*. Madrid: Alianza Editorial].

SUMAR (n.d.) accessed August 31, 2017, <www.sumaracciosocial.cat>

UN (2017) *ESA/P/WP/248 World Population Prospects. Key Findings and Advance Tables (2017 Revision)*. New York: UN. Department of Economic and Social Affairs. Population Division. Available at: <https://esa.un.org/unpd/wpp/publications/Files/WPP2017_KeyFindings.pdf>

UN (n.d.) accessed July, 17 2018, <www.un.org/en/sections/issues-depth/ageing/>

UPIMIR (n.d.) accessed August 31, 2017, <https://upimir.com>

Weicht, B. (2015) *The Meaning of Care: The Social Construction of Care for Elderly People*. Basingstoke, UK: Palgrave Macmillan.

Zárate, B. (2016) La familia en la Ley de Dependencia. Implicaciones sociosanitarias y jurídicas 10 años después. *Quaderns de Polítiques Familiars*, 2, pp. 4–13.

Chapter 3

The healthy home at early years

Cristina Costa and Asunción Esteve

Introduction

There is empirical evidence of the relationship between housing conditions and children's health. For example, children who live in houses occupied by low-income residents are more inclined to suffer from asthma (Krieger et al., 2000). Let's see a real case. Cecilia and Toni live in Barcelona. They have three children and they own a flat in the upper side of city, where the traffic jams are very intense. The building where Cecilia and Toni live was built more than 100 years ago and it has an old gas boiler system. The whole building consists of five floors and it only has one central boiler, which is located on the ground floor. That causes Cecilia and Toni serious problems because their flat lies on the first floor. For this reason, the upper floors only get heating after Cecilia and Toni's flat is overheated. When the boiler is switched on, the average temperature of their flat is 24 C° in the winter, day and night. They asked their neighbours to install a temperature regulator for the boiler, but their claim was dismissed.

The health problems began when their two youngest children started suffering from bronchitis in their early months. They both had repetitive respiratory infections and it took them a long time to get completely cured. When they were two and three years old, they got bronchitis quite often and they used to spend more than two weeks coughing, wheezing, and having shortness of breath. Then, Cecilia's realised that there could be a relationship between the extra heating of their flat and the children's long-term bronchitis. When the boiler was connected, the whole family felt their throat was dry when they woke up in the morning. Under these conditions, the doctor recommended that Cecilia and Toni move somewhere else, where the children could breathe fresh air. So, they decided to rent out their apartment and they found a house to rent in "Collserola" mountain, situated on Barcelona's western fringe. Since they have lived there, their children seldom suffer from bronchitis, and if they do, they get rid of it much faster.

This case shows how important is to provide children with a healthy home environment, especially from birth to five years of age. Studies show how childcare settings provide a valuable opportunity to promote health and physical activity (Risica et al., 2019: 2). Moreover, home is the place where children discover life and family; it is their small cosmos, where they will develop their first emotions, reactions, affections, and cognitive abilities. It is important to provide them with the most nurturing and healthy home environment as possible. In the case of families with small children that live in large cities, they are kept away from the benefits of natural surroundings. They must learn how to transform their "urban" homes into healthy environments.

The aim of this chapter is to give some guidelines to build a healthy home with particular attention to child development at an early stage. It will, firstly, describe how our homes, particularly in large cities, are affected by disturbances that may undermine our health, and it will, secondly, provide the main criteria to have a healthy house that provides a safe, quiet, and stimulating environment for children.

Urban environment and health

Large cities have experienced important population growth in recent years. In 1980, the urban population accounted for 39% of the world population. In 2015, the size of the urban population had increased to 54%. According to projections, the urban share of the world population will grow to 66% by 2050.[1] In large cities, such as New York, London, or Hong-Kong, the demand for urban living has increased faster than the supply of great urban spaces. The result is that most of the people who live in large cities can only afford small flats that lack good, healthy conditions.

Tiny apartments and lack of indoor spaces pose serious problems for having healthy homes in many cities worldwide. Toxic agents (such as radon, nitrogen dioxide, and carbon monoxide) are often concentrated in the indoor air environment as a consequence of energy conservation practices or inadequate ventilation. In a study conducted in public housing during the heating season, the increased frequency of respiratory symptoms among infants at risk for asthma was correlated with increased indoor levels of nitrogen dioxide. Another study (Spengler, 2005) that measured personal exposures to volatile organics with known carcinogenic risk potential in New York City and Los Angeles showed that contributions from the indoor air environment greatly exceeded those from outdoor exposure.

Furthermore, many massive buildings have been constructed in large cities with materials that may affect our health.

Use of building materials such as vinyl siding, aluminium studs, gypsum, and synthetic wood products reduce the water-holding capacity of homes. Inadequate ventilation and drainage practices can trap moisture behind siding, encouraging mould growth. Increased manufacturing and use of synthetic inorganic compounds have increased the presence of these compounds in the environment worldwide, and have also increased their concentration in indoor air and dust samples.

But there is a greater threat for health in large cities: outdoor pollution. Different types of pollution and disturbances may affect homes located in large cities. Excessive burning of fuel caused by traffic or smoke from factories and vehicles,

Figure 3.1 Example of flats in extremely bad condition in Hong-Kong

as well as industrial wastes, the excess heat in the environment, and noise cause disturbances and human diseases. Noise is a new type of urban pollution that is also disturbing the ecosystem (Buxton et al., 2017: 531–533). Researchers have investigated the impact of traffic noise on children from birth to the age of ten, and they have assessed behavioural problems at the age of ten. According to their research, children exposed to higher noise levels have greater problems of hyperactivity and inattention, and are more likely to display emotional problems.[2]

As the report "Planning horizons. Promoting Healthy cities" from the United Kingdom Royal Town Planning Institute states,

> "Health" is not limited to hospitals and clinics. The environment in which we live, work and spend leisure time has an enormous impact on our health and wellbeing. Health problems such as obesity, chronic heart disease, stress and mental health issues are intricately linked to the environments in which people live and work.[3]

For all these reasons, our present-day society should get more conscious about the importance of living in healthy homes. The problem is that only families with very high incomes can afford a flat with good healthy conditions in large cities. However, guaranteeing access to decent and adequate housing is an obligation of public authorities. The right of access to housing and to housing assistance is recognised in article 34 of the Charter of Fundamental Rights of the European Union, also in articles 30 and 31 of the revised European Social Charter, adopted by the Council of Europe, and in article 25 of the Universal Declaration of Human rights, as well as in many national constitutions.[4] In this respect, the Economic and Social Council of the United Nations has declared that "*access to decent, affordable housing promotes the right to physical and mental health, the right to education, the right to family, the right to work and the right to participate in the cultural life of the community.*"[5]

Public administrations from all over the world – especially in the so-called developed countries – are implementing housing policies to reduce energy poverty and adverse health effects. The European Union fosters housing policies throughout EU countries to reduce heating and cooling needs, and recommends constructing houses with sustainable building materials.[6] In the United States, the National Centre for Healthy Housing has developed the National Healthy Housing Standard to deliver housing policy that includes strong recommendations regarding air leakage and damp indoor environment to avoid respiratory illness in children.[7] In the United Kingdom, the Town and Country Planning Association (TCPA) campaigns for the "Healthy Homes Act" that sets out ten high-level principles that define what constitutes a decent home (such as adequate living space, access to natural light, walkable access to green space open to everyone, etc.).[8]

These are some examples of public initiatives to implement better housing conditions. However, much is still to be done in order to supply secure and decent housing to everyone. Although many people cannot even afford a "decent" house, we consider it important to give some guidelines to middle-class families in order to facilitate their decisions when choosing the type of house that they might have.

What follows is the exposition of the most relevant factors to set a healthy home. The most relevant factors to set a healthy home are, mainly, the following three:

1 *A suitable environment*
2 *The building materials*
3 *The indoor setting and equipment*

Let's explore them with particular attention to children.

Main factors to set a healthy home

A suitable environment

People who can afford to buy a flat or house choose their home's location according to criteria such us proximity to family, schools, or work. Most people choose the neighbourhood that is the closest fit to their lifestyle and personality, a place where they feel comfortable, and where they are likely to get along with their neighbours. It is obvious that a person's neighbourhood is a sign of their social and economic status. However, criteria related to the outdoor environment, such as the quality of the air and the closeness to gardens, parks, or nature, are also important. There is evidence (Bengtsson and Grahn, 2014: 1) that gardens and nature can have therapeutic benefits such as relief from physical illness symptoms, stress reduction, and improvement of the overall sense of wellbeing. Parks in urban areas are the alternative for private gardens. For many people in cities the park is a place that resonates with concepts of the original "garden" (Ward Thompson, 2002: 65). Moreover, a natural environment is a playscape for children and has an impact on children's learning and development (Fjurtoft and Sagei, 2000: 83).

It may be argued that having a house with a garden is a privilege, especially in large cities. This is absolutely right. But some large cities, like London, Berlin, or Rio de Janeiro, have huge and centrally located parks. In such cities it is recommended to choose a home location near a park, if possible. Other cities have preserved a natural environment that provides a healthy quality of living to their inhabitants. This is the case of Munich, Montreal, Stockholm, or Melbourne. Nevertheless, many large cities lack natural resources and public authorities are largely responsible for preserving parks and green areas.

If one lives in a large city that lacks natural resources, one may try to find a location outside the city. Land and housing prices are cheaper and more available in rural areas where everybody can live much closer to nature and breathe in the fresh air. Obviously, living in the countryside may pose a transport problem if parents work in large cities or if children go to schools located inside the city. In these cases, it depends on each family to decide if they prefer the advantages of a large city (shops, restaurants, museums, cinemas) or a healthy home.

It is also important to choose a home location away from pollutant and noise sources. Other important criteria when choosing a house or flat are the direction the house faces, the entrance of sunlight, and the humidity. Typically, a south-facing house gets sun for most of the day, especially at the front of the house, and is therefore usually brighter and warmer. A north-facing home gets sun at the back of the house and is typically darker and naturally cooler than a south-facing one.

The right decision about the location largely depends on the weather conditions of the town or city where we live; the sun shining into a house all day in a hot city like Barcelona can be problematic, but it is very nice in a house located in Norway, like Bergen. Sunlight helps to eliminate mould and bacteria and gives us energy. It is also important to maintain proper humidity levels at home. Indoor humidity levels should be between 45% and 60%, and they can be checked with a hygrometer. Proper sunlight and indoor humidity levels are especially relevant for children and adults that suffer from allergies and pulmonary infections. As we saw in the aforementioned case of Cecilia and Toni's flat, the lack of proper indoor humidity was the reason of their children's long and repetitive bronchitis.

Last but not least, there are also some invisible factors that may also affect our health and have become new areas of research: geobiology and electromagnetic radiation.

i) Geobiology

Geobiology is a new field of scientific research that explores the interactions between the physical Earth and the biosphere. The field of geobiology has recently energised the life and Earth sciences as geologists and biologists bring new tools to collaborations addressing fundamental problems that transcend the disciplines (Kump, 2008: 1). In very basic terms, geobiology studies the unseen and invisible energies that emanate from the Earth and influence living organisms. Although there is still a lot of scepticism regarding the effect of Earth's magnetic lines on our health, it may help to determine the best location for our homes.

Studies show that our bodies are sensitive to outside influences like Earth's magnetic lines and it is recommended that people avoid locations close to "geopathic stress zones," like underground water, earthquake faults and manmade lines, such as underground gas, sewers, and quarries (Guxens, 2011: 93). The Austrian school teacher Käthe Bachler studied the impact of flowing underground water, magnetic fields of the Earth, and geological fault lines on children at school. She used to test the effects of radiation on the classrooms, bench for bench, and how it affected individual scholars' behaviour and academic results. The results of her research showed a link between health problems and the Earth's radiation.[9]

Some experts on healthy homes recommend analysing the effect of Earth's magnetic lines on the different rooms of a house. The so-called Hartmann Grid was discovered in 1935 by German medical doctor Ernst Hartmann. The grid is believed to be a result of the electrification of the world and it encompasses the Earth in a net-life pattern, flowing from south to north and west to east. There appears to be a neutral area between the lines, but the intersection of lines is believed to be the most harmful place. Children are particularly sensitive to this radiation, especially when they are babies. If babies usually wake up and cry at night, they might have their beds or cradles in a "geopathic stress zone" (Guxens, 2011: 95).

ii) Electromagnetic radiation

Electromagnetic radiation may also pose a serious problem for health in our homes. Current technologies have become a source of electromagnetic radiation. Broadcast TV, digital broadcast TV, AM and FM radio, wireless internet, or devices in daily use such as cordless telephones, smartphones, tablets, and portable computers expose people to electromagnetic pollution every day. The harm caused by this pollution is still open to debate since there is no clear and definitive evidence of its negative influence on human beings. However, extremely low frequency electromagnetic fields were classified as potentially carcinogenic and some studies estimate that magnetic fields generated by high-voltage power transmission lines may develop leukaemia in children (Redlarski, 2015: 1).

Therefore, it becomes very important to appropriately protect our homes and children from electromagnetic pollution. The use electromagnetic radiation filters, and even special paint and fabrics, are recommended for use.

Some natural way to reduce electromagnetic radiation are:

1. *Unplugging appliances when not in use.*
2. *Keep bedrooms clear of mobile phones, tablets, and computers.*
3. *Avoid halogen and fluorescent lighting.*
4. *Unplug Wi-Fi when it is not in use and keep the router away from areas where children and family members spend a lot of time.*
5. *Avoid Wi-Fi technology, such as wireless pacifiers that monitor a baby's temperature and wireless diapers that alert when the baby's diaper is wet* (Shoemaker and Vitale, 1991: 161–171).

The building materials

Building materials have an important effect on human health. Many public institutions from different countries are getting more and more involved in building healthy homes and promoting healthy cities. Germany was one of the first countries to study the impact of building materials on health and to foster the bio-construction of homes and healthy living environments. The "Baubiologie" movement (Building biology) began in Germany in the 1970s by the "Working Group Healthy Building + Living" integrated by some German professors. They founded the Institute of Building Biology and Sustainability in 1976.[10] In the 2000s, similar international movements sprang up in North America, Australia, Japan, France, and Spain.

The so-called Building Biology studies how the environment of residential, commercial, and public buildings can affect the health of the occupants. The German Institute of Building Biology provides consumers with objective information and assessment of building materials, equipment, homes, and properties. It has released a comprehensive list of 25 principles about healthy building construction.[11] While all 25 principles are difficult to achieve, they are a guide to achieve a healthy home.

The 25 principles of Building Biology are:

Building materials and noise control

1. *Use natural and unadulterated building materials.*
2. *A building shall have a pleasant or neutral smell, not releasing any toxins.*
3. *Use building materials with the lowest possible level of radioactivity.*
4. *Protective measures against noise and vibration pollution need to be based on human needs.*

Indoor climate

5 *Regulate indoor air humidity naturally by using humidity-buffering materials.*
6 *The total moisture content of a new building shall be low and dry out quickly.*
7 *Strive for a well-balanced ratio between thermal insulation and heat retention.*
8 *Optimise indoor surface and air temperatures of a given space.*
9 *Promote good indoor air quality through natural ventilation.*
10 *Use radiant heat for heating.*
11 *Interfere as little as possible with the natural balance of nature's own background radiation.*
12 *Prevent exposures to human-made sources of electromagnetic fields and radio-frequency radiation.*
13 *Minimise exposures to mould, bacteria, dust, and allergens. The environment, energy, and water*
14 *Minimise energy consumption while using renewable energy whenever possible.*
15 *Prefer regional building materials, without promoting the exploitation of scarce and hazardous resources.*
16 *Building activities shall cause no environmental problems.*
17 *Choose the best possible drinking water quality.*
Interior design
18 *Take harmonic measures, proportions, and shapes into consideration.*
19 *Select light exposures, lighting systems, and colour schemes following natural conditions.*
20 *Base interior and furniture design on physiological and ergonomic findings.*

Building site

21 *Site buildings on land free from geological and human-made disturbances.*
22 *Locate residential homes away from pollutant and noise sources.*
23 *Provide low-density housing with sufficient green space.*
24 *Develop individualised housing and settlements in harmony with nature in ways that support human and family needs.*
25 *Building activities shall cause no social problems.*

This list shows how far we have strayed from natural building practices. It seems clear, though, that these principles require effort and investment of money from families. But most people are more interested in spending their money on home furniture and interior design than on getting a healthy home. Fortunately, some people are now beginning to understand the effects that their homes can have on their health and are placing a much higher priority on this issue. At minimum, it is a positive step to get familiar with these 25 principles and try to achieve the most relevant ones.

Building materials have an effect on our health, especially on children and elderly people. Buildings today often contain inherent chemical, physiological, and biological risks as a result of materials and processes employed by the construction industry in a drive to minimise costs and build times. The physical quality of housing may lead to childhood diseases including asthma, lead poisoning, and respiratory distress, as well as accident, injury, or even death. Factors that can lead to such diseases include structural house conditions relating to building quality and maintenance, safety hazards, functional systems (for example, ventilation, smoke alarms heating/cooling, plumbing) or environmental toxins including lead, asbestos, and neurotoxins. All of these hazards are preventable and treatable (Vandivere et al., 2006).

We should try to avoid homes whose floor and wall materials and finishes (paints, varnishes, etc.) are toxic. If we are renovating a house or an apartment, and if we can afford to build our own home, we should choose natural materials. Wood, ceramics, stone, and leather are grouped together as natural furnishing materials.

Wood environments positively impact people's emotional states, and therefore have the potential to improve their psychological health and wellbeing (Rice et al., 2006: 8). Like plants, products that appear to be wood fulfil an innate desire in humans to replicate nature in their indoor environments through the use of natural materials.

Regarding floors, wood floors are always a healthy flooring choice. Oak is the most common wood flooring material; maple, beech, or birch are more expensive, but a yellow pine floor can be an attractive, less expensive option. Other healthy flooring materials include ceramic tile, slate, terrazzo, brick, hardwood pine, natural rubber. and "true" linoleum.[12] Ceramic floor is a good choice for children's playrooms and bathrooms, but not for bedrooms. Linoleum is durable, resilient, thermally insulating, quiet, and low maintenance with natural antibacterial properties. It is important to avoid vinyl flooring, as vinyl chloride fumes are known carcinogens. Vinyl also traps moisture, which can promote delamination of subfloors and mould growth or rot, especially in hot, humid climates. In older houses, be careful removing vinyl flooring: they may be a source of asbestos.[13]

As for paint, the use of natural "eco" paint is recommended in all rooms. VOCs (volatile organic compounds) are essentially chemicals that are not acutely toxic, but over the long term can have "off-gas" toxins. The most harmful VOC is **formaldehyde**, which is present in most conventional **oil-based paints**.[14] *The use of natural materials that minimise or eradicate VOCs is a key element of the healthy home concept; low VOC or VOC-free paints are now commonly available.*

It is also important to take into account that, nowadays, conventional cabinets, doors, and shelfs are often composite wood covered with veneer to make them look like wood. These products contain large amounts of formaldehyde. In a healthy home, cabinetry, doors, and shelfs should be made of solid wood or formaldehyde-free wheat board, and finished with a low VOC paint or stain.[15] Regarding drywall, the most natural wall finish is additive-free plaster. Plaster has the added advantage of blocking VOC off-gassing present in the gypsum and taped joints of modern construction, but traditional plaster and lath construction is many times more expensive than drywall.[16]

The indoor setting and equipment

Interior design may be considered as a luxury, but instead of decorating our homes according to mere aesthetic criteria, we should try to concentrate on very basic elements that provide a safe and quite indoor setting for our family, especially for our children (Bueno, 2005: 17). It is important to choose the adequate furniture, lighting, and colour for every room of the house. We are going to focus particularly on children's bedrooms, as it is the place where they rest and spend most of their time at an early stage.

i) Furniture

Normal furniture has a surprisingly high number of chemicals that may be harmful for children. As previously mentioned, the most common chemical is formaldehyde, which has been scientifically linked to some forms of cancer, but other chemicals may cause irritations, breathing problems, and hormonal changes. Opting for furniture built from durable materials that are natural and healthy will solve these issues. Furniture made of wood and metal, bamboo, cork, stone, wicker, or rattan is recommended.

Contrary to popular belief, furniture made of natural materials is often more affordable than the regular type of furniture. Pine is less expensive than many other wood pieces, especially if you buy it unfinished, which makes it a very popular choice. It can be painted, stained, or covered with a clear coat of varnish. Unfinished pine furniture, which can be personalised by painting, allows great flexibility in a child's room. The furniture can be refinished and repainted as the child's tastes change.

Clear finishes, like varnish and lacquer, can contain high levels of volatile organic compounds (VOCs) which contribute to air pollution and can cause health problems. Varnishes use petroleum-derived and synthetic solvents that emit high levels of VOCs during application. For this reason, varnishes are not considered environmentally preferable, but they are the most durable floor finish. Water-based sealers are environmentally preferable, and they continue to be improved, both in terms of better performance and lower emissions.

Carpets can detract from good indoor air quality and are discouraged in general. Only carpets made with cotton are acceptable. Chairs, couches, and mattresses made from natural latex foam covered with wool, hemp, or natural textiles are highly recommended in all rooms, especially in children's rooms.

ii) Lighting

The effect of light on health and wellbeing is perhaps the most complex and least understood aspect of lighting. Lighting can affect many areas of our life, from how well we sleep to how we feel, to how susceptible we might be to a range of diseases and health disorders. We generally cannot control the lighting we

Figure 3.2 This three-year-old child's bedroom has wood flooring and furniture made from natural materials. The rug is made from natural esparto grass and cotton.

experience in public environments on a daily basis, like our workplace or school. Therefore, our home becomes the place where we can make adjustments to lighting to promote good health (Frering and others, 2013: 8).

Regarding lighting, it is of course much better to have as much as natural light as possible. A house filled with sunlight is cheery, warm, and inviting. It also has an effect in our biological rhythms. Generous use of glass is the most obvious way to get light into a home; but rather than simply getting as many windows as possible, it is important to balance light's benefits with its side effects such as heat gain or loss and glare. In the healthy home, electric lighting systems must provide proper conditions over time without any negative aspects. Lighting and control systems must be simple to understand, use, and adjust over time as needs change. They must also be robust and not need a lot of time or effort to program or maintain. It is better to use energy-efficient light bulbs such as halogen incandescents, compact fluorescent lamps (CFLs), and light-emitting diodes (LEDs).

All lighting technologies have pros and cons. Compact fluorescent lamps are diffusive sources of light that use energy efficiently and can last for many years under typical home use. However, they do not work well in applications where light is being directed to a small area. For this reason, fluorescent lamps are fine for kitchens but not for living rooms or bedrooms. All take time to "warm up" when switched on before providing their full light output. Many people find this a bit annoying.

Light-emitting diodes (LEDs) have characteristics that lend themselves to better matching the needs of each lighting application within a home in a very efficient manner, especially in situations where well-controlled, directional lighting is desired. However, LED products tend to cost more than conventional lighting products. The colour effect of the bulb is also relevant. Warm lights are recommended for use at night – to easily fall asleep. Cooler lights are recommended for in the morning to wake up and activate our bodies. Light from televisions, computers, and mobile telephones is cool, and for this reason, it is better to not use them before going to sleep.

iii) Colour

Colour is the most dominant and visible aspect of interior design, and studying its impact on our health and wellbeing is a complex subject. Many research experiments over decades have concluded that we are indeed influenced by colour in our interior environments. Colour is often the easiest aspect of an interior to change, altering the feel and characteristic of an interior environment, so it is important to understand something of this topic.

The UK Green Building Council provides some general principles regarding the use of colour for interior design:[17]

1. A tonally homogenous, monotonous colour scheme may result in under-stimulation, which can lead to restlessness, irritation, aggression, and difficulty in concentration.
2. A coloured environment of extreme complexity and contrast can lead to over-stimulation, causing physiological responses of increased pulse rate, blood pressure, and muscle tension.
3. As with natural environments, interior spaces require some variety of colour hues, saturation, contrast, light, and texture to provide balance, stress relief, and enhance a sense of wellbeing.
4. The degree of colour saturation will affect the way a space is perceived: paler tints make a surface recede and make rooms appear larger, or ceilings higher, and vice versa.

The use of colour (in walls, paintings, rooms decoration) also has an impact on our mind: blue is good for concentration (studies); violet is good for children's play rooms; green can be relaxing in bedrooms, bathrooms, or living rooms; and yellow is uplifting, so it is good for kitchens and living rooms.

To sum up, the interior setting of our homes is a key aspect for our wellbeing and health. Although some may consider it irrelevant or even a bit snobbish, it is important to be careful when choosing furniture materials and setting the lighting and colours of different rooms. Although the building materials can only be chosen when we are able to build our own home, being informed about the flooring, wall materials, and finishes of the house or flat that we want to buy or rent is recommended.

The home users: Age, habits, and healthy needs

Finally, we must also describe the relationship between home and its inhabitants. Home gives us protection as well as a place to experience a warm and safe atmosphere. It is the place that we share with our most loved ones, where we feel comfortable and protected. Shelter and protection are the most basic functions of a house.

Our home provides us with an environment that is often described as our "third skin" – it plays a similar role than our skin or our clothes. Apart from giving us shelter, our home also serves other purposes for us. It creates a healthy microclimate and supports our life and family processes (resting, nurturing, communicating, sharing, playing, washing); it contributes directly to our wellbeing. Creating an appropriate healthy environment at home is particularly relevant for the weakest inhabitants of the homes: the children, and most particularly, the newborn babies. After spending nine months in her mother's uterus (a warm and safe shelter), the newborn child starts to experience the external conditions of temperature, light, or noise. A newborn baby has specific emotional needs at the beginning of life. For example, newborn babies need a lot of sleep because they are growing and developing at such a fast pace. For this reason, a baby should sleep in a room that is quiet, dark, and kept at a slightly cool temperature (Sparshott, 1997: 12).

Additionally, one has to bear in mind that children in the early years spend most of their time at home. Their important activities of the day, like playing, eating, sleeping, washing hands, and going to the bathroom, take place at home.

The connection between children's development and their home environment is quite strong. The Italian physician Maria Montessori studied the impact of the environment on children at the beginning of the twentieth century. She viewed the child as one who is naturally eager for knowledge and capable of initiating learning in a supportive, thoughtfully prepared learning environment.[18] She developed the Montessori method which promotes the use of natural materials in furniture, finishing, and toys to provide a healthy environment for children. It also encourages freedom of movement, giving the child the space and opportunity to move around, and avoiding having them confined into one place, not being able to explore their environment.

As Maria Montessori said,

> We must give the child an environment that he can utilize by himself: a little washstand of his own, a bureau with drawers he can open, objects of common use that he can operate, a small bed in which he can sleep at night under an attractive blanket he can fold and spread by himself. We must give him an

> environment in which he can live and play; then we will see him work all day with his hands and wait impatiently to undress himself and lay himself down on his own bed.[19]

Nonetheless, getting a natural environment and choosing appropriate building materials and indoor settings is not enough to have a healthy home. Healthy life habits are also relevant, for example, balanced nutrition, keeping the home clean and tidy, and children's timetables and routines. Routines, indeed, make children feel safe and secure. These healthy life habits are the basis for children's education.

Order and cleanliness are habits to be acquired at home. Order is often seen as a huge challenge, but as Marie Kondo, the creator of the Konmari home organising method says, it creates multiple benefits at a wellbeing level, both physical and psychological; improving our mood, stimulating creativity, and relieving stress.[20]

From an inner perspective, the time we spend at home will build family and childhood memories. A house is full of these memories and we build our identity and sense of belonging in relation to our home (what type of space is, who we live with, which memories we have). These are key aspects for children in the early stages of life and they build children's confidence and self-esteem. If we help them to grow up in a peaceful and natural environment, they will do the same with their children. It is our way to contribute to creating a better society.

Figure 3.3 Floor beds and toddler-size furniture are recommended, but are not essential for children development

Figure 3.4 Responsibility and having to participate in housekeeping is good for children – it helps them to feel needed, important, and trusted. It helps them feel like they belong.

Conclusion

As we saw in the case of Cecilia and Toni at the beginning of this chapter, the home environment may determine the health and wellbeing of our children and family. When choosing our homes, we should all give more importance to closeness to nature than proximity to shops, work, or schools. The outdoor environment has

Figure 3.5 Cecilia and her family now live in much heathier home

a clear connection with the total moisture content of the house and the air quality through ventilation. Other important criteria that helps us to build or create healthy homes are the adequate flooring and furniture made from natural elements like wood, stone, or bamboo. Sunlight exposures, lighting systems, and colour schemes following natural conditions also help to provide a warm and healthy environment at home.

Home is a unique place for children; it the place where they start their lives and where they may discover family affection and happiness. It is the place where they grow up and become adults. Let's try to improve their health and wellbeing by making their homes a better place to live.

Notes

1 See www.urbanet.info/world-urban-population
2 "Noise impacts on health, Science for environmental policy", European Commission, January 2015, p. 10. http://ec.europa.eu/environment/integration/research/newsalert/pdf/47si.pdf
3 "Planning horizons. Promoting Healthy cities", Royal Town Planning Institute, 2014, www.rtpi.org.uk/media/1119674 /rtpi_promoting_healthy_cities.pdf
4 See European Parliament resolution of 11 June 2013 on social housing in the European Union (2012/2293(INI)).

5 "Decent, affordable and healthy housing for all." An introduction to the Ministerial segment of the 78th Session of the Committee of Housing and Land Management, United Nations Economic Commission for Europe, Geneva, November 2017, www.unece.org/fileadmin/DAM/hlm/sessions/docs2017/ Information_doc_10_Affordable_Housing.pdf
6 "Urban Agenda for the EU: The Housing Partnership Action Plan", December 2018, p. 37. https:// ec.europa.eu/futurium/en/system/files/ged/final_action_plan_euua_housing_partnership_december_2018_1.pdf
7 "National Healthy Housing Standard", US National Centre for Healthy Housing, 2018, pp. 48–51, https://nchh.org/resource-library/national-healthy-housing-standard.pdf
8 See www.tcpa.org.uk/healthy-homes-act
9 Käthe Bachler was born in 1923 and she wrote seven books on Earth radiation. See, for example, her book *Earth Radiation: Startling Discoveries of a Dowser*, 1988.
10 See https://buildingbiology.com/
11 See https://buildingbiology.com/principles-of-baubiologie/
12 True linoleum is made from wood, cork, limestone dust, pine resin, and colorants mixed with linseed oil.
13 See www.healthyhouseinstitute.com/a-799-Choosing-Healthy-Building-Materials
14 www.homebuilding.co.uk/is-your-home-making-you-ill/
15 www.healthyhouseinstitute.com/a-799-Choosing-Healthy-Building-Materials
16 Fortunately, veneer plaster systems are available and provide many of the same benefits of traditional plaster for a price similar to standard drywall. See www.healthyhouseinstitute.com/a-799-Choosing-Healthy-Building-Materials
17 See "Health and Wellbeing Homes," UK Green Building Council, July 2016, p. 23, available at www.ukgbc.org
18 www.montessori.edu/
19 See Maria Montessori, *The Absorbent Mind,* The Theosophical Publishing House, 1949, available at https://archive.org/stream/absorbentmind031961mbp#page/n7/mode/2up
20 Marie Kondo is the author of the best-seller book *The Life-Changing Magic of Tidying Up*. See https://konmari.com/

References

Bengtsson, A. and Grahn, P. (2014) "Outdoor environments in healthcare settings: a quality evaluation tool for sue in designing healthcare gardens", *Urban Forestry & Urban Greening*, 13(4).

Bueno, M. (2005) *El libro práctico de la casa sana*. Barcelona: RBA Libros.

Buxton, R.T, McKenna, M.F, Mennitt, D., Fristrup, K., Crooks, K., Angeloni, L. and Wittemyer, G. (2017, May 5) "Noise pollution is pervasive in U.S. protected areas", *Science*, 356(6337).

Fjurtoft, I. and Sagei, J. (2004) "The natural environment as a playground for children. Landscape description and analyses of a natural playscape", *Landscape and Urban Planning*, 48, 83–97.

Frering, D., Figueiro, M.G., Leslie, R.P. and Rea, M.S. (2013) *Lighting the Swedish healthy home*. Lighting Research Center, Rensselaer Polytechnic Institute. Available at: http://ceebel.se/wp-content/uploads/2013/12/Swedish-Healthy-Home-White-Paper-Final-Version.pdf.

Guxens, J. Método ARN (Alto rendimiento Natural) (2011). Barcelona: Instituto Guxens.

Krieger, J., Song, L., Takaro, T.K. and Stout, J. (2000, March) "Asthma and the home environment of low-income urban children: preliminary findings from the Seattle King county Healthy homes project", *Journal of Urban Health*, 77(1), 50–67.

Kump, L. (2008) "Geobiology–Quo Vadis", *Geobiology*, 6(5), 423–424.

Redlarski, G. and others (2015) "The influence of electromagnetic pollution on living organsims: historical trends and forecasting changes", *BioMed Research International*, 2015.

Rice, J., Kozak, R.A., Meitner, M.J. and Cohen, D.H. (2006) *Appearance wood products and psychological well-being*. Available at: https://wfs.swst.org/index.php/wfs/article/view/180.

Risica, P.M., Tovar, A., Palomo, V., Dionne, L, Mena, N., Magid, K., Ward, D.S. and Gans, K.M. (2019) "Improving nutrition and physical activity environments of family child care homes: the rationale, design and study protocol of the 'Healthy Start/Comienzos Sanos' cluster randomized trial", *BMC Public Health*, Available at: https://doi.org/10.1186/s12889-019-6704-6.

Shoemaker, J.M. and Vitale, C.Y. (1991) *Healthy homes, healthy kids: protecting your children from everyday environmental hazards*. Washington, DC: Island Press.

Sparshott, M. (1997) *Pain, distress and the newborn baby*. New York: Wiley.

Spengler, J.D. (2005) *What is the scientific evidence for health problems associated with the indoor environment*? Report of the surgeon general's workshop on healthy indoor environment, January 12–13, National Institutes of Health, Bethesda, MD. Available at: www.ncbi.nlm.nih.gov/books/NBK44634/.

Vandivere, S., Hair, E.C., Theokas, C., Cleveland, K., McNamara, M. and Atienza, A. (2006) "How housing affects child well-being", *Funders' Network for Smart Growth and Livable Communities*. Available at: www.fundersnetwork.org/files/learn/Housing_and_Child_Well_Being.pdf.

Ward Thompson, C. (2002) "Urban open space in the 21st century", *Landscape and Urban Planning*, 60, 59–72.

Chapter 4

Unsafe food handling and preparation in poor households

Nahieli Greaves-Fernández and Maria del Carmen Rabiela-Sotelo

Introduction

Traditionally, the home has been regarded as a place of wellbeing and safety, notwithstanding the fact that, within it, unsafe practices can take place that endanger its inhabitants' health. One such practice is the unsanitary handling of foodstuffs from the moment they are bought to when they are prepared, stored, and eaten. This chapter will explore, from the health and educational perspective, how different poor households handle their food and which are the risks posed by unsanitary handling practices. At the end of the chapter, a series of recommendations will be issued based on the findings.

The family home

Home and family are central to people's wellbeing and education. In the home, values that are important for each family are transmitted and family members learn the rules to live in a wider society. From home, deeper learning and experiences are promoted which help to consolidate growth, development, personality, habits, and social interactions of its members. Most of the behaviours and attitudes towards food, hygiene, and nutrition are acquired at home from an early age and they will last a lifetime. Within the family, the individuals learn different values such as respect, responsibility, generosity, order, and discipline which help them thrive in a wider society.

The home is also a place where healthy eating habits are developed. Parents have a great influence in promoting a safe and healthy diet for the family. This includes handling the food in a way that ensures its safety. Despite the fact that both parents have a role in the family dynamics, in Mexico, as in many other countries, the main workload of the domestic labour lies with the women, who take care of children, clean the house, and cook, among other chores. Besides, many women work outside the home without seeing the household tasks diminished (INMUJERES et al., 2016). Many women learn the basic aspects of homemaking by watching their elders, and the practices are passed down through generations. In many households, especially ones where the educational level is low, these practices may pose a risk to the inhabitants of the home. The present work will focus on how the women in charge of the families cook food for the family members, emphasising their food-handling practices and understanding the role of family dynamics in high-risk practices regarding food hygiene.

In Mexico, food-borne illnesses are one of the most frequent reasons why people visit a physician and one of the main causes of death, mainly of people of a low socioeconomic status. It has been estimated that among the poorest people in third-world countries, the probability of a child dying before reaching five years of age is as high as 50%, mainly due to food-borne illnesses. In 2003 in Mexico, 4,556 persons died because of these illnesses (Hernández Cortez et al., 2011). In Mexico City in 2017, 620,000 cases of gastrointestinal illnesses were reported (Sistema Nacional de Vigilancia Epidemiológica, 2017). They can be the result of consumption of contaminated food both at home and in the street. Even if the risks associated with eating in the street are well established (Quinlan, 2013), contrary to common belief, eating at home can also pose serious health risks (Wright et al., 2011; Wills et al., 2013).

Food-borne illnesses are produced by foods contaminated by bacteria or viruses at any point in the food production process – from the point food is harvested to the moment when it is eaten. A survey conducted in the United Kingdom (Prior et al., 2013) showed that most people know very little about food safety and, worse still, this knowledge does not lead to safer practices in the kitchen (Wright et al., 2011).

Most studies of how food is handled consist of surveys in which people self-report their own practices or behaviours. One of the limitations of such studies is that participants can report activities that they are aware they should perform but that are not put into practice regularly, such as washing their hands (Bermúdez-Millán et al., 2004). Alternatively, there are certain behaviours that, being routine, go unnoticed by people. In 2011, researchers from the University of Hertfordshire conducted a study about food safety in 20 homes of elderly people. The study revealed that there is a large difference between what people do, what they say they do, and what they know about the hygienic handling of food, which is why observing actual behaviours is essential for an in-depth understanding of the problems and risks associated with food hygiene (Wills et al., 2013; Dickinson et al., 2014).

Some studies have shown that populations with low incomes are at a higher risk of suffering from gastrointestinal illnesses (Bytzer et al., 2001; Gillespie et al., 2010; Hernández Cortez et al., 2011). Being prone to suffering from gastrointestinal illnesses, it is quite important to determine the factors associated with the food production process that endanger poor families.

Context of the study: MAPFRE community

The present study was carried out in the MAPFRE Community Centre, located in the borough of Santa Fe in the northeast quarter of Mexico City. The centre is a place where the inhabitants of the borough, most living below the poverty line, can take courses of different topics and exercise. The MAPFRE Community Centre offers cooking courses, and efforts have been made to adapt them to the economic and social conditions of the borough. However, it is still an open question whether the actual contents are suitable for the attendees, since the teachers do not reside in the borough and belong to a different, usually higher, socioeconomic and cultural level. When the context of the participants does not inform the design of the courses, it can be the case that they end up being irrelevant for the target audience, since they focus on topics participants do not know or do not do, framed from a perspective outside their experience (Wills et al., 2013).

This pilot study will deepen our knowledge of this particular population by identifying their buying habits, storage methods, and food preparation activities, with the ultimate aim of designing better courses and support materials, well-adapted to their specific needs, practices, and habits.

Aim: To carry out a pilot study in low-income homes located in the borough of Santa Fe, Mexico City, aimed at identifying cooking practices and kitchen spaces, and determine if these can influence the hygiene with which food is handled. By understanding the practices involved in the preparation of food, we will be better able to generate materials and courses adapted to the specific needs and context of the target population. It is worth noting that this study does not pretend to generalise the way that food is handled in poor households. It is an exploratory study that will allow the authors to better understand how to design applicable educational solutions for a group of families.

Methods: To carry out the pilot study, a qualitative approach was applied – namely, participant observation of actual cooking as performed in the homes visited (Kawulich, 2000). This method allowed us, the researchers, to collect data on the daily practices of participants in their own environments. It is worth stating at the outset that this chapter reports on results obtained from a small – but representative – sample of the population of interest. This pilot study is the basis of a larger study to be conducted in the near future. The study was conducted by two researchers from the Universidad Panamericana, both experts in the hygiene of food handling. During the visits to the selected homes, both researchers took detailed notes of their observations, conducted semi-structured interviews with participants, and recorded the spaces where participants normally cook, as well as their cooking practices, through photographs and videos.

Participant selection

The study took place from March to September 2017 and followed women that received assistance from the Mapfre-Universidad Panamericana Centre. The participants were selected according to the following criteria: they had to reside within the borough of Santa Fe and cook for other persons, as well as be willing to allow the researchers into their homes to observe their cooking facilities and

Table 4.1 Demographic data of subjects included in the study

Name	*Age range (years)*	*Number of individuals that eat meals at home*	*Number of individuals at risk of food-borne illnesses*	*Trade or occupation*	*Has participant received instruction in diet-related issues?*
Greta	30–40	5	3 children	MAPFRE Community Centre staff (part-time). Sells food in her spare time.	Yes, she has worked in a company cafeteria
Katia	30–40	3	1 child	Homemaker	No
Leslie	50–60	6	3 children	Homemaker	Yes, she has taken courses in the MAPFRE Community Centre
Maria	50–60	5	3 children	Homemaker	Yes, she has taken courses in the MAPFRE Community Centre
Paulina	30–40	12	4 children and 2 elderly adults suffering from diabetes	MAPFRE Community Centre staff (part-time)	Yes, from a nutritionist that provides care for her at-risk children (from diabetes)
Soledad	30–40	5	3 children diagnosed with pre-diabetes	MAPFRE Community Centre staff (part-time)	Yes, from a nutritionist that provides care for her at-risk children (from diabetes)
Telma	50–60	5	-	Homemaker. Sells food in her spare time.	No

practices. Participants of a wide age range and living in different family setups were selected. The socioeconomic status and the work conditions of participants were likewise mixed. Gathering data from a broad section of homes increases the credibility and relevance of the results (Mays and Pope, 2000), together with their applicability to the design and implementation of actions intended to minimise the potential risks of suffering from a food-borne illness. An invitation to participate in the study was published in the Mapfre-UP centre, while the centre's promoters also actively searched for suitable participants among the population they service. So far, the kitchens and cooking practices of seven homes in the borough met the aforementioned criteria and have been observed in detail. All persons accepted to participate in the study signed an informed consent letter. All of the participants in the study were women. This is because in Mexico, and especially in low-income households, most of the household work is carried out by women. Some of the participating women also worked away from their homes, a situation that influenced their cooking practices. In those cases where men were part of the family, their main role in the family was as breadwinners.

Research method

All research was conducted in the kitchens in participants' homes, and occasionally encompassed other spaces when cooking activities (such as washing, processing, and storage of food) took place outside of the kitchen. Spaces and practices were observed and detailed notes made for as long as participants cooked. Additionally, a checklist based on the Norma Oficial Mexicana [Official Mexican Regulation] that regulates the handling of food in commercial establishments and food-processing plants was adapted to ascertain the quality of cooking processes (Secretaría de Salud, 2009). Observations of both kitchens and practices were recorded with the aid of photographs and videos. Samples of the water used for cooking and washing the dishes were analysed using the Test Kit for Pool and Spa (Pentair) to determine their pH value and residual chlorine concentration. While participants cooked, the researchers interviewed them informally about the decisions they made when cooking, particularly decisions concerning the handling of food. All research notes were immediately transcribed after the visits came to an end.

Grounded theory methods were employed for data analysis, so as to derive categories from the data. A total of 152 documents – comprising photographs, videos, notes, and conversations with the participants – were analysed. All materials generated were repeatedly analysed and coded independently by each researcher with the aid of the AtlasTi (version 7.0), and discussed to create categories (Glaser and Strauss, 1967) and identify correct and risky practices enacted by participants, as well as common ideas and myths associated with cooking. The joint discussion of the researchers based on the notes and all other generated materials during the course of the research lent rigour to the qualitative research (Barbour, 2001).

Results

In the following, we present the results from the observations conducted in participants' homes, together with their analysis. The first part of this section summarises the features of the participants. Immediately after, a brief description of participants' kitchen facilities follows, focusing on their limitations. The discussion then centres on the thinking processes that underpin participants' purchase and storage of food. Approaches to cleaning and disinfection are also touched upon here, particularly as pertains to the source and quality of the water used for cooking tasks, the methods for washing both hands and foodstuffs, and the hygiene of work surfaces. This leads to an analysis of the consumption of potentially hazardous foods in the home. Finally, food service behaviours and the disposal of leftover food are assessed.

Participants

Table 1 summarises the characteristics of the participants in the study. All names have been changed to protect the participants' identity and ensure their anonymity.

All participants care for other family members, especially their own children or grandchildren. In some cases, participants even provide care to members of their extended families (such is the case of participant Paulina, who cooks for up to 12 people every day.) All participants remarked that the children eat food prepared at home, which places them at considerable risk of contracting food-borne illnesses resulting from poor handling and preparation practices.

The kitchen

Facilities and kitchen equipment

Visits to homes confirmed that all participants own stoves. Likewise, all participants own a refrigerator, although both Greta and Paulina stated that they do not make use of it. In Paulina's kitchen, where 12 people eat on a daily basis, a mini fridge with a broken freezer is used instead of a full-size refrigerator.

Size of the work area

Generally speaking, work areas in the kitchens were large enough to allow one person to move around comfortably. This space allowance minimises the risk of both accidents and the cross-contamination of food. The only kitchen small enough to be of concern is Greta's (Fig. 4.1) – its area is small enough that only one person can cook at any one time, a problem compounded by the large number of cooking utensils that clutter work surfaces.

In some cases, the kitchen area extends beyond the physical space normally allocated to cooking tasks. Katia, for instance, takes the food processor to the

Figure 4.1 Greta's kitchen

bathroom, placing it on the toilet seat cover to operate it in order to use the only remaining free outlet. In a similar vein, Soledad washes both dishes and food items in a basin where she also does her laundry because her home lacks a proper kitchen sink. Finally, Paulina lacks a kitchen sink and – like Soledad – has also resorted to washing vegetables in the same basin where she does her laundry. In Katia's home, the kitchen and the dining room share the same physical space. However, the dining table is cluttered with household items, both kitchenware and other housewares, drastically reducing the area available for cooking and preparing meals. Due to this circumstance, foods in different stages of preparation end up being in direct contact with items that can lead to cross-contamination (Fig 4.2).

Shopping

Each family possesses different shopping habits. Three of the participants (Greta, Paulina, and Telma) stated that they purchase their food on a daily basis from the public market. As mentioned previously, Greta and Paulina stated they have no need of their refrigerators because they shop for food every day due to an

Figure 4.2 Katia's work area

economically precarious situation. They decide on a daily basis what to purchase depending on what monies are available.

Both Paulina and Soledad explained that once a month they purchase foods in supermarkets. Soledad further commented that she buys bread for a whole month. She also gets one-kilogram packages of ham bought from a wholesaler. This amount of ham lasts her family a full month in the refrigerator.

Storage of food and kitchen utensils

Refrigeration

Two participants do not use refrigerators. In general, most participants keep an orderly arrangement of the contents of their refrigerators, with consumable goods and/or foods stored inside airtight containers or plastic bags, and meats and vegetables on separate areas. Telma and Paulina, particularly, left chopped onions outside the refrigerator for several days so as to keep them handy while cooking. In Katia's home, a couple of unrefrigerated yoghurts were placed on the crowded table.

Freezing

Five of the seven participants in the study referred that they rarely, if ever, freeze food. In some cases (Greta, Paulina, and Soledad), the precariousness of their economic situation has led to adopting the practice of eating the food on the same day it is purchased (so there is no surplus left to freeze); in others (Katia and Telma), participants or their families do not like to eat food that has been frozen. On the contrary, Leslie freezes the meat she buys in the street market if she is not going to cook it in the next couple of days, whereas Maria freezes all food left over on weekdays (Monday to Thursday) so as to serve it on Friday.

Dry storage

Leslie, Maria, and Telma have, in their kitchens, cupboards above waist level they can close, whereas Soledad stores her non-perishable products in shelves below both her stove and her worktable, hidden from view by a cloth curtain. Greta has no dry storage area, so she keeps a few things on her work area (Fig 4.1). Paulina uses open shelves attached to a wall close to the stove. Katia, like Soledad, keeps all her non-perishable products in a storage unit placed under the stove. This unit appears neither ordered nor clean, with bags containing unidentified powders stored with no information on when it was bought or its expiration date (Fig. 4.3).

Personal hygiene

All participants exhibited an overall appearance of cleanliness about their persons. However, several behaviours concerning their personal hygiene that put them at risk were observed. Only one of the participants (Soledad) washed her hands before starting to cook. All others began cooking without doing so, even though during the process several of them did wash their hands while washing vegetables. On multiple occasions, Greta touched both her face and her neck while cooking and, after doing so, handled the food with her bare hands. At Paulina's home, a six-year-old child entered the kitchen on several occasions, coughed without covering his mouth close to – or over – the food being prepared, ate from

Figure 4.3 Katia's dry storage. Her cooking utensils can be seen on the left.

the ingredients being used to cook, and cleaned his hands and mouth with the dishcloth normally used for cleaning work surfaces. Telma tasted what she was cooking by placing a small sample in her hand and then licking it. She afterwards kept cooking and handling foods without having washed her hands. Both Greta and Telma sell food in their spare time to increase their earnings.

Risk of cross-contamination

One of the most striking findings was the large number of behaviours that increase the risk of cross-contamination of foods. Paulina, for example, picked up a plastic bag that had contained raw meat and put it in her sweatshirt pocket. Soledad handled raw chicken meat and immediately after added, with her fingers, a pinch of salt taken from an open container, quite possibly contaminating it. She also placed the cheese with which she was going to fill the chicken breasts on the same chopping board where she had previously sliced raw meat. Leftover cheese was returned to its original packaging, even though it had come into indirect contact with the raw chicken. Soledad, Telma, and Paulina all failed to wash their hands after handling raw meat.

Among the most worrying behaviours – and the most likely to result in the cross-contamination of foods – relate to the use of dishcloths. In all kitchens, excepting that of Maria, dishcloths were not freshly washed when the visits took place. In most kitchens, a single dishcloth plays several roles during the cooking process. It is used as a work surface, as a sort of temporary trashcan for vegetable remainders, as a chopping board, to clean surfaces, to carry hot pots from the kitchen to the table, to dry one's hands after washing them, and to clean them after handling raw chicken or other meats. In Paulina's case, in addition to the aforementioned uses, her mother used the kitchen dishcloth to clean the chopping board where she had sliced tomatoes. Immediately after, a six-year-old child used the same dishcloth to wipe his hands. Soledad, likewise, left her dishcloth lying over the board where she had prepared a chicken-based dish and then used it to wipe all the kitchen surfaces clean.

Cleaning and disinfection of food, utensils, and work surfaces

Washing and disinfection of fruits and vegetables

During the preparation of food, several ways of washing and disinfecting fruits and vegetables were observed. Participants washed tomatoes, cucumbers, and cacti with tap water and detergent and the mechanical aid of a scrubber. In spite of this, in the case of chopped vegetables and long-leaf vegetables, such as lettuce, the disinfection practices observed did not follow established guidelines. For example, Paulina, Soledad, and Greta add a few drops of chlorine to an unknown volume of water where vegetables are soaking, pouring the water out only 15 seconds after adding the disinfectant agent. They then rinse the vegetables with tap water. Leslie and Maria did follow the instructions provided with the disinfectant agent (colloidal silver and chlorine, respectively). Greta, in her turn, washed boiled cacti with tap water.

Cleanliness of the work areas

The kitchens of Leslie, Maria, Telma, and Soledad appeared to be quite clean. Paulina commented that she had her kitchen painted before the visit took place, so it turned out to be impossible to ascertain if her kitchen was ordinarily clean or if it was cleaned for the occasion. The same uncertainty applies to the rest of the kitchens. Even though Katia's stove looked clean, the table where she prepares food was cluttered with objects that do not belong to a kitchen. The dirtiest kitchen was Greta's, where the stove and the walls were coated with a film of burnt residue of cooking oil (Fig. 4.4). During the interview, Greta pointed out that when she worked in a canteen as a cook she was responsible of deep cleaning the kitchen, so it is to be expected that she has some knowledge about cleaning practices.

Food preparation

Time of day

Four of the participants who work out of home (Soledad, Maria, Greta, and Leslie) cooked or started preparing the ingredients at night, when the rest of the family was asleep. Telma, Katia, and Paulina cook in the mornings.

Figure 4.4 Greta's stove

Storage of food after their preparation and eating schedule

Another high-risk situation uncovered pertained to the storage of food. In all homes, due to their work schedules, several members eat their main meal at night. When food is prepared in the morning, it is left on the stove or the table for three to eight hours before being eaten. When each family member arrives home, each eats a portion of food from a pot. When Greta, Katia, Paulina, and Soledad finished cooking, they covered the food with different items: dishcloths, plastic tablecloths, napkins, and plastic lids. Both Karina and Paula stated that if left uncovered, food "gets sour."

Leftover food

Six of the seven participants commented that they do not end up with leftover food after all family members have eaten. If anything is not eaten by midday, it is eaten at noon. They also stated that, due to their socioeconomic circumstances, they cook only the exact amount of food that will be consumed each day. However, if something remains uneaten after noon, this surplus is left outside the refrigerator. The only participant that stores surplus food inside her refrigerator was Maria, who cooks enough food to last two to three days. Inside her refrigerator, several closed containers were evident.

Discussion

All participants in the study are homemakers who cook on a daily basis for people at a high risk of suffering from gastrointestinal illnesses, such as small children and elderly people, as well as ill people (Cortez Cecilia et al., 2011; World Health Organization. Foodborne Disease Burden Epidemiology Reference Group, 2015). Greta and Telma even manage their own catering businesses. The fact that even professional food handlers lack a thorough knowledge of food hygiene is amply reported in the international literature on the subject and is a cause of concern for health authorities (Secretaría de Salud, 2009; Bessa Martins et al., 2012).

The kitchen

Home visits revealed that not all homes have kitchens that consist of enclosed spaces dedicated solely to the preparation of food. The fact that people have to physically displace themselves in order to wash their food or rinse their hands makes it especially important for them to be well aware of the risks associated with a lack of hygiene, since the need to save time or avoid going out into bad weather may lead them to cut corners by not washing their hands and/or foods. Wills and co-authors found out that the boundaries of the kitchen are usually not well defined and that spaces in a home have multiple uses – laundry room, recreational activities, communal living, homework, and office work (Wills et al., 2013). As in this study, especially in the case of Katia, other researchers have found objects in kitchens that do not belong in them, such as mail, magazines, keys, mobile phones, among others, all of which represent potential sources of contamination (Meadow et al., 2014). Another high-risk practice is using bathrooms as extensions of kitchens. Bathrooms can have higher levels of pathogenic bacteria associated to human waste that can end up in food (Flores et al., 2011).

Shopping and storage of foods

Shopping practices are closely linked to the socioeconomic status of the families. Participants that purchase food every day in public markets do so because their income varies on a daily basis. Purchasing food daily helps reduce the risk of suffering from food-borne illnesses caused by inadequate storage of food, especially in homes that do not have, or do not use, refrigerators (Greta and Paulina). According to criteria established in the Official Mexican Regulation (Secretaría de Salud, 2009), not more than four hours must elapse from the moment a food is bought to the moment it is consumed. In the case of some of the participants in this study, due to time constraints imposed by work schedules of family members, foods remain outside the refrigerator all day, increasing the risk of illness. Soledad's family purchases bread and ham once a month and make the effort to "make it last" for the whole 30 days. This is a risky practice, since the expiry dates or best-by dates of these products are considerably shorter than a month. Ignoring the expiry date is one of the most common mishandling practices when it comes to food, as demonstrated by a survey conducted in the United Kingdom (Wright et al., 2011). Ham can easily become contaminated given that it has a high water and protein content. As such, it is recommended that sliced ham be stored from three to five days once it is removed from its package (USDA, 2015).

Adequate storage of non-perishable products is a key consideration towards keeping them in optimal conditions and, thus, to insure food safety. Storage areas need to be cool, dry, and well-ventilated spaces, as well as arranged in such a way that labels of the products can be easily read. Contrary to this, in Katia's case, her cupboard was disorganised and filled with unlabelled foods, as well as being vulnerable to infestations and grime.

Hygiene

The finding that six out of seven participants fail to wash their hands agrees with Bermúdez-Millán and co-authors' finding that 90% of Puerto Rican women in their study did not wash their hands before cooking (Bermúdez-Millán et al., 2004). Studies that directly observe participants have the advantage of avoiding – or minimising – the over-reporting by participants of the frequency of actions such as washing both their hands and chopping boards, as was reported in work carried out in 2004 with a sample of Latin Americans residing in the United States

(Dharod et al., 2004). The present study also documented the use of dirty chopping boards. Additionally, Greta was observed rinsing her chopping board with only tap water and letting it dry in the dish rack. Chopping boards are a common medium of transmission of food-borne illnesses (Faour-Klingeil et al., 2016), which is why cleaning and disinfecting them requires careful attention, particularly after chopping raw foods.

Other high-risk behaviours associated with personal hygiene observed were as follows: licking one's hand to test the flavour of food after handling raw chicken (Telma); coughing on food being prepared (Paulina's child); and constantly stroking one's face and neck while cooking (Greta). In Telma's case, apart from the risk of cross-contamination of foods, handling raw chicken increases the risk of suffering from a *Salmonella* infection. Touching one's face or hair can contaminate foods. Between 30% and 50% of all adults carry *Staphylococcus aureus* in their nostrils, whereas 20% to 30% carry this bacterium in their skin. This microorganism is responsible for episodes of food poisoning (Ebert, 2018).

Cross-contamination

The risk of cross-contaminating food is difficult to ascertain from either interviews or from focus groups, since the process involves small everyday actions that people are not consciously aware of performing. In a survey answered by 3,231 persons in the United Kingdom, 96% admitted to cleaning kitchen surfaces at least once a week (Prior et al., 2013). This notwithstanding, the study did not determine whether this activity was carried out with a clean dishcloth. Our study suggests that people cling to an "illusion of cleanliness" even though their cleaning procedures might be doing more harm than good.

Not washing one's hands after handling raw meat is another of the observed behaviours that increases the risk of cross-contamination. Additionally, storing food in containers where raw chicken had been kept, as Soledad did when she stored cheese together with raw chicken in the refrigerator, also poses a health risk. In the survey conducted in the United Kingdom, 85% of respondents claimed they washed their hands after handling raw meat (Prior et al., 2013). However, given the nature of the research, it is not possible to determine if that is truly the case. The present study allowed us to confirm that participants are mostly unaware and unconcerned of the risk of the cross-contamination of food. De Jong and co-authors (2008) conducted a study in which chicken meat was inoculated with *Campylobacter jejuni* and asked volunteers to handle the chicken. Afterwards, the researchers asked participants to wash their hands and, in spite of the washing, found out that the hands of all the participants remained contaminated with the microorganism. This finding suggests that washing procedures were inadequate. Cross-contamination could be reduced if people washed their hands following an adequate protocol, but the processes commonly used do not appear to guarantee the removal of pathogens.

During the observations it also became evident that the use of dishcloths entails a serious risk of cross-contamination since multiple uses are given to a single dishcloth within the kitchen, and they are not replaced frequently. Dishcloths can carry large amounts of bacteria, such as *Enterobacteriaceae*, *Pseudomonas* spp., *Salmonella*, and *Staphylococcus aureus*, among other pathogens. Thus, through dishcloths, kitchen surfaces are contaminated (Enriquez et al., 1997; Hilton and Austin, 2000).

Washing food

In this study, three kinds of mistakes were observed in the handling of fruits and vegetables: a) inadequate concentrations of the disinfectant agents were used; b) the disinfectant agents were allowed to act for insufficient amounts of time; and c) disinfected foods were rinsed with tap water. Disinfectant agents, such as sodium hypochlorite and colloidal silver, eliminate microorganisms only if the instructions of use are followed. Tin cans should also be washed before being opened, since during storage dust and microorganisms can accumulate on their surfaces and contaminate the food inside when the can is opened (USDA, 2016).

Preservation of foods

In the present study, all participants left food outside the refrigerator for a period of time longer than is recommended as safe (Secretaría de Salud, 2009) in response to their family dynamics and work schedules. Several participants claimed that covering food protects it from spoiling, in spite of being at room temperature for a number of hours. Meer and Misner (2000), reported that 67% of participants in their study stated not knowing if it was necessary to let cooked food cool at room temperature before placing it inside the refrigerator. Another study that monitored the practices of a group of elderly people in the United Kingdom in detail found out that several of them left cooked foods for up to five days on the stove, and in spite of this considered the food as safe to eat (Wills et al., 2013; Dickinson et al., 2014). These types of practices, according to the participants, reduce waste and facilitate access to the food by other family members, but also puts them at risk of suffering from food-borne illnesses, especially in warm seasons.

Recommendations for safe food handling

The Mexican government has issued some campaigns about food handling, and also includes hygiene-related topics in the school curriculum. However, as the results of this small study show, some households do not carry out safe food handling practices. As a result of the observations during the study, the authors adhere to the World Health Organization's list of recommendations, which are applicable in any household, regardless of the socioeconomic status (World Health Organization. Department of Food Safety, 2006: 28).

1) *Keep clean: Wash your hands before handling foodstuff and after going to the toilet. Wash and sanitise surfaces and equipment used for food preparation. Protect kitchen areas and food from insects, pests, and other animals.*
2) *Separate raw and cooked food. Never mix raw meat with other foods.*
3) *Cook thoroughly: Especially meat, poultry, eggs, and seafood. Bring foods to boiling and reheat thoroughly after storing.*
4) *Keep food at safe temperatures: Never leave cooled food at room temperature for more than two hours. Refrigerate below 5°C. Do not store food too long and do not thaw frozen food at room temperature.*
5) *Use safe water and raw materials: Use clean water and select fresh and wholesome foods. Wash fruits and vegetables. Do not use food beyond its expiry date.*

Limitations of the study: This study has several limitations that need to be considered when analysing the results. First, the sample size is small due to the fact that few volunteers came forward and the privacy associated with the kitchen does not lend itself to repeated visits. Also, all of the participants in this study were women, as in Mexico the majority of the housework is carried out by women. Second, it is difficult to determine the extent to which the presence of the researches influences the behaviour of participants, the cleanliness of the spaces, and the preparation, previous to the visits, done by participants.

Conclusion

Homemaking is an activity that can be easily taken for granted. There is, however, some specialised knowledge that people should have to ensure the health and safety of the inhabitants of the home, especially when they are catering to vulnerable people who are at risk of food-borne illnesses. Participants relied on what they knew from watching their mothers when they were growing up, and they lack the knowledge to provide their families with a meal that guarantees their safety. This study provides an insight into their practices that will be helpful in the design of educational materials adapted to the needs of the community. This potential decrease in food-borne illnesses in low-income families can enhance their quality of life and minimise non-attendance at work and school, positively affecting both their income and their education, respectively.

So far, cooking courses offered by the community centre have not taken into account the limitations imposed by infrastructure, income, and education – nor the influence of culture – on cooking practices. Any intervention or educational initiative must by necessity take stock of the real conditions under which families operate in order to achieve a positive impact on their living standards. It will also be necessary to measure the extent of such an impact, so as to establish whether interventions have been adequate or not.

References

Barbour, R. S. (2001) 'Checklists for improving rigour in qualitative research: a case of the tail wagging the dog?', *British Medical Journal Publishing Group*, 322(7294), pp. 1115–1117. doi:10.1136/BMJ.322.7294.1115.

Bermúdez-Millán, A. *et al.* (2004) 'Food safety knowledge, attitudes, and behaviors among Puerto Rican caretakers living in hartford, connecticut', *Journal of Food Protection*, 67(3), pp. 512–516. doi:10.4315/0362-028X-67.3.512.

Bessa Martins, R., Hogg, T. and Gestal Otero, J. (2012) 'Food handlers' knowledge on food hygiene: the case of a catering company in Portugal', *Food Control*. Elsevier, 23(1), pp. 184–190. doi:10.1016/J.FOODCONT.2011.07.008.

Bytzer, P. *et al.* (2001) 'Low socioeconomic class is a risk factor for upper and lower gastrointestinal symptoms: a population based study in 15 000 Australian adults', *Gut*, 49(1), pp. 66–72. Available at: www.ncbi.nlm.nih.gov/pubmed/11413112 (Accessed: 27 October, 2017).

Cortez Cecilia, H., Arreola Ma Guadalupe, A. and Escarpulli Graciela, C. (2011) 'Situación de las enfermedades gastrointestinales en México', *Enfermedades Infecciosas y Microbiología*, 31(4). Available at: www.medigraphic.com/pdfs/micro/ei-2011/ei114f.pdf (Accessed: 27 October, 2017).

Dharod, J. M. *et al.* (2004) 'Influence of the fight BAC! food safety campaign on an urban latino population in connecticut', *Journal of Nutrition Education and Behavior*, 36(3), pp. 128–134. doi:10.1016/S1499-4046(06)60149-8.

Dickinson, A. *et al.* (2014) 'Food safety and older people: the kitchen life study', *British Journal of Community Nursing*, 19(5), pp. 226–232. doi:10.12968/bjcn.2014.19.5.226.

Ebert, M. (2018) 'Hygiene principles to avoid contamination/cross-contamination in the kitchen and during food processing', *Staphylococcus aureus*. Elsevier, pp. 217–234. doi:10.1016/B978-0-12-809671-0.00011-5.

Enriquez, C. E. *et al.* (1997) 'Bacteriological survey of used cellulose sponges and cotton dishcloths from domestic kitchens (PDF Download Available)', *Dairy, Food and Environmental Sanitation*, 17(1), pp. 20–24. Available at: www.researchgate.net/publication/281579647_Bacteriological_survey_of_used_cellulose_sponges_and_cotton_dishcloths_from_domestic_kitchens (Accessed: 28 October 2017).

Faour-Klingeil, D., Kuri, V. and Todd, E. (2016) 'The transfer rate of Salmonella Typhimurium from contaminated parsley to other consecutively chopped batches via cutting boards under different food handling scenarios', *Food Research International*. Elsevier, 89, pp. 495–503. doi:10.1016/J.FOODRES.2016.09.001.

Flores, G. E. *et al.* (2011) 'Microbial biogeography of public restroom surfaces', *PLoS ONE*. Edited by M. R. Liles. Public Library of Science, 6(11), p. e28132. doi:10.1371/journal.pone.0028132.

Gillespie, I. A. *et al.* (2010) 'Human listeriosis in England, 2001–2007: association with neighbourhood deprivation', *Eurosurveillance*, 15(27). Available at: www.cabdirect.org/cabdirect/abstract/20103238079 (Accessed: 27 October 2017).

Glaser, B. G. and Strauss, A. L. (1967) *The discovery of grounded theory: strategies for qualitative research*. Chicago: Aldine Pub. Co.

Hernández Cortez, C., Aguilera Arreola, M. G. and Castro Escarpulli, G. (2011) 'Situación de las enfermedades gastrointestinales en México', *Enfermedades Infecciosas y Microbiologia*, 31(4), pp. 137–151.

Hilton, A. C. and Austin, E. (2000) 'The kitchen dishcloth as a source of and vehicle for foodborne pathogens in a domestic setting', *International Journal of Environmental Health Research*, 10(3), pp. 257–261. doi:10.1080/09603120050127202.

INMUJERES *et al.* (2016) *Atlas de Género*. Available at: http://gaia.inegi.org.mx/atlas_genero/ (Accessed: 8 November 2017).

de Jong, A. E. I. *et al.* (2008) 'Cross-contamination in the kitchen: effect of hygiene measures', *Journal of Applied Microbiology*, 105(2), pp. 615–624. doi:10.1111/j.1365-2672.2008.03778.x.

Kawulich, B. B. (2000) 'Participant observation as a data collection method', *Forum Qualitative Sozialforschung/Forum: Qualitative Social Research*. Deutsche Forschungsgemeinschaft, 6(2). Available at: www.qualitative-research.net/index.php/fqs/article/view/466/996 (Accessed: 27 October 2017).

Mays, N. and Pope, C. (2000) 'Qualitative research in health care: assessing quality in qualitative research', *British Medical Journal Publishing Group*, 320(7226), pp. 50–52. doi:10.1136/bmj.320.7226.50.

Meadow, J. F., Altrichter, A. E. and Green, J. L. (2014) 'Mobile phones carry the personal microbiome of their owners', *Peer J, Inc*, 2, p. e447. doi:10.7717/peerj.447.

Meer, R. R. and Misner, S. L. (2000) 'Food safety knowledge and behavior of expanded food and nutrition education program participants in Arizona', *Journal of Food Protection*. International Association of Milk, Food, and Environmental Sanitarians, 63(12), pp. 1725–1731. Available at: www.cabdirect.org/cabdirect/abstract/20013004808 (Accessed: 27 October 2017).

Prior, G. *et al.* (2013) *Exploring food attitudes and behaviours in the UK: findings from the food and you survey 2012*. Available at: www.food.gov.uk/sites/default/files/food-and-you-2012-main-report.pdf (Accessed: 27 October 2017).

Quinlan, J. (2013) 'Foodborne illness incidence rates and food safety risks for populations of low socioeconomic status and minority race/ethnicity: a review of the literature', *International Journal of Environmental Research and Public Health*, 10(8), pp. 3634–3652. doi:10.3390/ijerph10083634.

Secretaría de Salud (2009) *NOM-251-SSA1–2009*. Ciudad de México. Available at: www.dof.gob.mx/normasOficiales/3980/salud/salud.htm.

Sistema Nacional de Vigilancia Epidemiológica (2017) *Boletín Epidemiológico. Vigilancia epidemiológica, semana 40, 2017*. Ciudad de México. Available at: www.gob.mx/cms/uploads/attachment/file/264542/sem40.pdf (Accessed: 27 October 2017).

USDA (2015) *Ham and food safety, United States department of agriculture. Food safety and inspection service*. Available at: www.fsis.usda.gov/wps/portal/fsis/topics/food-safety-education/get-answers/food-safety-fact-sheets/meat-preparation/ham-and-food-safety/ct_index/!ut/p/a1/jZFdT4MwFIZ_DZelB5kL846QmA0duCy6jpulg0MhgZa0Vaa_3jpv_Nh07VXPeZ605y0tKKOF5C-t4LZVkncf52K6gxVMg (Accessed: 29 October 2017).

USDA (2016) *Washing food: does it promote food safety? United States department of agriculture. food safety and inspection service.* Available at: www.fsis.usda.gov/wps/portal/fsis/topics/food-safety-education/get-answers/food-safety-fact-sheets/safe-food-handling/washing-food-does-it-promote-food-safety/washing-food (Accessed: 30 October 2017).

Wills, W. *et al.* (2013) *Domestic kitchen practices: findings from the 'kitchen life' study.* Available at: www.food.gov.uk/sites/default/files/818-1-1496_KITCHEN_LIFE_FINAL_REPORT_10-07-13.pdf (Accessed: 27 October 2017).

World Health Organization. Department of Food Safety (2006) *Five keys to safer food manual.* Geneva, Switzerland: World Health Organisation.

World Health Organization. Foodborne Disease Burden Epidemiology Reference Group (2015) *WHO estimates of the global burden of foodborne diseases.* Geneva, Switzerland: World Health Organisation.

Wright, M., Canham, R. and Masrani, R. (2011) *Food safety behaviours in the home final report for the food standards agency.* Reading. Available at: www.food.gov.uk/sites/default/files/700-1-1185_X04009_FINAL.pdf (Accessed: 27 October 2017).

Chapter 5

Responsible citizenship and our common home

Taking care of the natural environment in households and beyond

Maria Rosaria Brizi

Introduction

We all know that human behaviour has an impact on stocks of natural resources and the quality of the natural environment, which, in turn, can have tremendous effects on human health and wellbeing. The space and time scope of those effects cannot be completely predicted, yet they should be a matter of concern for all of us.[1] The environment responds to human activities, often in some unpredictable ways. Private actions can have significant consequences in terms of the environmental impact they generate. Households, in particular, have an impact on some crucial areas such as energy and water consumption, waste management, and food and transport choices – albeit the immediate and individual impact that they generate is not necessarily evident. Nonetheless, the households' pattern of consumption matters, as everybody's behaviour, at home and beyond, entails consequences. This chapter aims at investigating the role of the home in the collective sustainability challenge and its inner potential in terms of contribution towards the sustainability of the ecosystem. Our lifestyle, in the home and beyond, is often unsustainable, yet everybody's home can be turned into a sustainability practice. Drawing from previous reflections on ecological citizenship and assuming that environmental virtues are as relevant to the environmental sustainability challenge as legal instruments and economic instruments, this chapter highlights the crucial role of the home as a catalyst of change and a pivotal contributor to the end of the "sustainable environmental common good."

Furthermore, by acknowledging the existence of several political actors, the chapter reflects on the importance of developing a synergy between the home, the state, and the business world – synergy that can prove crucial in the pursuit of more a sustainable world. The assumption is that legal instruments and economic incentives certainly matter, yet there is more to that, which is about choosing a course of action instead of a different one whenever there is no mandatory option and beyond mere compliance with a set of rules. Often, acting responsibly towards the natural environment is a matter of knowledge, thus, the relevance of information, communication, and acquired awareness are also highlighted.

Throughout the chapter, the home appears as the site where all of us, in our capacity of householders, parents, and consumers, can contribute actively to the protection of the planet by taking an eco-friendly course of action and nurturing the virtues that ecological citizenship embodies. The home not only matters in its capacity of interacting with both business and institutions, but also as an incubator of good environmental practices. Above all, the home holds the promise of a sustainable future, being the experiential and educational site where the eco-citizens of today have the chance to contribute to the moulding of the responsible pro-environmental citizens of tomorrow.

Sustainability, the home, and the common environmental good

The home can widely contribute to the protection and enhancement of the natural environment by becoming an environmental sustainability practice. To this end, though, a preliminary understanding of the notion of sustainability seems particularly relevant. There are different definitions of sustainability. For instance, Barry specifies that "the core concept of sustainability is some X whose value should be maintained, in as far as it lies in our power to do so, into the indefinite future," whereas "the content of sustainability depends on what we think it matters" (Barry, 1997: 101). Those definitions normally encompass an idea of projection towards the future. For example, according to Murray (2011: 34), sustainability is "an aspirational expression that represents where we need to go as a species."

In environmental terms, we can start from assuming that "sustainability is about the relationship between human behavior and nature" (Murray, 2011: 172), in order to focus on the ongoing depletion of the Earth's natural capital and the urgency to challenge it. In this respect, nature, and therefore the ecosystem, is the X factor that should be maintained into the future. There is no denial that it matters, as the ecosystem is the provider for our basic needs and the needs of those who are going to walk in our footsteps. Nor can it be denied that a healthy and well-functioning natural environment is an indispensable condition for human welfare. Thus, given the instrumental value of the ecosystem as our life-supporting context, the importance of caring for the natural environment and preventing its further depletion is *in re ipsa*.

Preserving the natural environment is a huge challenge that has to be understood more as a process than an outcome. Besides, it is to be pursued both at a local and a global level. The local challenge, in particular, has to be started and pursued in the home, where unsustainable patterns of consumption can have a huge bearing on the natural environment both nearby and elsewhere, in the present as well as in the future. In this respect, the home, as local as it is, can have a global environmental impact and contribute to collective challenges such as climate change, excessive waste, air pollution, water shortages, and so forth.

It is therefore pivotal to practice, in the home and beyond, "mindful as opposed to mindless consumption" (Barry, 2006: 38) and start undertaking responsibilities for the sake of the natural environment.[2] Nevertheless, it is a fact that some people do better than others, although most people, at their deepest level, would like to be a "positive force in the world" (Murray, 2011: 71). In truth, most people agree about the importance of caring for the planet, although they do not necessarily behave accordingly, as taking care of the planet does not automatically imply immediate benefits for the individual and his private household. Rather, it might entail future and far afield advantages that may not necessarily justify the immediate cost. As a consequence, commitment to the care of the environment is an everyday challenge that not everybody is ready to embrace.

The question, then, is how to solve the dilemma between conflicting interests such as the immediate, individual good and the future common good. In this respect, we draw upon Connelly's notion of "sustainable, environmental common good," which is based on eco-virtues "that go beyond their bearers" (Connelly, 2006: 51), being social rather than private. According to Connelly, eco-virtues incorporate environmental concerns and can be described as "an internally motivated ecological thoughtfulness leading to action" (Connelly, 2006: 60). In fact, "a virtue, fully formed, transcends mere compliance with law or policy, because it includes as part of itself the appropriate motivation and intentionality" (Connelly, 2006: 52).

Amongst the eco-virtues, justice is crucial as it makes us accept that every human being is or should be entitled to an equal share of the natural resources as any other human being. In fact, as we inhabit the world and make use of its natural endowment, we inevitably affect the entitlement of others to their share of natural resources, the others being not only currently living creatures, but also those who are not yet borne (Di Paola, 2015).

Thinking that every human being is entitled to the same share of natural resources, though, may not suffice to justify an obligation to preserve the natural environment to the benefit of future generations, especially those who are far removed from us in time, while compliance with any such obligation entails costs and burdens at the expense of the current generations. Nonetheless, "care for future generations follows from the overlap of generations here in the present. This generation cares for the next generation, which will in turn care for generations yet to come" (Connelly, 2006: 56).

What should kindle our commitment towards the conservation and enhancement of the ecosystem is the reflection that we live on it and it is just fair to acknowledge the right of everybody else to the same opportunity. Thus, in order to bridge the gap between the self-interest and the common, environmental good, we need to draw upon our underlying norms and find intrinsic motivation as citizens of the planet where we belong and that we own. Eco-virtues, justice *in primis*, are the key. There is a nexus of mutuality between the self-interest and the sustainable, environmental common good, which draws upon our sense of belonging on the planet that we inhabit. The sense of belonging should make us feel like we are citizens of the planet, and also entails a sense of ownership, which, in turn, leads to an idea of self-efficacy. It has been argued that "self-efficacy is an important factor in determining pro-environmental action" (Nash and Lewis, 2006: 163).

Therefore, if we further argue the sense of belonging, ownership, and self-efficacy, while considering ourselves citizens of the natural environment that all of us inhabit and live upon, then we have to acknowledge that the conservation and sustainability of the planet are our duty that exists beyond any imposition by the rule of law. Basically, it is about doing the right thing and self-imposing self-constraint. As Dobson and Bell highlight, "some of us, some of the time, do things because we think they are the right thing to do, even if they conflict with our perceived self-interest"[3] (Dobson and Bell, 2006: 4). This is the mindset that is required to contribute to environmental sustainability, everybody in his own tiny domain, starting from the home.

In this respect, Connelly's construct of ecological citizenship is enlightening.[4] Basically, we incorporate environmental concerns into our daily routine because of those eco-virtues that make us find both the motivation and the intention to embrace a sustainable lifestyle. In doing so, we perceive ourselves and act as eco-citizens who restrain themselves and choose a certain course of action instead of another for the sake of the ecosystem. Ecological citizenship is non-territorial in nature, as environmental issues are transnational and intergenerational, inasmuch as centred on self-imposed duties "that are not limited in scope to time and place" (Connelly, p. 63). Basically, it encompasses "the ecological duties with the virtues appropriate to their fullfilment" (Connelly, 2006: 65), therefore a kind of citizenship worth exploring.

Polis, oikos

The way we behave and the decisions we make in the home are extremely relevant to the end of the environmental common good, yet private action is not sufficient when the conservation of the ecosystem is at stake. The state plays a crucial role in enabling and encouraging its citizens to adopt environmentally responsible lifestyles. What the state does, though, is not sufficient either. As Barry argues (Barry, 2006, quoting Barry and Paterson, 2003), "States do not become green by themselves." In those spaces where there is no action or standard mandated by the rule of law, everybody can deliberately choose how to behave. Such space of liberty encompasses the chance to take environmental considerations into account and transform everybody's home into a sustainable practice where eco-virtues unfold and ecological citizenship gets rooted. To this end, the synergy between the *oikos* and the *polis* is pivotal. In this respect, households matter, as they mediate the success or failure of environmental policies.

It is certainly for the state to generate the conditions and provide the right incentives to spur eco-friendly lifestyles. Many governments have actually introduced a wide variety of measures in order to encourage people to take environmental impacts into account in their daily life. Phasing out incandescent light bulbs, introducing energy-performance labels for homes, or providing tax incentives to purchase alternative fuel vehicles, inasmuch as price-based incentives aimed at fostering energy and water savings, are some of the possible measures that governments adopt in order to encourage greener choices.[5]

Of course, changing both mindset and subsequent behaviour is not going to happen overnight. It may take some time for households to adjust. Responsiveness depends on a number of different factors, including age, gender, income, education, housing conditions, working habits, and so forth. For instance, changes that entail investments in capital goods – such as cars or energy-saving equipment – may take some time and unfold at a different pace in various segments of the population.[6]

Adequate infrastructures also make a difference in encouraging green behaviour. Who wants to buy an electric car if charging it proves way too difficult? And how do you encourage the use of bikes if cycling in urban areas is dangerous? It is the role of politics to create the conditions for households to make green choices. Both economic incentives and the supply of environment-related infrastructures can bear a tremendous weight on households' choices and inherent consumption patterns.

Of course, budgetary considerations unescapably fall into picture, since many environmental policies may entail adverse distributional effects. For instance, low-income households are quite likely to be adversely affected by a rise in water and energy charges. Investment in efficiency equipment may entail costs, which are unbearable for certain segments of the population. Not only low-income households might prove unwilling to pay in order to switch to "green" energy, such as wind or solar, though. In rental properties, landlords are not as likely to invest in renewable sources as owner-occupiers, since the former seem to have little to gain from the investment. Likewise, tenants are quite unlikely to invest in the same kind of equipment to be installed in a property they do not own, particularly if they are not planning to inhabit it for a lengthy period of time.

The scenario is therefore quite fragmented and the effectiveness of environmental policies cannot be taken for granted. It is for governments to tackle possible disparities and address adverse distribution effects by introducing measures capable of mitigating those differences, thus ensuring any such effectiveness.

The state can rely upon a toolbox of standards, sanctions and incentives to promote eco-friendly lifestyles in keeping with sustainability targets. As Connelly points out, policy statements, legislation, differential taxation, charges, and appropriate intervention that somehow underlie a measure of approval or disapproval of certain courses of action have a bearing on encouraging people towards eco-virtuous behavioural patterns. "The encouragement of voluntary action, through encouragement and facilitation, is therefore vital" (Connelly, 2006: 69).

Nevertheless, albeit people certainly respond to economic incentives, penalties, and price policy matters, budgetary issues do not account for the overall picture. The implementation of environmental policies largely depends on the awareness of the impacts that households' consumption patterns have on the ecosystem. Therefore, policies aimed at raising the level of environmental awareness are also necessary, as awareness contributes to the acceptability of both policies and inherent costs.

Economic incentives, inasmuch as prohibitions and sanctions, may induce temporary behaviour changes, but it is a genuine pro-environmental state of mind that makes a difference and kindles a deep sense of ecological commitment. The latter is the key to transforming attitudes into behaviour change at home and beyond. As Connelly (2006) highlights, virtuous eco-citizens are those who are capable of internalising the purpose and worth of good environmental practices, thus adopting an eco-friendly lifestyle beyond the mere compliance with the rule of law.

The role for business: Corporate social responsibility and the creation of shared value

Business also plays a crucial role in tackling environmental issues. The civil society certainly expects companies to undertake responsibilities and take action for the sake of the natural environment. And society undoubtedly has some stake in how business is run and what externalities it causes. Through corporate social responsibility, more and more companies tend to include environmental concerns into their strategies, procedures, and processes, partly because they need to comply with the rule of law, and partly because their heightened awareness makes them go beyond the mere logic of short-term profit. Business has huge potential in tackling environmental challenges and contributing to the common environmental good.[7] The question, then, is whether business is ready to contribute and to what extent.

Companies definitely use more natural resources than other social actors, therefore they should undertake greater responsibilities in shaping a response to crucial environmental issues. For example, by assessing and enhancing their water performance, companies can certainly contribute their crucial share to global challenges, such as water scarcity and water pollution. Elsewhere, they can commit to greenhouse gas emission reduction targets, and invest in renewable energy and low-carbon technology, thus contributing to the world's climate change challenge. They can also pursue a circular economy, that is restorative by definition, by reconceiving products, especially long-lasting goods rather than disposable ones, or goods that can be easily repaired or disassembled and turned into something else. Besides, they can introduce further changes in the supply chain, regarding transport, distribution methods, and so forth.

Protecting the planet from degradation is now definitely acknowledged as a priority on a global scale, and is also one of the Sustainable Development Goals[8] that all global stakeholders, including business, are called to. Business seems quite responsive to the sustainability challenge, as the huge number of signatories to the UN Global Compact,[9] the world's largest corporate responsibility initiative with more than 10,000 signatories in over 135 countries, clearly illustrates. The Global Compact foresees a very prominent role for companies by specifying that business should "support a precautionary approach to environmental challenges"[10] and "undertake initiatives to promote greater environmental responsibility,"[11] inasmuch as "encourage the development and diffusion of environmentally friendly technologies."[12]

Thus, by undertaking corporate social responsibilities towards the planet as a whole and society at large, business has the opportunity and the responsibility to take the lead in ensuring that markets can advance in ways that benefit both economies and societies while preserving the natural environment. There are challenges, of course, and costs. Corporate decisions pertaining to environmental protection may imply trade-offs, since companies are constrained with limited financial resources. How do we prioritise corporate social responsibility, then? How can we align business and society in the common pursuit of the protection and enhancement of the natural environment? And, above all, why do we care?

The first and commonsensical reflection is that caring may entail good business, as pro-environmental practices can yield revenue in terms of brand perception, reputation, expanded market opportunities, and reduction of social pressure and litigation. Undertaking corporate social responsibility can therefore evolve into creating "shared value,"[13] which entails pursuing environmental protection or social development while acting in the self-interest of the company. Thus, pursuing environmental goals does not necessarily imply sacrificing profit.

Considering environmental protection, a productivity driver rather than a burden and a net cost is the key to the creation of shared value. For instance, through successful marketing, businesses can motivate customers to shift towards organic food or environmentally friendly products, thus facilitating a cultural change that contributes to the protection of the planet, while earning the company a larger segment of the market. It is a win-win situation where shared value is created. In terms of value chain, investing in a more efficient use of the water and energy not only benefits the natural environment, but also implies reduced costs for the company. Therefore, a better environmental performance both entails cost savings, much to the advantage of the company's budget, and contributes to putting the available stock of natural resources at more a rational level by reducing waste.

Nonetheless, it would be illusory to think that acting pro-environmentally always yields a business advantage and turns into a win-win situation. This is where the state needs to get involved, sometimes using fiscal instruments, sometimes relying on economic incentives, provided they encourage pro-environmental business strategies. Enforcing environmental performance measurement systems inasmuch as supporting innovation can also help. Basically, the state needs to facilitate the potential of business as a key driver of change. That said, and without overlooking the role of the public sector in supporting business, it is still for companies worldwide to make the right, pro-environmental choice and induce an overall level of integrity in business as a whole (Osorio-Vega, 2019). As a fundamental political actor, business has to find the foundation of commitment to environmental sustainability and a sense of belonging not only to its immediate, physical surroundings, but to the planet as a whole, and join in the idea of ecological citizenship as a long-term investment, beyond the logic of short-term profit. This is the core sustainability call that the UN Development Goals and the UN Global Compact basically entail and the expectation, no matter how ambitious, that society at large nurtures.

Information, knowledge, awareness

We have suggested that ecological citizenship is mainly about self-imposed duties. Nonetheless, taking care of the natural environment not only entails undertaking responsibilities and performing duties. It is our right to dwell in a safe, clean and healthy ecosystem and have access to both environmental information and environmental justice.[14] Therefore, being proactive and effective for the sake of the natural environment can also be about claiming our rights, especially the right to be informed. Namely, it is the duty of governments, companies, and service providers to disclose environmental information. It is our right as citizens to be duly informed.

An adequate level of knowledge can certainly affect behavioural patterns in households. For instance, it is pivotal for households to be aware of new charges, such as subsidies or taxes, in order to make greener decisions. Likewise, householders need to know what their level of consumption of environment-related resources amounts to, in order to start saving on them. Metering water or energy consumption is an option and a way to both increase the level of awareness and to send a warning message to householders. When implementing environmental policies, time is also a crucial factor as the short-term response of households, both in terms of use of natural resources and investment in capital goods, might be limited. Therefore, price incentives need to be complemented by different kind of measures such as awareness campaigns, labels on eco-products, and whatever instrument may provide households with sufficient information to start questioning their lifestyle. In this respect, availability of information and the subsequent level of acquired knowledge may prove crucial, albeit age, income, and ownership status, amongst other factors, inevitably have a bearing on the decision-making process in the home.

In order to develop a sufficient degree of awareness, all we need to grasp is a basic knowledge about the ongoing ecological crisis and a few facts about what we can do in our tiny domain. The kind of knowledge that behavioural change in the home requires is not necessarily sophisticated and elitist in nature. It is more about little gestures and common sense than charts and figures. In this respect, everybody's home can be turned into a sustainable practice for the sake of the ecosystem. Low-income households are no exception.

For instance, understanding that a large part of the trash that every household generates on a daily basis can be processed and put to new use is within everybody's reach. Likewise, the kind of knowledge that is required in order to dispose of hazardous waste simply consists of grasping what to do with unused medications or where to take old electrical equipment. By the same token, in order to start recycling, what recycling services are available is the only necessary information.

An increased level of awareness certainly affects the decision-making process, and also encourages changes on the demand side. Consumers' choices are no exception. On the contrary, even if consumers are concerned about the environmental effects of their purchase decisions and have strong pro-environmental beliefs, they may not behave accordingly if they lack the appropriate information.

Trust in the information and the inherent source matters as well. Eco-labels and environmental certification, for instance, need to be trusted to prove effective (Tinacci Mossello, 2008).

Confidence is also important. It is unlikely that we will turn to renewable energy if we do not believe that electricity can be totally produced from renewable sources. By the same token, it is dubious that we recycle plastic bottles if we ignore that plastic takes over 500 years to decompose. A few facts are all we need to know. Yet, such basic knowledge is crucial to behavioural change, as we need to internalise any such awareness in order to act on it whenever we can choose between different courses of action. The level of motivation, which is the key to taking certain tasks seriously, undertaking efforts, and bearing whatever burden may go with acting responsibly towards the natural environment, makes the difference. By internalising motivation, we become eco-virtuous. Motivation, though, does not come out of nothing. Rather it assumes some kind of knowledge, which is the key to making informed decisions. We need to know before engaging in eco-friendly practices. Therefore, for behavioural changes to happen, information has to be provided and communication becomes a task of paramount importance not only for governments and service providers, but also amongst members of a family.

Communication in the home

Making informed decisions is worth teaching. It is often a matter of waste management and energy efficiency but, above all, it is a matter of inner, environment-sensitive disposition and sense of responsibility. Through open and continuous communication, parents have the chance to raise the level of awareness and pass down to their children a concern for the environment that helps generate both motivation and commitment to act responsibly. Communication in the home is crucial to engage all the family members in an eco-friendly lifestyle. It is also the key to sharing and passing down environmental awareness, inasmuch as a sense of both self-efficacy and entitlement towards the care of the ecosystem, with a goal of a prospective greener society. For instance, as parents, we can encourage our children to make mindful choices by explaining the environmental impact that industrial production generates. Thus, when we purchase things, we can try to draw our children's attention to the product's characteristics.

We can also highlight the benefits associated with buying eco-products and try to make them understand why those products are often more expensive than non-eco products. The aim is showing that, whenever we consider purchasing an item, we need to take into account not only the economic value but also environmental concerns. Paying a little bit more for an eco-product equals bearing an extra cost for the sake of the environment, thus accepting the idea that a nexus of mutuality exists between common interest and individual interest.

Some issues may seem too remote or global in nature to be related to home-made solutions, though. For instance, climate change is huge in terms of importance and maybe too vast an issue to be confronted within the narrow limits of households (Payne, 2010). Therefore, it may sound unrealistic to associate global concern to our daily behaviour, whereas associating immediate personal consequences with the ongoing eco-crisis can help experiencing a sense of self-efficacy. When we realise that there is something we can do, we are probably more inclined to do something. It has been highlighted that people are more likely "to frame their attitudes depending on perceived personal consequences, and somewhat less on broad cultural values" (Nash and Lewis, 2006: 164).

Communication should not be prescriptive, patronising, or hypercritical, otherwise it backfires and turns off our children instead of making them understand that more a sustainable lifestyle is both possible and desirable. For instance, in order to enhance the effectiveness of our communication, we can start explaining that caring for the environment entails both collective and individual benefits, such as reduced energy bills resulting from energy-saving behaviour or personal health benefits related to the consumption of organic food.

At the same time, we can explain to our children how powerful consumers' choices are in order to convey a strong message to the business world. Those choices will not go unnoticed: sooner or later, the inner intelligence of the economic system will respond to the message, as demand drives the supply. Customers are the key drivers of companies' environmental initiatives, after all.

Communication is no simple task, though. If environmental education is to prove a story of home success, we need to strike a balance between different factors. When conveying our eco-friendly message, we need to consider the enormous pressure children are exposed to, as different sources convey dissimilar and often conflicting messages.

For example, how do we suggest cutting down on consumption if advertisements continuously generate new needs and desires? Hence, we can suggest our children find creative ways to fix and reuse items that they already own or take them in to second-hand stores.

Also, we can invest some of our time to teach them how to make mindful choices. Let us consider clothing. We cannot outright ignore that it is often a matter of identity amongst peers (Payne, 2010). Nonetheless, we can explain to our children that the fashion industry is now trying to become eco-friendly, therefore even the most callous amongst fashionistas can wear sustainable items. Why not give eco-friendly options such as vintage and "eco-cool" a chance?

Answering questions and offering convincing explanations is probably the hardest of tasks. In fact, in environmental matters, many of the answers involve value judgments that, as such, do not necessarily rely upon unquestionable objectivity. There are plenty of data and statistics, of course, but they do not necessarily account for it all.

Environmental education in the home

The home is the first site where our values and beliefs are moulded. Therefore, it is the right place to start experiencing a caring attitude towards the ecosystem by embracing those concerns that go beyond our self-interest. As Payne (2010: 213) depicts it, "the home is probably the most significant experiential site of an embodied, inhabited and place-based environmental education (or not) – well before and beyond the classroom, the playground and the school."

In the home, those who perceive themselves as eco-citizens can therefore contribute to the environmental sustainability goal not only by adopting a pro-environmental lifestyle, but also by passing down awareness, concern, and motivation to the next generation of responsible, pro-environmental citizens. The values children are exposed to in the home are actually likely to linger long into their adulthood. It is therefore for parents to consider it a priority and undertake responsibility in this respect. If the parents are committed to the care of the natural environment, then the children have a chance to follow suit.

As Gaugh and Scott (2006) suggest, there must be a connection between environment, citizenship, and education. Thus, trying to build on environmental education in the home is a way of investing in the citizens of tomorrow. The children of today are those that will soon make informed decisions, take risks, undertake responsibilities, seize opportunities, and choose one pathway instead of another, in keeping with the sense of ethics and the beliefs they will have started developing in their own homes.

The environmental education that we can give children in the home is therefore the bridge that we build in order to take them into an adult, pro-environmental, responsible world where they are going to act as leaders, householders, innovators, consumers, and, above all, parents that are going to pass down the concern for the planet to those who are going to follow, that is to say yet another generation of possible eco-citizens. Education is the tool by which responsible behaviour towards the environment is framed, explained, and encouraged. Helping our children understand that they will be capable of interacting with the ecosystem and impact it is crucial for them to engage in the broader framework of society and make their own contribution as prospective eco-citizens. By gaining a sense of awareness of the ongoing eco-crisis inasmuch as some experience, our children actually develop motivation and start to perceive themselves as members of a larger community whose behaviours and decisions make both an individual and a collective difference. Above all, they start growing a sense of belonging in a double dimension: the individual home and the common one. It is a sense of membership, belonging, and ownership that nurtures eco-virtues and leads towards the undertaking of responsibilities towards the natural environment.

Obviously, education develops an attitude but not necessarily leads to environmentally responsible behaviour. There is more to that. Concern generates the desire to change and leads towards ecological commitment, whereas the latter is the key that makes the action match the intention. Nonetheless, education is the foundation of responsible behaviour: what we do, how we manage issues, and what decisions we make largely draw upon what we know and the issues we have been exposed to, not only through formal education but also in the home. Of course, it is a long way before education builds an eco-friendly attitude that develops into behaviour change. Yet, again, the longest of journeys starts with the first step.

A genuine sense of commitment can be transferred to children by doing, showing, and explaining, thus nurturing those eco-virtues that are the key towards ecological citizenship. Children must be shown what to do, of course, but, above all, they need to understand why they should care. In this respect, we need to convey a message of hope and a vision of the future that includes both ourselves and everybody else if the final aim is bridging the gap between our individual households and the common home that we all inhabit, inasmuch as the further gap between the common home where we dwell now and the common home somebody else will inhabit in the future.

The home is the site where eco-virtues can be nurtured and a vision of an eco-friendly lifestyle fostered, shared, and turned into reality. Above all, it is probably the primary and most important place to learn by doing and to treasure the experience, before or while being exposed to formal education in schools or other institutions. In a nutshell, the home is the place to start building the foundation of environmental education and the laboratory to generate eco-virtues as a precondition to assume, later on in life, the responsibilities that go with ecological citizenship and the inherent self-imposed duties.

The daily routine and the relevance of little gestures

Most of the learning actually occurs when the children get involved in doing practical things that are somewhat related to environmental issues. Therefore, it is pivotal to integrate those gestures that underlie concerns for the natural environment and embody an attempt at taking care in the daily routine. Even little gestures, as meaningless as they may seem, can make a difference. For instance, while exposing our children to the idea that water is too precious a natural resource to be wasted, we can show them that turning off the tap while brushing our teeth, or taking a shower rather than a bath, has an impact on the level of the household consumption. With regards to air pollution, we can suggest walking and cycling as healthy and eco-friendly activities. In addition, we can highlight the value of green mobility by introducing them to environmentally friendly options: public transport is often an alternative to private transport, whereas carpooling and car-sharing are smart solutions if we cannot do without a car. The key is explaining to our children that what we need in our daily routine is more often a transport service than a tangible asset.

Energy saving can also be taught. Apart from showing our children the inner magic of a candlelight dinner, we can try to explain the importance and availability of renewable sources. In addition, we can try to involve them in coming to terms with those electrical appliances that seem to pile up in many households. For instance, before buying new electrical appliances, we can take our children to talk to the retailers and ask them what to do with old ones. Most retailers can probably offer useful hints about possible take-back schemes. Moreover, instead of denying access to the computer and other electronic devices, we can suggest that the energy that we need in order to power a device for a given amount of time may equal the energy that we save by choosing recycled paper instead of first-generation paper, since the production of the former is more energy efficient than the production of the latter.[15]

By the same token, we can show our children how to reduce household waste. Composting is one way to reduce waste that can easily be explained. What it takes is no big deal: it is all about setting aside fruit peels and other vegetable food waste that can be piled up into a heap which, in turn, can be used as nutrient for one's garden, if any. The idea is circular in nature – what comes from the ground can feed the ground as well, which is an idea children might consider exploring.

Purchasing products in bulk is one more way to reduce waste, as it results in avoiding excessive packaging. Another way is saving on paper waste by having paper stuff, such as bills or bank statements, e-mailed instead of mailed. We can show our children how much paper we can save by not printing documents whenever storage in an electronic device is an option.

Home eco-politics is a major theme in both reusing and recycling.[16] Using reusable bags when buying groceries is one example. In addition, we can show our children that if we do not have a reusable bag with us, we should purchase paper bags rather than plastic bags. Paper provides a great example as it can be both reused and recycled, to again serve as well as brand-new paper. Paper bags for presents are just one striking example of reusable items. Wrapping paper is yet another. By the same token, there is no need to use more cardboard than necessary, especially when it comes to disposable items. Even on a picnic, we can bring our glasses, cutlery, and pottery and simply avoid paper plates, cups, and utensils that would end up in the trash after the first and only usage. The aim is explaining to our children that first-generation paper requires the pulp of trees that can only be obtained by cutting down those trees. Therefore, controlling the demand can lead to a reduced exploitation of natural resources.

Of course, when it comes to recycling, there is a lot that we can do at home not only with paper but also with other materials such as metal or plastic. Adding recycling to our daily routine is no big deal. In the first place, we can reduce the amount of trash that our households generate by cutting down on the amount of non-recyclable materials that we discard. It is a simple, yet important contribution that all of us can make to the benefit of our common home and one everybody, including our children, may take immediate credit for. All it takes is considering and explaining that the trash we produce, inasmuch as the way we dispose of it, is our own responsibility.

We can also show our children that buying products that have been made from reused materials is simple and often cost-effective: all it takes is looking for the recycling symbol and phrasing on the packaging. Paper towels, cardboard boxes, plastic containers, ink cartridges, paint, and furniture are amongst the many items that are often produced by recycled materials. And, again, we can insist on the importance to convey another useful message to the industries by showing a preference for recycle-friendly products.

Conclusion

The Earth is our common home, where we all belong, as we are all part of the natural environment. The ecosystem is the supplier for our basic needs and those of future generations. Therefore, its conservation and enhancement should be a matter of concern for all of us. The future of the ecosystem actually depends upon everybody's sense of responsibility and commitment, albeit this often generates immediate costs and burdens for the individual, whereas the inherent collective benefits may be far afield and even hard to localise, both in space and time. This potential asymmetry can be tackled only by drawing upon eco-virtues and justice in the first place that make us accept self-imposed duties for the sake of the sustainable common environmental good.

Only by acknowledging the nexus of mutuality between our self-interest and the said common good can we undertake responsibilities for the ongoing environmental sustainability challenge and bear the costs and burdens that any such challenge entails for the individual. Only by perceiving ourselves as citizens of the natural environment and embracing ecological citizenship can we feel the importance of taking care of the ecosystem and infer a sense of self-efficacy. If we realise that there is something we can do for the planet, then we are probably more inclined to do something.

We can embrace ecological citizenship as individuals, companies, or organisations alike. What it takes is nurturing eco-virtues and actively engaging in the environmental sustainability challenge even when there is no immediate advantage ahead to be yielded. It is about undertaking responsibilities for the sake of the planet and performing self-imposed, pro-environmental duties beyond mere compliance with what is mandatorily established by the rule of law. Basically, it is about doing what is right and making the pro-environmental choice.

There is a connection between ecological citizenship, the environment, and the home. This chapter has tried to illustrate the said connection by viewing the home both as a mediator of eco-friendly governmental policies, a driver to pro-environmental business, and an incubator of environmental virtues and belief. The home is actually the first place to start engaging in the environmental sustainability challenge, both as individuals and as members of a community. Therefore, the course of action that we take and the decisions that we make in the home can have a constructive bearing on the conservation and enhancement of the natural environment or, on the contrary, contribute to its further depletion.

The work of the home in building environmental awareness and upholding environmental values is therefore pivotal to the greening of societies. Furthermore, the work of the home is fundamental to advancing the concept of responsible pro-environmental citizenship into the future by nurturing the next generation of eco-citizens with appropriate values, beliefs, and motivation.

This is a crucial contribution to the collective sustainability project. Of course, many more contributions are indispensable – governments and business are obviously pivotal actors in this respect. Nonetheless, the collective sustainability challenge cannot succeed without the work of the home – everybody's home. In fact, the home is the site where to start feeling the challenge of sustainability and consider it not only an individual responsibility, but also a collective opportunity to join hands for the sake of the entire planet. We should therefore invest further, both theoretically and practically, in investigating and implementing the great potential of the home as a catalyst for genuine change.

Notes

1 According to UNEP, more than 2 million annual deaths and billions of cases of diseases are related to environmental degradation (UNEP, 2015a). For facts and data, see www.unenvironment.org

2 Of course, there is more to sustainability than the greening of societies and a genuine sense of commitment to environmental conservation. It is largely a matter of tackling world poverty, addressing social injustices, challenging human rights abuses, and so forth. Nonetheless, in this chapter, the focus is on environmental conservation and enhancement as part of the much broader picture of sustainability.

3 Dobson A. and Bell D. (2006), "Introduction," in: Dobson A. and Bell D., eds., *Environmental citizenship*, The MIT Press, Cambridge, MA, pp. 1–17

4 It is beyond the scope of this chapter to give an outlook of the theories regarding citizenship in general and environmental citizenship in particular, albeit it a fascinating domain of conceptualization and investigation, which entails ethical and political issues, social and economic trade-offs, not to mention legal aspects.

5 Studies conducted within the OECD suggest that price-based measures with regard to electricity, water, fuel, or waste disposal services is necessary in order to cut down on emissions and maintain the endowment of natural resources. Environmental indicators and data pertaining to different countries can be found at www.oecd.org. Further environmental reviews can be found at www.unenvironment.org.

6 OECD studies show the importance of the right incentives. For instance, households charged for their consumption on a volumetric basis consume approximately 20% less water than those that are not charged. Moreover, they are more likely to invest in water-efficient equipment at home. By the same token, charging households for the mixed waste that they produce increases recycling practices. Finally, higher fuel costs seem to reduce car ownership and use. See Nauges (2014), Ehreke et al. (2014) and Kriström and Kiran (2014).

7 For the connection between the common good and stakeholder theory, see Argandona A. (1998), "The Stakeholder Theory and the Common Good", *Journal of Business Ethics*, 17(9/10), How to Make Business Ethics Operational: Creating Effective Alliances: the 10th Annual EBEN Conference, pp. 1093–1102.

8 The other goals consist of ending extreme poverty and fighting inequality and injustice. In 2015, all 193 Member States of the United Nations adopted a plan for achieving a

better future for all, the so called "Agenda 2030" (UNGA A/RES/70/1), which states 17 Sustainable Development Goals (SDGs) to define the world we want (UNEP, 2015b). It acknowledges that "social and economic development depends on the sustainable management of our planet's natural resources" and stresses the intention "to conserve and sustainably use oceans and seas, freshwater resources, as well as forests, mountains and drylands and to protect biodiversity, ecosystems and wildlife," inasmuch as the intention "to promote sustainable tourism, to tackle water scarcity and water pollution, to strengthen cooperation on desertification, dust storms, land degradation and drought and to promote resilience and disaster risk reduction."

9 The UN Global Compact, which was launched in 2000, is a call to companies around the world to align their strategies and operations with ten universal principles in the areas of human rights, labour, environment, and anti-corruption, and to take action in support of broader UN goal, at www.unglobalcompact.org

10 UN Global Compact, Principle 7.

11 UN Global Compact, Principle 8.

12 UN Global Compact, Principle 9.

13 Porter M.E. and Kramer M.R. (2011), "Creating shared value," Harvard Business Review, 89(1–2), pp. 62–77. They define shared value "as policies and operating practices that enhance the competitiveness of a company while simultaneously advancing the economic and social conditions in the communities in which it operates." For a criticism of the shared value construct, see Crane A., Palazzo G., Spence L.J., Matten D. (2014), "Contesting the Value of "Creating Share Value"," *University of California Berkeley*, 56(2), pp. 130–153.

14 If citizens have substantive environmental rights, they also should have procedural rights, that is to say the right to defend their substantive rights. This also implies the right to be informed. In this respect, see the Aarhus Convention on Access to Information, Public Participation in Decision-Making and Access to Justice in Environmental Matters. The Aarhus Convention was adopted on 25 June 1998 in the Danish city of Aarhus, at the Fourth Ministerial Conference, as part of the "Environment for Europe" process. It entered into force on 30 October 2001.

15 It has actually been estimated that 24 trees need being cut down to make one ton of printing paper, whereas recycled paper creates 70% less pollution than first-generation paper production.
www.dartmouth.edu/~cushman/courses/engs171/Paper.pdf

16 Practically, 60% of what ends up in the trash bin can be recycled, whereas certain items, such as aluminium cans or glass bottles and jars, can be recycled completely, which entails saving energy and reducing pollution. Around 16% of the cost of a product is spent on its packaging which is completely wasted if not disposed of properly. See Palatnik et al. (2014).

References

Barry B. (1997), "Sustainability and intergenerational justice", *Theoria: A Journal of Social and Political Theory*, 89, pp. 43–64. Available from: www.jstor.org/stable/41802067.

Barry J. (2006), "Resistance is fertile: from environmental to sustainability citizenship", in: Dobson A. and Bell D., eds., *Environmental citizenship*, The MIT Press, Cambridge, MA, pp. 21–48.

Barry J. and Paterson M. (2003), "The British State and the environment: New Labour's ecological modernisation strategy", *International Journal of Environmental and Sustainable Development*, 3(2), pp. 237–249.

Connelly J. (2006), "The virtues of environmental citizenship", in Dobson A. and Bell D., eds., *Environmental citizenship*, The MIT Press, Cambridge, MA, pp. 50–73.

Crane A., Palazzo G., Spence L.J. and Matten D. (2014), "Contesting the value of 'Creating Share Value'", *University of California Berkeley*, 56(2), pp. 130–153.

Di Paola M. (2015), *Cambiamento climatico*, Luiss University Press, Roma.

Dobson A. and Bell D. (2006), "Introduction", in: Dobson A. and Bell D., eds., *Environmental citizenship*, The MIT Press, Cambridge, MA, pp. 1–17.

Ehreke I., Jaeggi B. and Axhausen K. (2014), "Greening household behaviour and transport", OECD Environment Working Papers, No. 77, OECD Publishing, Paris. Available from: https://doi.org/10.1787/5jxrclmd0gjb-en.

Gaugh S. and Scott W. (2006), "Promoting environmental citizenship through learning", in: Dobson A. and Bell D., eds., *Environmental citizenship*, The MIT Press, Cambridge, MA, pp. 263–285.

Kriström B. and Kiran C. (2014), "Greening household behaviour and energy", OECD Environment Working Papers, No. 78, OECD Publishing, Paris. Available from: https://doi.org/10.1787/5jxrclm3qhr0-en.

Murray P. (2011), *The sustainable self*, Earthscan, New York.

Nash N. and Lewis A. (2006), "Overcoming obstacles to ecological citizenship", in: Dobson A. and Bell D., eds., *Environmental citizenship*, The MIT Press, Cambridge, MA, pp. 153–184.

Nauges C. (2014), "Greening household behaviour and water", OECD Environment Working Papers, No. 73, OECD Publishing, Paris. Available from: https://doi.org/10.1787/5jxrclrr79f7-en.

Osorio-Vega P. (2019), "The ethics of entrepreneurial shared value", *Journal of Business Ethics*, 157(4), 981–995.

Palatnik R. et al. (2014), "Greening household behaviour and wate", OECD Environment Working Papers, No. 76, OECD Publishing, Paris. Available from https://doi.org/10.1787/5jxrclmxnfr8-en.

Payne P. (2010), "Moral spaces, the struggle for an intergenerational environmental ethics and the social ecology of families: an 'other' form of environmental education", *Environmental Education Research*, 16(2), pp. 209–231, doi:10.1080/13504620903580545

Porter M.E. and Kramer M.R. (2011), "Creating shared value", *Harvard Business Review*, 89(1–2), pp. 62–77.

Tinacci Mossello M. (2008), *Politica dell'ambiente*, Il Mulino, Bologna.

UNEP (2015a), *Annual report*. New York: United Nations Environmental Program.

UNEP (2015b), The United Nations environment programme and the 2030 Agenda. New York: United Nations Environmental Program.

Part 2

Home and people

My home, my life

Aspirations of people with intellectual disability for an ordinary home and an ordinary life[1]

Sheila the Baroness Hollins

Background

In 2018, Penny Mordaunt, then Secretary of State at DFID, spoke about disabled peoples' rights to full inclusion at the opening of the first Global Disability Summit in London, which was co-hosted with the government of Kenya and the International Disability Alliance. She said: "*This is not just the right thing to do for a common humanity – it is the smart thing to do. When disabled people are included great things happen.*" I agree with this sentiment, and further suggest that if we can get things right for people with intellectual disabilities, then we will get them right for everyone.

My interest in the barriers to living an ordinary life, in a place that people can call home, deepened when I was appointed consultant psychiatrist to a long-stay mental handicap hospital.[2] I had already been aware, as the mother of a child with an intellectual developmental disability (IDD), just how many obstacles there were to my son's full inclusion in our local community. The majority of people with IDD lived at home with their families into and beyond early adulthood, with families typically battling to find and fund the support their children need to live harmonious and fulfilling lives. I had not known just how many of those who could not live with their family of origin were living in a children's home or other long-stay institution. More recently I have become aware of the work of the international development charity Hope and Homes, which quite simply aims to close down orphanages worldwide and instead support local communities to find substitute family homes for abandoned and orphaned children.

The evidence for institutional harm

Hope and Homes point to evidence that 80% of children in orphanages have a living parent but were often abandoned because of disability.

www.hopeandhomes.org: "*Orphanages do not care for orphaned children. There are 8 million children across the world confined to institutions. Over 80% of them are not orphans.*"

My early experiences in the long-stay hospital prompted two ethnographic research studies, for which I recruited social anthropologist Jane Hubert. The first was a participant observation of men with IDD living in a locked ward, which found institutional attitudes and practices and very low aspirations for these men's lives (Hubert and Hollins, 2006, 2007). As still being evidenced by Hope and Homes today, these men had been admitted in childhood when a parent died or was unwell, or following the birth of another child. The second was a similar study of 16 women who had also spent their lives since childhood in a long-stay hospital and were being prepared for a move to a community home. This study was funded by the Judith Trust, which had a particular interest in the mental health of women with intellectual disabilities, inspired by the life of Judith, who herself had an IDD (Owen et al., 2007).

In response to widely reported concerns about disabled children living in institutions, particularly those in Romania, Bulgaria, and the Czech Republic, and the observed care practices so obviously deeply detrimental to these children's health and wellbeing, I was asked to chair a WHO Europe working group. Children who were not born with developmental disabilities were at risk of acquiring impairments because of the neglect they experienced. The remit of the working group, whose members included people with intellectual disabilities, was to review the health and wellbeing of children and young people who were living in institutions and orphanages (many of the residents having been abandoned by their parents for financial reasons or because of the perceived stigma and lack of state support if the child had physical or mental impairments) (WHO Euro 2010). In 2012, the resulting Declaration about the health and wellbeing of children and young people with IDD and their families was signed by the health ministers of all 52 countries in the WHO Europe region. The Declaration identified ten priorities. The first was that all children and young people need to be kept safe from harm, neglect, and abuse. The second was that every child needs a home and a family, with each of the priorities and action plans backed up with research evidence.

Community responses

For 18 years I co-facilitated a psychotherapy group for adults with intellectual disabilities with psychoanalyst Dr. Valerie Sinason. There was a lot of effort in the UK at the time to move people from institutional care into what was loosely called "the community." We asked each of the members for their thoughts and feelings about the place they currently lived in, some being residents in long-stay hospitals, and others living in residential settings known as "group homes." Only one person lived in his own home. We often used wordless books in the group to help the group explore an issue in more depth, and we read books called *A New Home in the Community* and *Peter's New Home* together (Hollins et al., 2017, 2nd edition).

Figure B.1 "A New Home in the Community" and "Peter's New Home" together (Hollins et al., 2017, 2nd edition)

The group members discussed what these transitions from institutions to communities actually meant in practice, and we wrote a chapter for a book aimed at mental health practitioners drawing on their words, stories, hopes, and thoughts. We concluded:

> *People with intellectual disabilities are citizens with a right to a home. If they are given adequate help in working out their dreams and needs, most can become full members of a community. . . . The key issue is one of choice. As*

> *with all other people, those with intellectual disabilities do not form a homogeneous group. They have many different needs and wishes. The attitudes of social workers and disability specialist staff play a central role in the provision of real choice. If low expectations are the norm, individual dreams may simply not be heard.*
>
> (Sinason and Hollins, 2004)

A pioneering theatre company called Access All Areas engaged me to help with a user-led research project examining the history of institutions for people with IDD, and to explore how far institutional attitudes still restrict people's lives in the twenty-first century. The project led to a challenging performance piece by five disabled actors, a historical exhibition, a wordless book (Hollins et al., 2018), and the BELONG Manifesto (see Figure B.4).

Similar dehumanising practices and attitudes have been found in some mental health services. Professor Peter Tyrer developed Nidotherapy (from the Latin word "nidus" meaning nest), which aims to help create a safe nest or home environment for people with long-term mental health problems and personality disorders. Tyrer says that it's not about changing the person or requiring the person to be motivated to change, but about changing their environment and providing the supports they need to enable them to live an ordinary life that keeps them safe and well (Tyrer, 2009). It's less about doing things to support people, and more about accompanying them to belong.

At the moment, when people do move into a community setting and need support outside of their family, they are likely to receive very little support unless something goes wrong. Staff who are supporting them tend to be minimally trained and poorly paid. Meanwhile, the most skilled staff – the specialist workforce – do not work flexibly and responsively enough in the community, but deliver crisis interventions, often requiring admission a long way from home. It should be the rarest thing to admit somebody because their home circumstances have broken down (Hollins, 2018).

Living an ordinary life – influencing policy

It was back in the 1970s that the ordinary life movement began in response to some of the scandals being reported in UK mental handicap hospitals, and because of the predominance of institutions in people's lives. The King's Fund led the initiative with a paper called "An Ordinary Life" (King's Fund, 1980). David Towell was one of the leaders of the new movement, and was personally influenced by the fact that in 1945, on the day before he was born, his sister was admitted to a long-stay hospital (Rix, 2006). At that time, it was very common for children to be admitted to hospital and, as it were, put away and forgotten. After meeting her for the first time in adulthood, his new awareness changed the course of his life, as he tried to persuade people of the importance of an ordinary life (Towell, 1990).

When I first started teaching medical students, I would ask them to give me the names they knew to describe such children and adults, and to tell me where they lived. People only knew pejorative words such as spastic, cretin, or retard, and used expressions such as "put away." Unless they had had somebody in their family or had met someone at school, they did not have the language or know how to talk about intellectual disability. We all have a right to a family life including children and adults with intellectual difficulties and impairments. My role as an advocate in many leadership positions is to invite others to stop and think and ask, what about people with intellectual disabilities and/or autism?

How many people considering a situation will ask themselves how would this affect people with intellectual disabilities? If we all asked this question, perhaps we would be more likely to get it right for the majority of people from the start. But if the needs of people with intellectual disabilities are not thought about from the conception of the project or policy, such projects rarely, if ever, work without major adjustments for this group.

Back in the 1980s and 1990s we had hopes that closing the institutions would lead to better support and care, and more ordinary lives for people. But, unfortunately, although the last of the old long-stay hospitals in the UK closed in 2009, the change hasn't quite delivered everything that we expected. And although the NHS hospitals did close, they were soon replaced by private assessment and treatment units which in turn have provided lengthy hospital stays, often far from a person's home community. The Transforming Care programme, set out in the NHS England's "Building the Right Support" strategy, was launched in October 2015 and aimed to close 35–50% of beds in these ATUs by March 2019. Only 20% of beds were closed by that deadline, and there is no ongoing strategy to address the programme's failings. Often people are not discharged because of an assumption that their behaviour is just too difficult.

A former trainee of mine approached me at an event and said

> that man who gave you the picture he'd painted, you won't remember him, but he used to be in that hospital. . . . I thought that he was one of the people who would never be able to leave the hospital, the things he did there were terrible . . . we were convinced he would never cope. He lives on his own in a flat in the middle of the town now. I said to him one day, "I don't understand what happened." He replied, "I didn't like being locked up."

Very simple, "I didn't like being locked up." None of us would like to be locked up either. We would like to be in our own home, and to be able to make some decisions for ourselves, and, crucially, to be supported to develop the homemaking skills we need to live a fulfilled life.

David Towell (1990) says that our homes are central to our way of life, and "the fulcrum around which all else turns":

It's a supportive place to go out from.
It's a nice place to be.
It's a place where you can be alone.
It's a place you don't get turned out from.

It's a place to unwind.
It's a place where you can do what you like.
It's a place where you choose who else lives there, who comes to visit, and for how long.
It's a place that expresses who you are.

Unfortunately, people with intellectual disabilities don't usually have the skills needed to create a good home life for themselves without the right support, with the decisions about how they live their lives often being made by strangers. And the intimacy of home can be intruded upon in a number of different ways. Perhaps it's a person's neighbours who get too involved. Take a disabled adult living in his own home whose neighbour knocked on his door and complained that she had heard him climb the stairs to bed after midnight. To his family, she said, "don't you know this is a private street? I shouldn't have to live next door to somebody like that, he should be living with his own kind, people like him."

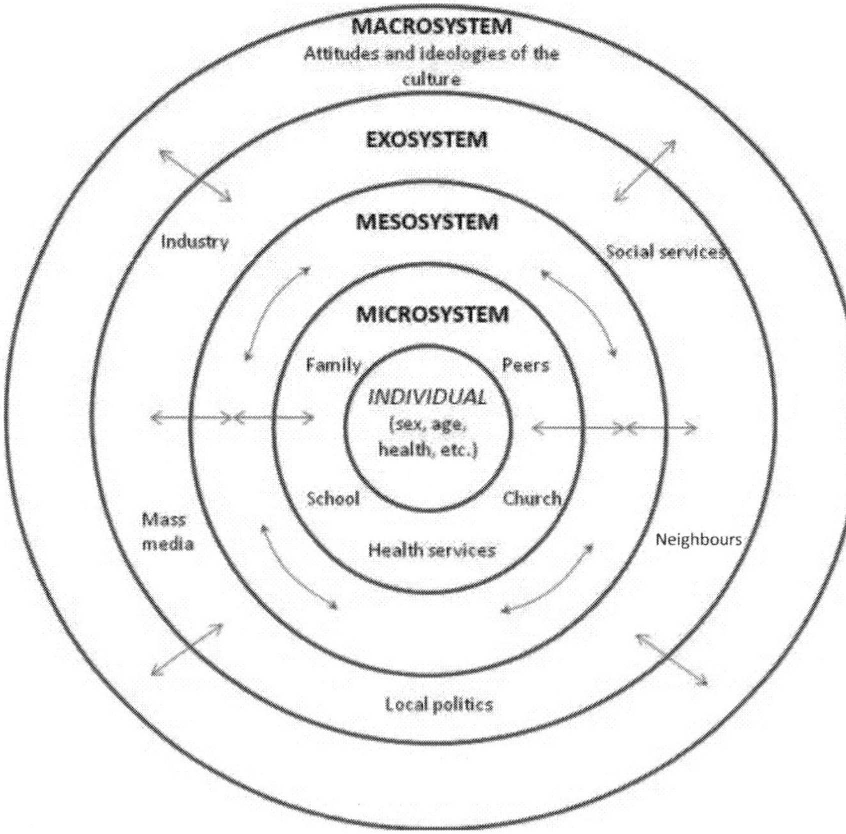

Figure B.2 Bronfenbrenner's Ecological Theory of Development

Families come in different shapes and sizes. Bronfenbrenner's Ecological Theory of Development puts each of us at the centre of our own little world. Explained simply, there are people and systems at varying distances from us with more distant people and networks usually being less personally helpful to us (Bronfenbrenner, 1979). Sometimes a person is so separated from those wider systems and communities that nobody really knows about them, and for example, this can happen to people living in institutions. Their little circle becomes very small with even their family becoming remote.

Disseminating best practice

Throughout my academic and clinical career, I have endeavoured to explain best practices to the people most affected by a particular life situation. During my work with institutionalised people, I had discovered the power of wordless stories to communicate, and this discovery led to the Books Beyond Words (Books Beyond Words, 1989 to 2019) series being co-created with subject experts and experts with lived experience. These stories, told entirely in pictures, epitomise my approach in trying to understand their perspectives and to empower people with IDD. There are nearly 60 books in print at the time of writing, and they cover many aspects of people's lives and experiences providing a mini "curriculum" for life. It is much harder to create a picture book which tells the essence of the subject than it is to write an academic paper. Each book takes 18 months to research, co-create, and trial with people with IDD. The power of the books is in their empowerment of a marginalised minority who seek to belong but face barriers of ignorance and attitudes which exclude (Strnadová et al., 2018).

Learning to listen

When we are trying to understand people's hopes, we have to find ways of inspiring them and of listening to them, and sometimes their non-verbal cues are going to be the most important. During Pope Francis' Year of Mercy in 2016, I gave a number of talks on the subject of listening, compassion, and empathy – attributes which all involve listening. On World Communications Day in 2016, Pope Francis said:

> Listening means paying attention, wanting to understand, to value, to respect, and to ponder what the other person says. Knowing how to listen is an immense grace; it's a gift which we need to ask for and then make every effort to practice.
>
> (Pope Francis, 2016)

To me, some of these words have a particular resonance; wanting to understand, pondering, and practicing. These relate closely to a number of similar methods used in the psycho-therapeutic world, such as watch, wait, and wonder (Muir et al., 1999).

Books Beyond Words are a tool to help us listen. They are stories about life – about people living ordinary lives. Storytelling goes back to the earliest of times and anthropologists have been re-evaluating the purpose of storytelling traditions in cultures around the world. Smith et al. (2017) suggest that people who read stories are more empathic and more in touch with others in their community and that storytelling is a valued leadership skill which promotes community cooperation.

One important characteristic of a story is that it has a beginning, a middle, and an end. Its helps if there is a little bit of excitement or something unexpected to excite the imagination. Our wordless stories always include an intervention, often a listening intervention, which helps to change the outcome for the person or people in the story. The books are read alone or in reading groups by disabled people and others who find pictures easier than words, and they tell stories that people can identify with. Several hundred people meet weekly or monthly to read together in a book club, in a library, a cafe, a church, or school. And because the books are not language dependent, they are now being read in a few different countries.

Growing up and leaving home

Why do people with intellectual disabilities leave their family home, and what will home mean to them when they become adults? A typical pattern when you become an adult is to seek a greater separation from parents as you become your own person and make your own life. But it's much harder for people with IDD to have a sense of who they are and to develop their own identity. It's much harder for parents to let them separate in any ordinary, adult way and to encourage more independence with the inevitable risks that it may entail. And, of course, another reason why people leave is to form a loving relationship and create a family. There is a continuing reluctance in most cultures to support people to develop intimate relationships with a focus instead on determining incapacity or being concerned about safety (Bates et al., 2017). Sadly, the majority of women with IDD who give birth will have their babies taken into care rather than be given the support they need to make a family home themselves.

People read different stories into the wordless book *Sonia's Feeling Sad (*Hollins, Banks et al., 2011). Some people decide that it's a story about Sonia's own baby being taken away – perhaps to be adopted – and they relate to her distress. Others think that Sonia's place as the baby in the family has been taken by a new arrival in the family. Another interpretation is that she sees her sister having a baby and realises that there's no chance for her to have similar opportunities. Here she is, stuck at home with mum and dad with no opportunities, no aspirations, no life of her own. During a workshop in Portugal, a Portuguese man with IDD who was part of one of the groups became very animated and said it was just how he felt when his mother had a new baby. For the first time, he saw that other people had the same feelings that he'd had.

Figure B.3 Cover page of "Sonia's Feel Sad" by Beyond Words

Who decides what's going to happen to you when you become an adult? Typically, there is a rather paternalistic attitude that people with intellectual disabilities don't have the capacity to make decisions or to make the "right" decisions. In English law, there is provision under the 2005 Mental Capacity Act for a best-interest meeting to be held to make decisions that an individual is deemed not to have capacity to make themselves. Sometimes it's to escape domestic violence or other difficult dynamics at home when home doesn't feel safe, as in the books *When Dad Hurts Mum* and *Finding a safe place from abuse* (Hollins et al., 2014, 2015). The most common reason people leave home, sometimes to go into residential care, is because somebody has died (Hollins et al., 2004).

In my clinical work as a young psychiatrist, I had observed that neither hospital nor outpatient services seemed to recognise the emotional needs of children or adults with intellectual disabilities. My first book, *When Dad Died*, was developed when I was working in a long-stay hospital, still unsure about my role as a child psychiatrist and psychotherapist. My first psychiatric referral there was to see a man of about 40 with no spoken language and a diagnosis of Down's syndrome. He was refusing to get out of bed, refusing to eat, and beginning to injure himself. The nurses rather unrealistically wanted a prescription of something to "get him up." They didn't know why his behaviour had changed until a member of the kitchen staff was able to tell us that his father had previously visited every Sunday, but hadn't been seen for several months. His Dad had died. I could find no way of getting the staff to recognise and understand that this man was grieving, or to be able to explain his father's death to him. We made a video called "The Last Taboo: Mental Handicap and Death" in which we re-created a funeral involving some of the patients to mourn one of their number who had died. Then we created our first book *When Dad Died* (Hollins, Sireling et al, third edition, 2004). People with IDD generally don't get invited to funerals of either family or friends. The subject of dad or mum or friend is not raised by staff, and mementoes are not offered as these classic ways of remembering "might upset them." But actually, remembering helps all of us. Our wordless books try to model good practice. In *When Dad Died*, the characters in the story are fully involved with other family members in grieving at home as well as in the funeral rituals, and are encouraged to choose a memento to help them remember their father.

In the assessment and treatment units (ATUs) in the UK, most of which have grown up since the long-stay hospitals closed, people are admitted when their behaviour has deteriorated or changed. They may be described as having behaviour that challenges the service provider, but rather than seeing it as a communication of distress, their behaviour may become a diagnosis. It's usually a symptom of something difficult that's happened in a person's life – something that has not been understood. As many as half of people are admitted to ATUs within two years of a parent dying. Often the professionals admitting them don't realise that the behaviour leading to admission may have been because of a change in the support a person needs to continue living at home and because of a delayed grief reaction. Behavioural treatments are not the recommended first treatment for people showing behavioural change following trauma. But delays in returning people to their own homes are exacerbated by a lack of adequate locally based psychological therapies such as the service offered in South West London before my retirement.

Conclusion

Enjoying valued social relationships of different kinds goes hand in hand with a feeling of empowerment. Our mental health is better when we feel, in some small measure, in control, and that we aren't always being told what to do.

Most of us, when confronted with a choice about where we would want to be cared for at a time of deep care, assume that we will feel safest in our own place. But a colleague studying end-of-life care for people with intellectual disabilities was surprised that a woman she knew who had spent the first two decades of her life in a large and impersonal institution had moved into a residential/nursing home when she was terminally ill. My colleague hypothesised that as she approached the end of her life, this place, which she shared with so many other people, was more familiar and actually felt more like home to her given her own particular life experience (Tuffrey, 2010 & Living with LD). Choice is indeed the point.

An ordinary life depends on having a personal narrative and relationships of our choice. An ordinary home is the place where we feel safe, sometimes with

ACCESS ALL AREAS MADHOUSE re:exit Beyond Words empowering people through pictures

A living manifesto for a better life for people with learning disabilities

When the institutionalisation of people with learning disabilities has ended...

- and there is enough money to spend on food and essentials
- and there are opportunities to make some choices in life
- and people with learning disabilities feel good about themselves and their friends
- and there is an end to being bullied, assaulted, and called names
- and everyone can access health care, education, and employment on equal terms

We will all **BELONG**

Six ways we can be sure of feeling good about ourselves and our friends:

B Be active and be healthy – like eating well, dancing, swimming, and joining in.

E Enjoy our friends and family and show them we care.

L Love ourselves, and welcome the love and support of others. And if things go wrong, say yes to help.

O Ordinary things like choosing where we live, and what we do and share.

N New things to make our lives more interesting - like drama, drawing, singing, and sharing stories - with the support we need.

G Give something nice - like our time, our work, a hug every day.

©Belonging (Books Beyond Words, 2018)

@AAATheatre www.accessallareastheatre.org
@uk_beyondwords www.booksbeyondwords.co.uk

Figure B.4 MadHouse: Re:Exit by Beyond Words

support. Some years ago, I helped to form a new organisation we call the Institute of Psychotherapy and Disability with the strapline "treating with respect." Respect is fundamental. A disabled person living on his own, who falls out with a support worker in his own home, is typically reacting to a felt lack of respect. He has picked up that they've seen him as somehow lesser; not as an agent in his own life, and someone of equal human value.

In this chapter I have tried to unpick some basic aspects of home and what it might mean to people who may have few choices about where they live and who they live with.

Notes

1 Based on a talk given in London on 17 November 2017
2 *Different words are used in different countries to describe people with intellectual disabilities. Learning disability is the term used in the United Kingdom to describe people with a developmental condition occurring before adulthood and who need extra help to live an ordinary life (it does not include specific learning difficulties such as dyslexia). In some countries, the terms mental handicap, developmental disability, or intellectual disability are used. Intellectual disability is often associated with autism, although not everybody with autism has an intellectual disability.

References

Bates, C., Terry, L. and Popple K. (2017) Supporting people with learning disabilities to make and maintain intimate relationships. *Tizard Learning Disability Review*, 22(1): 16–23. https://doi.org/10.1108/TLDR-03-2016-0009

Bronfenbrenner, U. (1979) *The ecology of human development: experiments by nature and design*. Cambridge, MA: Harvard University Press.

Hollins, S. (2018) *The long-term sustainability of the NHS and adult social care–motion to take note (26 Apr 2018) Hansard*. London: UK Parliament. https://hansard.parliament.uk/lords/2018-04-26/debates/F523BB19-90B8-4AA9-BCC0-7B8AA92AD6DE/TheLong-TermSustainabilityOfTheNHSAndAdultSocialCare.

Hollins, S., Banks, R. and Webb, B. (2011) *Sonia's feeling sad. london: books beyond words*. Mental Capacity Act 2005.

Hollins, S., Hutchinson, D., Towell, D. and Webb, B. (2017 second editon) *Peter's new home*. London: Books Beyond Words.

Hollins, S., Scotland, P., Blackman, N. and Perks, A.-M (2014) *When dad hurts mum*. London: Books Beyond Words.

Hollins, S., Scotland, P., Blackman, N. and Perks, A.-M. (2015) *Finding a safe place from abuse*. London: Books Beyond Words.

Hollins, S., Sireling, L. and Webb, B. (2004) *When mum died* (3rd ed.). London: Books Beyond Words.

Hollins et al. (2018) *Belonging*. London: Books Beyond Words.

Hubert, J. and Hollins, S. (2006) Men with severe intellectual disabilities and challenging behaviour in long-stay NHS hospital care: qualitative study. *British Journal of Psychiatry* 188: 70–74.

Hubert, J. and Hollins, S. (2007) Ethnographic research in closed institutions: ethical issues. *Research Ethics Review* 3(4): 122–126.

Kings Fund. (1980) *An ordinary life*. London: Kings Fund.

Muir, E., Lojkasek, M. and MCohen, N. (1999) *Watch, wait and wonder: a manual describing a dyadic infant-led approach to problems in infancy and early childhood.* Ontario: Hincks-Dellcrest Institute.

Owen, K., Hubert, J. and Hollins, S. (2007) Moving home: the experiences of women with severe intellectual disabilities in transition from a locked ward. *British Journal of Learning Disabilities*. doi:10.1111/j. 1468–3156.2007.00484.x.

Pope Francis. (2016) *Message for the 50th world communications day. Communication and Mercy: a fruitful encounter*. http://w2.vatican.va/content/francesco/en/messages/communications/documents/papa-francesco_20160124_messaggio-comunicazioni-sociali.html.

Rix, B. (ed.) (2006), *All about us*. London: Mencap.

Sinason, V. and Hollins, S. (2004) The ideal home and community for people with learning disabilities. In: Campling, P., Davies, S. and Farquharson, G. (eds.), *From toxic institutions to therapeutic environments*. London: Gaskell.

Smith, D., Schlaepfer, P., Major, K. et al. (2017) *Cooperation and the evolution of hunter-gatherer storytelling*. doi:10.17863/CAM.22555.

Strnadova, I., Johnson, K. and Walmsley, J. (2018, May 15) "But if you're afraid of things, how are you meant to belong?" What belonging means to people with intellectual disabilities. *Journal of Applied Research in Intellectual Disabilities*. doi: 10.1111/jar.12469.

Towell, D. (1980) (reprinted 1990) *An ordinary life in practice*. London: King Edward's Hospital Fund.

Tuffrey-Wijne, I. (2010) *Living with learning disabilities, dying with cancer: thirteen personal stories*. London and Philadelphia: Jessica Kingsley.

Tyrer, P. (2009) *Nidotherapy: harmonising the environment with the patient*. London: RCPsych Publications.

WHO Euro (2010) *Better health, better lives: children and young people with intellectual disabilities and their families*. European Declaration on the Health of Children and Young People with Intellectual Disabilities and Their Families, EUR/51298/17/6, November 26, 2010. www.euro.who.int/__data/assets/pdf_file/0015/121263/e94506.pdf.

Chapter 6

The home as the primary source of intellectual development

From a phenomenological and anthropological perspective

Usochi Ilozumba

Introduction

There would be no earth if there were no continents; there would be neither continents, nor countries, nor communities if there were no people; and obviously, there would be nobody if there were no homes. The home has the right to the claim as the nub from which sprouts human existence. "Home" here is taken to mean the irreducible smallest unit of society – the family. It is consistent with Argandoña's (2018) outlook on the home as "a community of people (a family) who live together in a place (a house), with a more or less explicitly shared common project." No human being falls from the sky. Each life is transmitted to the other, thanks to the progenitors who are collaborators in its conception, protection, nurture, and growth. There, in the cosy nest of the family's private and shielding embrace, emerges each human life to add to the population scale of an already existing community. The notion of the home which I hope to transmit in this chapter is that which is primarily defined by the different and complementary functions of the masculine and feminine anthropological makeup to give rise to a new life. Little matter if the aforesaid home is left with one or both or none of its principal creators. Each human existence, from its defenceless stage to its mature years, is born into a context. A context where, for Torralba (2005), both the inexorable human dependency and pursuit for autonomy are mixed in a most intricate liaison of full self-donation to give care, complete surrender to receive care, and openness to enrichment derived from individual self-expression of personal freedom. In other words, the home is the nook within which human life blossoms, develops in all its aspects, finds shelter, and learns to enter and take its place in its larger community.

A country such as Nigeria, with a remarkably high estimate of a youthful population less than 15 years of age, is plagued with an alarming rate of incarcerated adolescents in juvenile remand homes. About 96% of these children had a problem with their primary support group even before they were taken into these institutional homes. Problems such as separation from parents, family dysfunction or disruption, abandonment, etc. are but a few of the grave issues that curb the appropriate development of these children (Bella et al., 2010). But what is, one might ask, the root cause of youth misconduct? Could it be due to lack of formal education? Or could it point to a deficiency in the adolescent's early formation and imitable parental model due to instability in families? What's more, recent studies have shown that a greater part of a child's subsequent misconduct, especially at adolescence, can be traced to early neglect within the family in nurturing a wholesome development, beginning from the child's sensory-motor stages to periods of self-knowledge and self-affirmation when the rational faculties are more employed (Parks, 2013; Kreppner, 2000; Price MA and Kunz, 2003). Many organisations and public policies concerned with child developmental psychology, family enrichment programs, parenting skill acquisition, etc. have proposed tangible ways of improving the child's general home formation since whatever is or is not given at these primal stages of development has repercussions in later years, whether in a positive way or otherwise. In the case of Nigeria, the legislation termed *The Children and Young Persons Act II,* operating under the Children and Young Persons Law (CYPL) whose principal objective is to rehabilitate and incorporate these children back into society as "renewed" individuals, has utterly failed to meet its goals due to gross deterioration of the remand facilities, stagnant public policies, want of good governance, and widespread corruption (Bella et al., 2010). Indeed, the situation is alarming.

To tackle the issue of adolescence rebellion and social delinquency, perhaps, there is more to it than changing school curricula or providing more accessible counselling programs by public policies. There is need to go to the root – the home/family – which is the place of nurture and the ambit for achieving direct contact with the person so as to achieve a sustainable impact in the society at large. It is in the home that the first-ever intellectual operation of its new human life is exercised. It is in the home – thanks to the intrinsic relational quality of the human being's rational nature – that the mental faculties of a new and developing life learn about the world through observation from its parents. From there it builds up its own singular intellectual capacities for its eventual contribution to the good of its family, as well as that of the common good of its society.

The *return* to a philosophical insight of the family and its lasting effect on the intellectual maturation of its members is the main relevance of this chapter. It proposes one palpable way of grappling with this societal problem. Why? It is for no other reason than this: societal problems are first and foremost family issues, because the family is the nucleus of society. And by family, we have a network of strong interpersonal bonds of parent-parent (or just single parent), parent(s)-child, child-parent(s), child-child(ren), child(ren)-child, and the chain goes on to other extended family relations. Not to mention the wider circle of neighbourhood, church, school, community, state, and country. For the sake of brevity, the chapter focuses on the intellectual development of the child within the immediate circle of the family, as well as the roles the family – concretely, the primary caregivers – have in contributing to the overall developmental harmony of the child. Here, this chapter sustains the theoretical models of Bronfenbrenner (1979) and Belsky

(2011) to bring to focus the most distinguishing operation, called the intellectual operation, and the home's role in ensuring the attainment of the intellectual height of its members. Both experts in human and child development studies, respectively, underscored the need to analyse development within contexts.

A contextual setting, or more precisely, a system, whether open or closed, provides an undivided margin for applying a theoretical framework in the studies of human development. Bronfenbrenner, in particular, adopted concepts of a family system called the microsystem in his model. The microsystem is that of a complex of interrelations within the immediate setting of the person, which directly contributes to his development, and whose lasting effect can be traced even up to his adult years. The latter, on the other hand, established that

> children who experience a higher rather than a lower quality of childcare evince somewhat higher levels of cognitive-linguistic functioning at two, three, four and five years of age; and children who spent more time in any kind of non-familial childcare . . . were more impulsive and engaged in more risk-taking behavior at age 15.
>
> (Belsky, 2011)

Furthermore, Minuchin (1985), who was quite influenced by Bronfenbrenner, maintained the systems theory and seconds the view that the family is a relevant context for the genuine consideration of the individual development since each of the members is conceptualised and interdependent. Landry (2008) proposed an approach of responsive parenting for achieving a higher cognitive upgrade in children, especially during the early stages of their growth. More recent studies confirm that family relationships are associated with cognitive development (Shin et al., 2019). Concretely, the fourth part of this chapter builds on the cognitive theories of Jean Piaget (1965) and traces the part played by the family in the early stages of intellectual development alongside it.

Grounded in basic anthropological principles of human cognition and building on the aforesaid theoretical assumptions, this chapter proposes a deepening of the idea of the home as an essential unit of nurturing the rational faculties towards cognition and intellectual excellence. A brief exposition of the nature and dynamics of the human intelligence will be done by means of a descriptive method to engage in a review of three authors – Eugenio Sarti, Jean Piaget, and Juan José Sanguineti. Each of these authors, in their fields of experimental science, psychology, and philosophy, respectively, has contributed to the understanding of human cognitive development. The review serves as a basis for experts in child development, family therapists, public authorities, and all who are concerned with individual and social welfare to seek solutions that accommodate and promote the paramount role of the home as the nurturing environment for the newborn's cognitive activities. Additionally, some insights on some ordinary phenomenological experiences and the roles, both major and subtle, that the home plays throughout the child's stages of sensory-motor, operation, and intellection will be touched.

The dynamics of human intelligence

Intellectual operations are the exercise of the rational faculties in the acquisition of knowledge. Transitive actions, as the name implies, whose effect is directed towards an object external to the acting agent, and immanent actions – whose effect rests in and is auto-determinant of the agent, are the two main types of operations of human beings. The latter constitute the intellective acts after it has been preceded by the possession of sensible forms of a concrete external object in an immaterial way (Malo, 2013). Thanks to the immateriality of the sensible form, human beings can operate on a higher level of intellection where there is total immateriality and the possession of universal concepts which can be applied to other objects of the same sensible forms. The intellectual operations are carried out by the rational faculties when engaged to a higher level of knowledge that, on the one hand, derive data from the external senses by its contact with external realities; and on the other hand, are separated from them and independently operate on their own.

Thinking, judging, willing, and intuiting are categorised as intellectual operations carried out by the two rational faculties of human intelligence. The operations of these faculties are not limited to the delicate organs scientifically held to be sites where these faculties function. There is an "absolute transcendence of human intelligence over the body" (Sanguineti, 2007: 98). They are not constrained by the brain or the nervous system. Indeed, the way these organs function can have repercussions on the proper exercise of the faculties; but the brain cannot be strictly taken as their *organ*. When we think, the produced concept is simultaneously interpreted in a linguistic image, such that the concept has a *name*, or at least can be described. Again, every concept comes about by a sense transmitted image; since, according to Aristotle (2016), "the soul can never know without the help of an image." Therefore, although intellectual knowledge (being on the spiritual sphere) is high and above corporeal restrictions, it is strongly linked to the brain in such a way that the cerebral activities are essential conditions for its production. Thus, they facilitate intellection but they are not exclusive conditions for intellectual acts (Sanguineti, 2007, 2005).

Faithful to the Aristotelian conception of cognition, it is appropriate to affirm that the first step to knowledge is an *extro*spection of the external world. We learn from the moment we open our eyes to the world. The eyes that are looking at the world at that first instance do not deceive in themselves. There is, therefore, a need for an openness to the external world from which knowledge begins. The question now remains: how does the needed *extro*spection take place?

Eugenio Sarti's response-transmission as extrospection of external stimuli

We are immersed in a world that is in constant transmission. "Transmission" here implies a two-fold significance: the first is the presence of external objects that can be known by the intellect in act. The second is the openness of the same intellect to the external world to give rise to knowledge. And all these would not take place without the access provided by the sense organs; so that humans are able to receive information from the outside and after having undergone the necessary cognitive processes, would arrive at the cognitive act called knowledge. For Sarti, "information is at the root of every transmission of knowledge . . . We learn in as much as we are informed. Information is, therefore, a vehicle for knowledge" (2002).

Consequently, the singular link between the external world and the human intellect is highly essential to a person's life to such an extent that failure to be affected by this transmission, or the failure of one's response to the external stimuli, would imply a breakdown of the vital organism and even death. Indeed, every organism receives and elaborates the information in its environment for its vital growth. Sarti (2002: 6), explaining the information in the world of living organism, affirmed that "it has been discovered that the life of every organism, whether simple or complex, depends in an essential way on the circulation of biochemical signal that transmits information necessary to the harmonious development of the vital processes." For instance, from the moment a set of newly born senses of a human individual are immersed in the world, there is a simultaneous collation of external data that fills up the once-empty little mind. The child, from the very moment of the development of his auditory glands in the womb, is already able to pick up its mother's voice and the common sounds of the environment where it is carried. From that moment, a new form of musical sensitivity develops so that the child grows with a particular affiliation to the sounds of the environment into which it has been born.

Our connection with the external world sometimes presents us with realities and experiences that cause a *reactional* surge from us so that we are no more than passive recipients and reactors. In a very impressively mysterious, albeit, scientifically proven way, babies in their most early stage of intellectual development are *active* observers, receptors, and reactors. Often, they are thought to instinctively react by means of their ever-resounding wails or heart-warming smiles. At this early stage, there is a noticeable temperamental distinction as well as a rapid internal cognition of their environment. Here Sarti's *transmission-reaction* relation between the environment and the living being can now be interpreted in the light of Piaget's theory of cognitive development in children.

Piaget's theory (1965) holds that the cognitive process is founded on biological determinants within the living being. That is, the child is born biologically prepared for motor responses, which provide them with the framework for the thought processes that follow. Thus, intelligence is rooted in two biological attributes of organisation and adaptation. Organisation, on the one hand, is the tendency of every living organism to integrate processes into coherent systems. It occurs, for instance, when an infant, originally capable of either looking at objects or grasping them, integrates these two separate processes into higher-order structures which enable him to grasp something at the same time he looks at it. Adaptation, on the other hand, is the innate tendency of a child to interact with his environment. This interaction fosters the development of a progressively complex mental organisation. Each stage in this sequence of development provides the foundations for the next stage, permitting progressively complex and effective adaptations to the environment. Adaptation comprises two complementary processes of assimilation and accommodation. The child assimilates experiences and fits them into the expanding structure of the intellect when he encounters new experiences which he cannot fit into the existing structure (Simatwa, 2010). Piaget's revolutionary classification of intellectual development into four main stages became the model for a duration-scaled study of human cognitive progress. He identified four major stages: sensory-motor, pre-operational, concrete operational, and formal operational. He held that

> all children pass through these phases to advance to the next level of cognitive development. In each stage, children demonstrate new intellectual abilities and an increasingly complex understanding of the world. For Piaget, stages cannot be "skipped"; intellectual development always follows this sequence.
>
> (Wood et al., 2011, p. 2)

Piaget's stages of early intellectual development and role of the home

The sensory-motor stage

In the sensory-motor stage between zero to two years, "cognitive activity is based on immediate experience through the senses. The major intellectual activity here is the interaction between the senses and the environment" (Simatwa, 2010: 2). Here, the aforementioned extrospection of external reality corresponds to Piaget's sensory-motor phase of cognition. When the child is in his zero age, the first major intellectual activity would be the interaction of his senses with his environment. And the senses which are extremely active at this early stage take in every data around them. However, there is little or no capacity for relating the experiences in a temporal scale of past, present, and future because memory, which is crucial for the acquisition of experiences, is not yet developed. Also, "infants cannot predict reactions, and therefore must constantly experiment and learn through trial and error. Such exploration might include a rattling or putting of objects in the mouth. As they become more mobile, infants' ability to develop cognitively increases" (Wood et al., 2011: 4).

> During this stage, a phenomenon known as "visual pursuit" is manifested. The child will visually pursue an object relentlessly, long after an older child would have lost interest. Such visual pursuit develops the capacity of "object permanence," a primitive form of memory. As children begin to develop intellectually, they understand that when an object disappears from view, it still exists even though they cannot see it.
>
> (Simatwa, 2010: 2)

At this key phase, the home is endowed with the singular task of assuring a rich and receptive sensory environment.

A remarkable example is the acquisition of a special human act: smiling. It is a semi-conscious action that oscillates between voluntary and involuntary acts. It is deeply rooted in natural neuro-muscular responses that are more or less concomitant with cognition. For instance, if I remember something agreeable and I smile, that facial response is a voluntary act that is laden with knowledge and therefore something quite different from a mere reflex smile. But when it comes to babies who have not yet developed the cognitive capacities, Melinda Beck (2015) would argue that scientists have distinguished between four different kinds of smiles: the spontaneous smile (also known as *sognando gli angeli – dreaming of angels*) that have no known cause and seem to not mean anything; the stimulus-response smile, also called social smile (or *Duchenne* smile), is considered the complete smile that is learned from interaction with older humans and indicates a particular social response to some cause of happiness or contentment; there is also the anticipatory smile, that appears when babies increasingly integrate objects into their interactions with other people; and, of course, laughing, which babies exhibit long before they can speak.

Undeniably, the above conforms with Bronfenbrenner (1979) in his claim that

> the environmental events that are the most immediate and potent in affecting a person's development are activities that are engaged in by others with that person or in her presence. Active engagement in or even mere exposure to what others are doing often inspires the person to undertake similar activities on her own.

The baby's smile may be either of these four types of scientifically proven smiles; the bottom line is that if the older persons who are members of the home of the newborn take advantage of the rapidly developing sensory operations of the baby at this early stage, the (pleasant) external data of smiling would be picked up so that the baby *learns* to smile. In the long run, the acquired habit would contribute to the unfolding of an agreeable personality when the age of free cognition is reached.

Pre-operational stage

The pre-operational or intuitive stage, mainly from two to seven years of age, is characterised by "the use of language and the development of memory and imagination" (Wood et al., 2011). The development of a "one to one correspondence is crucial for the acquisition of the number concept. And until then, Piaget affirms that the child would not know how to count" (Simatwa, 2010: 2–3). Again, the home has the first responsibility for encouraging the development of the child's linguistic and imaginative ability. Language is an important medium of thought. Growth in the knowledge and skills of children are associated with growth in the number of words that represent and convey facts and procedures. The needed one-to-one correspondence is formed in the child by means of dialogues, that is, by simply speaking *with* the child. The more parents and/or other caregivers speak with their children, the greater the opportunities for children to learn vocabulary and a slew of other cognitive skills (Lao, n.d.). With their newly found power of speech, some children may succumb to the appeal of vulgar words. This is where the attentive guidance of primary caregivers is crucial for the child's redirection. One effective means of correction is through words – dialogues – which the child finds especially fascinating at this stage. What's more, the traditional "bedtime" stories help in the development of his imaginative ability as well as his capacity to distinguish between the real and what is make-believe. All these play crucial roles in the child's growth into a balanced adult with little or no problems of adjustments or personality disorders.

Concrete operational stage

The concrete operational stage develops between the ages of seven and 11 years. Intellectual development at this stage is demonstrated through "the use of logical and systematic manipulation of symbols, which are related to concrete objects" (Wood et al., 2011: 4). And even more notable is the child's impressively high enthusiasm to learn (Simatwa, 2010: 4). Here home caregivers, backed up by the school's support, can make the best of the child's fervour. With their close observance, the child is exposed to varied learning fields to detect, from which sprouts a special affinity. Encouragement in the development of a particular field of interest is vital, although such encouragement should not be done in a constraining way. Exposure of the child to books (always appropriate to age), educational games, walks in the parks, sightseeing in art galleries, and musical skill acquisition all help to stimulate interest and learning.

Furthermore, in this phase of maturation, "concepts of right and wrong begin to develop. Usually, these are concerned with specific acts at first and only gradually become generalized" (ibid, p. 5). Here, the development of the aforementioned second rational faculty – the will – is noticed. The child's moral culpability and sense of fairness come to the fore. Children at this phase are "still moral realists, having difficulty comprehending the subtleties involved in various situations. And since they see rules as absolute, good judgment must be exercised to prevent manipulation of their literal interpretation of rules" (ibid). The use of dialogues serves to unlock seemingly complex ethical situations. Still maintaining the one-to-one correspondence, parent(s) and/or hired professional caregivers could rightly inculcate a wider understanding of morality by signalising to the child the end and consequences of his/her concrete acts. The awareness of the end, extensively explained by Aquinas (1964), is essential for the authentic self-realisation of the human person in his actions. The human person's free actions are morally implicating because one is imbued with the capacity to direct oneself to one's ultimate end by means of these concrete free actions. Hence, the connection between the use of reason and the moral life in which rationality is seen as an essential factor for authentic self-realisation.

In addition, the arrival to the *age of discretion* is a critical period. The intellectual judgment of the child at this phase is influenced by the will whose object is the good. With his capacity for temporal relation of past experiences, present acts, and possible future consequences (thanks to the work of the memory and imagination), the child is now able to choose between two or more possible ends in a freeway and devise the means to realise them. Herein lies the parents' pivotal task of teaching that human life is not a juxtaposition of various disconnected events that is stored into a pack with little or no effect on the pack itself. Thus, it is necessary that a closer non-restricting and trusting guidance is called for. Usually, the child begins to feel part of an important whole. His intellectual keenness needs to be adequately directed. On the one hand, introducing him into new responsibilities; and on the other hand, giving him the support needed for the field of interest he finds particularly attractive. Thus, parent(s) and/or other caregivers contribute to opening new horizons for a fuller and more integral intellectual development. Indeed, the school plays a decisive role, but that of the primary caregivers is particularly decisive since the home would always be the most intimate social circle of the child.

Formal operational stage

In the formal-operational stage, usually between 11–15 years, adolescents "use symbols related to abstract concepts. They can think about multiple variables in systematic ways, can formulate hypotheses, and think about abstract relationships and concepts" (Wood et al., 2011: 5). In addition, an ever-increasing understanding of the intertwining laces of every human life is developed. That is, the fact that the *others* are not merely outside of one, as a chair is separately well situated in a room with little or no consequence with the person inside the room. Each human life is linked to another in an unimaginably intimate way. It is at this critical stage that such a challenge is first encountered. Now the home unrolls the path for the child's confrontation with the real world. In this semi-adult phase, the manner in which the sensory-motor, pre-operational, and concrete operational stages have developed configures the way the young adult lives and interprets reality with all its challenges. Hence, the current period of formal operation is well defined by how much impact the home has contributed to his earlier developments.

The paramount task of adequately directing the insatiable curiosity and hunger for the high ideals of the teenager falls directly on primary caregivers. Now, the adolescent tends to easily pick up models different from his parents since he begins to realise the need to assert himself. There is the tendency to experiment with different adventurous and sometimes conflicting experiences with continuous alterations of interests. The

> shifting from one interest to another does not necessarily mean a lack of mental discipline. Many [fix] unrealistically high standards for themselves

> and tend to be perfectionists. The inability to live up to such standards leads to feelings of frustration and guilt.
>
> (Simatwa, 2010: 5)

The case at hand is a very difficult moment for both the adolescent and the parents. Above all, the fundamental upshot at this phase is a widening of the adolescent's knowledge of sense of self. He feels the compelling need for contributing, but with little or no means of making it happen. The primal duty of the parents here is their nearness, encouragement, understanding, and patience. The child is

> taught to develop realistic levels of aspiration by having him start out doing simple tasks and working up to difficult ones. In doing so, he does not only test his capabilities but would also have some experience with success. The latter makes it easier to accept failure when he reaches his limits. Usually, adolescents want to become independent while still in need of adult guidance and support. This ambivalence may cause disorganized, unpredictable, or inappropriate behavior which defies rational analysis.
>
> (Ibid)

Herein, the parents' (and professional caregivers') understanding is crucial for proper orientation and assistance without falling into any form of paternalism. The adolescent's sense of importance is not to be disregarded; rather, it should be encouraged and well moderated, hence contributing to the growth of a wholesome personality needed for society.

The above elaboration – from Sarti's response-transmission relationship between the living being and its environment to Piaget's stages of early intellectual growth – gives insights on the progressive scale of intellectual operations. Knowledge which begins from the senses forms the basis for the human person's cognition, although it is not reduced to it alone. It is at this point that Sanguineti's unparalleled elucidation of the absolute transcendence of the intelligence becomes useful.

The human intelligence in its excellence

The absolute transcendence of the intellect makes the human person

> capable of understanding whatever type of reality there is, over and above the space-temporal conditions. In this sense, the human being is the *master* of space and time. He is conditioned by time and only lives in a period of history, but simultaneously, he can understand the history of all times, he can write atemporal novels and project the construction of all types of things in any place or at any time. Each person, if well prepared, demonstrates this inexhaustible capacity which could be impeded but never eliminated.
>
> (Sanguineti, 2007: 99)

Thus, a new human life, born in the nurturing shelter of the home, finds the required duration and care for the actualisation of its intellectual capabilities. All that is needed for the acquisition of the highest level of knowledge that transcends the realm of the sensible is contained in the little life. It is in the home that its earliest linguistic expression "*mummy/daddy*" is uttered; it is there that one's capacity to love freely and disinterestedly is fostered as a consequence of having received and experienced the same. And, ultimately, the home is where his acquisition of an essential "settled disposition – habits – which determines the choice of actions and emotions" (Aristoteles, 1987) is facilitated. Family life is a rich site for the experience and acquisition of high humane inter-relational skills through the carrying out of disinterested services and mutually sharing experiences, intimacies, and deepest yearnings.

Piaget's contribution to the study of the child's intellectual development is inestimable. His constructivist claim that each child singularly develops his/her intellectual ability without any influence from adults is right, although it leaves much to be questioned. Piaget understood that children "are not limited to receiving knowledge from parents or teachers; they actively *construct* their knowledge" (Wood et al., 2011: 1). But the contextualised form of human nature, with its essentially rational identity, reaffirms that the human being comes into the world already occupied by objects; most especially, by other subjects so that his existence is not that of an isolated species lost in space and devoid of any form of communication. He is essentially born into a community and called to engage in a relational experience of the *other* equal to him in nature. His life is composed of a long chain of entangling lives, beginning from the most basic and smallest community called his home. Thus, if the very first context of human existence is the home and its early developments occur there, it would, therefore, be appropriate to reiterate that the home has an indubitable impact on the mental progress of a child.

Furthermore, since every human being is born absolutely dependent on another for its nourishment and growth, it is requisite that much has to be invested in the promotion of authentic homes to meet the needs of its reliant members. In addition, although an

> empirical, statistical and sociological investigation can demonstrate the characteristics (or stages) of human intelligence, they do so in a partial or non-definite way. Indeed, they are useful psychological and sociological investigations, but they normally remain on limited experiences. Since the human person is both corporeal and spiritual, natural scientific methods [like those of Sarti and Piaget] do not totally explain the infinite potency of the intelligence. We know our universal cognitive capacities only thanks to a metaphysical study that points out who we are and what we do. The metaphysical experience of our intelligence does not focus on only isolated acts. It comprises of the ontological capability of the human being to know and value reality as *reality* (and this forms the basis of what we mean when we say that

> someone *is intelligent*). It is also observed in the human person's infinite capacity for linguistic expression
>
> (Sanguineti, 2007: 102–103)

which we had earlier shown to be principally developed in the home. Conclusively, the metaphysical experience of our intelligence consists in the experience and exercise of our freedom, thanks to which we have an infinite capacity to want and desire anything as long as there is the possibility of achieving it (Sanguineti, 2007). Freedom is, thus, best made attractive when primary caregivers, with their loving guidance, present opportunities for self-mastery and an upright choice of action in the children. For instance, in the child's training in responsibility for himself and for the people around him, especially his siblings.

Moreover, the parents' role is shown through a flexible and prudent direction of their young adult's career choice, whereby the child's moral formation is channelled towards his making free and responsible life decisions. All these refer to intellectual growth beyond mere sensible or psychological analysis, and the achievement of such mental excellence remains the prevalent duty of every parent.

Re-examining all the above, it would be apt to summarise the nature and role of the home in Argandoña's (2018: 13) own words:

> in the home we have, give or do. When we show ourselves as we are, we reveal ourselves as vulnerable beings who need material, cognitive or spiritual protection; human vulnerability receives protection on a physical level from the house as a structure and on a personal level from the home's members. So, vulnerability means dependence on the help received from others; therefore, it is complementarity and reciprocity.

Therefore, since the home is the source from which proceeds all human beings who collectively form the larger societies, the complex relationship between family and state is one that this chapter does not fail to ignore. For there to be a conducive family environment for attaining intellectual excellence, a well-ordered and just public arena is needed. In the first place, the provision of a social support network for parents and other hired caregivers is pertinent. "At some stage in the lives of each of us, we face at least one period of utter dependency . . . all [persons are], at least potentially dependent" (Kittay, 1995: 8). Within the caregivers' (single, married, separated, or an outsourced professional) nuclear and extended family, friends, neighbours, worship groups, colleagues, etc. there is a need for the presence of and support from all inter-connected human bonds. Again, furnishing social supports for parents who are at risk, especially single parents, by the state would somewhat alleviate heavy financial burdens and help the parent(s) focus their energy into parenting.

Furthermore, job security and exposure to more parenting skill programs should be implemented by public policies. New skills such as responsive parenting, contingent responsiveness (Landry, 2008), family orientation programs, etc.

should be developed. The nature of these programs ought to be inclusive in order to embrace all varying family situations and social circumstances. What's more, optimal education for parents and professional caregivers is crucial, thus public policies ought to create avenues and education advancement opportunities for adults in need of financial support for getting a higher education so that they serve as intellectual models for the children, and likewise assist them to overcome the possible obstacles inherent in their development.

Also, the mental health and stability of parents and caregivers need particular attention from mental health organisations and policymakers. These mental health aides have to be accessible, personalised, and laden with competent professionals because if caregivers play crucial roles in the intellectual development of younger persons, their own stable mental health is of even more paramount importance since no one can give what he or she does not have. Moreover, funding for more research on the remarkable functions of the family in fashioning a good citizen should be taken into consideration by the state. A good society fosters the development of good homes, but the relationship is reciprocal: "human development and the advancement of society will only be possible if it is based on societies made up of stable families organised in a personalised home environment; this is what will lead to a stable and personalised society" (d'Entremont, 2018) in (Argandoña, 2018).

Finally, the joint tasks of parent(s) and teachers in the educational system cannot be overlooked. Mutual respect should prevail between the parent(s)' autonomy to choose what is best for their child's development and the teachers' commitment to ensuring the adequate means to achieve the highest intellectual good of the child. Hence, the school, engaged in a subsidiary system with the state, should employ well-coordinated structures to make these two important sources of human development work together towards a common good. The good in question is a well-directed project of development of all the aspects of a growing person. In this way, with the subsidiary function of the state with respect to the person and the family, a wholesome maturation of its citizens is made possible. And the home, where a most basic and affectionate trust and where each person is known, loved, and cherished for who he is reigns, (Francis, 2016) is the principal source of intellectual growth.

Conclusion

In this chapter, we have placed the home at the centre of the review on the root of a person's intellectual flourishing. The utmost aim of all that has been elaborated so far has been to enlighten, by means of cues given us by Sarti, Piaget, and Sanguineti, on the initial happenings within the intelligence of a newborn, its eventual social integration, as well as its expression of actions of ethical nature; and all depend on a well-formed cognitive capacity.

As a conclusion, it would be appropriate to ask a lingering question which the limit imposed on the chapter has constrained from further elaboration: at the attainment of adulthood, does the home continue to influence one's intellectual excellence, whether one still resides in the home of birth or in one's newly established home?

There could be varying answers to the question; all reasonable, relevant, and even contradictory. However, as a logical conclusion of everything we have examined so far, an affirmative answer is most suitable. The reason being that since the intrinsic form of a person's relational nature is primarily realised within the home; and the home, likewise, depends on and fosters human relation; and since cognitive development depends on these interpersonal links and on the exemplary human models that are present in human relations; consequently, even in adulthood, the home would continue to influence one's intellectual maturity. But all these are nothing but a quick response to a question that requires methodical research and deeper reflection.

Perhaps all we have seen so far serves as a prelude for scholars, government agencies, and all who have an interest in reflections on the home. It, however, beckons for more scholarly works on sound philosophical reflections of the human person, together with the unparalleled contribution of the home to society.

References

Aquinas, T., 1964. *Summa theologiae: latin texte and English translation, introduction, notes, appendices, and glossaries*. Blackfriars Publications: Eyre and Spottiswoode; McGraw-Hill Book Company, London; New York.

Argandoña, A., 2018. *The home: multidisciplinary reflections*. Edward Elgar Pub, Cheltenham, UK; Northampton, MA, USA.

Aristoteles, 1987. *The nicomachean ethics, great books in philosophy*. Prometheus Books, Buffalo, NY; New York.

Aristotle, 2016. On the Soul. *Univ. Adel. Libr.* https://ebooks.adelaide.edu.au/a/aristotle/a8so/ (accessed 8.11.18).

Bella, T.T., Atilola, O., and Omigbodun, O.O., 2010. Children within the Juvenile Justice system in Nigeria: psychopathology and psychosocial needs. *Annals of Ibadan Postgraduate Medicine*, 8, 34–39. https://doi.org/10.4314/aipm.v8i1.80344

Belsky, J., 2011. Childcare and its impact on young children. *Encyclopedia on Early Childhood Development*. http://www.child-encyclopedia.com/sites/default/files/textes-experts/en/857/child-care-and-its-impact-on-young-children.pdf.

Bronfenbrenner, U., 1979. *The ecology of human development*. Harvard University Press, Cambridge, MA.

d'Entremont, A., 2018. *Spatial relationality and domesticity: reality and functions of the home from a human geography perspective*. Edward Elgar Publishing, Cheltenham, pp. 163–176.

Francis, P., 2016. Pope Francis–Amoris Laetitia' frRick Healey. *FrRick Heal.* www.frrick.com/ebooks/amoris-laetitia/ (accessed 8.11.18).

Kittay, E.F., 1995. Taking dependency seriously: the family and medical leave act considered in light of the social organization of dependency work and gender equality. *Hypatia*, 10, 8–29. https://doi.org/10.1111/j.1527-2001.1995.tb01351.x

Kreppner, K., 2000. The child and the family: interdependence in developmental pathways. *Psicologia: Teoria e Pesquisa*, 16, 11–22. https://doi.org/10.1590/S0102-37722000000100003

Landry, S., 2008. The role of parents in early childhood learning. *Encyclopedia on Early Childhood Development.* http://www.child-encyclopedia.com/parenting-skills/according-experts/role-parents-early-childhood-learning.

Lao, Joseph, n.d. Intellectual home environment. *Parent. Lit. What Parents Need Know.* http://parentingliteracy.com/parenting-a-z/55-home-environment/94-intellectual-home-environment (accessed 8.11.18).

Malo, A., 2013. *Essere persona: Un'antropologia dell'identità.* Armando, Roma.

Melinda Beck, 2015, November 23. What your baby's smile can tell you about her development. *What You Baby's Smile Can Tell You about Her Development.* www.wsj.com/articles/what-your-babys-smile-can-tell-you-about-her-development

Minuchin, P., 1985. Families and individual development: provocations from the field of family therapy. *Child Development*, 56, 289–302. https://doi.org/10.2307/1129720

Parks, A., 2013. *The effects of family structure on Juvenile Delinquency.* Electronic Theses and Dissertations. Paper 2279. East Tennessee State University.

Piaget, J., 1965. *The moral judgment of the child* (19th print ed.). Free Press, New York.

Price, C., and Kunz, J., 2003. Rethinking the paradigm of Juvenile Delinquency as related to divorce. *Journal of Divorce & Remarriage*, 39, 109–133. https://doi.org/10.1300/J087v39n01_07

Sanguineti, J.J., 2007. *Filosofía de la mente: un enfoque ontológico y antropológico.* Palabra, Madrid.

Sanguineti, J.J., 2005. *El conocimiento humano: una perspectiva filosófica.* Palabra, Madrid.

Sarti, E., 2002. Information. *Interdisciplinary Encyclopedia of Religion & Science.* http://inters.org/information

Shin, E.K., LeWinn, K., Bush, N., Tylavsky, F.A., Davis, R.L., and Shaban-Nejad, A., 2019. Association of maternal social relationships with cognitive development in early childhood. *JAMA Network Open*, 2. https://doi.org/10.1001/jamanetworkopen.2018.6963

Simatwa, E.M.W., 2010. Piaget's theory of intellectual development and its implication for instructional management at pre-secondary school level. *Educational Research and Reviews*, 6.

Torralba Roselló, F., 2005. *¿Qué es la dignidad humana? ensayo sobre Peter Singer, Hugo Tristram Engelhardt y John Harris.* Herder, Barcelona.

Wood, K.C., Smith, H. and Grossniklaus, D., 2011. Piaget's stages of cognitive development. http://epltt.coe.uga.edu/index.php?title=Piaget%27s_Stages.

Chapter 7

The ageing of parents in the home of an adult person with disability

Horacio Joffre Galibert

Introduction

The role of the family is paramount for the socio-affective development of its members. Expectations, bonds, and ways of relating to other people are all built into its daily context; and if the family is the first model, the home is the space, both physical and emotional, where all this occurs and where a large part of a person's life is spent. It is also the most influential environment of a person's life. Argandoña says (2017) that the notion of "home" focuses in three internal components: people, family, and shared space. It also focuses on two external components: the social and the material environments. People are therefore placed in the centre, and this is unified through the proper conception of home. But creating an environment to foster a person's development is not something that just happens; building it demands work and energy. In a harmonious home, each member has a fundamental role to play – a role assigned at a very early age. In this regard, a home can be thought of as a system of parts interacting in a dynamic and ever-changing way. Moreover, a home could be conceived as an organism, with a life-cycle with a beginning and an end, with breaks produced by specific events, and with a life curve determined by the biological cycle of its founders. The addition of a new member, for instance, is a disruption that will necessarily trigger a rearrangement of roles and interactions.

The arrival of a person with a disability in the home has a powerful effect on the family. It creates feelings of bewilderment, perplexity, distress, anxiety, and unease. It is a milestone establishing a "before and after" in family life, which will never be the same again. Certain life events, such as the coming of age of other family members and their departure from the home to start their own families, or the ageing of the parents, bring a degree of additional anxiety. If the future usually causes uncertainty, having an adult with a disability in the home intensifies this, and planning for the future becomes crucial. All of this has a relation with the notion of home, which goes through a temporary dimension – as a group of processes through time – and a spatial dimension – in a not only physical context (Argandoña, 2017).

In recent years, the ageing of people with disability has become the target of greater attention. There has been an increase in awareness of the issue, including the proposal for specific public policies and services aimed at that stage in life, which is now understood to be a social problem that needs to be addressed. However, the treatment of the question as a whole, and in a scientific manner, has been long-winded. This chapter aims to contribute to the awareness of life in the home of a person with autism: the struggle for social inclusion, the building of spaces to "catch one's breath," the exercise of rights, the enjoyment of free time, the concern for self-esteem, and maintaining family bonds and the way the parents join forces to design a life project, in view of both their own ageing and that of their children.

Relevance of the home in an individual's development

In the *First Global Home Index*, Bryan Sanderson, chairman of the Home Renaissance Foundation, states that the home is the most important place for people's development, the first contact a human being has with society: "the first place one feels part of and the roof under which one receives the care and the education needed for one's development" (Debeljuh et al., 2017: 7). A substantial home is a key condition for the development of an individual. However, to build this home is not a simple enterprise: it demands both tangible and intangible resources. In order for each of its constituent members – children, teenagers, adults, and elderly – to receive the care needed for their wellbeing, it is necessary to manage the resources and distribute tasks and responsibilities. The effective functioning of a home requires the involvement of all of its members.

When a child with a disability is born into a home, there is no doubt that this is an event that will affect every one of its members. Sometimes, parents may find themselves wondering whether they will even be capable of coping with the situation. The equilibrium which they had previously managed to forge will be altered in such a way that it will require redefining everyone's role. If before, teamwork was important, now the environment and the family will be vital for achieving a positive and harmonious home, capable of providing the support needed for a person with disability.

Children with autism, for example, have the very same needs as other children of their same age. This seems obvious, but it is sometimes forgotten: the routines and tasks at home should be the same for them as for the other siblings, along with the specific care they may need. By routines, we mean the daily life activities of the child and his/her family. A routine has to arouse curiosity, directing a child's focus of interest. Rules must be flexible, and not just imposed by the adult, and they should certainly fulfil a clear objective: for instance, eating for nurturing and being healthy in order have a good life, playing for having fun, dressing to be protected and warm.

For a person with autism, routines have a preponderant place in their way of facing daily life. These interests, according to the NAS (2017), can provide them with structure, order, and predictability towards daily activities. In the familiar environment, this results in a rigid schedule to be fulfilled with the intention of removing the greatest possible amount of anxiety that could disrupt the routine of a person with autism, no matter how minimal, like a meal out of time. In that context, the entire family group must work considering prevision and preparation over a change, so that the impact generates the least possible amount stress.

According to the systemic approach, the family is a whole and it works as a whole. People living with an individual with autism learn that each case is unique, and that answers need to be both specific and flexible. However, a common obstacle that has to be overcome is the frequently voiced concept that the child with autism will always remain a child. Including the person in the workplace could be a major step in correcting this false notion.

ASD: Autism spectrum disorder

Austrian psychiatrist Leo Kanner (1896–1981) was the first to produce a full clinical description of infantile autism using that term in the way we understand it today.[1] His first book was *Child Psychiatry*, but his most prominent paper was *Autistic Disturbances of Affective Contact* (Kanner, 1935; 1943), in which he laid the foundations for the awareness of autism, followed a year later, entirely independently, by Hans Asperger's 1944 article (Asperger, 1991). Until that time, children with autistic behaviour were confused with people with schizophrenia, but in the ensuing decades, the criteria for diagnosis changed.

Autism acquired "fame" thanks to Hollywood, in particular the film *Rain Man* starring Dustin Hoffman and Tom Cruise, winner of the 1988 Oscar for best actor, best director, best film, and best original screenplay. Dustin Hoffman's role was partly inspired by Joseph Sullivan, the autistic son of Ruth Sullivan, one of the founders of the Autism Society of America.

The mainstream media began to publish articles on autism, its characteristics, and even its alleged cures. Asperger's syndrome was included for the first time in DSM-4 (*Diagnostic and Statistical Manual of Mental Disorders*), published in 1994 by the American Psychiatric Association (1994), as well as in ICD-10, the World Health Organization's International Classification of Diseases (1990). Autism was bracketed under Pervasive Developmental Disorders (PDD), defined by severe deficits and impairments in diverse developmental areas, such as social interaction and communication, and with the existence of restricted or repetitive interests. Today, with a new update of this manual, the DSM-5 (2013), all these conditions are considered part of Autistic Spectrum Disorder,[2] putting an end, once and for all, to the concept of PDD, which was not just confusing but ambiguous.

Many TV series and movies today include at least one character with autistic features, often specifically based on a limited area of the spectrum: namely, the "savants" or people with gifts or a wide knowledge in a particular field but with socialisation problems. In the developed countries, various associations and organisations have managed to broaden society's awareness of autism spectrum disorder and have promoted greater tolerance towards the behaviour of many children with autism, both in public spaces and in schools. With both progress and setbacks and nothing too well-defined beforehand, these organisations were able to bring about the general acceptance of different paradigms based on integration and inclusion.

At the University of California in Los Angeles, a tenacious team of researchers led by Dr. Ivar Lovaas (1932–2010) introduced the ABA (Applied Behavioural Analysis) method. This educational tool, created by, among others, Dr. Charles B. Ferster in 1960, uses a process known as Discrete Trial Training (DTT), consisting of successfully applying principles of behaviourism based on the reward of desired behaviours and the punishment of undesired behaviours in children with autism at the Linwood Children Centre in Maryland. ABA, applied at a very early age and adapted to each child, may positively transform the present and future of the infant with autism. Soon, other methods based on the same principle, such as the Picture Exchange Communication System (PECS), Pivotal Response Training (PRT), Verbal Behaviour (VB), the Comprehensive Application of Behaviour Analysist of Schooling (CABAS), etc., would also bring about improvements in the wellbeing of people with autism.

The impact on the home and family

The impact on families is defined, above all, by the permanent presence of stress within the family unit. It begins with the uncertainty of the diagnosis, as in many cases an accurate identification of the problem can take a long time, arriving many years after the first signs are detected. This is followed by major concerns and questioning posed by the very own characteristics of the syndrome: severe communication difficulties, feelings of being rejected by other people, and other behavioural problems. Then, there are the uncertainties related to the causes of the disorder, the appropriate intervention programmes, and the future evolution of the condition (the prognosis).

The severity of the impact is different for each case and depends on three variables: family resources (psychological, socioeconomic, and social support); alignment of the couple (the mental health and quality of the conjugal relationship), and the individual characteristics of the child's autism spectrum disorder. The diagnosis, in itself an extended process of uncertainty, is the beginning of a crisis which manifests itself in the four well-known phases: shock, denial, depression, and reality, or reaction (Cuxart, 1995). Parents need regular professional support and counselling in order to be able to face the challenges of living with a child with ASD. Without professional help, which should include access to quality services and attention to the siblings as well, cohabitation can be very complex and the consequences for family members can prove substantial.

The stress may strengthen (when it results in adaptation) or weaken (when it results in crisis). Adaptation is the desired positive outcome of the interaction between stressors, endurance capacity, value judgements, and coping strategies. Crisis is the negative result, but may be used as a signal to help us realise that a change is urgently required, that things are not functioning well, and that a greater effort must be undertaken to adapt or to overcome a particular situation. Neither outcome is bad *per se*. Both are part of the process, and all families must go through them. Moreover, adaptation will never be definitive, given that the family is not a stable and closed system, but one which goes through different processes and stages, constantly facing new situations and having to re-adapt over and over again.

It is important to be aware that both stages, crisis and adaptation, must be understood as opportunities for the family to learn to balance and manage situations of chaos, bearing in mind that these states are dynamic and constantly changing, i.e., they are part of a never-ending process. Therefore, once the family has passed through the adaptation or the crisis, the entire process recommences. In their model, Cunningham and Davis (1988) point to three different sets of consequences for each member of the group:

- For siblings: they must often fulfil the role of caregivers, face their friends' reactions, fear being isolated due to the lack of information, and feel the need to compensate for their sibling's "deficiency."
- The figure of the father and his need for assistance has not received the same attention as the figure of the mother. He is often less aware of the demands of the disability.
- The mother is the one who often carries the daily burden, and she is the one who has the greatest possibility of suffering physical and emotional distress. Often, she feels isolated due to a lack of understanding from other people and to the severity of the demands posed by a child with high levels of dependency.

In the systemic model, the family is a system and its parts – fraternal, conjugal and paternal subsystems – work together. Their relationships will be defined by the way the disability affects each one of these elements. Therefore, each family can go through a different adapting process, depending on how their members react. Regarding the parents' subsystem, the relationship between the parents and the children without a disability will be affected in several ways (Roche y Arozarena, 1997). It is possible that difficulties will arise in explaining or discussing the autistic sibling's disability. The brothers and sisters may feel that they have been abandoned by their parents. Or they may at least feel that they have been receiving far less attention than the child with autism, leading to a sense of burden of responsibility on the part of the siblings.

Concerning the relationships within the conjugal system, a study conducted by Blair (1996) showed that 35% of the participating couples expressed the view that having a child with autism had added stress to their marriage. Nonetheless, only 31% stated that having a child with autism had ultimately had an adverse impact and 34% believed that the experience had brought the couple closer. As stated previously, it is generally accepted that the relationship between the parents will be adversely affected only if there were already problems prior to the birth of the disabled child, as the disability can reinforce the union or trigger mismatches depending on the previous quality of the relationship. Over time, many families confront a surviving scenario. These circumstances unleash a situation of insanity for the couple, framed by a chronic and sustained period of stress (Cuxart, 1995), which tests both the bond between the couple and the very existence of the family.

As regards the relationships within the fraternal subsystem, the behaviour of the child with autism spectrum disorder may be difficult for siblings (because of the autistic child's problems with communication, language, and relationships, difficulties with imagination that will affect the development of play, destructiveness, aggressive, or violent behaviour, etc.). Anger towards the child with autism may arise due to the degree of attention he/she receives, and the life of the child's brothers and sisters can also be affected because they cannot enjoy moments of peace or fun with their peers. There may also be feelings of embarrassment or rejection towards the child with disability (Rivière, 1999). However, a sibling may become the greatest defender of the person with autism. In addition, due to the difficulty children with autism have in relating to their peers, the relationship with their brothers and sisters could be therapeutic for him/her. Siblings cohabiting with a child with a disability will mature ahead of time and this will have a major influence on the way they face the world. In conclusion, a person with ASD cannot be treated in isolation because their life is immersed in a family context, as the centre of contention, conforming their support network. It is essential to treat the family as a system: each of its members will be affected by the disability, which will, in turn, affect the relationships between the different subsystems that make up the family.

Ageing

As mentioned above, ageing parents in a home with an adult with a disability will have greater concerns and will have to start thinking about the time when they are no longer alive to protect the vulnerable child. Vulnerability is determined by our condition of being living creatures (animals); in other words, by the susceptibility to be hurt, and this is strongly linked with dependence and aspired autonomy (Argandoña, 2017). In order to ensure that their children receive the appropriate care, they must know and exercise their rights, which are the responses provided by the state to their concerns. Public policies should guarantee that these rights are fulfilled.

In this respect, it is important to mention the regional statistic where it is observed that, in the year 2010, 9.9% of the Latin American population was at least 60 years old; however, it is projected that this percentage will increase to 14.17% in 2025, and to 24.5% in 2050. This demographic growth with respect to the ageing of the population must be projected in the planning of the countries and in the design of public policies. Regarding the ageing process of people with disabilities, the Inter-American Convention on the Protection of Human Rights of Older Persons (Organisation of American States General Assembly, 2015) considers that disabled people are potential subjects who could suffer multiple discriminations. A positive arrangement for protecting people with disabilities in their ageing is the one implemented in Argentina in the reform of the Civil and Commercial Code in 2015, with the modification of the legal parts of succession rights. It incorporates an upgrade of a third additional part in favour of the disabled heir. It is illustrated hereunder:

Symbolic cypher: $100,000.00
Available part: $33,333.33 (1/3)
Legitimate part: $66,666.67 (2/3)
Improvement in favour of Ignacio (disabled son): $14.814,81 (1/3 of legal part)

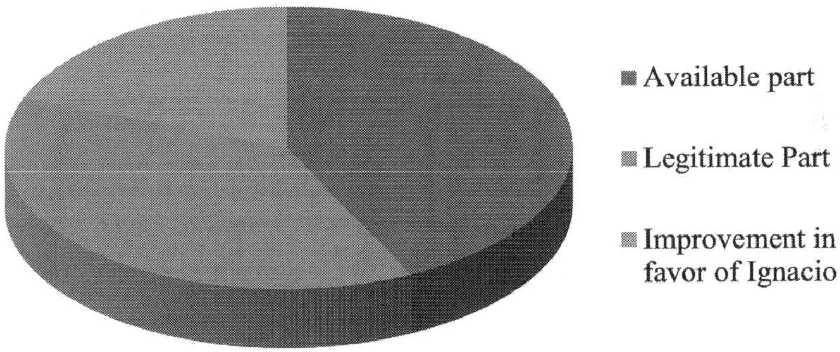

Figure 7.1 Initial situation (Galibert, 2019, p. 84)

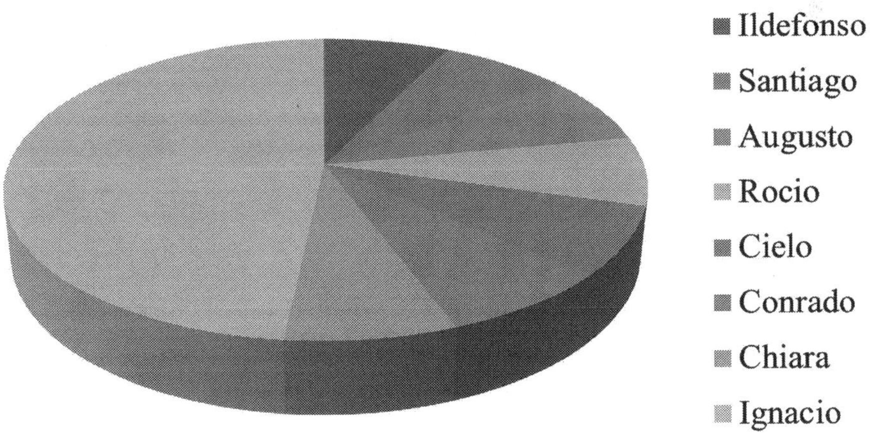

Figure 7.2 Final result (Galibert, 2019, p. 84)

As it can be seen, the best result for Ignacio is $56,851.85 (2/3 as he is a descendant + 1/3 because of improvement + 1/3 available). In addition, this reform incorporates new figures, like partnership agreements and trusts, which can also be used in favour of people with disabilities.

Alternative homes

Considering the predecease of the parents and the eventual losing of the home of a person with autism who hadn't achieved a desirable degree of autonomy, it appears the need of creating homes where they could develop themselves. The "new stars" are the people in charge of their care – people trained to treat the residents in a one-to-one setting. Those homes where the members are educated in cohabitation, in the spirit of solidarity, and in the exercise of desire for exceptional deeds, will no doubt have better resources to assist the person with disability in their adult life stage and to provide them with a dignified and worthwhile quality of life. The challenge of building a space with the required love and support to grow old in an environment where the person with ASD can give and receive love has already been addressed. The home should be designed to allow the assistance required to suit the particular needs of its residents.

Figure 7.3 Nacho with his brother Augusto Galibert, current director of the San Ignacio community

The reality is that in Argentina, there are very few places for adults with ASD. One such places is the San Ignacio community, under the direction of Augusto Joffre Galibert, brother of 37-year-old Ignacio, who has severe autism (Galibert, 2004). This community, which works as a "respite home" (in Spanish, "casa de respire") and includes recreation, holiday, and camp activities, was established in 2000 and it has grown since then. It started as a small property funded by APAdeA and it has grown to include recreation activities (Galibert, 2019). Today, it is the only residential home of its type in the province of Buenos Aires. It is the permanent residence for Ignacio and four or five other people with ASD, and it receives up to 20 adults during the weekend so their families can catch their breath.

When a state fails to offer tangible responses, the need to strengthen the civil associations and entities seeking to change this illogical and absurd state of affairs becomes critical: in the United States, the Autism Society of America (ASA), founded in 1965 by Bernard Rimland with Ruth Sullivan, managed to create a "system" consisting of a small group (up to 10 residents) cohabiting in homes in society, self-managed – when possible – or assisted by trained collaborators and controlled by civil institutions. Such an environment enables the preservation of a sense of individuality, activates the potential for work and for friendship among peers, develops the control of their belongings, and creates comfort and the possibility of enjoyment and caring for themselves and their personal environment in a responsible manner through the fulfilment of "obligations" – housekeeping tasks such as cleaning and general organisation for shopping, meal preparation, and visits outside the residence – while enjoying the comfort of living in a community and not being abandoned as an outcast. Does this sound like a dream? Maybe, but its implementation has proved to be a more effective way of achieving wellbeing, independence, and health of residents, and it is much more economical for the state than the total institutions.

The way the state cares for its most vulnerable people is a sign of the quality of its citizenship and this does not speak well for our social structure. Autism is caused by enigmatic genes not yet identified, and manifests itself in the strange and intense reactions of people affected with ASD, some exotic, others logical, most indecipherable. Over the past 20 years, scientific knowledge has allowed us to understand, communicate, and socialise with these individuals to a degree that nobody had thought possible before and, as they grow older, they continue to be the most interesting human beings inhabiting our planet.

The parents' association movement and public policy

Autism is a life-long condition. The statistics are not encouraging. According to the new criteria, one in 68 children have autism (CDC, 2018). The prevalence has increased 15% in comparison with the report of 2016 (which estimated that one in 59 had the disorder). People with autism have a life span similar to the rest of the population, yet the future of today's children and young people diagnosed with autism does not look very different from that of adults with autism today. While the parents are alive, the child will be under their care. After that, the decisions about their future will be taken by third parties and they will be moved into a system of overcrowded residences and "homes" or psychiatric institutions, to what Michel Foucault (2009) refers to as "where society confines its madness."

In a social reality where intellectually disabled individuals and their families are among the most vulnerable groups, the United Nations Convention on the Rights of Persons with Disabilities acknowledges that only adjustments or the provision of services will be insufficient to ensure the full enjoyment of human rights (United Nations General Assembly, 2006). Thus, the Convention is not the end but the beginning of the journey. Its immediate objectives are promoting the self-management and self-determination of people with disabilities. The effective fulfilment and full exercise of these rights translates into the access of people with disabilities to the right to happiness, essential for the development of all human beings. It is a priority to provide the necessary support to their families, and to build support in the community so that inclusion becomes a reality in the twenty-first century. Associative movements arise as a *life project*, specifically to provide concrete answers and to help build a future for both the parents of disabled people and for individuals themselves. As mentioned before, a child with autism or another disability can bring high levels of stress for the parents because of the way they behave as well as their symptomatology and evolution.

Once the last stage of the shock process is reached (the acceptance), many parents and relatives decide to create or join an existing civil organisation. The underlying belief is that, in seeking a comprehensive solution for the group, every individual will find his/her own answers. In fact, the state has finite resources and faces infinite demands from society. There are problems which remain outside the state's remit, beyond its obligation to develop public policies to meet the needs of disabled people's life cycles, and its duty to monitor services and provisions, and maintain funding for public policies. There are requirements which cannot be absorbed by the governmental system. Therefore, it is the responsibility of civil organisations to detect the actual needs of people with disabilities during their lifecycle, to provide answers and support to their families, and generate and provide the necessary funding to fulfil the social objectives of wellbeing, empowerment, and community representation.

The perspectives and the contributions of the family are essential for this task and for the development of health and education professionals. Parents, who know their children better than anyone else – their ways of relating to others, their preferences, and motivations – can contribute with crucial information, allowing effective solutions to be implemented. The parents also play an essential role in the effectiveness of the introduction of state support programmes and public policies. In this regard, Capalbo and Maniei (2007)maintain the following:

The role of NGOs (non-governmental organisations) today should not be overlooked. National, transnational, and continental associative movements organised around the topic of disability, with the involvement of the family environment as a whole, in all their social spectra and all parts of the country, have been crucial players and revolutionary managers of rights and policies in the international arena – the new actors in the global order. In all human activities, they constitute the most significant social factor of our times. For this reason, NGOs emerge as a new, parallel constructive and foundational process in the world. They provide protection and hope in many other campaigns, such as the prevention of the destruction of the ecosystem, the battle against social injustices, political conflicts, poverty, disability, and the exercise of new third-generation rights.

The NGOs of disability have distinctive features, both in their formation and functioning. Their mission and vision are lifetime projects. And parents of people with disabilities, the nuclear family, and sometimes the extended family are incorporated into its mission. It can be said that, among other aspirations and immediate needs of the parents of disabled people, when they don't receive any answers from the social system (the government system included) they shield themselves, sometimes desperately, in the NGOs of parents, founding them together with other parents or adhering to the existing ones, wherever these could be. Apart from the first contention, they follow the possibility of a real and concrete solution for their distress and their suffering, as well as a way to battle the public authorities or to articulate the struggle of the cause of the disability as a mission.

What sets the specific associative movements by disability apart, like APAdeA, is its philosophy based on the thoughts of a group of parents (expressed by the founder parents as the APAdeA "mystique"), which seeks, within a general solution for the population with autism, a singular solution for each individual case (Galibert, 2005, 2013). Another important element of a disability NGO is the high percentage of people whose commitment will last for life. In the best-known cases of these NGOs, the lead parent is most often the mother, reducing the secondary

Table 7.1 ALaFe composition. Own elaboration.

No	*Country*	*Organisation*	*Leader/Founder*
1.	Argentina	APAdeA	Father
2.	Bolivia	Bolivian Network of Parents of People with Autism (Red Boliviana de Padres de Personas con Autismo)	Both of them (father and mother)
		TEAcompaño Foundation	Mother
3.	Brasil	ABRA	Both of them (father and mother)
4.	Costa Rica	ASCOPA	Mother
5.	Ecuador	Isaac Centre	Mother
6.	Guatemala	AGUA	Mother
7.	Paraguay	EPA	Mother
8.	Perú	ASPAU	Mother
9.	Uruguay	Encuentro TEA	Mother

role to the father or partner. This pattern is at least appreciated in the organisations of familiars of people with autism which conform the ALaFe – Autismo Latinoamérica Federación – whose founder is APAdeA.

As it can be seen in this table, in nine of the ten organisations, the mothers are involved in the leadership and in the foundation of these associative movements, whose purpose is guaranteeing the welfare and the life quality of people with autism. In the case of APAdeA, it has been working for the past 25 years on how to mitigate the impact of disability for the families through counselling, guidance, escorts, and the provision of advanced and free legal service on issues related to health, education, job training, transportation, and specialised care.

Argentinian case

Despite being a country with a strong psychoanalytical culture, the contribution of psychoanalysis to the problems of parents of people with disability in Argentina has not been significant. The parents were the ones who, alongside prominent professionals and prestigious entities, took control of the debate and achieved, among other measures, the passage of the exceptional Law 24.901, which mandates the coverage of 100% of all benefits required by people with a disability. Through this law, which puts Argentina in the forefront of Latin America, a "reasonable" yet very slow evolution towards educational and social integration of individuals with autism was set under way. APAdeA played a historic role in what has been considered the continent's greatest social achievement in legislation on disability. Nevertheless, despite the law, there is still the need for awareness (and public policies) on the early detection of autism and early intervention, although the instruments to perform this detection with a simple test, applied at the ages of 18 and 24 months, already exist. In addition, there are very few specialised centres for the education and treatment of the most severe cases.

There is no support from the state for the maintenance of the existing centres or the creation of new ones. In higher-education or college courses related to health or education, autism is not even mentioned. Another problem is the lack of facilities to provide emotional support to families suffering long-lasting personal stress and the sense of isolation that, despite the greater awareness of ASD, persists to this day. This sense of isolation is further enhanced by the process of seeking a diagnosis, obtaining a disability certificate, joining a health plan or registering the child in a kindergarten, as well as the search for a special-education teacher, special school, or therapeutic education centre. Not to mention the anxiety produced by birthday parties, going to restaurants or other public spaces, visiting the dentist or friends, or going on holiday. And particular anxiety awaits: the arrival of puberty and the bitter feeling overtaking parents facing the uncertain future when they will no longer be there to care for the child.

In that context, APAdeA has made great efforts through its entire track record to support families and provides services that should be granted by the government. This work started with programs of *Padres a la Escucha* (Parents Listening), in

Figure 7.4 San Ignacio community, founded by Ignacio's family

which a group of parents of people with autism attend to inquiries from other parents, who contact the organisation looking for information and advice. This involves legal affairs to exercise rights, as well as contention. The founders of the organisation worked very hard and found new methods and applications, which were being used successfully elsewhere in the world, to treat their children when they imported the first franchising (as a successful product, the "know-how" and the "my book" on paper/digital) from UCLA (University of California, Los Angeles), United States, after having an interview with the previously mentioned Dr. Ivar Lovaas.

APAdeA has been contributing by accumulating information on its experiences and practices. Furthermore, since its establishment as a parents' association, it has played a vital part in establishing national legislation. It has also been advising many Argentine provinces on institutional development. All this has been based on a lifecycle perspective and consequently, nowadays, APAdeA offers services for school inclusion, home treatments, employability with support, as well as home and respite home aimed at adults with autism.

Conclusion

The history of the role of parents in the treatment of their children with autism can be summed up as the shift from the family's influence on autism to the influence of autism on the family (Rivière, 2001). Associations made up of families are rarely considered objects of direct intervention because they are involved in the hope that this will positively affect the child's treatment. Another, less common approach, is precisely the opposite: in an association formed by families, there may be services directed at the family, considered the object of intervention, so that treatment of the child is expected to have a positive impact on the functioning of the family as a system.

But whichever approach is adopted, what is important is to provide answers to both the person with ASD and his/her family. Parents have been so profoundly concerned with finding the right treatment for their children that when they created the associations or battled with the authorities, they focused almost exclusively on obtaining services to meet the needs of their children appropriately. Currently, most families, at least those with children attending schools, have achieved this goal, which was probably the most pressing one. But once this goal is attained, the associations and institutions face further challenges. One of these is obtaining quality services for themselves, as families exposed to the risks of suffering high levels of stress, which in turn undeniably has a negative effect on the individuals with autism.

Interventions relating to the child will improve the general functioning of the family, in the same way that interventions relating to the family will improve the functioning of the person with autism. This is why no aspect should be neglected. This chapter has sought to contribute to society's awareness of the life of a person with autism in the home and to the critical importance of the home as his/her privileged living space, where values are learned, happiness is enabled, and the future is planned. The place where a person with a disability lives should receive state assistance and guaranteed rights, through public policies that provide education and integral services. The struggle for social inclusion, for respites homes, for opportunities for free time, for appropriate care which will enable the couple's development, as well as planning for the old age of the parents and the evolution of the family in a home with meaning is not finished; it is the battle that still has to be won.

Notes

1 Nevertheless, Adam Feinstein, in his authoritative history of autism, published in 2010, points out that Asperger was already using the term "autism" from the early 1930s.

2 Lorna Wing (1996) was the first scientist who used these words in her work *The Autistic Spectrum: A Guide for Parents and Professionals*.

Bibliography

Argandoña, A. (2017) *The home: multidisciplinary reflections*. United Kingdom: Edward Elgar Publishing. pp. 8–54.

Asperger, H. (1991) 'Autistic psychopathy' in childhood (U. Frith, Trans.). In U. Frith (ed.), *Autism and Asperger Syndrome*. New York, US: Cambridge University Press. pp. 37–92.

Blair, P. (1996) *Parental perceptions of the lifetime changes associated with having an autistic child: a gender comparison*. https://files.eric.ed.gov/fulltext/ED390236.pdf.

Capalbo, L. and Maniei, H. (2007) *La expresión social de la conciencia planetaria*. Buenos Aires: Centro Integral Comunicación, Cultura y Sociedad, CICCUS. p. 101.
Centres for Disease Control and Prevention (CDC) (2018) *CDC Increases estimate of autism's prevalence by 15 percent, to 1 in 59 children*. Website Autism Speaks. Available from: www. autismspeaks. org/science-news/cdc-increases-estimate-autisms-prevalence-15-percent-1–59-children (accesed July 15, 2019).
Cunningham, C. and Davis, H. (1988) *Trabajar con los padres. Marcos de colaboración*. Madrid, Spain: Siglo Veintiuno Editores.
Cuxart, F. (1995) *Estrés y psicopatología en padres con hijos autistas*. Barcelona, Spain: Servicio de publicaciones de la Universidad Autónoma de Barcelona.
Debeljuh, P., Mesurado, B. and Idrovo, S. (2017) *Primer informe global home index: un estudio comparativo en 20 países* (1ª ed.). Buenos Aires: Baur.
Feinstein, A. (2010) *A history of autism: conversations with the pioneers*. Chichester, England: Wiley-Blackwell.
Foucault, M. (2009) *Historia de la locura en la época clásica* (2 Volúmenes). Buenos Aires, Argentina: Fondo de Cultura Económica.
Galibert, H. (2004) *Ignacio. Un niño. Un universo* (3ª edición). Buenos Aires, Argentina: Editorial Dunken.
Galibert, H. (2005) *Creación de ONG. Cómo estructurarlas legalmente. In: Primer Congreso Iberoamericano Discapacidad, Familia y Comunidad*. Buenos Aires, Argentina: Asociación Amar, Fundación Telefónica.
Galibert, H. (2013) *ONG Movimientos asociativos. Las asociaciones de padres y las Organizaciones en Discapacidad*. Buenos Aires, Argentina: Fondo Editorial APAdeA.
Galibert, H. (2019) *Autismo: Cuadernos de APAdeA*. Buenos Aires, Argentina: Fondo Editorial APAdeA.
Kanner, L. (1935) *Child psychiatry*. USA: Springfield.
Kanner, L. (1943) *Autistic disturbances of affective contact*. USA: Nervous Child.
Lovaas, O.I. (1977) *The autistic child: language development through behavior modification*. New York and USA: Irvington publishers.
Lovaas, O.I. (1981) *Teaching developmentally disabled children: the ME Book*. Nerang, Australia: Pro-Ed Books.
National Autistic Society (NAS) (2017) *Identify the behavoir's porpuse*. Website National Autistic Society. Available from: www. autism. org. uk/behaviourguidelines (accesed: September 13, 2019).
Organisation of American States General Assembly (2015) Resolución 2875: Convención Interamericana sobre la Protección de los Derechos Humanos de las Personas Mayores (June 15, 2015). AG/RES. 2875 (XLV-O/15). Available from: http://scm. oas. org/doc_public/SPANISH/HIST_15/AG06943S04. doc (accesed July 15, 2019).
Rivière, A. (2001) *Autismo: Orientaciones para la intervención educativa*. Madrid, Spain: Editorial Trotta.
Rivière, J.W. (1999) Sibilings relationships when a child has autism: marital stress and coping. *Journal of Autism and Developmental Disorders*, 33. Berlin, Germany: Springer Science+Business Media. pp. 383–394.
Roche, R. and Arozarena, E. (1977) *Hijos con problemas: ¿la familia a prueba?* Pamplona, Spain: Eunante.
United Nations General Assembly (2006) Resolution 61/106: Convention on the rights of persons with disabilities (December 13, 2006). A/RES/61/106. Available from: https://undocs. org/en/A/RES/61/106&Lang=E (accesed July 15, 2019).

Chapter 8

Taking care of a severely disabled child at home: Caregivers' burden and chance of personal growth

Aleksandra Kroll

Introduction

This article elaborates on the life circumstances of an exceptional group of homemakers who are family caregivers. The presented study is based on analyses of interviews with Polish participants who all provide constant care for children suffering from cerebral palsy and moderate to profound intellectual disability. All the participants are homemakers who, because of unchosen life circumstances, which the disability of their children definitely is, have chosen to live a life full of additional duties, which include basic nursing, therapy coordination, daily preparation of extra meals adjusted to special medical needs, etcetera. In a country where the social welfare system isn't as supportive as in many other parts of Europe, day after day they persist to create unique homes where a permanently ill person is an important and central figure.

Every newborn is completely dependent on the care provided by adults from the nearest surrounding. As time passes, a child becomes more and more self-sufficient as a result of natural, healthy developmental processes comprehensively supported by closest carers. Nevertheless, in some children this natural process is strongly interrupted on the biological level. Due to a permanent and irreversible health condition, they are not able to develop in the same way as their typically developing peers and they do not reach the level of independence adequate to their age, which means that they require constant care or help with fulfilling basic life needs. As it is necessary to provide safety, which often means that a caregiver needs to be physically present and by the patient almost all the time, and it impossible to decide if and when the situation may improve, one of the major decisions that needs to be made is to choose between residential or home care. In some situations, professional home carers are entrusted with providing care, in others, the care is provided by family members. In the majority of EU countries, informal caregivers provide, on average, about 60% of the care needed. The estimation varies when it comes to particular countries, from only 15% of the care tasks performed by family members in Denmark up to 90% in Greece, as well as in central European countries, including Poland (Genet et al., 2012).

The viewpoint that addressing the needs of chronic patients should be based on family and social bonds with resorting to residential care only when the immediate environment lacks sufficient resources is widespread in Polish society (Kowalik, 2012), e.g., an opinion poll conducted by the Centre for Public Opinion Research (CBOS) at the end of 2007 showed that 94% of respondents claimed that caring for people with disabilities is primarily a family responsibility (www.cbos.pl/SPISKOM.POL/2007/K_169_07.PDF). When it comes to disabled children, the vast majority of them are being cared at home by mothers, e.g., in research among families of disabled children from the city of Łódź, 80% of participants declared that the mother was the main caregiver (Mikołajczy-Lerman, 2011). According to a Generations and Gender Survey (GGS), the same tendency is observed in all European countries, and mothers more frequently than fathers give up their career or job in order to be able to provide care to a disabled child (Di Giulio et al., 2014).

The situation of study participants is to some degree also influenced by the cultural context. The culture is understood as a set of beliefs and values shaped within a community for generations and can be expressed through behaviour, tradition, customs, works of art, or literature. Individual experiences may confirm the cultural message or deny it, and the specific decisions may be aligned to or remain in contrast with generally accepted standards of behaviour. Among the cultural factors that have a strong impact on the situation of the Polish family caregivers is religion. In Poland, close to 90% of people declare themselves as Roman Catholics, and around half of them practice their faith regularly. The religion calls to respect the body of a human sufferer and the care is considered a moral obligation, although there may be different forms of complying with it. One of the main documents covering this subject is *Salvifici doloris* (John Paul II, 1984). However, at the same time, this seems to be contradicted by the influence of current popular culture. In the middle of the last century, Viktor Frankl said, in the culture, in which productivity, youth, and vitality are becoming the biggest virtues, sick people suffer additionally from a sense of shame, that they are suffering (Frankl, 2009). The emphasis put on productivity today and the appearance of people with idealised beauty affects the self-confidence of even healthy young people, not to mention anyone who has some serious and visible medical problems (Warren, 2014, Thompson et al., 1999, McCabe and Ricciardelli, 2004, Haller Beth et al., 2006). Although there are specialised targeted publications, magazines, and TV programs dedicated to the issues of disability and diseases in Poland, they are addressed to a relatively small group of receivers. Undoubtedly, new possibilities have been created by the internet, but the coverage of people with problems similar to those the family caregivers are facing on a daily basis is still assessed as minimal (Haller et al., 2006).

To make their voice more widely heard, the study has been conducted. It concerns Polish family caregivers of children suffering from cerebral palsy, which is one of the most frequent causes of severe disability among children. It is estimated at between 2 and 2.5 cases per 1,000 births (Odding et al., 2006) and defined as

> a group of permanent disorders of the development of movement and posture that are attributed to non-progressive disturbances that occurred in the developing fetal or infant brain. The motor disorders of cerebral palsy are

> often accompanied by disturbances of sensation, perception, cognition, communication, and behavior; by epilepsy, and by secondary musculoskeletal problems.
>
> (Rosenbaum et al., 2007)

Although in this definition, the motor nature of the disorder is emphasised, problems in other areas may also occur, such as intellectual disability or communication disorders. The emotional state of a patient, a possible result of the awareness of his or her condition, could pose other difficulties. Additionally, in neurological diseases, changes to the emotional state and personality could appear because of structural damage to the nervous system that is hard or even impossible to treat. Such behaviours as uncontrolled aggression, disinhibition, and sudden outbursts of dejectedness or crying are even more difficult because of very limited verbal communication with the patient that often occurs in intellectual disability, and the patient is often not able to reflect on his or her behaviour later on. Although cognitive and emotional disturbances may be concomitant or not, if present, they can impose even greater burdens on people from the nearest social surrounding than the physical disability itself (Bax et al., 2005; Bottcher, 2010).

OBJECTIVES: The aim of the study was to get to know the life circumstances of Polish family caregivers of severely disabled children better. The focus was on their assessment of experienced burdens and risk factors, as well as the ways of coping and possibilities for personal growth.

MATERIAL AND METHODS: The participants of the research were Polish family caregivers of children with cerebral palsy and mild, moderate, or severe intellectual disability. There were 21 participants (15 women), aged between 28 and 51. They participated alone in an interview, held partially as structured and partially as semi-structured. In the first part of the interview, participants were asked about the main medical conditions their child is diagnosed with. Then they used a Likert scale (point 1 to 5, where 1 was the lowest score) to assess their child's independence, specific communication competencies, and the quality of relationship they have. They also assessed the general possibility to communicate with the child (point 1 to 10, where 1 was the lowest score) and listed the ways of aiding communication they use. In the semi-structured interview, they answered open-ended questions concerning their general situation as a family caregiver.

RESULTS: Participants provided information about the disabled child they care for at home. All the children were diagnosed with cerebral palsy, intellectual disability, and severe communication problems. Twelve patients suffered from aphasia and severe speech impairment, three from dysarthria, and three were reported to have other communication disorders. Ten patients suffered from poor movement control, eight were paralyzed and had paraplegia, six had uncontrolled face expression, six impaired sight, and four had poor face expression. More than half of the caregivers were not aware of the connection between poor communication and poor intellectual capabilities of the patient.

Regarding the assessment of independence, the average general independence mark was 33 points (SD=13.96, MIN=14, MAX=59) and the typical assessment of independence in the examined group was between 17 and 44 points. Despite the difficulties with voluntary movement control, most of the patients were able to move within their homes thanks to the support of modern technologies +($\bar{x}$ = 3.41). The ability to independently execute certain actions, such as drinking from a mug with a handle ($\bar{x}$ = 3.23), eating with their own hands ($\bar{x}$ = 3.14), and independently handling physiological needs ($\bar{x}$ = 3.14) were assessed relatively highly. The lowest scores were achieved for the ability to use cutlery ($\bar{x}$ = 1.41), handwriting/drawing ($\bar{x}$ = 1.59), and also for the ability to use electronic devices, including a mobile phone ($\bar{x}$ = 1.00). Details are shown in the Table 8.1.

Regarding the general assessment of communication abilities (on the 10-point scale), the average answer was $\bar{x}$ = 5.45 (SD=2.22). The most common result was M=5 and M=3. Seven out of 21 carers assessed the possibility to communicate with the child as 6 or more. Regarding particular communication abilities (on the 5-point scale), the competencies with the highest scores were the abilities to: communicate the need to eat or drink ($\bar{x}$ = 4.50), create an emotional bond ($\bar{x}$ = 4.35), react adequately to funny situations ($\bar{x}$ = 4.35), communicate feeling unwell or experiencing pain ($\bar{x}$ = 4.25), react to emotional states of other persons ($\bar{x}$ = 3.90), and have own sense of humour ($\bar{x}$ = 3.85). The competencies with lowest marks showed that patients had troubles with: introducing themselves and giving information about themselves ($\bar{x}$ = 1.72), giving information when they want to go outside of the home ($\bar{x}$ = 2.53), as well as trying to offer comfort when they see someone sad ($\bar{x}$ = 2.70), having an interesting conversation ($\bar{x}$ = 1.50),

Table 8.1 Assessment of independence

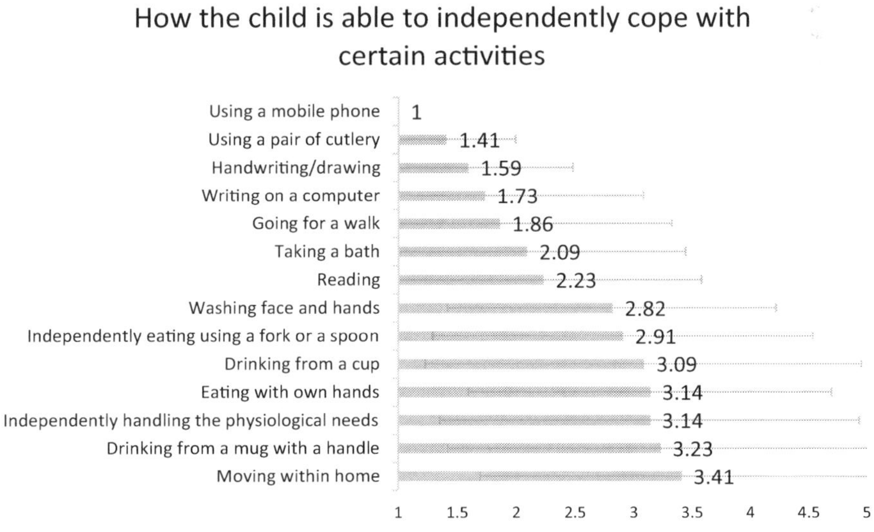

taking up a discussion ($\overline{x}$ = 1.48), or talking about existential issues ($\overline{x}$ = 1.33). Details are shown in Table 8.2.

These abilities are connected with using speech and performing the discursive-information function of communication, which is severely damaged if not completely absent in persons with a mild or severe intellectual disability. The caregivers were also asked to assess their relationship with the child. There were much more *positive* ($\overline{x}$ = 20,95, SD=4.12) indications than *negative* ($\overline{x}$ = 9,67, SD=3.01) ones.

The highest level of agreement was with the statements *I enjoy the situations when I am able to achieve particularly good communication with the patient* ($\overline{x}$ =4.52), *I like to stay with that person* ($\overline{x}$ = 4.43), and *I am eager to take care of her/him* ($\overline{x}$ = 4.33). The lowest score was returned by the statements: *the patient is indifferent to me* ($\overline{x}$ = 1.33), *I am tired of her/his company* ($\overline{x}$ = 1.71), and *I find it irritating when facing difficulties in communicating with the patient* ($\overline{x}$ = 1.81). Details are shown in Table 8.3.

The carers were also asked to describe the ways of aiding communication with the patient. Among the most commonly mentioned ways are: touching, stroking, hugging (61.90% of carers considered this to be effective), pointing at items or places connected to the question asked (52.38%), caring for good mood (47.62%), encouraging (47.62 %), showing pictures or familiar items (42.86%), talking about family and relatives (38.10%), recalling earlier events (38.10%), repeatedly asking the same question (33.33%), repeating the same commands (33.33%), using single sentences (28.57%), using special gestures (28.57%), talking louder (23.81%), using single words (23.81%), searching for topics which are of special

Table 8.2 Average score of communication competencies assessment

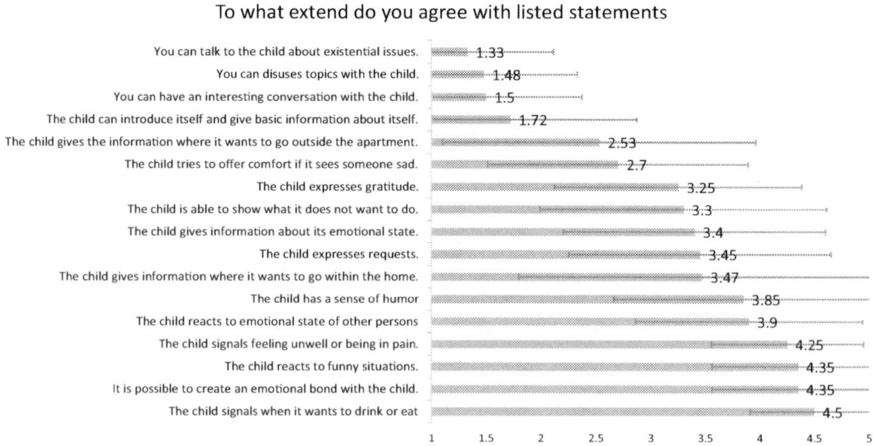

Table 8.3 A detailed assessment of the carer's relationship with the child

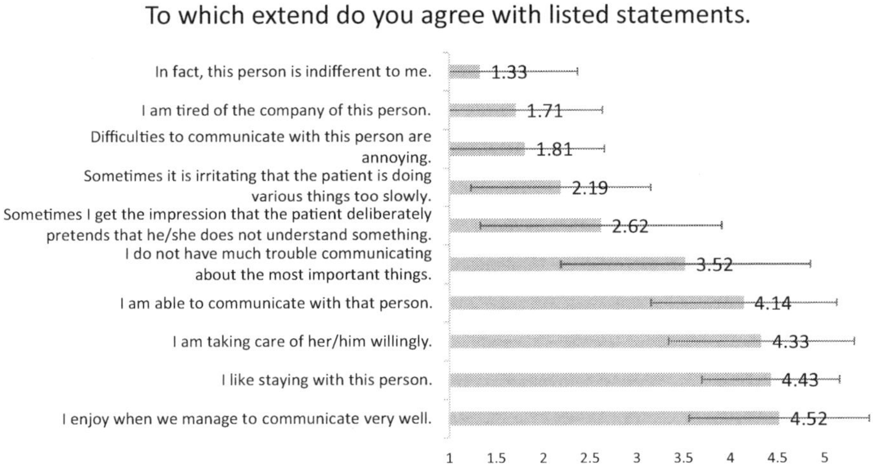

interest to the patient (23.81%), standing in front of the patient (23.81%), slower pace of speaking (19.05%), talking more clearly (19.05%), speaking in a higher tone of voice (19.05%), drawing (14.29%), using the same command in different forms (9.52%), listening patiently (4.76%), using special pseudo-words to name something (4.76%), and others (38.10%). No one considered sign language as an effective method, and there was no carer in this group who would say that no methods can significantly help with communication with the patient.

Information obtained in a semi-structured interview

As a result of the analysis of the participants' responses, the following topics were distinguished: attitude towards their own child's disability, woman as a family caregiver, difficulties in communication with the child, attitudes of local communities, social support, main difficulties, and possibilities for personal growth. Regarding attitude towards their own child's disability, the participants talked about a lack of understanding related to unestablished reasons for the disease, for some of them interpreted as a sign that it is surrounded by a mystery. Everybody agreed that it is difficult for them to think about the disabled child they look after as a "patient" due to a close relationship they have created. They admitted that they learned to live with the situation throughout the past years although they considered their current attitude a result of a long process, which usually included a personal fight for health, attempting consecutive "miracle therapies," and shattered hopes. The doubts raised by increased knowledge of CP risk factors and potential opportunities to avoid disability often returned during interviews. *"During these years I have grown accustomed to it. It is just the way it is and that's all about it." "At first nobody wanted to tell me anything. You know, I am a nurse by profession." "Still, nobody knows what causes that illness. Nobody can say what the cause is." "I have been through it all: space suit, healing with diet, massages, biofeedback . . . Now, I simply laugh about it all."*

Regarding the woman as a family caregiver, women declared that their direct engagement in care for a sick child is bigger than their husbands', who to a larger extent, accepted the duty to provide for the family. Two mothers brought up their children on their own, and one said directly that her husband had left her because of the child's irreversible disability. Exemplary statements typical for this category included: *"I look after her better than anyone else. My husband is immediately nervous." "I am the housekeeper and I look after the child, my husband earns." "My child does not have a father. He simply does not have a father, and that's it." "The dad of my sons failed. He left us. But we manage."*

Regarding the difficulties in communication with the child, the carers emphasised that they are perfectly able to communicate, however, it took them a lot of time to achieve this level of competence. The strategies they developed are often difficult to classify (e.g., child takes off cotton nappy from the shoulder to signal that she is hungry). The participants did not believe that the difficulties they had experienced in communication with their child brought problems to their family relationships. Modern techniques and tools supporting the communication process are seen by the participating group as mostly ineffective. Some said they were trying to implement them, but their efforts did not produce expected results. Exemplary statements included: *"Communication is not a problem" "We have our ways" "Those modern methods are not helping at all. They are not for us."*

Regarding the attitudes of local communities, the participants emphasised that they have been seeing an improvement throughout the past years. They jointly claimed that they do not encounter unfriendly conduct on an everyday basis. More often, they experience unwanted attention, the fear expressed by healthy people, or unwanted pity, which they take as outsiders' illegitimate attempt to encroach on their territory and a lack of understanding of the nature of the illness their loved one suffers from. Most of the participants of the research are not engaged in any associations apart from branches of the Polish Association for Persons with Intellectual Disability. Some people who participated in the research pointed out a necessity to appreciate non-governmental organisations and volunteers, but it would certainly require defining the scope of support provided by volunteers first, as some ideas about potential work volunteers could do were very extensive. Exemplary statements included: *"We are not experiencing discrimination." "Prying and being sorry for this child is annoying." "People have different experiences. We personally meet mostly with kindness."*

Evaluating their possibility of getting social support, in general, the participants said it is changing mainly because of the Internet, which enables communicating with other parents of disabled children. The participants admitted that they have a sense of being slightly different, though they provided various reasons for that feeling. Some claimed that families that do not have to care about a disabled family member do not understand their problems at all, whereas others disagree. However, many of them claimed that most of the friends from the time before having a disabled child abandoned them, but they made some new friends, especially among the other family caregivers. Exemplary statements included: *"If someone is not in this situation, he can't understand our problems at all." "We have the same problems as everyone. It does not differ."*

Regarding the main difficulties, participants mostly complained about financial difficulties and the lack of practical solutions. E.g., in Poland, it is not always easy to find external help or a hostel for disabled children, which could allow their parents to go out together with their children for a night. Participants also complained about the way supporting institutions, both governmental and non-governmental, work. The lack of cooperation as well as a turf war among institutions supporting the disabled was a problem that was emphasised. Health care professionals were praised and described as friendly, and some memories about bad experiences were accompanied by a claim that they should not give grounds for conclusions about the entire profession. Exemplary statements included: *"There are not enough hostels, even for weekends, that we could go somewhere together. That's how we're tied down, especially me." "It's difficult to understand ambitions between people from different associations for the disabled. Instead of supporting one another, they are sometimes harming one another." "The hardest thing is to get information. As soon as a new problem arises, it turns out that nobody knows anything. You have to know someone who knows the system well." "Individuals are usually kind. The problem is in the system."*

Regarding possibilities of personal growth, the possibility most frequently pointed to was a close relationship with the disabled children who are honest and grateful, although not able to express their gratefulness verbally. Participants declared that the disabled child encouraged them to rethink their priorities and put values such as family, love, friendship, and spirituality first. They also claimed that healthy siblings and cousins can learn a lot from having a disabled relative. Exemplary statements included: *"Thanks to such a child you know better what is important in your life." "Other children can learn a lot. They can be more generous in the future." "I couldn't put her into some institution. She is very important to me and always so close."*

Discussions

Environment which supports development of every child

All the participants of this study are family caregivers and simultaneously homemakers. This means, according to the view presented by Argandoña (2018), that they all are the main person in their households who is responsible for coordinating the activities of all the people creating that small community – the family – caring for the shared space while at the same time being present in the external environment. What distinguishes participants of the presented study from other homemakers is that in the small community they are responsible for, one of the children demands extra care and attention.

A severe disability of the child distorts or even reverses the order typical for that phase of human life. According to Erik Erikson's theory, each stage of psychosocial development is characterised by a specific nature of tasks assigned by a developing human body, as well as required by society (Erikson, 2004). Childhood and adolescence are characterised by a great number of changes leading to gradually growing independence and maturity. The pace at which a healthy child acquires new skills makes adults look at this process with hope, try to foresee a child's future, and help to prepare for independent life. But when a child is diagnosed with a severe disability, different and mixed reactions may occur. Happiness is often replaced by fear about the future, by sadness and anger, and after that critical phase, usually by attempts to fight for the highest possible level of abilities (Mikołajczy–Lerman, 2011). When it comes to the period of adolescence, it is typically characterised by a profound rise in the level of independence and self-reliance in healthy individuals, which may, on the one hand, be a source of joy and, on the other, a concern for parents. In the case of disabled teenagers, these feelings are replaced by concerns about the future and an awareness of a need to provide constant care if parents die or, for some reason, become significantly less efficient in providing care (Hallum, 1995, Kościelska, 2007).

Although the developmental processes are not progressing correctly they are still active in children. therefore it is often not clear for many years to what degree functions and abilities can develop (Baxter et al., 1995). For this reason, the developmental process in such children is stimulated with available therapeutic methods for as long as it seems to bring results (Blair, 2010). As the participants claimed, one of the most difficult things is to obtain reliable information and understandable diagnosis. Hence, the main caregiver of a disabled child has to become competent in the area and, despite the other duties, he or she usually has to coordinate the cooperation among specialists involved in the process of rehabilitation and developmental support. Because of this fact, participants considered such personal traits as flexibility and adaptability as particularly important for caregivers. Moreover, like participants noticed, depending on the developmental stage of a child and his or her individual needs, caregiving may become more and more demanding over time.

The necessity of focusing so much on the disabled child carries the risk of neglecting their healthy siblings. None of the participants note that risk. They claimed that the other children become more responsible, empathetic, and resourceful because of having a disabled brother or sister, and that the additional obligations resulting from such life circumstances can teach them generosity and tolerance. Although they most certainly have a point, on the other hand, it has to be admitted that there are some proofs of greater risk of interpersonal and psychopathological problems in siblings of children with disabilities (Goudie et al.,

2013). Hence, parents must remember that one child's special needs should never be used as an emotional operant to force healthy ones to do something or to prevent them from some actions unwanted by parents. True arguments should always be shown without using the disability of one of the children as an excuse.

The importance of social support

Numerous factors are affecting caregivers' lifestyles. One is the fact that the lifestyle becomes less regular and more dependent on improvements and deterioration of the patient's health. This is also connected with the threat of family isolation from the community (Surender et al., 2016). Among the participants of the study, people with poor social support declared they dedicated all their free time to caring activities, treating the medical community as a kind of substitute for their relationship deficiencies. As a result of such an attitude, they lose motivation to attempt to open up to their local or professional environment. Such an attitude may result in focusing too much on the child's disease, excluding oneself from other areas and creating a hospital-like atmosphere at home. Family caregivers engaged in social groups and non-governmental organisations more often declared to receive emotional support. They were also well informed about changes in the law, opportunities to raise funds, and all sorts of other ongoing projects. Similar advantages of being engaged in supportive organisations are mentioned by Mikołajczy-Lerman (2011). During interviews, these caregivers more often declared being open to support from both professionals and volunteer organisations. In contrast, people who declared in the interviews they had no need or time to deepen social relationships more often reported a need for some practical solutions, not knowing that such solutions are already available to them and reimbursed by the state, and also offered additionally by non-governmental organisations. The analysis of their declarations indicates that isolation of the family because of caring for a disabled

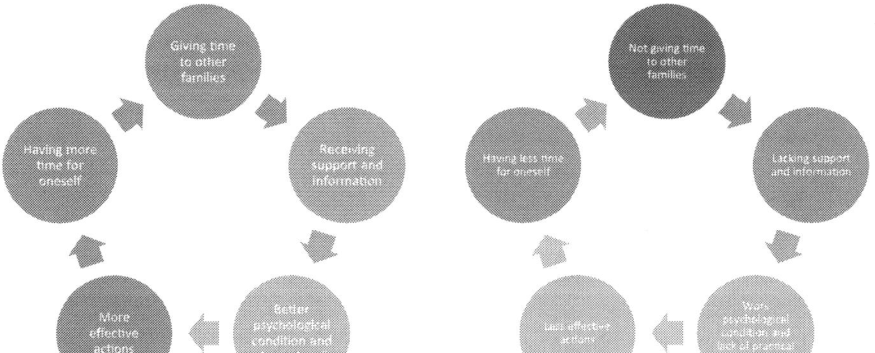

Figure 8.1 The circle of social support (left) and the circle of social isolation (right).

child increases isolation and adds, even more, to the burden of the main caregiver. Ending the reluctance to meet with others results in reversing that negative effect.

The need of financial stability

One of the families' concerns that study participants mentioned most frequently was a financial hardship. In Europe, the risk of economic difficulties in families with disabled children is bigger than in those without. The family's financial situation may differ depending on the law of the country they reside in. Di Giulio et al. (2014) report that this is seen in every country examined, except Russia. The percentage of families declaring that they "*make ends meet with difficulty or great difficulty*" is different across European countries, with the lowest values in Austria and the highest in Bulgaria (*ibidem*). The biggest difference reported within countries by child disability status are in Romania (22.3 pp), Lithuania (12.5 pp), and Austria (21.1 pp). State aid, as well as aid from NGOs, seems to be needed so that in the case of financial deficiencies, the family could avoid health or rehabilitation negligence of the patients. Among the participants, a need to earn money in a legal way was also frequently expressed. In some countries, including Poland, any paid activity of main caregiver results in losing a profound part of the benefits the families are entitled to because of raising a child with a disability. This situation was considered unfair by all participants of the study, especially those with older children who usually spend a couple of hours a day at school. Their mothers declared that they would be glad to engage in some kind of telework or online small business, and that they have the organisational capacity to do so. Interestingly, regardless of the financial problems mentioned, the main declared motivation of taking additional activity outside the home was not the intention to avoid poverty but to prevent social isolation. It turns out that some mothers of older children voluntarily engage in an additional activity for the benefit of others: three moms have reported running a blog, whereas two of them declared being engaged in some administrative work in parents' associations.

Smart solutions to prevent physical stress

Family burdens result mainly from a limited autonomy of the patient, disturbances in the family system, and difficulties in treatment and therapy participation (Taranowicz, 2001). The limitation of mobility and strain of somatic illness are among the most often mentioned factors, which definitely concerns participants of the presented study, regarding their assessment of child independence (Arnaud et al., 2008, Surender et al., 2016). The severity of disability can be classified at many levels, e. g., in the Polish law, there are three levels that are distinguished and named as *light*, *moderate,* and *severe*. The latter is defined as a person with a congenital birth defect, long-term illness, or bodily injury. The disabled children looked after by our participants are all included in this last category, and are not able to fully and independently address their basic needs, like eating or having a glass of water. This means that the constant presence of a person who is able to help them is necessary. Consequently, all other duties that a caregiver has to perform have to be coordinated to secure the needs of their disabled child.

The organisational problems caregivers of disabled children are facing may be compared to those which parents usually have when caring for a newborn or toddler. The main differences stem from physical features of a dependent child, such as their height and weight, and include a necessity for additional help or special equipment, or more frequent physical fatigue. Researchers share numerous diseases which carers are suffering from. Among them, back pain and joint pain resulting from overload, chronic fatigue, headaches, and insomnia (Zysnarska et al., 2010). To prevent this physical stress, the home environment has to be adjusted by means of appropriate ramps, adapted bathrooms, special elevators, and the presence of medical equipment. Participants frequently mentioned that modern technology makes these solutions not only more and more functional, but also aesthetic, which is important because a nice environment can have a profound and positive effect on the patient as well as people close to them (Cattell et al., 2008), and allows them to avoid the dangers of focusing on the disease and suffering, and to lead a so-called normal life instead despite the disability.

The chance of personal development

Although from the medical perspective the home environment is not as professional as a special care facility, being cared for at home has a lot of benefits for disabled children. The most important include daily contact with close relatives, a stable group of people providing care throughout the day, s smaller risk of infections, and more flexible timing of feeding, bathing, and resting (Friedman and Kalichman, 2014). The home environment enables a more personalised approach towards caregiving, which is especially apparent in the sensibility which participants of the presented study showed towards the communication difficulties their children had. Interestingly, their general assessment of a possibility to get through to the child was relatively high, taking into consideration that the children are not able to produce verbal language and only understand very simple messages. Nevertheless, their parents are creative and persistent in searching for ways to understand them. One significant example was a mother whose daughter signalled that she finished her meal by taking off the cotton nappy from her shoulder. (Fig. 2.) To establish such a way of communication with the girl, who due to the intellectual impairment is not able to cooperate, a great amount of time and an individual approach towards the ill person was needed. This is easier to achieve in home surroundings than in a congregate care setting.

Interestingly, many participants noticed that they have the impression that most of the specialists are too focused on their problems and burdens. One mother said, "One might think that a man is obliged to be unhappy. That we are must be sad, suffering and not to be able to cope." But caregivers noticed many valuable aspects of their special situation. The most commonly mentioned are getting support from others, satisfaction from providing care, and the patient's gratitude. They also noticed a field for personal development, claiming that over the years, they have learned to maintain emotional stability in emerging crises associated with the disease and calmly resolving emergency situations. They also emphasise the ability to enjoy little things and seeing the positive side of difficult situations, as well as not focusing too much on troubles and laughing frequently. One should seek to offset the effects of the heavy burden carers are facing. As claimed by Viktor Frankl, not fighting with unnecessary suffering is a variation of mental masochism. The decision to care for a child with disabilities at home is, in a sense, in contradiction to current trends defined by Frankl as avoidance of suffering at all costs. One must note, however, that many carers mentioned the satisfaction that they draw from the relationship with their sick child. Similarly to the Zysnarska's studies (2010), although more than 80% of respondents reported resorting to dreaming of a life without the burden of caring for a close person frequently, almost the same number of people declared that they would be willing to take the

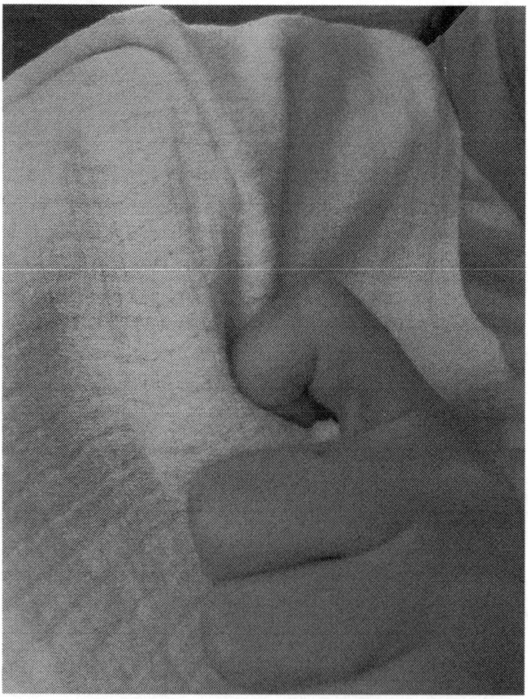

Figure 8.2 One of the participants noticed that her child put off cotton nappy from her shoulder sometimes during her meal and everytime at the end of it. She guessed that maybe her daughter did it when she is not hungry anymore. From this moment every time when the girl performed the gesture during a meal the mother stopped feeding her. It appeared that after mothers reaction girl calmed down. In this way mother established this simple behavior as a sign which is useful in communication.

same decision of caring again. It suggests that many caregivers find the role of a carer to be of higher value than their subjective sense of life comfort, which can be referred to as the concept of happiness, which is achieved not through a deliberate search for it, but by the pursuit of good (Frankl, 1984).

One of the participants noticed that her child took a cotton nappy off her shoulder sometimes during her meal and every time at the end of it. She guessed that perhaps her daughter did it when she was no longer hungry. From then, every time the girl performed the gesture during a meal, the mother stopped feeding her. After the mother reacted in this manner, the girl calmed down. In this way, the mother established this simple behaviour as a sign which is useful in communication.]

Conclusions: A child with disabilities co-creates home

This study's sample is not fully representative of the population because the research procedure (direct talk with the researcher) tends to exclude people with profound psychopathology. Participants of this study, together with their families, are all rather good examples of how such homes can work despite many difficulties if the main caregiver accepts their role and is fully engaged in it. Therefore, the decision to care for a physically and intellectually disabled child at home can be taken only in freedom. To those who decided to take this responsibility on their own, every possible support should be provided (Soto-Rubio et al., 2017). The family members know the patient well and are able to provide care in a sincere and delicate way. Treating the disabled child with adequate respect allows her or him to grow, though in a way limited by the disease.

If we consider the home as a secure place, where one is loved and accepted regardless of achievements or personal advantages (Patrão Neves, 2018), the homes with disabled children emphasise this aspect. Although in the fast pace of life which our civilisation experiences there is a greater risk of forgetting about kindness or thoughtfulness, presence of a seriously disabled child prevents this. It also encourages a more personalised view of humanity in the sense that the person who is absolutely vulnerable in some way reminds others that this is the potential reality of every human being. The situation of patients and their families goes beyond the perspective of a contemporary *homo faber* who is driven by the ethics of success. A lot of caregivers mentioned that they face questions of an existential nature: about the meaning of life, suffering, and relationships. The simple optimism which discards the presence of suffering does not give an answer, however, it can be found in caregiver's new perspective on life, sense, the essence of interpersonal relationships and love.

References

Argandoña, A. (2018) The home: multidisciplinary reflections. In The Home. Cheltenham, UK: Edward Elgar Publishing. doi: https://doi.org/10.4337/9781786436573.00009.

Arnaud, C., White-Koning, M., Michelsen, S.I., Parkes, J., Parkinson, K., Tyen, U., et al., (2008) Parent – reported quality of life of children with cerebral palsy in Europe. *Pediatrics*, 121: 54–64.

Bax, M., Goldstein, M., Rosenbaum, P., Leviton, A., Paneth, N., Dan, B., et al. (2005) Proposed definition and classification of cerebral palsy. *Developmental Medicine and Child Neurology*, 47: 571–576.

Baxter, Ch, Cummins, R.A., Polak, S. (1995) A longitudinal study of parental stress and support: from diagnosis of disability to leaving school. *International Journal of Disability, Development and Education*, 42(2): 125–136, doi:10.1080/0156655950420204

Bieganowska, A. (2005) Model niepełnosprawności w mediach a postawy wobec osób niepełnosprawnych. *Szkoła Specjalna*, 5: 362–371.

Blair, E. (2010) Epidemiology of the cerebral palsy. *Orthopedic Clinics of North America*, 41(4): 441–445.

Bottcher, L. (2010) Children with spastic cerebral palsy, their cognitive functioning, and social participation: a review. *Child Neuropsychology*, 16(3): 209–228.

Cattell, V., Dines, N., Gesler, W., Curtis, S. (2008) Mingling, observing, and lingering: everyday public spaces and their implications for well-being and social relations. *Health & Place*, 14(3): 544–561.

Di Giulio, P., Philipov, D., Jaschinski, I. (2014) *Families with disabled children in different European countries*. Family and Societies Working Paper Series.

Erikson, E. H. (2004) Tożsamość a cykl życia. Zysk i S-ka. [Identity and the Life Cycle: Selected Papers, 1959].

Frankl, V. (1984) Man's Search for Meaning. New York. Touchstone.

Frankl, V.E. (2009) *Człowiek w poszukiwaniu sensu, przeł. A. Wolnicka, Wyd.* Warszawa: Czarna Owca.

Friedman, S. L., Kalichman, M. A. (2014) Out-of-home placement for children and adolescents with disabilities. *Pediatrics,* 134(4): 836–846. https://doi.org/10.1542/peds.2014-2279

Genet, N., Boerma, W., Kroneman, M., Hutchinson, A., Saltman, R.B. (2012) *Home care across Europe: current structure and future challenges*. Geneva: World Health Organization.

Goudie, A., Havercamp, S., Jamieson, B., Sahr, T. (2013) Assessing functional impairment in siblings living with children with disability. Pediatrics, 132(2): e476-e483. https://doi.org/10.1542/peds.2013-0644

Haller, Beth, Dorries, Bruce, Rahn, Jessica (2006) Media labeling versus the US disability community identity: a study of shifting cultural language. *Disability & Society*, 21(1).

Hallum, A. (1995) Disability and the transition to adulthood: issues for the disabled child, the family, and the pediatrician. *Current Problems in Pediatrics*, 25(1): 12–50.

John Paul II, *apostolic letter Salvifici doloris*. http://w2.vatican.va/content/john-paul-ii/en/apost_letters/1984/documents/hf_jp-ii_apl_11021984_salvifici-doloris.html

Kościelska, M. (2007) Sens odpowiedzialności. Perspektywa psychologa klinicznego, Oficyna Wydawnicza "Impuls". *Kraków*, 96–97.

Kowalik, G. (2012) Praktyczne zastosowanie modelu pielęgnowania Doroty Orem. *Studia Medyczne*, 26(2): 107–111.

McCabe, M. P., Ricciardelli, L. A. (2003) Sociocultural influences on body image and body changes among adolescent boys and girls. *The Journal of social psychology,* 143(1): 5–26. https://doi.org/10.1080/00224540309598428

Mikołajczy-Lerman, G. (2011) Kobiety i ich niepełnosprawne dzieci. *Acta Universitatis Lodziensis Folia Sociologica*, 39: 73–90.

Odding, E., Roebroeck, M.E., Stam, H.J. (2006) The epidemiology of cerebral palsy: incidence, impairments, and risk factors. *Disability and Rehabilitation*, 28(4): 183–191.

Patrão Neves, M. (2018) Self and others: home as a cradle of a non-violent relationship. In *The home: multidisciplinary reflections*. Edward Elgar Publishing, pp. 8–25.

Rosenbaum, P., Paneth, N., Leviton, A., Goldstein, M., Bax, M., Damiano, et al. (2007) A report: the definition and classification of cerebral palsy. *Developmental Medicine and Child Neurology*, 109(Supplement): 8–14.

Soto-Rubio, A., Pérez-Marín, M., Barreto, P. (2017) Frail elderly with and without cognitive impairment at the end of life: their emotional state and the wellbeing of their family caregivers. *Archives of Gerontology Geriatrics*, 73: 113–119.

Surender, S., Gowda, V.K., Sanjay, K.S., Basavaraja, G.V., Benakappa, N., Benakappa, A. (2016) Caregiver-reported health-related quality of life of children with cerebral palsy and their families and its association with gross motor function. A South Indian study. *Journal of Neurosciences in Rural Practice*, 7: 223–227

Surveillance of cerebral palsy in Europe (2000) A collaboration of cerebral palsy surveys and registers. *Developmental Medicine and Child Neurology*, 42: 816–824.

Taranowicz, I. (2001) Rola rodziny w opiece nad człowiekiem przewlekle chorym, w: Rodzina w czasach szybkich przemian, Roczniki Socjologii Rodziny, t. 13, Wyd. *Naukowe UAM, Poznań*, 209–228.

Thompson, J. Kevin, Heinberg, Leslie J., Altabe, Madeline, & Tantleff-Dunn, Stacey (1999). *Exacting beauty: Theory, Assessment, and Treatment of Body Image Disturbance*. Washington, DC: American Psychological Association.

Warren, C. S. (2014) Body area dissatisfaction in white, black and Latina female college students in the USA: an examination of racially salient appearance areas and ethnic identity. *Ethnic and Racial Studies,* 37(3): 537–556. https://doi.org/10.1080/01419870.2012.716520

Zysnarska, M. (2010) i wsp., Kobieta – opiekun osoby przewlekle chorej – wyznaczniki przeciążenia. *Nowiny Lekarskie*, 79(5): 386–391. www.cbos.pl/SPISKOM.POL/2007/K_169_07.PDF

Chapter 9

A "sense of home"

Perceptions and expectations of elderly people about residential care facilities

Gabriella Facchinetti, Marco Clari, Michela Piredda, Stefania Abbondanza, and Maria Grazia De Marinis

Introduction

The declining mortality and rise in life expectancy over the past 20 years has led to an increasing number of older adults living in high-income countries (World Health Organization, 2015). Age brings changes in lifestyle, social relationships, and health. Older people have specific and complex social, relational, and health needs. Ageing is associated with a number of diseases and conditions (Brody and Grant, 2001). In particular, chronic diseases rise exponentially with age, affect quality of life, and are the main cause of disability of elderly people (Rozzini et al., 1997). Living with one or more chronic diseases means that the activities that were once easy to accomplish (related to domestic, relational, and disease management) are now becoming difficult. So, the need for support becomes fundamental and increases. According to the Italian Ministry of Health, elderly people who are non-self-sufficient are characterised by functional deficits due to a loss of physical, mental, or psycho-physical abilities connected to illness-related events, which determine handicap and some levels of care dependency.

Health care outside the hospital is provided in residential or semi-residential settings as a response to the needs of the older and non-self-sufficient people who cannot be assisted at home. Consequently, extra-hospital residential facilities take the form of a range of care homes offering different levels of health care (with medical, nursing, and rehabilitative components), accompanied by social-assistance services to facilitate connection to and, when possible, reintegration in the patient's home environment. The residences' specific characteristics are related to the type of guests, and their degree of dependence or psycho-physical problems.

Thus, extra-hospital residency can be divided into:

- Rehabilitation facilities for subjects suffering from physical, mental, and sensory impairment. In these facilities, the rehabilitation of people suffering from physical, psychological, or sensory impairments, dependent on any cause, is implemented through a high level of health protection, which contributes to the functional recovery of the disabled person, and through diagnostic and therapeutic-rehabilitative services using interdisciplinary clinical, psychological, pedagogical, and social contributions. These rehabilitation services may either be full-time, day-time, outpatient, or domiciliary. The rehabilitation benefits are aimed at restoring and maintaining the highest level of acquired autonomy, as well as reducing relapses.

- Residential care facilities: Residential care facilities differ from rehabilitation facilities because of the high intensity of health care involved and the longer periods of stay of those assisted, who, depending on their psycho-physical state, can also be permanent residents. Residential care facilities are long-term care given to the aged who live in a residential setting rather than in their own home or family home. They offer health care (medical, nursing, and rehabilitation) supplemented by a high level of protection and residential care to non-self-sufficient elderly people who can no longer live alone.

Therefore, when the elderly and their families realise that their homes and competences are no longer sufficient to support the high complexity of their needs, they start thinking about moving to residential care facilities.

The choice to move to residential care facilities is crucial in the lives of the elderly. Therefore, they "*should do so by positive choice*" (Wagner, 1988) and their participation is vital for the success of admission (Nolan et al., 1996). The literature explains that the majority of elderly people may enter residential care at the instigation of their carers or even professionals (Allen, 1992). The decision to move into residential care is often seen as a last resort because older people may prefer to stay at home (Falk et al., 2013). Memories embedded in the home and the passing of time tend to deepen the sense of rootedness and increase the desire to age in place (Saunders, 1989; Lawrence, 1995; Després and Lord, 2005). However, sometimes this is not possible for one or more of the following reasons: a fall/fracture and an acute illness, a general deterioration in their health and ability to look after themselves, as a result of increasing pressure on their carer, and loneliness (Allen, 1992). Moreover, moving into residential care might be the culmination of a number of events and illnesses that have taken place over several years.

Moving to residential care might lead to an increase of anxiety (Biedenharn and Normoyle, 1991), depression, fear, and stress for older people (Lee, 1997). Furthermore, unfortunately stereotypical views of residential care involve older people being left to themselves, and also reflect older residents' experience of being left without doing anything for extended periods in a common room (Lee et al., 2013).

On the other hand, some older people have reported positive experiences of moving into residential care, including feeling less lonely, feeling more financially secure, and with increased personal safety (Edwards et al., 2003). It is important to note that when the elderly move away from their home, they still have the need to feel at home.

Theoretical framework

A concept analysis of *home* (Gillsjo and Schwartz-Barcott, 2009) revealed that a *home* is much more than a house, a physical structure, or a dwelling devoid of or unrelated to its inhabitants. It is argued that the *sense of home* is created through a special relationship between people and the environment. This "emotional based relationship with the dwelling place is what defines the very nature and essence of home as distinguished from a house" (Moore, 2000). It takes time for this relationship to develop and it does not happen immediately or spontaneously. Indeed,

> the understanding of the home rests on the ontology of the person, who is presented simultaneously as vulnerable and dependent and also as independent, albeit an independence at the service of dependence, and the mediation between the two corresponds to the role of care.
>
> (Argandoña, 2018, Introduction)

Therefore, there is a strong relationship between the place people call home and their self-identity (Falk et al., 2013; Dovey, 1985), and the latter becomes more and more important with age (Gillsjo and Schwartz-Barcott, 2009). To be at home is to inhabit a "lived space" and a secure centre, where bodily and personal routines and cycles repeated over time make for complete insideness (Dovey, 1985).

Understanding the "sense of home" is critical to older people because the place in which people live can be a source of support and opportunities or constraints that affect nearly every aspect of the ageing experience (Wahl and Lang, 2003). The literature tries to explain the multifaceted nature of home and its impact on elderly people. Studies by Rapoport (1988, 1995) describe two different roles of the home: a functional role (i.e., privacy, usability) and an abstract role (i.e., identity, status). In fact, home is not merely a house or any other type of living space, but it holds emotional and personal significance for individuals. According to Cristoforetti et al. (2011), home also symbolises an extension of the self that is often understood as expression, identification, belonging, power, and appropriation. This symbolic feature of home reflects many aspects of individuals' lives, including personal background, life experience, and culture. What makes a house into a home? Despite the amount of literature about the experiences of older people in residential care facilities, there is a lack of literature about the sense of home in residential institutions. In addition, no study has been conducted to describe the perception of the sense of home and housing needs of elderly Italians.

Aims of the study

The aim of this study was to explore what contributes to the feeling of the "sense of home" and what are the housing needs of elderly people.

Methods

Study design

A qualitative descriptive study was carried out. This approach allowed researchers to explore the relevant phenomenon in its artless state (Guba and Lincoln, 1994).

Participants

A community-dwelling sample of aged people was used to obtain information deriving from the main stakeholders in this phenomenon. A maximum variation purposive sampling was recruited to reach a high level of heterogeneity among participants (Palinkas et al., 2015). The sample was chosen to provide the most relevant information in response to the research questions (Patton, 1990).

Inclusion criteria were: aged 65 years or older, with no cognitive impairments, and able to speak Italian and reside in Italy. The participants' age ranged from 65 to 94 years. Detailed socio-demographic characteristics are reported in Table 9.1.

Data collection

Data were collected from a sample of 14 aged persons between June and July 2017 using semi-structured face-to-face interviews. The interviews were conducted in a quiet place in the "Alberto Sordi" Senior Day Centre by an interviewer trained in qualitative interviewing to improve data collection. The interviews lasted between three and 21 minutes, and were audio-recorded and transcribed verbatim.

Table 9.1 Socio-demographic data sample

Sample (N) 14	
Year (DS)	83.5 (7.27)
Range year	94–64
Gender	
Female (%)	12 (85.71%)
Male (%)	2 (14.28%)
Education	
None	2 (14.28%)
Primary school	6 (42.85%)
Secondary school	2 (14.28%)
High school	3 (21.42%)
Bachelor degree	1 (7.14%)

Open-ended questions were used to explore participants' perceptions about residential care facilities, and about barriers and facilitators of inclusion and stay in a residential care facility. Socio-demographic data, which included age, level of education, and previous work, were collected.

Setting

Older adults attending an "Alberto Sordi" Senior Day Centre, named in honour of the famous Italian actor who financed the centres in Rome (Italy), were invited to participate in the study. This "Alberto Sordi" Senior Day Centre is managed by the Alberto Sordi Association and hosts 30 seniors a day who attend from a minimum of two to a maximum of four days a week.

It was inaugurated in 2002 with the following general aims:

- To support elderly persons in the delicate and difficult phase of life that is old age, trying to improve the quality of life and support of the family;
- To prevent or delay their possible institutionalisation;
- To support and strengthen frail elderly persons by helping them to identify and face psycho-physical weakness with awareness, and also by increasing their resilience.

Specific aims were also:

- To promote the maintenance of the residual cognitive, physical, and relational skills of the elderly by designing and proposing targeted activities that strengthen them and allow their empowerment in fundamental personal areas (intellectual, bodily, relational, emotional, and spiritual). In this way, older adults are helped to recover self-esteem, safety, and interpersonal skills, improving their quality of life, helping them maintain their independence for as long as possible, and making them feel that they are still an "active" part of society.
- To promote the social inclusion of older people in order to prevent and/or reduce the consequences of prolonged isolation. For this purpose, the day centre offers possibilities for company and socialization inside and outside the centre, linking the elderly among themselves and with their families, as well as with community services.
- To give respite to families by providing concrete help to their elderly relatives in order to alleviate their care task, supporting families with psychological counselling, and providing a social administration service able to support them in identifying and making contact with institutional community services that can help and support them in care tasks.

In accordance with the aims of strengthening the elderly and encouraging their social inclusion, the planning of the activities that take place in the day centre follow an inclusive educational approach, starting from the analysis of real-life stories, i.e., from the special and singular needs of the elderly and their interests, as the most up-to-date pedagogical literature indicates. Today it is clear that inclusive education has extended to all ages and, as John Dewey taught, can be achieved by connecting with people's interests, i.e., the autonomous and spontaneous activities that determined learning throughout the life course of a human being (Pennacchini, 2015). Therefore, educational attention focuses on identifying the most suitable activities for the elderly designed to maintain, recover, and, where possible, develop their psycho-physical conditions. These activities can be attributed to lifelong learning, and aim at empowering the elderly by involving them in practical activities, in doing things together with others, and being active subjects and actors in their lives. Therefore, it is not a matter of occupying their time, but of involving the whole person.

The methodology used in the project is summarised in the words "didactic teaching," a phrase very reminiscent of learning by doing, which is also used in continuous education in all ages of life. This methodology tries to actively involve them in activities. The individual appropriately developed activities have a specific instrumental value, involving the elderly from the cognitive, motor, relational, and emotional aspects. Personal gratification, obtained at the end of the activity, increases self-esteem, an essential condition for the recovery of self-confidence and for the empowerment of the elderly.

In order to encourage every elderly person's engagement to this methodological approach, each new member is teamed with another elderly member who has been attending the day centre for a long time, and who is charged with introducing him/her into the social-relational context (peer-tutoring) and supporting him/her in the activities (peer-education).

The strengthening of the resilience of the elderly and their families is pursued through the synergistic action of all those who work directly and indirectly in the day centre. Plentiful recent research shows that resilience is not a purely individual capacity, as was previously thought, but involves the whole nuclear family. The association benefits from the continuous and regular collaboration of 30 expert volunteers who support the staff and the elderly. Most of the volunteers are elderly people who take care of other seniors, and in this way not only enhance their self-care skills, but also show the importance of self-care by implementing a form of intra-generational education for users of the day centre.

Data analysis: Data were analysed immediately after the transcription of the interviews. A deductive content analysis was carried out. A categorisation matrix was created on previously identified sub-categories (Elo and Kyngäs, 2008). Transcripts were read in an iterative process and data were coded according to the recognised sub-categories. Similar sub-categories were then gathered together to create more comprehensive content categories.

Trustworthiness: Four investigators reviewed the coding process and agreed on the analysis to establish dependability. A continuous discussion between members of the research group enhanced the confirmability of the analysis process (Graneheim and Lundman, 2004).

Ethical consideration: This study was approved by the Ethics Committee of the Campus Bio-Medico di Roma University. An information letter was provided to all study participants to explain the aim of the study and informed consent was obtained. The contact details of the researchers involved in the study were provided in case the participants needed more information or had psychological issues during the interviews. During the interviews, participants were free to not respond to questions they wished to omit. All data obtained from interviews were anonymised and treated as confidential.

Results

The analysis of the 14 interviews generated five categories: *the residence: a safe and quiet place; need for privacy; contact with reality; freedom of choice;* and *keeping human interaction.*

The residence: A safe and quiet place

The residence is considered a safe place by the elderly. A place where they can be quiet and be themselves. The residence should be an "elderly friendly" place where they can live their daily lives in full freedom. This place should have at least one lift that enables older people (whether or not they have trouble with walking) to move around autonomously. Or, better still, there should be no stairs. The residents must be able to explore their new home, to get to know every corner of it, so that they can feel it as their own.

> *It would be better not to have the stairs to not have to go up and down. [P12]*

In the residence, there must also be a comfortable dining room that allows the elderly to enjoy their shared meals, which must be of good quality. Mealtimes are very important to the elderly because there is nothing more family-like and intimate than eating with somebody. They also see company during meals as a key element that makes them feel good.

> *Eating alone makes me sad. [P14]*

Contact with nature: time spent in and around tree-lined streets, gardens, parks, and forested and agricultural lands is consistently linked to objective, long-term health outcomes (Kuo, 2015).

The elderly in particular seem to agree with this view, and appreciate and require the presence of green spaces inside the residence.

> *The residence should have a little garden, terrace . . . in short, a bit of green!* [P12]

According to the elderly, in order to become a home, the residence should be a place where they feel safe and secure, where facilities are elderly friendly and comfortable:

> *If there is comfort for the elderly, in short, things that make life a bit restful, a bit quiet, because it is said to be a little rough, somewhat sacrificed in so many ways!* [P1]

It must also be a serene, familiar, and welcoming environment:

> *Familiar! Like at home, familiar, serene. That would be the ideal environment.* [P16]

And, finally, light in the rooms and fresh air in the residence are extremely important for the elderly:

> *A sociable environment that treats us well. If you are treated well in an environment it is logical that you like to stay there. It must be an airy building, a building where, let's say, if one wants a little rest there has to be a bed, there must be an armchair, there must be television . . . these things that make you stay active because if there isn't, it's like . . . you're dead!* [P3]

Need for privacy

Living in a residence together with other people brings to mind in the elderly the fundamental need for privacy, understood as the need for protecting their intimacy. Every person in his/her home has full control over his/her privacy. Instead, in a residence, the presence of other rhythms, other environments, and other people leads to the loss of this control. The elderly manifest the need to recover it by choosing a single room that preserves their intimacy and protects them from strangers.

> *I would like a room of my own, otherwise I will not go, because I do not feel like living with a stranger. No, I do not like it.* [P11]

Contact with reality

The external reality in a residence may become increasingly strange with the passing of time. In the residence, each of the elderly re-creates their own environment, their small reality, and they can often lose contact with the outside world. Thus, the elderly could feel alienated and away from the events surrounding them. Their life before residency becomes a remembrance. It is therefore essential for them to participate in activities or to take action that creates a link between the reality within the home and the outside world. One of the activities suggested by the elderly is shared reading and discussion of newspapers in the morning. But also, activities of daily living that imitate the activities they used to do previously in their home.

> *I'd love to do what I do at my home! I live alone with a dog and a cat. Then, I get up in the morning, I see if they want to eat, if the litter is clean, if they have some water, I stroke them, talk to them, sit down to rest, listen to music, switch on television. Then, some phone calls, some friend who comes to see me and with whom I can talk. [P12]*

In addition, excursions, trips, and opportunities for a family holiday can help the elderly to keep the sense of contact with people, places, and environments outside the residence. Also, they can help them to maintain vitality by exploring new places and making new experiences.

> *So . . . you go out, you live, you go out for a short excursion . . . I could not visit many places because I had a very hard life! And now it seems like a dream to me that I can see the world, see the museums for example. [P1]*

Freedom of choice

When thinking about moving to a long-term facility, the elderly think that having the opportunity of choosing freely between different activities and interpersonal relationships plays a pivotal role. This theme is central among participants; in particular, the possibility of moving to a long-term facility is a self-determined choice made not to be a burden for the family in case of need. Long-term facilities are viewed by participants as a good alternative when elderly live alone, as they can socialise, stay with people, and share their daily life with them.

> *In a future, when I will be alone, I could move to a long-term facility as I would like to stay with other people, socialize, speak . . . to be helped in everyday life and have someone to cheer up with. [P1]*

Even though the choice of moving to a long-term facility is easier if shared between the family members, the elderly do not want their family carers to push them to make a choice that they dislike. The elderly want to choose on their own, and to continue to be as independent as they can. Even when moving to a long-term facility is considered a good choice, the elderly perceive this as break from family ties.

> *Moving to a long-term facility means going away from home, and going away from home means being out of the family . . . doesn't it? [P12]*

Maintaining the usual pace of life while living in a long-term facility is reported as a milestone of a successful stay in a long-term facility. Participants reported the urge to keep control of the schedule of their daily activities. Moreover, they want to continue to decide for themselves which activities to participate in, and the people they want to keep in contact with to have a good quality of life.

> *It depends on one's expectation, being obliged to go to hear a conference or a debate that she doesn't care about is bad. Even if you want to play cards and you cannot, or listen to some music and others say "you cannot," worsens your quality of life. [P12]*

The freedom to choose between a variety of different activities contributes to a sense of self-determination. The activities available should reflect the spare capacities and preferences of people living in a long-term facility. The continuous involvement of the elderly in the care environment helps to attribute a meaning to their reshaped everyday life.

> *I am not able to do many activities, for example, I can't sew . . . other elderly women can . . . but even if I don't sew I like to be with other people, and talk with them!!! [P10]*

Keep human interaction

Participants described two main types of human interaction: interaction among elderly people living in the same facility, and between the elderly and the health personnel. In particular, living in a long-term facility is fundamental to maintaining sociability and making new friends. In all the interviews, it is reported how having satisfactory relationships gives the elderly identity and a sense of community. However, sometimes sharing spaces and experiences with other people with different temperaments can be challenging.

> *The temperament is fundamental, as I'm very friendly, everyone helps me in many ways . . . but in long-term facilities, you can find someone who bothers you. [P8]*

Being with other people helps to distract the elderly from their problems. Furthermore, the possibility of sharing experiences could help them to put things into perspective. Even helping other people in need and being helped in return by others are pleasant activities.

> *Doing little services is nice, if a friend is down I would like to meet her to take a coffee, or if I'm in need I think that a friend comes and visits me . . . when you see other elderly more sick than me, I feel better!!! [P11]*

The relationship between health care professionals and aged people is also expected to be of central importance. The participants described the need for staff who are not only professionally competent, but also able to make the elderly feel at home. Health care professionals should treat the elderly as humans.

> *In long-term facilities, I would like to find a family atmosphere, because we lived with a family and in these facilities, you nurses will be our family . . . and you have to treat us well! [P3]*

In particular, participants considered it essential that health care professionals present in long-term facilities are, on the one hand, trained and competent in elderly care. On the other hand, nurses and assistants have to be smiling and cheerful; it could even be useful to have young personnel to help produce a joyful atmosphere. In contrast, other participants required qualified and expert health care professionals, as they have to be vigilant and anticipate the needs of elderly people.

> *I would like to find smiley people, people able to laugh, able to feel when you need to talk with someone, but able not to talk if you don't want to . . . Staff have to be young but experienced, trained for working with the elderly . . . you know, they have to understand our needs. [P12]*

Discussion

The aim of this study was to explore what contributes to the feeling of the "sense of home," and what are the housing needs of elderly people. In this study, 14 older adults who do not live in residential care facilities were questioned about which factors could contribute to a good/bad experience of living in a hypothetical residence. Our findings show that to generate a sense of home, the physical environment should offer opportunities for people to obtain satisfaction within the environment, such as opportunities to carry out activities, to do things that make people joyful, and opportunities for personal growth, in accordance with Gustafson (2001) and Manzo (2003). In fact, the five categories generated from the interviews, *a safe and quiet place; need for privacy; contact with reality; freedom of choice;* and *keeping human interaction* are all related with the physical environment.

A "sense of home" is a complex and multifactorial phenomenon, linked to a sense of identity and wellbeing (van Hoof, 2015). In fact, our results underline the importance of personalising their rooms or feeling free to interact with co-residents and nursing staff when and how they want. All of these elements strengthen the sense of identity in line with Falk et al. (2013), who found the following strategies constructed a sense of home for older people:

- *Attachment to space* consisted of three dimensions: taking part in activities with others, expressing personality, and making friends. In this way, an important factor for the creation of attachment to space was the ability to make independent decisions about activities and social relationships.

- *Attachment to place* included two dimensions: nesting and being in charge. Nesting allows the elderly to personalise and privatise their own room; being in charge enables them to decide whom to include or not include in their daily life.
- *Attachments beyond the institution*: communication with family members and friends outside the residence is fundamental "*to pursue their self-determined goals and to keep up appearances*."

Finally, our results confirm that social factors such as relations with staff, interaction with other residents, interaction with family and friends, and activities not only play a pivotal role in the wellbeing of older people, but are also factors that compose a sense of home (Rijnaard et al., 2016).

Conclusion

Feeling at home in an elderly residential facility is not always easy. Very often their bond with their own home, their environment, and objects connected with their life memories make it difficult for elderly people to feel at home in another environment. At other times, the elderly feel they have been abandoned and forced to live in a residence. This does not favour their integration and stay in the facility, but such integration is crucial from the physical and psychological point of view, and for the quality of life of the elderly. Factors hindering them from "feeling at home" can be multiple, and many strategies can be adopted to facilitate the successful integration of elderly people in residential homes.

This study is a first step towards understanding what an elderly person means by "feeling at home," and how to re-create this intimate and caring environment that we all call home. Our results underline the importance of the sense of independence for older people: they want to be respected in their choices and to maintain their residual autonomy. To do this, they should be left free to re-create their own home environment. It is important that managers of residential care facilities become aware of this in order to improve the experience of being in the residence for older people, which in turn contributes to their quality of life and wellbeing.

Implication for practice

The findings of this study need to be viewed in the context of health care and policy. Enhancing a *sense of home* in residential care facilities is of fundamental importance for the wellbeing and autonomy of older people (Board and McCormack, 2018). To this end, health care professionals working in residential care facilities should be trained to invest time in building helping relationships with residents to better meet their psychological and social needs (Westin and Danielson, 2007). In addition, policies related to nursing home organisation and construction methods should take into account the needs of residents as derived from literature data such as this study.

References

Allen, I. (1992). *Elderly people: choice, participation and satisfaction*. Policy Studies Institute, London. Chapter 8.

Argandoña, A. (ed.). (2018). *The home: multidisciplinary reflections*. Edward Elgar Publishing, Cheltenham.

Biedenharn, P. J., & Normoyle, J. B. (1991). Elderly community residents' reactions to the nursing home: An analysis of nursing home related beliefs. *The Gerontologist*, 31, 107–115.

Board, M., & McCormack, B. (2018). Exploring the meaning of home and its implications for the care of older people. *Journal of Clinical Nursing*, 27(15–16), 3070–3080.

Brody, J. A., & Grant, M. D. (2001). Age-associated diseases and conditions: Implications for decreasing late life morbidity. *Aging Clinical and Experimental Research*, 13(2), 64–67.

Cristoforetti, A., Cennai, F., & Rodeschini, C. (2011). Home sweet home: The emotional construction of places. *Journal of Aging Studies*, 25(3), 225–232.

Després, C., & Lord, S. (2005). Growing older in postwar suburbs: The meaning and experience of home. In G. D. Rowles & H. Chaudhury (eds.), *Home and Identity in Late Life–International Perspectives*. Springer, New York, pp. 317–340.

Dovey, K. (1985). Home and homelessness in human behavior and environment: Advances in theory and research. In I. Altman & C. M. Werner (eds.), *Home environments* (Vol. 8). Plenum Press, New York, pp. 33–64.

Edwards, H., Courtney, M., & O'Reilly, M. (2003). Involving older people in research to examine quality of life in residential aged care. *Quality in Ageing: Policy, Practice and Research*, 4, 38–43.

Elo, S., & Kyngäs, H. (2008). The qualitative content analysis process. *Journal of Advanced Nursing*, 62, 107–115.

Falk, H., Wijk, H., & Persson, L. O. (2013). A sense of home in residential care. *Scandinavian Journal of Caring Science*, 27(4), 999–1009.

Gillsjo, C., & Schwartz-Barcott, D. (2009). A concept analysis of home and its meaning in the lives of three older adults. *International Journal of Older People Nursing*, 6, 4–12.

Graneheim, U. H., & Lundman, B. (2004). Qualitative content analysis in nursing research: Concepts, procedures and measures to achieve trustworthiness. *Nurse Education Today*, 24, 105–112.

Guba, E. G., & Lincoln, Y. S. (1994). Competing paradigms in qualitative research. In N. K. Denzin & Y. S. Lincoln (eds.), *Handbook of qualitative research*. Thousand Oaks, CA, pp. 105–117.

Gustafson, P. (2001). Meanings of place: Everyday experience and theoretical conceptualizations. *Journal of Environmental Psychology*, 21, 5–16.

Kuo, M. (2015). How might contact with nature promote human health? Promising mechanisms and a possible central pathway. *Frontiers in Psychology*, 6, 1093.

Lawrence, R. J. (1995). Deciphering home: An integrative historical perspective. In D. N. Benjamin & D. Stea (eds.), *The home: Words, interpretations, meanings, and environments*. Avebury, Aldershot, pp. 53–68.

Lee, D. T. F. (1997). Residential care placement: Perceptions among elderly Chinese people in Hong Kong. *Journal of Advanced Nursing*, 26, 602–607.

Lee, V., Simpson, J., & Froggatt, K. (2013). A narrative exploration of older people's transitions into residential care. *Aging & Mental Health*, 17(1), 48–56.

Manzo, L. (2003). Beyond house and haven: Toward a revisioning of emotional relationships with places. *Journal of Environmental Psychology*, 23, 47–61.

Moore, J. (2000). Placing home in context. *Journal of Environmental Psychology*, 20, 207–217.

Nolan, M., Walker, G., Nolan, J., Williams, S., Poland, F., Curran, M., & Kent, B. C. (1996). Entry to care: Positive choice or fait accompli? Developing a more proactive nursing response to the needs of older people and their carers. *Journal of Advanced Nursing*, 24, 265–274.

Palinkas, L. A., Horwitz, S. M., Green, C. A., Wisdom, J. P., Duan, N., & Hoagwood, K. (2015). Purposeful sampling for qualitative data collection and analysis in mixed method implementation research. *Administration and Policy in Mental Health and Mental Health Services Research*, 42(5), 533–544.

Patton, M. (1990). *Qualitative evaluation and research methods*. Thousand Oaks, CA, Sage.

Pennacchini, M. (2015). *L'interesse in John Dewey e l'educazione dell'anziano*. Armando, Roma.

Rapoport, A. (1988). Levels of meaning in the built environment. In F. Poyatos (ed.), *Cross-cultural perspectives in nonverbal communication*. Hogrefe, Toronto, pp. 317–336.

Rapoport, A. (1995). A critical look at the concept home. In D. N. Benjamin, D. Stea, & D. Saile (eds.), *The home: Words, interpretations, meanings, and environments*. Avebury, Aldershot, pp. 25–53.

Rijnaard, M. D., van Hoof, J., Janssen, B. M., Verbeek, H., Pocornie, W., Eijkelenboom, A., Beerens, H. C., Molony, S. L., & Wouters, E. J. M. The factors influencing the sense of home in nursing homes: A systematic review from the perspective of residents. *Journal of Aging Research*, 2016, Article ID 6143645.

Rozzini, R., Frisoni, G. B., Ferrucci, L., Barbisoni, P., Bertozzi, B., & Trabucchi, M. (1997). The effect of chronic diseases on physical function. Comparison between activities of daily living scales and the physical performance test. *Age and Ageing*, 26(4), 281–287.

Saunders, P. (1989). The meaning of "Home" in contemporary English culture. *Housing Studies*, 4, 177–198.

van Hoof, J., Verhagen, M. M., Wouters, E. J., Marston, H. R., Rijnaard, M. D., & Janssen, B. M. (2015). Picture your nursing home: Exploring the sense of home of older residents through photography. *Journal of Aging Research*, 2015, Article ID 312931.

Wagner, G. (1988). *Residential care: A positive choice. report of the independent review of residential care*. London: HMSO.

Wahl, H. W., & Lang, F. R. (2003). Aging in context across the adult life course: Integrating physical and social environmental research perspectives. In H. W. Wahl, R. J. Scheidt, & P. G. Windley (eds.), *Annual review of gerontology and geriatrics*. Springer Publishing Company, New York, pp. 1–33.

Westin, L., & Danielson, E. (2007). Encounters in Swedish nursing homes: A hermeneutic study of residents' experiences. *Journal of Advanced Nursing*, 60(2), 172–180.

World Health Organization. (2015). *World report on aging and health*. World Health Organization, Geneva.

Part 3

Home and work

Feature Article three

UpToYou, emotional education for personal growth in the early years Educating interior dispositions

José Víctor Orón Semper

Introduction

UpToYou is a proposal of emotional education (www.uptoyoueducacion.com) that directly influences family coexistence and the way parents interact with their children and the spouses among them, as reported by the testimonies of the people who have done the training (see web). In the present chapter we will present the basis of the proposal of UpToYou in the development of the first years of the child's life promoting health and the emotional development of children.

Childhood is the time to lay the foundations that will be the starting point for future life, as the studies of psychoanalysis clearly show: "everything starts at home" (Winnicott, 1986). The dispositions acquired at that time towards oneself will last throughout life. This educational key is not usually considered in the day to day of the family when a family focuses on behaviour (behaviour routines) and not on those interior dispositions. For example, a child is playing and it is time to eat. When the father or mother tells the child that it is time to eat and the child wants to continue playing, conflict arises. The child lives a correction and a frustration. We could ask ourselves what is the most important thing: that the child learns to sit down early to eat or that the child knows how to deal with frustration? We will see that it is one thing to educate pretending to acquire behaviours, and a completely different thing to educate pretending to learn how to situate oneself before the person's inner complexity. It does not mean that you do not have to pay attention to behaviour, but that if you focus primarily and exclusively on the behaviour, it can generate contrary provisions to it. Besides, if you learn to deal with frustration you will learn not only how to sit down to eat, but also to face other common and varied experiences of frustration that we encounter throughout life. It was Erikson who explained how, in fact, during the first years of a child's life they acquire a series of dispositions both towards themselves and towards the world (Erikson, 1963).

UpToYou wants to invest in the future child's life and focuses on educating to generate appropriate dispositions in diverse emotional situations. In this sense, from a general perspective, we seek that the person gets to know themselves starting from the emotional reality they live, and, secondly, that they learn to make choices considering the complexity of different decisions (Orón Semper, 2016). But, in the first years of life, there are not many decisions to make. Instead, as we shall see, it is a time when the child will grow a lot in self-knowledge based on his interaction with his mother and father. Therefore, what we can educate on are the proper dispositions towards oneself. In the first years of life, it is more important to educate about the dispositions than specific behaviours. For example, the psychoanalyst Winnicott comments that it is more important for the child to develop creative dispositions than being successful according to the adult's evaluation (Winnicott, 1986: 53). For instance, developing the initiative to move one object is more important than putting the object in the right place. These dispositions are going to be the rulers of your future behaviours and even thinking styles. Since the child, according to Piaget, reasons not according to conceptual chains, but according to psychological principles (Piaget, 1928: 91), at UpToYou we ask ourselves about the non-rational logic (psychological principles) that the child uses. From there, assuming it and making a proposal according to it.

Let's go deeper now to discover the child's logic, and his way of understanding the world and himself, to end up showing an educational proposal of emotional education in childhood according to this investigation.

The development of the child in trust, attachment, and social reference

Erikson, whose studies are very relevant in the field of the psychosocial development of the human being, pointed out (1963) that in the first two years of life, the child lives a series of experiences that will lead him to adopt an attitude of basic trust or basic distrust. If the child discovers that his needs are known and met by the caregiver, father or mother, the child will grow in basic confidence. If the experience is that these needs are not covered or only some are covered – for example, only the physical ones, but not the psychological ones (playing, caressing, etc., which implies spending time interacting with the child) – then the configuration that child acquires is basic distrust according to the type care missing. Basic trust and basic mistrust are two models, between which there are all types of gradation. It is called basic trust because it refers to a basic disposition of the child to the world and to himself or herself and it would mean that basically he or she can trust what is presented to him or to her and does not adopt any defensive posture. The basic distrust would lead to the opposite disposition.

In the 1980s, new literature in psychology illustrated the power of the affective bonds between the mother and the child showing how the child learned a concrete evaluation of the context in relation with the mother's understanding of the world, and also in relation with the quality of the relationship between the mother and the child. The first is called "social referencing," and the second "attachment theory." Children appreciate the emotional meaning of the affective samples of caregivers. Not as mere modulators, but as what allows or impedes the development of the child (Tronick, 1989). Experimentation discovered that the communication was fundamentally due to the visual triangle son-carer-object by which the child learns the meaning and guides its behaviour based on the facial expression of the caregiver. This phenomenon coined the term "social reference" (Walden and Ogan, 1988). In attachment theory, Trevarthen, a reference author in psychology who has been studying this phenomenon for years, said that attachment is not a simple matter of feeling safe, but is the basis in order to get to know the world and to reach a meaning (Colwyn, 2005).

Studies on "social reference" discover that, in humans, the social is not simply the environment in which learning takes place. In such a case, the social would be just one more modulator more among many, simply because learning happens in that context. But that would be an understatement. The social is a guarantee of significance. The presence of the other human being makes the world significant and valuable enough to be known. For example, learning a language for young children requires the presence of the person (Kuhl et al., 2003), otherwise the sounds of language are treated as noise. For the young child, things have no meaning by themselves, but their meaning is taken, we could say "borrowed," from the emotional reaction of the adult. This is the theoretical basis of the "social reference" most evident in situations of ambiguity (Klinnert et al., 1986, Mireault et al., 2014, Pelaez et al., 2012), although we might think that when something new is presented it has an ambiguous character. The social reference will not only provide emotional meaning to the world of objects or events, but also to other people, because if the mother engages in positive communication, the child will also welcome the stranger positively (Feinman and Lewis, 1983). It is possible that this explains that the social reference is affected by the marital satisfaction expressed by the father (Dickstein and Parke, 1988), since in the usual social context, the mother presents the father to the child. The influence of social reference in form and intensity will change throughout life (Striano and Rochat, 2000, Walden and Baxter, 1989, Walden and Ogan, 1988). The social reference also explains the phenomenon of emotional "contagion" of the emotional experience of the mother to the child in pathological cases (Rosnay et al., 2006; Pelaez et al., 2013). Therefore, the social reference is giving meaning to objects, events, and personal relationships.

Attachment theory, which is closely related to what Erikson pointed out about basic trust or mistrust (Pittman et al., 2011), has not changed since the 1980s. The emotional attachment of the child who feels safe and protected by his parents enables him to exercise his search of the world under the paradigm of exploratory curiosity (Carson, 2012, Hong and Park, 2012, L'Ecuyer, 2014). Current research shows how the child's dependence on the mother affects not only the healthy development of the child, but also the child's psychopathologies. The mother passes her psycho-emotional state to the child. A longitudinal study of children aged 0 to 11 years verified that exposure to early and chronic maternal depression significantly increases a child's susceptibility to psychopathology and socio-emotional problems, including social withdrawal, bad emotional experiences, and reduced empathy towards others. When the mother is not in a depressed state, it is evident that the greater the mother-child synchrony, the better cerebral functioning of the child. Sadly, statistics indicate that 15–18% of women in industrial societies and up to 30% in developing countries suffer from maternal depression (Pratt et al., 2017).

There are other series of studies that clearly support similar conclusions. The depth of the bonds of the mother or primary caregiver with her son or daughter, and the social sensitivity of the child with the mother and vice versa, are no longer doubted. The brain of mothers is especially sensitive to the crying of their children, which activates the relevant areas to detect the intention of behaviour (Bornstein et al., 2017). We have cells sensitive to caress and these (not touching or rubbing) lower the pulsations of the heart, relaxing the child while increasing brain activity (Jönsson and Emma, 2017). The sensitivity of a mother towards her child affects the mother's own brain function (Atzil et al., 2017) and the same with the child. Maternal sensitivity and maternal genetics affect the emotional configuration of the child (Zhang et al., 2014). The way in which the parents care for their children conditions the affection, sociability, and brain configuration of the latter (Silk et al., 2014).

All these investigations and theories lead to the fact that there is no neutral access of the child to the world, but rather that the child projects the quality of the caregiver-child relationship onto the world. We could say that the mother or primary caregiver "lends" her mind to the child. We understand "mind" in this case as the way to understand the world. That is, the child knows the world based on the presentation made by the mother. For example, if the mother presents a ball to the child, the child will hold the ball in a trusting relationship and will not see the ball as a hostile object. The child projects onto the object the relationship of trust or distrust it has with the mother. However, not only does it serve to know the world, but also oneself. The way the child is treated is the basis for knowing himself. Therefore, the way to access the world and oneself is always a social access. Even if the child is alone, the child's social relationships are equally present.

That is, the dynamic of trust makes the child perceive the new thing with astonishment and makes him want know more about it. The dynamic of distrust makes the child perceive the new thing with some mistrust and look for a way to feel safe in the face of this unknown thing, which is more or less hostile. But in a child's emotional experience, what is new for the child, the object to be known, is the same child. For this reason, we need to go deeper in the child's emotional experience.

The emotional development

Katherine Bridges (1932) already showed the process by which the child is gaining expressiveness in his emotional repertoire. Contrary to what is usually believed, Bridges postulated that there are no basic emotions (joy, sadness, fear, disgust, and anger), but the child is simply born with a capacity for basic excitability. Bridges assumes that we can recognise that the child differentiates two different emotional situations if he or she offers different bodily expressions. For example, if something disgusts, scares, or hurts him or her, and the child has the same body reaction, it means that the child does not distinguish between disgust, fear, or pain. Bridges observed that at birth, the child has the same corporal expression before any event. Very soon he learns to differentiate the unpleasant from the pleasant. At this moment, their differentiation and emotional knowledge is simply dual: pleasant-unpleasant. But, for example, everything pleasant – being satiated after eating or the caresses of the mother – is not differentiated since they have the same corporal expression. This Bridges proposal is similarly followed, more or less, by other authors (Campos et al., 1989, Jack et al., 2014). But the key point is that this emotional development is not merely driven by biological processes but also social, cognitive, intentional processes, etc.

The baby needs to understand that duality, which requires a cognitive exercise to understand the sources of the pleasant and the unpleasant, and to reconcile experiences. That is, the emotional and cognitive development concur at the same time as the child has to know the world to recognise the cause, so the child knows oneself and knows the world at the same time. It is a *pari passu* process. The child knows the world and expresses what is known in his or her emotional experience. Thus, the child knows what is pleasant and unpleasant because the child needs to reach a coherent interpretation and relates these two experiences, which in turn allows them to differentiate and identify them, and this process allows their own maturational development.

Other authors support the same theory. To the extent that the child relates the diversity lived and integrates emotional diversity, at the same time, the ability to differentiate and identify emotional situations will arise and thus its development and growth will proceed. That is, integration, differentiation, identity, and growth co-occur through the emotional reality of the child (Camras, 2011). That is, emotional development is not biologically programmed but instead depends on the social interaction and the child's own inner activity. After two years, with the appearance of language, the child will have to make a similar but much more socially complex journey to acquire a different emotional linguistic expression (Lewis, 2007).

Towards the educational proposal

We will connect what Erikson indicated, the theory of attachment and social reference, with what Bridges showed in order to make a proposal of emotional education within the family. What is suggested is that the state of basic trust will allow the baby to make a path of differentiation much closer to reality, because it approaches it without prevention. It is being educated in some provisions that will allow a better development. Astonishment, amazement, or wonder does not seek to control, but to know reality as it is. We could say that the wonder approach facilitates unintentional and respectful knowledge. In contrast, the situation of basic mistrust makes the child not approach the world from an attitude of amazement or wonder, but of distrust, and therefore his approach will be intentional because he or she will want to identify to control, to feel safe.

That is, when the path of identification progresses, the emotions are not a mere affective question of reaction to the stimulus, but they are actually the crystallisation or condensation of a whole-body, intentional, emotional, social, and cognitive experience. Emotion is, therefore, a condensation of the understanding of personal experience in the world and in a social network (Jack et al., 2014). Well, as we have already indicated, it is known that the child identifies and gives meaning to reality in terms of the relationship he or she has with the mother. The reactions of the mother's behaviour serve the child to identify the emotional meaning of the different events.

The disposition that the child acquires about his own emotional reality will be key in adulthood. In order to support this idea, we need to introduce the experience of Carl Rogers (1961) as psychotherapist. Adults who live in mistrust do not recognise their feelings as their own, nor can they think that those feelings are due to something that happens in them. But feelings are provoked by something external and feelings occur in oneself, but they do not belong to the person properly. Feelings happen in the person, but they do not belong to the person because they are a mere reaction to what happens outside of the person. Thinking that way, people do not accept responsibility for their feelings or behaviour. And they take a defensive position towards the world and to their emotional reality.

Certainly, Rogers is speaking from adult therapy, but he indicates what it is necessary to live in a state of health, and I believe that same internal dispositions are needed for every age. That is, the state of health involves recognising feelings as their own and not as merely awakened "from outside." Only then will the person take responsibility.

Roger points out that the person needs to welcome or accept inner complexity. Thanks to this, the client can discover the world of meaning. In such a case, emotions no longer need to be controlled. They are fine as they are, because they "talk" about the complexity of one's life and from them one can grow in self-knowledge. Denying or controlling an emotion would literally prevent growth in one's knowledge, which would lead to situations of unreality. It is not proposed to control, but to receive and accept in order to know them. When the person accepts without wanting to change, then the change occurs without being noticed (Rogers, 2000: 28). This requires the client to perceive that the therapist accepts his emotional reality without trying to change it. The reception of the therapist enables the client to accept its complexity. Without the acceptance of one's own reality, there is no possibility for growth.

Two proposals of emotional education

This brief journey is drawing us a double perspective in the face of emotional education that coincides with the two basic approaches that are being proposed today on the emotional issue: emotional regulation focused on the control and acquisition of routines, and emotional integration focused on the reception and development of adequate provisions. The "emotional regulation" is the prevailing approach (Gross, 2014, Vohs and Baumeister, 2011). This proposal seeks to identify the emotion to channel it. In such a case, emotions occur in oneself, but outside one's own subjectivity, because it is thought that an external stimulus is what has caused that emotion. Looking at is this way, it is normal that the elimination of the stimulus is proposed, or, if this is not possible, a psychological resource is sought to increase the distance to the stimulus.

In the family environment and with the child, this approach to emotional regulation is concretised in a control of the stimulus and in a control of the internal reactions in the presence of the stimulus. The mentality with which the situation is addressed is that of "solving problems." This mentality assumes that before the problem everything was fine and the event has generated a problem and we must intervene to recover the previous situation. For instance, the child was calm, but now has a tantrum in the supermarket, so we need to recover the previous calm. But we think that focusing on education to avoid problems (the tantrum) is not educating the person to develop. The child does not know what a tantrum and the frustration associated with it is, but if the child notices that the mother does not like it, the child will learn that it is bad and will try to remove it (self-regulation). He or she will be scared from the frustration experience and does not want to learn what a frustration is because the child just wants to remove it. Attitudes of self-control are not the necessary attitudes for personal development.

The approach of emotional regulation ignores the complexity of the formation of emotions described by Bridges because it attributes the emotion to the stimulus and assumes Erikson's model of basic mistrust that seeks to control what is around. Bridges helps us to understand that emotion does not arise from stimulus, because the significance of the stimulus depends on the cognitive, social, and experiential development that the child has had. Without discovering the complexity of that process, the reason for a behaviour cannot be known. Emotional regulation proposal is contradicted by what Rogers indicated: a child will only recognise as his own what an adult accepts. And it also ignores what is shown by the social reference that the child projects on the object (in this case, the same person of the child) the meaning of the adult. Besides, attachment theory contradicts emotional regulation because the child will not develop a secure attachment since he or she is the cause of the mother's discomfort.

Another approach, which we will call "emotional integration," follows the line of Erikson's basic trust and the theory of attachment and the complexity of the emotional world shown by Bridges, and Roger's proposal of self-acceptance and what is indicated by the Social Reference. In this line, emotions are the condensation or crystallisation of a vital state at a specific moment in one person. The child lives in confidence and is astonished by the emotional and unknown reality lived, but does not feel the need to control them, because they do not perceive the world as hostile. The unknown world is not harmful, so I do not need to protect myself from that. And in an emotional experience, the new world to be known is oneself. In emotional integration, the approach to the emotional reality is much more respectful because it allows to ask oneself: what is all that happens in me? And why does it happen?

Threat does not awake desire of knowing but desire of controlling. Reality is known when we approach it from an amazement, astonishment, or wonder disposition, not from a control disposition. Wonder approach can know and respect the reality as it is, without trying to manipulate it because the encounter is worthy. This way all the nuances of the emotion are discovered and also the causes for that.

It is not advisable to propose reconciliation between the "emotion regulation" and "emotional integration" because, philosophically speaking, these positions are described as "contrary non contradictory" (Altarejos, 2004). They are "contrary" because those who bet on one reject the other. And they are "not contradictory" because they both develop human proactivity, but from very different frames.

We think that, if we bear in mind the theory of attachment and social reference, together with the healthy dynamic of trust that Erikson indicated, along with the need to believe in the acceptance of the emotional reality that Rogers showed and complexity of emotional development that Bridges showed, we discover that the most coherent proposal of emotional education is emotional integration, since it takes place in the climate of acceptance and awe and appreciation and intensification of social relationships as the child needs. In this case, control is not sought, but rather the acceptance of the complexity of interpersonal relationships.

That is, just as the child needs the mother to introduce the outside world, the same should be assumed in relation to the inner world. In such a case, with the behaviour of the mother before the emotions of the child, the mother is telling the child what his emotional reality is. The emotional world of the child appears as something unknown by the child himself, but if the mother accepts the emotional reality of the child in an environment that safeguards the interpersonal relationship, then the child can approach his own emotional reality with ease, in a dynamic of amazement, to get to know its interior and grow in self-knowledge.

But if the main caregiver reacts to the emotional situation of the child as if it were something tragic (which is usually shown when adults try to avoid problems), he will perceive his own emotional situation as something negative and disruptive that will have to be controlled to eliminate, which prevents self-knowledge and the acceptance of one's own reality.

UpToYou's proposal

This proposal is in line with emotional integration and generates the suitable dispositions. UpToYou (www.uptoyoueducacion.com) is an educative program that understands that the emotions are information on the convenience of all the elements of the complexity in a concrete person at a certain time.

This program understands that emotional education consists of helping the person to consider their given emotional situation as a starting point for personal growth within the paradigm of personal integration. As an educative program, it has its own way of understanding what education means (Orón Semper, 2018).

In a schematic way, UpToYou points out that feelings are, in the first place, result or effect, because who lives as one lives (vital state) and does what one does and how one does it (event), then, one feels what feels (feelings). The cited authors' research discovers a complex game of social interactions in the emotional experience. In outline, it would be as follows:

Life status (1) + Event (2) = Feeling (3)

This formula is a simplification because the reality is that the event is not understood apart from the vital situation (life status). But feelings are not only results but also generate a trend. But the trend is subsidiary to the interpretation of feeling. For instance, if I understand frustration as something bad, it will promote one trend, but if I understand frustration as a normative experience of life, it will promote another trend.

The pedagogical proposal of the program has two steps: first, to help people to walk a "backwards" path, that is to say, to start from the feeling (3) to get to know the vital state (life status -1) and second, to promote people to face their vital state and make a decision about how to live while promoting personal growth and what is understood as to increase personal relationships with others. We call these two moments: "knowing the information" and "maximising the trend" (Orón Semper, 2015). The first moment ends when all the causes of a specific feeling are known and people learn the intrinsic logic of feeling and inner complexity. The second moment ends when people make a decision to do a global-personal act (Orón Semper, 2017) facing the issue of identity that entails personal growth.

This process is really an endless process, as it introduces the young person into a spiral of growth, because after global-personal acts, a new life status (1') will emerge and with new events (2') and other feelings (3') will show up and the process begins again. This is how the person is introduced to unrestricted growth.

Now, although the dynamic is always the same, it is not done in the same way in different moments of life since the capacities and dispositions of the person are different. Let's focus on seeing how UpToYou understands the proposal for the first years of life.

While the model of regulation applied to young children seeks to acquire specific behaviours, the integration model seeks to educate in appropriate inner dispositions that promote growth. The problem is the difficulty of characterising what growth means.

While acquiring a specific behaviour can be clearly characterised as an objective, and it can be evaluated if it has been reached or not, we find that growth cannot be categorised as an objective since it is not identifiable as a particular purpose. For characterising growth, let us see how different philosophers and psychologists understand it. The philosopher Leonardo Polo (2007) pointed out that growth is unrestricted and not in any particular direction, but in that which allows the human being to reach what he is called to be, which is recognised in the development of his personal transcendentals (co-existence personal, personal freedom, personal knowledge, and personal love). In addition, he also shows a dynamic of accepting what is received to deliver it. It means welcoming what we are and delivering ourselves to others. Wang Yangming (Frisina, 2002), neocunfunciónist of the fifteenth century, proposes that the growth is played in winning in harmony between everything created uniting sky and earth. Whitehead (Frisina, 2002), mathematician and philosopher, proposes to understand growth as maximising experience that is fundamentally relational. Carl Rogers (2000) points out that the starting point of the reception is followed by the response to the call to be what one is called to be. Victor Frankl (1991) emphasises the call to the meaning of life and personal devotion. Erikson (1959, 1997) discovers in personal identity the theme that accompanies and invigorates all of life. Kohlberg (Kohlberg and Mayer, 1972) picks Piaget's indication that a stage is superior to the previous one because it allows for a better resolution of complexity; Kohlberg applies it to the moral realm, and says that moral development makes it possible to better solve social conflict, and it facilitates reconciliation and social growth. In all of these authors, growth cannot be identified by a point, but as an improvement of interpersonal relationships being creative in complex situations. But it does not mean that all development is growth. For example, a type of development that divides the personal life into sectors is not a growth.

The regulatory model applied to the small child would be as follows:

- **Point of arrival defined**. There is a starting point characterised by an emotional situation and with a disruptive behaviour, and the point of arrival is determined by emotional situation with an associated defined behaviour (routine).
- **The regulator changes to the regulated while it remains stable.** The caregivers act so that the child changes and reaches the preset behaviour by regulators, but caregivers do not undergo any change.
- **Problem vision**. The starting point is seen as a problem that needs to be fixed. Seeing it as a problem implies that action steps are detection, definition of the point of arrival, and action.
- **Process with end.** Once the problem is over and a new emotional situation is reached, the intervention stops until a new disruption.

The integrative model applied to the small child is explained as follows:

- **There are references, but no point of arrival.** The starting point is not a problem but a personal state and a normal life situation. There is not specific point of arrival, but the aim is to develop the appropriate dispositions about oneself and interaction skills with the mother through play.

- **Everyone changes, the caregiver and the child**. In the growth of a system, all the elements change by the relations between them. There is no sectoral growth.
- **Growth vision**. The personal situation is not considered a problem. There is nothing to correct, but to help to grow. While problem mentality seeks to go back to recover the lost equilibrium, growth mentality is always going forward, trying to improve or intensify personal relationships by taking advantage of the past event.
- **Endless process**. The process never ends because growth is always open. New events will be the excuse for starting again and, even more, caregivers will create new events for improving relationships.

The educational activity that the mother or father performs to achieve this also follows the two indicated steps of "knowing the information" and "maximising the trend." The child knows himself by projecting on the mother's way of understanding the child. Therefore, if the mother does not condition the reception of the child to the emotional behaviour of the child, then the child will acquire a disposition of amazement of himself that opens the door to a more detailed knowledge in the future. On the other hand, the education of children is carried out through play, as indicated by great references (Montessori, 2013, Piaget, 1965, Piaget et al., 1982, Vygotsky, 1978) because we are not facing behaviours that need to be corrected, but capacities that need to be developed. And the game's main rule is how to use the object for playing. It is meant for the enjoyment of the experience of being together. As the child has not developed one's agency yet, the key point is how the caregiver will creatively use the event (2) to improve personal relationships with the child (enjoying the experience of being together). We are not saying to not pay attention to the event: the tantrum when the child lives the frustration because they want to play when it is time to eat. In our proposal, the caregiver creatively uses the child's frustration (normal experience that we live all days) as an excuse for enjoying the experience of being together. It allows the child to reach a good internal disposition about one's frustration, to learn how to eat, and to improve relationships.

But, if the mother focuses on the acquisition of routines by acquiring behaviours, the child will not appreciate an unconditional reception of his or her person and, instead of a disposition of amazement, he or she will acquire a disposition of fear and distrust of oneself, which will lead him to exert control over himself and with it a prevention for future growth.

UpToYou understands that the acquisitions of routines are an effect of the game, but the goal is the game in itself. If the caregiver considers as an objective what an effect is, the person will be blocked for growth. It is pedagogically decisive not to confuse the objective and the effect.

This academic journey ends up proposing a double alternative way: the "emotional integration" that starts from amazement and leads to know and acquire adequate provisions for the growth, and the "emotional regulation" that starts from distrust and leads to the search for control and the acquisition of routines. We have also presented how UpToYou's pedagogy understands these ideas at theoretical level.

Bibliography

Altarejos, F. (2004). 'Autorregulación e integración: dos propuestas en la educación de la afectividad (D. Goleman y Tomás de Aquino)'. *Estudios sobre Educación*, *7*, 45–66.

Atzil, S., Touroutoglou, A., Rudy, T., Salcedo, S., Feldman, R., Hooker, J. M., . . . Barrett, L. F. (2017). 'Dopamine in the medial amygdala network mediates human bonding'. *Proceedings of the National Academy of Sciences of the United States of America*, *114*(9), 2361–2366.

Bornstein, M. H., Putnicka, D. L., Rigo, P., Esposito, G., Swaind, J. E., Suwalskya, J. T. D., . . . Venutib, P. (2017). 'Neurobiology of culturally common maternal responses to infant cry'. *Proceedings of the National Academy of Sciences*, *114*(45): E9465–E9473

Bridges, K. M. B. (1932). 'Emotional development in early infancy'. *Child Development*, *3*(4), 324–341.

Campos, J. J., Campos, R. G., & Barrett, K. C. (1989). 'Emergent themes in the study of emotional development and emotion regulation'. *Developmental Psychology*, *25*(3), 395–402.

Camras, L. a. (2011). 'Differentiation, dynamical integration and functional emotional development'. *Emotion Review*, *3*(2), 138–146.

Carson, R. (2012). *El sentido del asombro*. Madrid: Encuentro.

Colwyn, T. (2005). 'Stepping away from the mirror: Pride and shame in adventures of companionship'. In C. S. Carter, L. Ahnert, K. E. Grossman, S. Hardy, M. E. Lamb, S. W. Porges, & N. Sachser (Eds.), *Attachment and bonding: A new synthesis* (pp. 55–84). Cambridge, MA: The MIT Press.

de Rosnay, M., Cooper, P. J., Tsigaras, N., & Murray, L. (2006). 'Transmission of social anxiety from mother to infant: An experimental study using a social referencing paradigm'. *Behaviour Research and Therapy*, *44*(8), 1165–1175.

Dickstein, S., & Parke, R. D. (1988). 'Social referencing in infancy: A glance at fathers and marriage'. *Child Development*, *59*(2), 506–511.

Erikson, E. H. (1959). 'Identity and the cycle of life: Selected papers'. *Psychological Issues*, *1*(1), 5–165.

Erikson, E. H. (1963). *Childhood and society* (2nd ed.). New York: W.W. Norton.

Erikson, E. H. (1997). *El ciclo vital completo* (Española). Bracelona: Paidos.

Feinman, S., & Lewis, M. (1983). 'Social referencing at ten months: A second-order effect on infants' responses to strangers'. *Child Development*, *54*(4), 878–887.

Frankl, V. E. (1991). *El hombre en busca de sentido*. Madrid: Herder.

Frisina, W. G. (2002). *The unity of knowledge and action. Towards a nonrepresentational theory of knowledge*. New York: State University of New York Press.

Gross, J. J. (2014). *Handbook of emotion regulation*. (J. J. Gross, Ed.). New York and London: The Guilford Press.

Hong, Y. R., & Park, J. S. (2012). 'Impact of attachment, temperament and parenting on human development'. *Korean Journal of Pediatrics*, *55*(12), 449–454.

Jack, R. E., Garrod, O. G. B. B., & Schyns, P. G. (2014). 'Dynamic facial expressions of emotion transmit an evolving hierarchy of signals over time'. *Current Biology*, *24*(2), 187–192.

Jönsson, & Emma. (2017). *Affective touch throughout life: from cortical processing in infancy to touch perception in adulthood*. Gothenburg: University of Gothenburg.

Klinnert Mary, D., Emde, R. N., Butterfield, P., & Campos, J. J. (1986). 'Social referencing: The infant's use of emotional signals from a friendly adult with mother present'. *Developmental Psychology*, *22*(4), 427–432.

Kohlberg, L., & Mayer, R. (1972). 'Development as the aim of education'. *Harvard Education Review*, *4*(4), 449–496.

Kuhl, P. K., Tsao, F.-M., & Liu, H.-M. (2003). 'Foreign-language experience in infancy: Effects of short-term exposure and social interaction on phonetic learning'. *Proceedings of the National Academy of Sciences of the United States of America*, *100*(15), 9096–9101.

L'Ecuyer, C. (2014). 'The wonder approach to learning'. *Frontiers in Human Neuroscience*, *8*(764).

Lewis, M. (2007). 'Early emotional development'. In A. Slater & M. Lewis (Eds.), *Introduction to infant development* (2nd ed., pp. 217–224). Oxford: Oxford University Press.

Mireault, G. C., Crockenberg, S. C., Sparrow, J. E., Pettinato, C. A., Woodard, K. C., & Malzac, K. (2014). 'Social looking, social referencing and humor perception in 6-and-12-month-old infants'. *Infant behavior & development*, *37*(4), 536–545.

Montessori, M. (2013). *El método de la pedagogía científica* (Tercera ed). Madrid: Biblioteca Nueva.

Orón Semper, J. V. (2015). 'Consecuencias de la dinámica de la integración de Leonardo Polo sobre la acción humana, la cognición y los sentimiento'. *Cuadernos de Pensamiento Español*, *57*, 201–217.

Orón Semper, J. V. (2016). 'Nueva propuesta de educación emocional en clave de integración y al servicio del crecimiento'. *Metafísica y Persona. Filosofía, conocimiento y vida*, *16*, 91–152.

Orón Semper, J. V. (2017). 'El acto global-personal'. *Colloquia*, *4*, 23–44.

Orón Semper, J. V. (2018). 'Educación centrada en el crecimiento de la relación interpersonal'. *Studia Poliana*, *20*, 241–262.

Pelaez, M., Virues-Ortega, J., Field, T. M., Amir-Kiaei, Y., & Schnerch, G. (2013). 'Social referencing in infants of mothers with symptoms of depression'. *Infant Behavior and Development*, *36*(4), 548–556.

Pelaez, M., Virues-Ortega, J., & Gewirtz, J. L. (2012). 'Acquisition of social referencing via discrimination training in infants'. *Journal of Applied Behavior Analysis*, *45*(1), 23–36.

Piaget, J. (1928). *Judgement and reasoning in the child. Trans*. London: Routledge and Kegan.

Piaget, J. (1965). The rules of the game. In *The moral judgement of the child* (pp. 1–104). Glecone: The free press.

Piaget, J., Lorenz, K., & Erikson, E. H. (1982). *Juego y desarrollo*. Critica, Grupo editorial Grijalbo.

Pittman, J. F., Keiley, M. K., Kerpelman, J. L., & Vaughn, B. E. (2011). 'Attachment, identity, and intimacy: Parallels between Bowlby's and Erikson's paradigms'. *Journal of Family Theory & Review*, *3*(1), 32–46.

Polo, L. (2007). *¿Quien es el hombre? Un espíritu en el tiempo* (sexta edic). Madrid: RIALP.

Pratt, M., Goldstein, A., Levy, J., & Feldman, R. (2017). 'Maternal depression across the first years of life impacts the neural basis of empathy in preadolescence'. *Journal of the American Academy of Child & Adolescent Psychiatry*, *56*(1), 20–29.e3.

Rogers, C. R. (1961). *On becoming a person*. Boston: Houghton Mifflin Company.

Rogers, C. R. (2000). *El proceso de convertirse en persona, mi técnica terapéutica*. Barcelona: Paidos Iberica.

Silk, J. S., Redcay, E., & Fox, N. a. (2014). 'Contributions of social and affective neuroscience to our understanding of typical and atypical development'. *Developmental Cognitive Neuroscience*, *8*, 1–6.

Striano, T., & Rochat, P. (2000). 'Emergence of selective social referencing in infancy'. *Infancy*, *1*(2), 253–264.

Tronick, E. Z. (1989). 'Emotions and emotional communication in infants'. The *American Psychologist*, *44*(2), 112–119.

Vohs, K. D., & Baumeister, R. F. (2011). *Handbook of self-regulation*. (K. D. Vohs & R. F. Baumeister, Eds.). New York and London: The Guilford Press.

Vygotsky, L. (1978). *Mind in society: The development of Higer psychological processes*. Cambridge, MA: Harvard University Press.

Walden, T. A., & Baxter, A. (1989). 'The effect of context and age on social referencing'. *Child Development*, *60*(6), 1511–1518.

Walden, T. A., & Ogan, T. A. (1988). 'The development of social referencing'. *Child Development*, *59*(5), 1230–1240.

Winnicott, D. W. (1986). *Home is where we start from. Essays by a psychoanalist*. London: Penguin books.

Zhang, M., Chen, X., Deng, H., & Lu, Z. (2014). 'Infant behavior and development identifying the interaction of maternal sensitivity and two serotonin-related gene polymorphisms on infant'. *Infant Behavior & Development*, *37*, 606–614.

Chapter 10

Work at the home

Purpose, function, and care

Antonio Argandoña

Introduction

In the home, we find a community of people (the family) who share a living space (the house) with an intention of continuity, serving a social purpose (Argandoña, 2018). The main element is undoubtedly the community of individuals, but keeping for each one their personal dignity and rights. This article attempts to explain work in the home as the action of the individuals who make up the home. It does not involve making a list of tasks which will change in time and space, will have numerous exceptions, and will end up being of little use, but rather it concerns finding a connecting thread that unifies these tasks. For this purpose, we will use the theory of human action in organisations, as developed by Pérez López (1991, 1993; cf. Argandoña, 2008a, 2008b, 2015b). In the following I will present individual human actions and shared actions, ending with the conclusions.

Individual human action

By "action" we understand any act carried out by a person in a rational, deliberate, and voluntary manner (Aquinas, 1990: 1–2, qq. 6–21).[1] These acts are very varied in the home; some are foundational, such as the decision to form a family, buy a house, or have a child. Others are occasional, such as painting a room, taking out a loan to pay for a child's education, or receiving a visit from relatives. The majority of these actions fill daily life: grocery shopping and preparing meals, accompanying an elderly person to the doctor's office and relaxing together, and many others that go unnoticed even though they may be very important: chatting about trivial matters, being pleased with the growth of children, caring about the health of a spouse, arguing and making up, expressing love between spouses, and many other things.

The concept of action is broader than the concept of work, although it includes both the voluntary work of members of the home and paid or unpaid work by other people (González and Iffland, 2014). Thus, we try to avoid the bias within the concept of work in the home introduced by neoclassical economic theory (Becker, 1981) or in some Marxist and feminist approaches, which take paid work as a reference when giving visibility and value to work of the home (Carrasco, 1998).

Action and results

In the origin of an action there is a need, broadly understood as the step from one given situation to another that is expected to be better, to the extent that it provides a good or corrects a shortfall or limitation (the improvement of which is also categorised as a good). The need may be of the agent or another person, and always appears as an opportunity for action. The action is justified by the goods the agent aims to achieve, which are the purpose of the action; the mere existence of means or resources is not enough to account for the action (Aranzadi, 2011).

The results of the action may be very varied, but can be grouped into three categories:

1. *Extrinsic, resulting from the environment's response to the agent's action: e.g., in the case of a worker who is not part of the family, the salary received and the recognition.*
2. *Intrinsic, produced by the agent himself and not received from an external source, e.g., the knowledge learnt and skills developed from the action, or the satisfaction from the task carried out.*
3. *External, i.e., the effect of the action on another person, which may or may not be determined and known by the agent.*

Motives and motivations

The expected or desired effects of the action determine the motives of the agent. Only the agent can give the reasons that drive him to act, and these reasons are his motives. This is important because human action is more than a process determined by physical, biological, or sociological laws, or according to criteria of efficiency or social influence or power. The motives for an action can be divided into three categories:

1. *Extrinsic motives, when the agent seeks extrinsic results provided by the environment.*
2. *Intrinsic, related to the learnings, satisfaction, and self-fulfilment of the agent.*
3. *Transcendent, in other persons, which "indicate a genuine interest in the development and motives of the other person"*

(Rosanas, 2008, 455, cf. Pérez López, 1993).[2]

Various motives are usually present in each action: e.g., the family member who spends a few hours on a holiday mowing may be doing so to avoid an expense (extrinsic motive), because he likes exercise and feeling useful (intrinsic), or to teach others to care for the home (transcendent). We will call the principal motive of the action the intention, which gives it unity and connects it to other actions, which form a group the meaning of which stems from the shared intention (Anscombe, 1957).

At this point, the agent has identified the need, has formed an idea of the possible results, has evaluated the desirability, and has a plan to accomplish the action; this includes the succession of action plans and controlling the course of action that should lead to the expected results. But the agent has not yet made the decision: the motives must become motivations, impulses to fulfil the motives. If the agent has sufficient willpower, he can develop three types of motivations: extrinsic, intrinsic, and transcendent, corresponding to the three motives and three types of desired results (Pérez López, 1991, 1993). The main or dominant motivation will be the one that puts the intention into practice.[3]

The nature and soundness of the motives determine the commitment to carry out the action, before oneself and before others. Commitment gives continuity to the intention and, as we shall see, it plays an important role when the action is carried out with others.

Once the action is performed, the different types of results will always be produced, to a greater or lesser extent, even if the agent has not sought them, and even if the agent is not aware they have been produced. Therefore, they will have consequences. For example, the person (whether in the family or hired) who prepares meals will likely develop operational skills related to their intrinsic motives, which will be translated into the better quality of their future work. And if this is done as a service to the family, that is, for transcendent motives, the person will be learning to take into account the needs of other people (evaluative learning). The person will be acquiring virtues (or vices) that will facilitate his future actions not only in that particular family, but also with other persons or even themselves.[4] And the recipients of the actions, in addition to the service provided, can also learn from this attitude of service, dedication, and generosity: that is, they can also develop their virtues.[5] But it is not the achieved result that is important, but rather the intended motive of the agent.

Therefore, the action should not be evaluated only for its extrinsic results; the other results, especially the external ones, are usually more difficult to recognise and value, but they may have very important consequences in the long term, since these results may be prolonged in time and affect the conduct of other people. The motives and intentions will likely change as the action takes place as a result of the learnings gained by the agent and other people. For example, what would appear to be a boring task that is only done for extrinsic motives may become a fun task with the possibility of developing new knowledge and abilities, which also pertain to intrinsic motivation, or show the social projection of the action, driving the transcendent motivation.

Shared, joint, or collective actions

A home is an organisation, that is, "a group of individuals who coordinate their actions to achieve common objectives that are of interest to everyone, although this interest may be due to very different motives" (Pérez López, 1993: 13). The main elements that comprise an organisation are: (1) its members, the persons who form part of or participate in it; (2) the motives that drive the actions of these individuals; (3) the common purpose that drives them and what this entails; (4) an intention to participate; (5) forming part of a community, the family, and (5) coordination of these individuals' activities.

Many of our actions are individual, in the sense that we do not need the collaboration of other people to achieve the goal or result we want. We will call collective, shared, or joint actions "any form of social interaction whereby two or more individuals coordinate their actions in space and time to bring about a change in the environment" (Sebanz et al., 2006: 75). This is the resolution of a problem (Andreu and Sieber, 1998) that is the opportunity to move from one situation to another that is considered more desirable, with the collaboration of other people. In all collective action there is a group of people who work collectively. This work is interdependent, and there is a goal or task to be achieved together (Okhuysen and Bechky, 2009, 469).

As we have explained, every human action requires an agent, an object or purpose (what I am going to do), and some motives (why I am going to do it). In the shared action we find several agents, each with his own purpose and motives, but also a shared purpose (what we want to achieve together), the cooperation of all and the coordination of the actions that each one will carry out will also be necessary. And there may also be some shared reasons.

Purpose in the joint action

To know the purpose of a voluntary organisation, such as a company, a numismatic fan club, or a group of friends who meet to play music on weekends, we would have to ask its members what it is that binds them together and why they meet. And each one would tell us their personal motives: make money, make friends, learn, develop personal relationships – that is, a set of particular "goods." But all this cannot be the purpose of that organisation, because those "goods" are not shared.

However, we could say that everyone will agree that they want the very existence of the organisation as a means for each person to achieve their personal goals. The existence of the organisation is, then, a "common good" to which everyone contributes and of which everyone participates, although for different reasons; they do not participate and enjoy it in the same way and in the same proportion, but it is a common good (or a common bad), and society benefits from it (Argandoña, 2015a). And, along with the common good that is the organisation, each one will find the private goods that he wanted – or, at least, he will hope to find them.

This can help us understand the shared purpose of the human community that forms the home. But, keep in mind that the home is not a "voluntary" organisation in the same sense as a company, an association, or a group of music lovers since some members cannot choose whether they belong to one home or another, and for many years their capacity to make independent decisions is very limited. This is an essential part of the home and, to some extent, it defines its social purpose:

the home is a "natural" organisation specially prepared to serve the individuals during long periods of vulnerability and dependence. Or, better, throughout his life, because home is a place where vulnerability is prevented and means are provided to face it.

Moreover, the home is a multipurpose institution unlike, say, a hospital or school which, despite their complexity, are relatively specialised. It is "a general service utility, an institution whose uses cannot be defined except as a presentation of a general plan for meeting future needs" (Douglas, 1991: 295). The literature on the home has listed its many functions: reproduction, nurturing, learning, socialisation, production of goods and services, care of the sick and elderly, provision of physical and ontological security, a place to act freely without worry, reproduction of social identity, restaurant, hotel, school, hospital, place of recreation, school of virtues, etc. (Alvira, 2010; Argandoña, 2018; Douglas, 1991; Heywood, 2005; Kearns et al., 2000; Saunders, 1984; Somerville, 1997). And these functions change over time and are passed on from one generation to another, not without significant changes (Regnerus, 2018). Somehow, a person who forms part of a home must be willing to undertake very varied tasks, because, as we said before, the contribution and enjoyment of the common goods is not fixed, nor proportional, nor responds to tit-for-tat criteria.

The home is a place where one "learns to live" during a long and changeable process, assuming various tasks. It is here that children acquire knowledge and develop abilities, and internalise rights, autonomy, participation, mutual respect, and freedom. It is a place where the other is recognised and accepted, not by what he has or does, but by what he is; and where one learns how to manage disputes and diversity, and this is learnt precisely in coexistence with the rest of the home's members – it is a joint and shared learning.

The previous list of needs includes, probably, many of those that all the people have and, maybe for that reason, we want to be members of a home. It is true that our needs will not always be the same, and that we can satisfy many of them by other means outside the home, but this does not prevent the "joint production" of private and common household goods from being very "efficient," not only from the economic point of view, but especially when we take into account the common goods (learning, development of virtues, trust, respect, and many more) that accompany them. That is to say, in the home there is a shared purpose, although it is not easy to define it in each moment.

Motives in the shared action

The personal motives of the agents are still active when the joint actions are performed. Even if these are mere exchanges ("I help you so that you help me"), they also produce intrinsic and external results: learnings, satisfactions, sympathy, trust, etc., that can generate shared social motivations. And this contributes something new to the collective action.

Godman (2013) mentions the example of two workers who are undertaking a cumbersome and tiresome task, such as moving a piano, but while doing so they discover that they were born in the same city, or are supporters of the same soccer team, or have family ties, common friends, or shared interests and tastes, and end up enjoying that very action, precisely because it is done together. The intrinsic motives (enjoy the relationship) and transcendent motives (make the other person happy) are brought to the fore. The action creates connections that produce both personal and social benefits: the relationships that arise from the action are a source of shared motivations that demonstrate the existence of commitment to the activity and to the individuals (Godman, 2013, Ihlan, 2014).

A joint action always implies a shared purpose. For the agent, this may stem from extrinsic, intrinsic, or transcendent motives, as we have already stated. These motives may or may not coincide with those of the other agent. For example, one may seek service to other people (transcendent motive), and the other may only be concerned by remuneration (extrinsic). Or both may have the same motive (remuneration), but this is not shared (each individual is only concerned with their own remuneration). Or they may have a social motive (they desire the relationship), but it is not shared (they only desire it to the extent that it favours them personally, e.g., working together allows them to achieve better results and receive higher remuneration). Or there may be a shared social motive, as in the case of those that carry the piano. It is the purpose that is relevant, not the motives, although the motives are also important.

In practice, it is likely that some of these situations will occur simultaneously in variable proportions that change over time. The relative importance of the shared purpose and the shared social motives may change, and the action may continue even if some of its causes have ceased. It is also possible that continuity in the joint action gives rise to new intrinsic and transcendent motivations both on a personal and social level. Therefore, carrying out actions with others may (although not always) facilitate the practice of virtues, and above all charity, which encompasses affection, sympathy, and comradeship, and are usually "lesser," often unforeseen consequences of an ongoing relationship (Argandoña, 2011b). In the home, the shared motives are obvious because the relationships that are formed in it are much stronger than those of companionship. But they can lose strength, by accustoming, the passage of time, frictions or difficulties, and many other reasons.

Cooperation, coordination, and trust

Many of the actions that take place in the home are purely individual or private. This is normal because the home is the ideal place for such actions; what is more, it is also a space for privacy where the individual retires to in order to keep his life in order and recover control over it:

> the most recondite, private, secure and comfortable place for the self, where it takes shelter from the natural world, to where it belongs as its innermost

shelter, and where it addresses the world and the other, opening itself to transcendence.

(Patrão Neves, 2018: 73; cf. Somerville, 1997)

But even this intimate sphere supposes a relationship: respect for privacy requires a shared purpose which is the first condition for a joint action. "The home is also a place where privacy is shared, where others become part of my privacy" (Yepes and Aranguren, 1996: 89).

Collective or shared action implies interdependence among people, and demands, as we said, cooperation and coordination. Cooperation or collaboration occurs in any collective action in a group or human organisation aimed at completing a task or achieving a result sought by the members of that group. There are many forms of joint action, according to the degree of interdependence of the agents, but they can be grouped into four types: pooled, sequential, reciprocal, and comprehensive interdependence (Thompson, 1967), which give rise to different forms of coordination:

1 Pooled interdependence. An agreement by family members to spend an afternoon cleaning and tidying the garden together may serve as an example of an elementary form of what Ihlan (2014) calls a coordinated collective action. There is a common purpose, but each member performs individual actions that are not particularly connected. One member waters the lawn, another trims the trees, and someone else sweeps up dry leaves. The possibilities of conflict are reduced, and it is enough for each agent to know what the others are doing.

   Coordination, in this case, may be established in the form of rules that govern the operating processes: in which part of the garden each one will start working, do not water the paths before collecting the dry leaves, what tools each will use, where they will collect the waste, etc. Coordination does not require an explicit social motivation to collaborate with the others, although such motivation may exist, and in many cases there will be, even if it is without external manifestations (Kort, 2008).
2 Sequential interdependence. It is a form of strategic interdependence in which, for example, the output of the work of one agent is the input of the next, which makes the results of the second dependent on those of the first. Many collective tasks in the home have this type of interdependence. For example, the order of preparation of meals, or the organisation of morning tasks, from the awakening of parents and children to the departure of each one to school or work, etc. Coordination is usually carried out in this case in the form of adaptive planning and scheduling, often informal.
3 Reciprocal interdependence. It occurs when the actions of each agent have effects on those of others, and vice versa. For example, one of the children got disastrous grades in his studies, and the parents create a plan that combines work and rest time, positive incentives and punishment, moments of more

pressure and others of relaxation, restrictions on the use of the mobile and remote monitoring, etc.

The coordination in this case is more complicated, and requires mutual adjustment. In the proposed example, parents will need (1) responsiveness: each parent should try to understand the intentions of the other in order to judge the other's actions and coordinate them with their own (Bratman, 1992); (2) dialogue between them; (3) commitment, at least, to carry out the joint activity ("if I cooperate, the other will also cooperate") and better still if it is a commitment of mutual support ("if I need the other's help, they will give it to me");[6] and (4) as a result, trust – not just in a functional or technical capacity, which exists when it is expected that the other person knows what he has to do and is capable of doing so, but rather personal trust, because one knows that the other wants to do what is best for everyone, i.e., act mainly due to transcendent motives (Rosanas and Velilla, 2003).

4 A more complete form of joint action is group agency (Ihlan, 2014). For example, musicians in an orchestra have a shared purpose; they have also shared social motives derived from the experience of playing together and the satisfaction that this gives. In the event of a dispute, the goals of the group take precedence over private goals; they all make efforts to achieve the best coordination and are willing to help those who need it. They all trust that everyone will act with the utmost professionalism and quality; each individual commits not only to the purposes but also to the actions he/she will perform (Godman, 2013).[7] The home is probably an environment in which group agency most frequently occurs.

Organisation theory points out the key factors of shared actions, namely, criticality (the probability of a fault, error, or failure) and uncertainty; the latter, in turn, is related to dependability and ambiguity (Worren, 2012). Obviously, the importance of these factors in the home will be variable; for example, the probability of an error in the action of a small child will be high, but its importance will be reduced by the nature of the task assigned to him and by the vigilance exercised over it. In any case, the main objective of this type of action is not so much the direct result (for example, a table perfectly prepared for dinner) as the child's learning about how to prepare a table and, above all, the development of the child's capacity to carry out actions in the service of others. Hence the importance of learning processes in the home (of all its members, according to the stages of life in which they are found), the development of skills, flexibility in the application of coordination mechanisms, and creation of trust.[8]

Solidarity, love, care

In the home, the "value" (economic or not) of the organisation is greater than the sum of the contributions received because the participation of everyone creates "external effects" or common goods that spill over the others (Douglas, 1991).

But this creates the risk of free riding, of opportunistic behaviour by those who wish to enjoy the benefits and appropriate the surplus without incurring the costs. Resolving this problem requires solidarity. For this reason, gifts and donations have an important place in the home. Services and transfers between members of the home form part of a comprehensive system of exchanges in which all are involved, including different generations, because some of these transfers occur in moments that are far between: it is not possible to compensate each service separately because it is not possible to determine its value; there is no direct reciprocity, but there are many forms of unplanned compensation – material goods can be distributed, spiritual goods can be shared. And the most intense way of sharing is love (Yepes and Aranguren, 1996).

Love may exist in many human relationships, but in the home it is key. Love is not only a sentiment but, above all, the virtue par excellence in relationships between couples and with children, and other relatives and collaborators. Love-need is the most natural and immediate form of love: we need something that is a good for us, we desire it, and when we have it we love it, enjoy it, and are happier with it; it seems like a selfish love, but it is the simplest form of love and preparation for other more generous forms. Love-gift or benevolent love consists of wishing the good for the loved one, not for oneself; and not only to wish the good, but to act on it, adding affection to love (Aquinas, 1990: II-II, q. 27, a. 2).

The home gives rise to the most elevated forms of benevolent love: conjugal love (*eros*), whereby the gift is the very person, beyond attraction, possession, and benevolence (Wojtyla, 1996); and friendship, i.e., mutual love, returned and reciprocated, selective (one may have many companions, but probably few friends), and constructed on the common purpose of the home. In the theory of action previously presented, benevolent love exists when a person acts with transcendent motivation, that is, when the person takes into consideration the needs of the other person and seeks a good for the latter, not for the benefit it may yield for the agent (Pérez López, 1991, 280–281). "Love, in its proper and full sense, is the impulse of an agent for the achievement . . . of perfect unity with other individual agents" (Pérez López, 1991: 271), which arises when all members in a home act in search of the good of the others, ensuring that they all feel appreciated and respected.

"The family experience leads us to a civilization of care" (Pérez Soba, 2016: 88). Love ethics has many points of contact with care ethics (Gilligan, 1982; Noddings, 1984; Tronto, 1993), in so far as it focuses not on abstract individuals, but on the needs of concrete persons, in their environment and particular situation, i.e., the home (Liedtka, 1996).[9] Care is provided to the individuals when they are treated as an end in themselves and not to obtain something else, and seeking not just the satisfaction of specific needs, but their personal development and improvement, respecting their autonomy and decision-making ability.[10] "The care of the home forms one platform on which the daily ritual of receiving and giving takes place" (Nwosu, 2011: 4).

The relationships of interdependence mentioned here are often mutual, but others represent a dependency, for example in the case of children, the sick, the elderly, or the disabled. In civil society, this may be a reason for undervaluing or discrimination, because our developed societies value the autonomy of the individual as an ideal of conduct, and consider that vulnerability means a lack of humanity. But vulnerability cannot be understood solely as a deficiency (Marcos, 2012).

At home, dependence is a normal situation. In the first years of life, children are completely dependent upon their parents and carers, and this situation is repeated, with more or less intensity, during periods of disability or illness, and again towards the end of life. The home is the first natural place where vulnerability does not provoke rejection. It is also the place where one can always seek refuge because it is where one will always be accepted for what one is, not for what one can do or give, or for one's qualities and strengths. Action in the home cannot be correctly understood if it is not taken into account that a person is a rational and social animal, but also dependent and vulnerable (Marcos and Bertolaso, 2018). In the home, the autonomy of some individuals is at the service of the dependency of others. Ultimately, to care is to look out for the other person (Frezza et al., 2017: 3).

If the transcendent motives are dominant, love is the main virtue in the family, and the relationships should be led by generosity and the gift, that is, by care. Coordination of actions is possible beyond technical or sociological reasons by the unity achieved by virtues led by love. It is possible to "explain" what an organisation-home "does" from the description of its common purpose and the existence of common intentions that are derived from and strengthened by virtues, the results of which will be commitment and trust. Similarly, failures in the family community can be explained by the failures in the common purpose, on the basis of the absence of virtues, in particular, love. The home "model" that the family chooses will depend on this. This also indicates the possibilities and limitations of external influences on the home: current ideologies, institutions, laws, culture, and social norms, etc. The home "model" will be influenced (but probably not determined) by such ideological, cultural, political, social, economic, and technological factors.

Conclusions

In human organisations, people carry out actions – some individual and some joint or collective – in order to achieve the organisation's objectives or purposes that serve the interests of all involved, albeit for different motives. Motives are the driving force of personal action; the impetus behind the attitude of cooperating with others in the organisation is the common purpose, which is a necessary but not sufficient condition to attain the results that drive the agents' motives – and joint actions may also give rise to shared motives. The interesting thing about joint action is the need for everyone's cooperation, which is what gives the organisation its strength.

Every action gives rise to a series of results, some known and desired, and others not known and not anticipated, but in any case, realised and important. Some results are given by the environment in which the agent acts, others are produced by the very agent, and others (transcendent or prosocial) occur in other persons but also leave a mark in the agent. Learnings that result from the action cause changes in the conduct of the agent and other persons, and here lies its importance, principally the changes that produce learning on virtues (or vices). And this depends on the motives of the agent, especially the transcendent motives.

In every organisation it is important that the agents are motivated to belong to the organisation, and this depends on the relationship between the agents' motivations and the organisation's objectives. In the case of the home, the transcendent motivation (which is the key to unity) puts the acquisition of virtues, mainly love, at the core of the home's objectives. And love is manifested in the home as care, thus becoming the key variable to the actions in the home.

The home is both a transitory and permanent institution. Transient, when the people who form it know that they will probably cease to belong to it in the future, or that, if they remain in it, they will do so in conditions very different from those of the past. But it is permanent in the sense that what has been learned in it in childhood will serve as the basis for the repetition of the model in the future (Regnerus, 2018). In other words, the "failure" of a home model can be projected in future generations.

The home can be a very pleasant organisation that encourages everyone to "return" and prompts affectionate memories of the past. But it can also be an unpleasant, hostile, rigid, oppressive place where "even its most altruistic and successful versions exert a tyrannous control over mind and body" (Douglas, 1991: 303). Whether it is one or the other will depend on many factors, as well as the actions of the individuals who make up the home. To the extent that the home is an irreplaceable institution as regards some of its functions, the efforts we make to further understand these actions will be more necessary.

Notes

1 Instinctive and vegetative-animal acts are excluded, but not habits to the extent that these originate from voluntary and rational acts.

2 The motives that Pérez López calls transcendent are known as prosocial motives by other authors (Batson et al., 2008; Frey and Meier, 2002; Grant and Berg, 2011). But not all behaviour that is called prosocial corresponds to transcendent motives: e.g., when a person does something for another person because he expects a reward from the latter, the motive is extrinsic.

3 Emotions, affection, and feelings that occur in relationships with other people are also involved in the action, and influence the spontaneous motivation to act in a particular manner, prior to the rational reflexion about it (Pérez López, 1991).

4 Virtues are acquired operational habits that develop through the deliberate, earnest, and voluntary repetition of acts that try to continuously improve (Alzola, 2015; Argandoña, 2011a). This process of acquisition and growth of moral virtues occurs when the decision-maker endeavours to achieve what is good for himself and for others, resisting the temptation to do something more pleasant or that brings immediate benefits in order to do something that the decision-maker believes is best for himself or for others.

5 The appraisal, whether or not favourable, that other people make of the agent's work does not reduce the learning of virtues by the latter.
6 "Commitment is seen as the glue of the group, of collective activity: it links the agent with the joint goal and the common solution, it links members' actions with the collective plan, it links the members with each other" (Castelfranchi, 1995: 41).
7 As we have seen, there are degrees of cooperation, from the "I-mode," whereby each agent acts independently of the others, to the "we-mode," whereby each person takes into account the purposes, values, norms, and beliefs of the group, that is, acts as a member of the organization (Tuomela and Tuomela, 2005).
8 "Coordination is enabled when the interdependence among parties, their responsibilities, and the progress of the task are all made visible through accountability. Additionally, coordination relies on the ability of interdependent parties to anticipate subsequent task related activity, that is, predictability. Finally, a shared conception of activities and how they are performed, or common understanding, also enables coordination. Through coordination mechanisms that produce these conditions, people succeed in integrating interdependent tasks in organizations" (Okhuysen and Bechky, 2009: 491).
9 "Care ethics is a discipline that concerns responsible relationships and moral relationships between individuals, motivated by a request, and whose ultimate purpose is the care of their fellow man or themselves" (Alvarado, 2004: 31). This definition directly refers to medical and nursing care, but the literature on the home also includes these medical and affectionate aspects; cfr. Bratt (2002), Burns (2018), Fox O'Mahoney (2013), Libman (2011).
10 Care ethics often identifies with feminist ethics, but this implies confusing the virtue of love or care (which can and should be experienced by any person) with some more or less constitutive psychological elements pertaining to a particular sex.

References

Alvarado, A. (2004), La ética del cuidado, *Revista Aquichan*, 2(4), 30–39.

Alvira, R. (2010), *El lugar al que se vuelve. Reflexiones sobre la familia*. Pamplona: Eunsa.

Alzola, M. (2015), Virtuous persons and virtuous actions in business ethics and organizational research, *Business Ethics Quarterly*, 25(3), 287–318.

Andreu, R. & S. Sieber (1998), Knowledge and problem solving: a proposal for a model of individual and collective learning. Occasional Paper No. 99/1, IESE Business School.

Anscombe, G.E.M. (1957), *Intention*. Ithaca, NY: Cornell University Press.

Aquinas, T. (1990), *Summa Theologica*. Notre Dame, IN: Ave Maria Press.

Aranzadi, J. (2011), The possibilities of the acting person within an institutional framework: Goods, norms, and virtues, *Journal of Business Ethics*, 99(1), 87–100.

Argandoña, A. (2008a), Integrating ethics into action theory and organizational theory, *Journal of Business Ethics*, 78(3), 435–446.

Argandoña, A. (2008b), Anthropological and ethics foundations of organization theory. In S. Gregg & J.R. Stoner (eds.), *Rethinking Business Management. Examining the Foundations of Business Education*. Princeton, NJ: The Witherspoon Institute, 38–49.

Argandoña, A. (2011a), Las virtudes en una teoría de la acción humana. In P. Requena & M. Schlag (eds.), *La persona al centro del Magistero sociale della Chiesa*. Roma: Edusc, 49–71.

Argandoña, A. (2011b), Beyond contracts: love in firms, *Journal of Business Ethics*, 99(1), 77–85.

Argandoña, A. (2015a), The common good, stakeholder theory and the theory of the firm. In M. Schlag, J.A. Mercado & J.E. Miller (eds), *The Challenge of Charity. Freedom and Charity Working Together*. Rome: Edusc, 195–216.

Argandoña, A. (2015b), Consistencia y ética en la toma de decisiones. Research Paper WP-1128, IESE Business School.

Argandoña, A. (2018), The home: Multidisciplinary reflections. In A. Argandoña (ed.), *The Home: Multidisciplinary Reflections*. Cheltenham: Edward Elgar, 8–31.

Batson, C.D., N. Ahmad, A.A. Powell & E.L. Stocks (2008), Prosocial motivation. In J.Y. Shah & W.L. Gardner, eds., *Handbook of Motivation Science*. New York, NY: The Guilford Press, 135–149.

Becker, G. (1981), *A Treatise on the Family*. Cambridge, MA: Harvard University Press.

Bratman, M.E. (1992), Shared cooperative activity, *Philosophical Review*, 101(4), 327–341.

Bratt, R.G. (2002), Housing and family well-being, *Housing Studies*, 17(1), 13–26.

Burns, H. (2018), The impact of the home environment on children's health and cognitive and social development. In A. Argandoña (ed.), *The Home: Multidisciplinary Reflections*. Cheltenham: Edward Elgar, 79–93.

Carrasco, C. (1998), Género y valoración social: la discusión sobre la cuantificación del trabajo de las mujeres, *Mientras Tanto*, 71, 61–79.

Castelfranchi, C. (1995), Commitments: from individual intentions to groups and organizations. In *Proceedings of the First International Conference on Multiagent Systems*. Menlo Park, CA: The AAAI Press, 41–48.

Douglas, M. (1991), The idea of a home: a kind of space, *Social Research*, 58(1), 287–307.

Fox O'Mahoney, L. (2013), The meaning of home: from theory to practice, *International Journal of the Law in the Built Environment*, 5(2), 156–171.

Frey, B.S. & S. Meier (2002), Pro-social behavior, reciprocity, or both? CESIFO Working Paper N 750, Munich.

Frezza, G., H. Keefe & M. Bertolaso (2017), Work of the home and social relationships as a guide to domestic care for the elderly. In F. Cavallo, V. Marletta, A. Monteriù & P. Siciliano (eds), *Ambient Assisted Living*. New York, NY: Springer.

Gilligan, C. (1982), *In a Different Voice: Psychological Theory and Women's Development*. Cambridge, MA: Harvard University Press.

Godman, M. (2013), Why we do things together: the social motivation for joint action, *Philosophical Psychology*, 26(4), 588–603.

González, A.M. & C. Iffland (eds.). (2014), *Care Professions and Globalization. Theoretical and Practical Perspectives*. New York, NY: Palgrave Macmillan.

Grant, A.M. & J.M. Berg (2011), Prosocial motivation at work: when, why, and how making a difference makes a difference. In K. Cameron & G. Spreitzer (eds.), *Oxford Handbook of Positive Organizational Scholarship*. New York, NY: Oxford University Press, 28–44.

Heywood, F. (2005), Adaptation: altering the house to restore the home, *Housing Studies*, 20(4), 531–47.

Ihlan, A. (2014), Leadership, collective action, and common goods. Presentado a la International Philosophy of Management Conference, Chicago.

Kearns, A., R. Hiscock, A., Ellaway & S. Macintyre (2000), "Beyond four walls". The psycho-social benefits of home. Evidence from West Central Scotland, *Housing Studies*, 15(3), 387–410.

Kort, E. (2008), What, after all, is leadership? "Leadership" and plural action, *The Leadership Quarterly*, 19, 403–425.

Libman, K. (2011), Housing and health: a social ecological perspective of the US foreclosure crisis, *Housing Theory and Society*, 29(1), 1–24.

Liedtka, J.M. (1996), Feminist morality and competitive reality: a role for an ethic of care? *Business Ethics Quarterly*, 6, 179–200.

Marcos, A. (2012), Dependientes y racionales: La familia humana, *Cuadernos de Bioética*, 23(77), 83–95.

Marcos, A. & M. Bertolaso (2018), What is a home? On the intrinsic nature of a home. In A. Argandoña (ed.), *The Home: Multidisciplinary Reflections*. Cheltenham: Edward Elgar, 35–56.

Noddings, N. (1984), *Caring: A Feminine Approach to Ethics and Moral Education*. Berkeley, CA: University of California Press.

Nwosu, B.U. (2011, March), A training and development model for the professionalization of housework. Home Renaissance Foundation Working Papers, N 27.

Okhuysen, G.A. & B.A. Bechky (2009), Coordination in organizations: an integrative perspective, *The Academy of Management Annals*, 3(1), 463–502.

Patrão Neves, M. (2018), Self & others: home as a cradle of a non-violent relationship. In A. Argandoña (ed.), *The Home: Multidisciplinary Reflections*. Cheltenham: Edward Elgar, 57–76.

Pérez López, J.A. (1991), *Teoría de la acción humana en las organizaciones. La acción personal*. Madrid: Rialp.

Pérez López, J.A. (1993), *Fundamentos de la dirección de empresas*. Madrid: Rialp.

Pérez-Soba, J.J. (2016), *La familia en la actualidad, profecía de una nueva humanidad*. Madrid: Unión Editorial.

Regnerus, M. (2018), Reproducing homes: intergenerational transmission of marriage and relationship legacy. In A. Argandoña (ed.), *The Home: Multidisciplinary Reflections*. Cheltenham: Edward Elgar, 97–119.

Rosanas, J.M. (2008), Beyond economic criteria: a humanistic approach on organizational survival, *Journal of Business Ethics*, 78(3), 447–462.

Rosanas, J.M. & M. Velilla (2003), Loyalty and trust as the ethical bases of organizations, *Journal of Business Ethics*, 44(1), 83–96.

Saunders, P. (1984), Beyond housing classes: the sociological significance of private property rights in means of consumption, *International Journal of Urban and Regional Research*, 8(2), 202–227.

Sebanz, N., H. Bekkering & G. Knoblich (2006), Joint action: bodies and minds moving together, *Trends in Cognitive Science*, 10(2), 70–76.

Somerville, P. (1997), The social construction of home, *Journal of Architectural and Planning Research*, 14(3), 226–245.

Thompson, J.D. (1967), *Organizations in Action*. New York, NY: McGraw-Hill.

Tronto, J. (1993), *Moral Boundaries: A Political Argument for an Ethic of Care*. New York, NY: Routledge.

Tuomela, R. & M. Tuomela (2005), Cooperation and trust in group context, *Mind & Society*, 4, 49–84.

Wojtyla, K. (1996), *Amor y responsabilidad*. Barcelona: Plaza y Janés.

Worren, N. (2012), *Organization Design: Re-defining Complex Systems*. New York, NY: Pearson.

Yepes, R. & J. Aranguren (1996), *Fundamentos de antropología. Un ideal de la excelencia humana*. Pamplona: Eunsa.

Chapter 11

Aligning the on-demand economy with the home as a workplace

Teresita Abay Krueger

Introduction

The chief aim of this review is to convey a level of inquiry worthy of a novel study that illustrates the home as a workplace and creative economy arena. My casual observations led me to seek confirmation of Maslow's (1943) Hierarchy of Needs; the theory offers a basis for organizational development with high employee motivation to achieve company objectives. An organization that satisfies Maslow's principles can feature high employee satisfaction, excellent employee retention and cohesive teams. Maslow's theory offers some theoretical support regarding why people strive to achieve a healthy work balance. This approach provides a conceptual foundation to research the literature and provide insight that economic disruption does more than reshape work and increase output, it also implies organisational structural changes in employment, and cultivates new environments such as the home as a workplace.

The revolutionary movement of the on-demand economy has inspired the work-at-home (WAH) opportunities that have been gradually appearing in the economy worldwide while remaining ignored. In this literature review, an analysis of the WAH sector and associated economic circumstances are investigated. This is for the purpose of identifying how the WAH sector is becoming a factor in the social and economic welfare of families, careers, compensation, and business outcomes. To bring to light the factors that WAH present, empirical data is covered and viewed within the theoretical framework of Maslow's Hierarchy of Needs. This will aid in expanding the awareness of how WAH interplays with society as an economic unit, and viability as a rapidly growing trend within today's workplace.

In defining the on-demand economy and aligning with the home as a workplace, this chapter looks at five dimensions (see Figure 11.2), depicted conceptually, as: job types/occupations now and in the future, home social implications, wages and benefits, technology enablers, and at the center of all this, the **New Geography of Work – The Home**.

This literature review made use of keywords, titles, and abstract information. The main search terms included, but are not limited to, "future of work," "information revolution," "workplace 4.0," "on-demand workplace," "work from

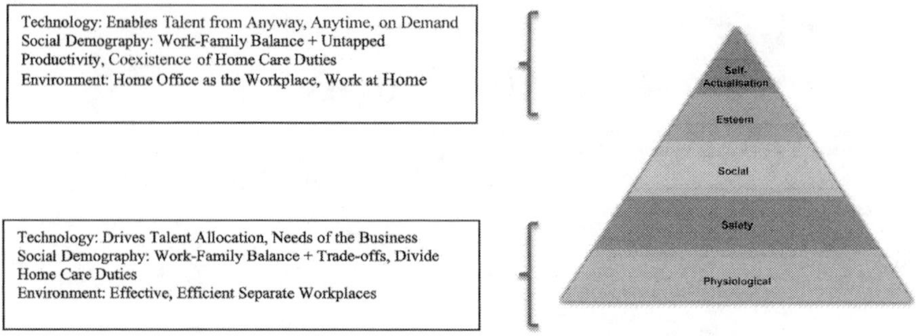

Figure 11.1 Applying Maslow's Hierarchy of Needs to the workplace

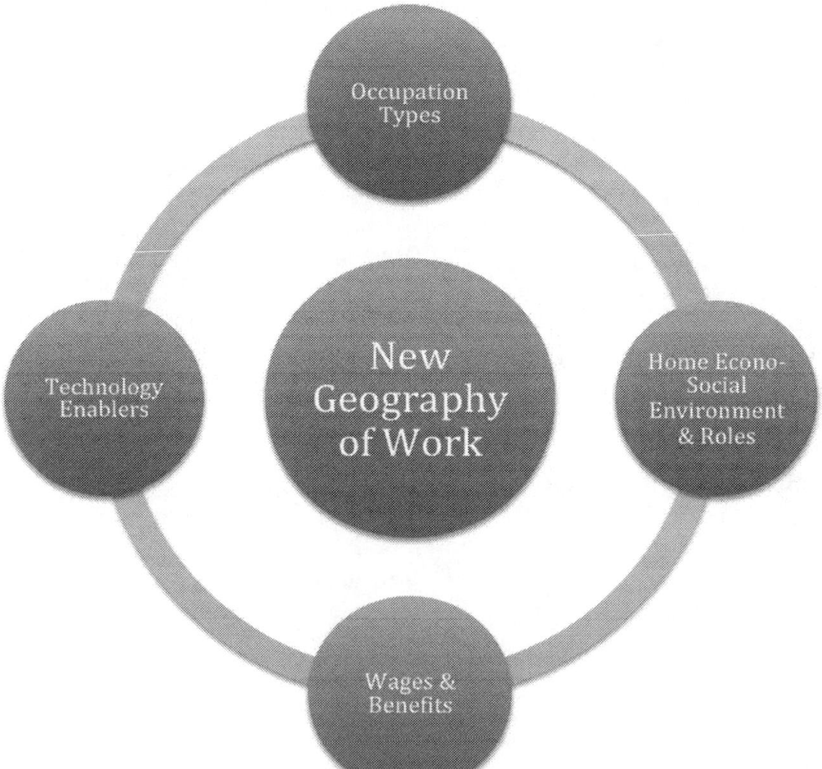

Figure 11.2 Implication – New Geography of Work

home," "demographic shift," "shared (gig, platform) economy," "stay at home moms and parents," "freelance," "independent consultant," "creative disruption," and "entrepreneurship."

Broad terms associated with work were also used, such as "social security," "working conditions," "wage inequality," and "job opportunities." Also, terms associated with social outcomes, economic outcomes, or technical enablers such as "work-life balance," "flexible-schedule basis," "family-related," "apps," and "platforms,"

Additionally, lists of references obtained from reviewed papers, book chapters, websites, and reports are included in this study and other relevant pieces of literature were systematically reviewed and experts were consulted to identify further additions. Most of the literature used is from sources and studies in English. Figure 11.3 provides an overview of the type of studies reviewed. Academic or intergovernmental publishing organisations, law firms, and consulting firms, such as Cornell University, Edward Elgar Publishing, Comparative Labor Law and Policy Journal, and the McKinsey Institute, wrote the majority of studies.

Literature review

In general, a career is perceived as the activity or pattern of work-related experiences that progress over a period of time, or even the life of every individual. This career "pattern" is seen as a growth or evolution of career activities (Greenhaus

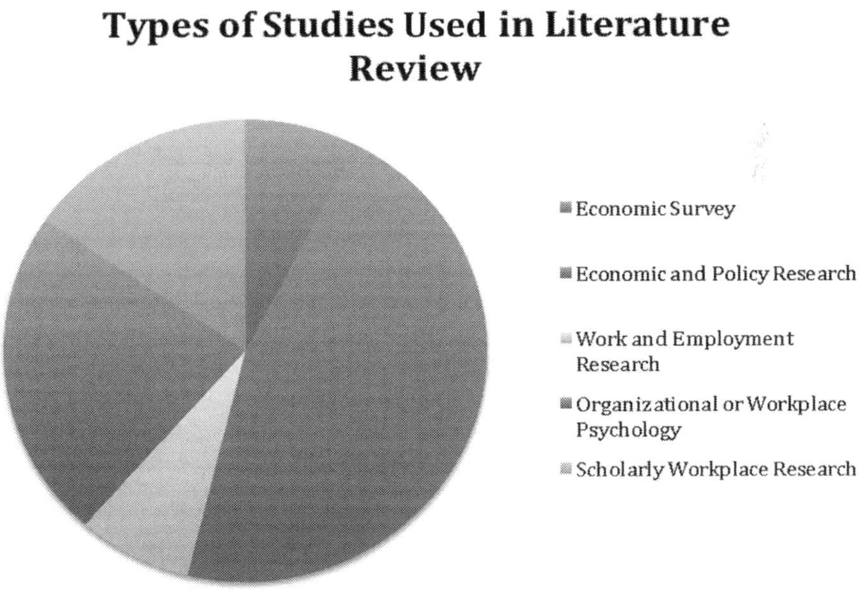

Figure 11.3 Types of studies used in the reviewed literature

and Kossek, 2014). However, this is not universal as not every individual has a stable career or is involved in a persistent or predictable pattern of work-related activities, which means that not everyone can relate to having a professional corporate or company-supported career within modern-day society. This also means that the classic idea of a career being related to a deep level of work commitment and stability, being tied to professional status and upscale socioeconomic opportunity, no longer holds true. Contemporary careers now incorporate a variety of trends, such as individuals who have combined income from multiple streams of revenue or provide consulting in different fields. Because of this, individuals who develop their careers at home are now becoming the forefront of career development. This includes individuals such as stay-at-home mothers and fathers, single parents who juggle work positions, dual-earner partners, students, handicapped individuals, and more. This allows for the flexible and mobile availability of jobs that aren't tied down to a specific location or region for work. Additionally, it provides some evolution in the social aspect of a career, where the lines between home and work begin to overlap.

The WAH job sector has been growing exponentially within the last ten years. Job activities such as outsourced vendors, independent contracting, freelancers, temps, or salaried virtual work, now contributes to 20% of the individuals who are influential in the economic outcome of the United States today (Cappelli and Keller, 2013). This was found to be in a higher percentage internationally. It is a trend that has been only expanding with time and appears to thrive even in uncertain economic environments, where layoffs and job insecurity are more pronounced in today's job market (Greenhaus and Kossek, 2014). A poor performing job economy only contributes to this trend, as innovation makes some human labour obsolete and new business models often reinvent or repurpose established careers, changing people's lives. These also change the environment of the home and provide new social implications as well.

WAH individuals are not only mobile within the US career market, but also globally. This presents a new dynamic, where global career problems become more important locally due to the globalisation of businesses as a whole (Greenhaus and Kossek, 2014). New occurrences, such as the propagation of international careers and the unprecedented interaction of international cultures across the globe, also influence how careers are constructed and developed within this new phenomenon. These new developments can no longer be ignored, as the face of contemporary economy diverges from the traditional and predictable facets of the classic job economy. Especially with the innovation of technology, and other inventions and advancements that become enablers for the WAH economy, many more changes are to come. Currently, a fifth of US workers, and a larger percentage globally, are involved in on-demand work that is an alternative to working for an employer full-time and from a centralised location (Cappelli and Keller, 2013). Also, the rise of "entrepreneurs [to] create new businesses in response to unmet needs and demands in the market" (Sappin, 2016). Old perceptions of the economy are based upon the full-time employment model. It is also difficult to create new economic models for alternative careers and WAH job positions due to the fact that they are varied and do not currently have classification systems by which to categorise them (Greenhaus and Kossek, 2014). Additionally, social trends among WAH workers are different from that which works within the office environment. For example, self-management is a practice that is crucial to WAH employees due to the fact that they do not invest in long-term careers and have to somehow remain employable despite the unpredictable fluctuations in the economy.

Defining the work-at-home economy for a new workforce

Creating a categorisation system for the introduction of WAH careers can take additional research, due to the fact that the variety of alternative work is often too differentiated. Many studies, in general, will combine these job activities as non-standard work, which can include anything that is not full-time or consistent employment. Another term for this form of work is contingent work, which refers to the inconsistency of employed terms (Cappelli and Keller, 2013). Often, these classifications revealed the economic influence of these positions, and whether they were high-rated jobs with good wages, or low-rated jobs with poor wages. However today, even high-wage IT contractors often work virtually or work on a project-by-project basis, while low-wage retail or restaurant workers have full-time employment. Some positions require full-time employment that is consistent, however employees can work offsite, such as at their home office (telecommute), throughout the duration of their career. This implies that the old classification systems of careers and work labels are mostly obsolete and need intensive research in order to redefine these distinctions that once separated the socioeconomic value of different career positions.

Another dilemma pertains to the identification of workers within this economy. Many businesses don't reveal this data, and don't want to reveal the level of outsourced work that they provide (De Stefano, 2015). This is now becoming known as the gig economy, where many workers may be registered to work at several companies over a shorter period of time. This contributes to the lack of reliability of an accurate estimate, with the lack of information and data, which reveals how the WAH economy is functioning over time.

However, despite its mysteries and obscurities, employees and contractors within the WAH workforce are benefiting from these new standards of living. The job opportunities allow flexible work schedules, which provide the opportunity for workers to maximise on multiple positions (De Stefano, 2015). The theories being developed behind this phenomenon are now creating new titles for job assignments, such as tasks or gigs, and are labelling this sector as the gig economy. Employment status can go unrecognised, or employment labels and titles are mis-classified. Many economic authorities have seen these roles as parallel to the work and career economy, rather than incorporating this sector as a part of the modern workforce. This could be seen as a way to dematerialise risk when approaching the contemporary labour markets, rather than considered an alternate or sub-wage form of income. It is also more economically advantageous due to the fact that many individuals within this field develop a variety of talents and skills due to the different roles they have to partake in. This is often essential in times where it is common for individuals who, despite having been committed to established corporations for many years, are laid off or simply lose their career because an organisation suffered loss, has to shut down, or reorganises its core businesses.

The social and emotional aspects of WAH work have also developed its own cultural environment. For example, WAH is more of a responsibility than a burden, and is dependent upon an individual's pace as opposed to a preset expectation (Kumar and Aithal, 2016). Additionally, technology has a multiplier effect. For example, the integration of computers and information technology that aid in carrying out job-related tasks are a big part of WAH. Employees also are able to complete work with little to no supervision, and are able to function more efficiently due to the less stressful environment. There are a lot fewer workplace stressors due to the fact that these individuals are mostly in control of their own environment. While some families may not have any control because of family members, they can set up their own office environment and quiet space for work. This has the ability to maximise output and reduce job-related burnout. The increase of women within the workforce don't seem to suffer the consequences of not being able to rear children within this sector, as they can adjust the level of work they commit to, have more flexibility in timing and pace, and are able to balance domestic chores with their work assignments (Kumar and Aithal, 2016). Additionally, they can continue maternal and gender roles, which is different from the once blurred lines between traditional male and female expectations. It is thought that the next generation of women may desire to be more present within the household, where men would be more present in business offices and centres. This helps diminish issues that deal with maternity leave in the work office environment. Quoting a Pew Survey, "about four in ten stay-at-home moms (SAHM) say that their ideal situation would be to work part-time" (Vanderkam, 2017). This number equates to 5 million women.

In many ways, this also changes workplace culture. Supervisors expect to see their workers in-person, visually and physically, but instead, individuals are mostly self-managerial (Kumar and Aithal, 2016). Managers have to be in charge of a more complicated remote workforce, which can detract from the organisational structure of a traditional workplace environment. This may seem impossible, as managers cannot necessarily contact these individuals in a time-efficient manner. However, technology has vastly improved the speed and reliability of communication. Task and project management software, and many other innovations, now exist for these exact types of scenarios.

Technology has advanced WAH and made it possible as a feasible and steady form of work. Not only do technology and WAH go hand-in-hand, but also this workforce has become very skilled in managing the sophisticated technologies that are introduced into this sector (Kumar and Aithal, 2016). This has led to the massive adoption of technology, and sharing of ideas, along with collaboration between technology platforms. Technology has become a proponent of speed, which is now more important than time or distance. It has also made communication simplified; making technology a standard by which it can be performed. How technology is perceived, and how it is utilised, has changed due to the environment it is being applied in. For example, as WAH becomes progressively more globalised, this means that the workforce will become more multicultural and multilingual. This is resulting in new ways of organisational structure – developed in addition to new policies, and ways of interacting with teams and co-workers. Technology has also improved the dissolution of gender barriers within their roles, as the ground is levelled by the equal use of technology. Technology helps to advance work performance and provide work-life options. The attitude of employers also has changed within this sector, as management leans more towards providing job enrichment and more flexible hours, rather than supervision alone.

In a study on the performance of WAH employment benefiting a national call centre, several surprising outcomes were discovered. This study was done on a large group of employees, where it was found that WAH was valued most in comparison to other offers (Mas and Pallais, 2017). Research revealed that job applicants would rather take an 8% decrease in wages in order to work at home. This was unexpected, as the concept of WAH was still widely unknown in call centres. Although a wage cut is costly, many employees valued this trade-off more so than receiving additional pay. However, if given the option to work longer hours rather than more flexible options, employees chose to work longer hours. When given the choice to work 50 hours, as opposed to 40 hours which provided more flexibility, 55% of the individuals chose the role with 50 hours.

The introduction of a new economy for work-at-home roles

The workplace environment has been changed into a deeply unstable and uncertain atmosphere, while adding to the globalisation of business which contributes to the switches in market demands, where there are several factors at play. Not only are there more competitors, but also disruptive technology often transforms the face of how business is enacted. Many organisations have also evolved to accommodate this new environment and have undertaken many of the more considerable changes (De Hauw and Greenhaus, 2015). For example, some organisations have become "leaner," as well as more adaptive, which allows them to moderate their organisational structure more effectively and more rapidly within a fluctuating market. Many have created more simplistic job structures, and even reduced the opportunity for employees to be promoted due to job uncertainty. However, this has allowed for more flexibility, in addition to the introduction of short-term transactional contracts (De Hauw and Greenhaus, 2015).

Due to the high level of uncertainty, where lifetime employment is most often not possible, employees have begun to start their own trends. In order to create their own careers and hone their own talents, they are able to aspire to more (De Hauw and Greenhaus, 2015). Employees, thus, have begun to increase their talent base in order to continue to be attractive as a job candidate, while also remaining adaptive in appealing to future employers. A key observation is that employees are able to advance themselves as career professionals in non-traditional ways.

Additionally, women have changed the shape of the economy, as they are now a stable part of the workforce. Today, nearly 50% of professionals and managers are female, as increasingly more women now work outside of the home (De Hauw and Greenhaus, 2015). This changed the traditional male and female roles, where the modern family is usually supported by dual-career professionals and single parents. Both genders are typically expected to manage domestic and work responsibilities, and because of this, often work and home are seen as one, rather than separate, entities. Because of this, the socioeconomic role of male and female individuals, whether married or single, has drastically changed. The home and work environments now influence one another. Only recently have scholars begun to see the effects that family life has on the careers of individuals, where some careers are customised to fit around personal goals. Careers are now seen as opportunities that consider the personal life decisions of every individual. The opening for older people to join the work force is also available, as the flexibility in work arrangements provides additional opportunities for those who are unable to fulfil in-person roles, whether due to the role's physical expectations or inconvenience, although the technological barriers can provide some setbacks.

In a traditional work economy, employees worked full-time schedules at established locations. Part-time work, job sharing, and other new forms of work contributions have begun to change the shape of how employees work and how they are compensated (De Hauw and Greenhaus, 2015). Employees can increase or decrease the amount of time they work, and also work on a schedule of their choosing. Companies cannot expect employees to stay with them for a lifetime, but rather, for a temporary career which works to meet the needs of the business. Discontinuities and interruptions in work are slowly becoming the norm. Some employers can expect employees to take time off, either to travel, to raise children, or for more personal reasons (such as a sick family member). Many simply resign from the company to begin a new business, or a new career, or shift job roles. Here is where entrepreneurship and innovation fuel economic growth.

The once permanent contracts that are associated with being an employee are now being exchanged for temporary contracts which have different durations. Some contracts are for independent employees, and others are even more transient and can be ended based on verbal notification (De Hauw and Greenhaus, 2015). This seems to take into consideration an enhanced level of personalisation regarding how contracts are made. For example, employees can create their own work parameters and negotiate terms with their employers. Flex arrangements, tele-work, and flex-time can all be decided upon according to the employee's unique needs. This includes work arrangements such as changes in employment relations, switches in location, changes in time and continuity, as well as the duration of the role. Job titles are also more flexible and can be negotiated on terms.

The job economy is now largely determined by globalisation. This is due to the fact that multinational growth has advanced, in addition to the progression of international careers and expatriate roles (De Hauw and Greenhaus, 2015). This has also increased the level of employee demand for global work experiences, where there are more international short-term assignments available to those who are working as expatriates, whether permanently or temporarily. The level of competency and job skills is more important than other aspects of employee work. The flexibility of employees is enhanced, which allows for their employability to be boosted by their wide range of skill sets and availability. The increase of working hours helps to expand the level of personal resources that an employee can afford, as well as devote to their work.

Issues with work-at-home opportunities

Some of the job-security problems that gig-economy workers have to undergo are due to the inconsistent nature of their occupation. For example, similar to part-time workers, temp-workers, and other contingent forms of work, independent contractors have to adjust to a lack of stability in their career (Berg, 2015). This means that oftentimes, these jobs are not really career level but are more often secondary income, which means that the tasks require minimum comprehension or training. While this may provide additional income, there is a loss of standards for these work opportunities. Other issues include the fact that there is no traditional relationship between employer and employees. The lack of protection makes it difficult for employees to continue to work long-term in an environment where tasks are mostly on-demand. It is not feasible long-term if no job security exists, whereas these tasks are only completed for compensation, rather than to hone a talent, skill, or future career.

Many a time, the outcomes of crowdwork(ers) invited legal challenges. Some high-profile lawsuits were the result, where US plaintiffs requested employee status in order to comply with the Fair Labor Standards Act (FLSA) in order to reveal that their job required higher expectations than an independent contractor (Berg, 2015). New movements are being created to protect individuals despite their role, regardless of the title they are provided. There has been a call for the creation of a system which protects independent workers missing out on such standard assurances as paid leave, employer-sponsored health care, retirement contributions, and disability insurance (Brookings, 2018). On balancing work and family, one study (Pew, 2013) offered a positive expectation of working parents in the workplace. It showed the rise in the notion of "shared responsibilities in the resources necessary to balance the responsibilities of work and family life (see Figure 11.4).

Although these flexible work arrangements provide an opportunity for individuals to work, which can contribute to a better work-life balance, it is not always

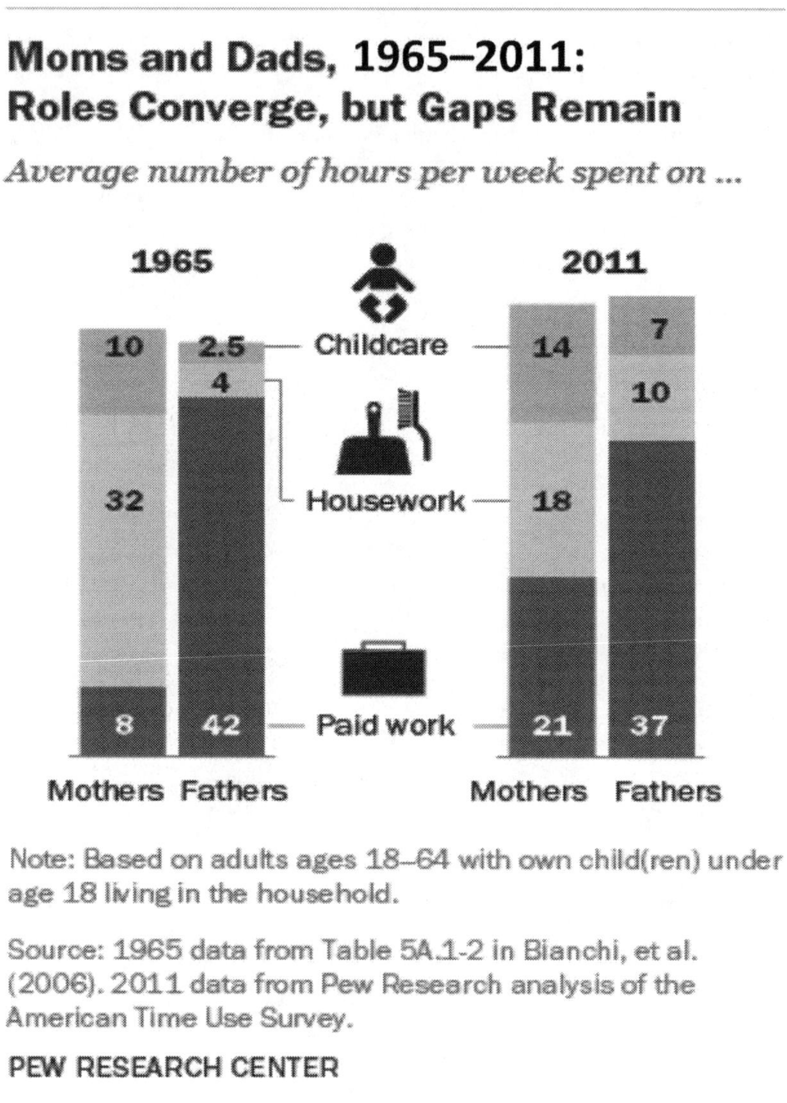

Figure 11.4 Balance work and family – parental roles converge

to the benefit of the worker (Mas and Pallais, 2017). These jobs can have irregular or unplanned schedules. For example, some workers may be expected to work weekends and nights. This can create a negative fragmentation of the workplace environment (home), although flexibility can also be beneficial in other ways. Independent contractors also benefit organisations in that these organisations need not address holidays, sick pay, Social Security, or anti-discrimination regulations (De Stefano, 2015). This translates as a cost savings to the business and benefits the employers more from independent contractors than the employees themselves. However, many believe that despite these risks, they are balanced by the flexibility proffered by job opportunities. The self-employment status affords a lack of fixed hours, which provides many chances to gain new wages and skills that wouldn't have occurred previously.

Globalisation, economy, and the work-home environment

As time progresses, multinational corporations, worldwide societies, globalisation, and the world economy continues to diversify the workforce. Nowadays, economists need to observe careers from a global perspective, rather than by country (Greenhaus and Kossek, 2014). Global careers are certainly becoming a staple, where career experiences are being developed internationally. They allow employees to become competent in a multicultural way, as they have to perform job tasks which are considerate of people from different nations. This means that they have a global approach to their work, and perspective, which is more collaborative than independent. This is widely unstudied in literature, as multicultural careers are a new occurrence within the job market. These careers are mostly related to projects which involve stakeholders that are sourced from two or more international regions. These global careers are entirely multicultural in essence, where there is a combination of both domestic and international cultural mechanisms.

For WAH workers, the involvement of being in a domestic atmosphere can either contribute to or harm their ability to manage global projects. For example, family members can create complications or distractions for expatriates who take on a project assigned to them (Greenhaus and Kossek, 2014). This ultimately affects job performance and completion. More research is necessary to discover how the new global workforce functions in a way that they can successfully perform their duties within a global workplace. Additionally, limited research is available on individuals who have cross-cultural differences, and how they interact with their employees and clients.

Economic outcomes of work-home opportunities

Temporary agency work is very provisional during economic downturns. It is found that temp workers are more employed during recovering economies and the rate remains high until the growth of the economy comes back to good health (Cappelli and Keller, 2013). This means that this trend continues as long as there is a fluctuating economy. Not much literature is provided on theories which analyse how these trends continue over time.

This also reveals a new dynamic, where there is a massive shift from long-term career work with a well-defined role. For example, in the past, most individuals expected to be a permanent employee with a set income based on a minimum wage. However, once this role is terminated and there is no feasible way to keep a consistent job, these individuals still have recognizable skills. There already exists a market for these types of talents, regardless of there being a long-term contract available. As the economy becomes more disrupted, as defined by the convergence of manufacturing, services, and technology to produce high-valued/adaptable industries, with fewer predictable careers and roles, the application of *lean* production and just-in-time staffing creates roles despite the volatile nature of the market. These individuals have specific skills and a knowledge base which can provide for companies that are outsourcing.

The factor of technology also provides breakthroughs, as well as disruption to the workforce. For example, during the Industrial Revolution, the workforce was separated into an assembly line (Osnowitz, 2010). Workers only provided skills for one aspect of the job, but didn't know how to wholly create the ultimate product. In this sense, there were some insecurities where employees lost their ability to have a full set of skills.

A new form of entrepreneur also develops itself in disrupted economies. Individuals may see themselves as successful when they are self-motivated and independent, where their personal talents can be tied to career achievements (Osnowitz, 2010). Individuals are able to manage their own resources, maintain their own business relationships, create new trades, and are more ambitious and ready to work self-directed. They receive project fees and work for clients or contracting employers on short-term agreements. Although, in some situations these employers may work as third parties, they still have more control over their job situation within the labour market. Clients go from individuals to large companies, and from corporations to non-profits, which can vastly diversify their client portfolio and skills.

This can create a new national economy which allows for greater collaboration, use of technology, and overall creativity within business societies (Sung, 2015). Additionally, information technology and knowledge can be easily accessed and shared between these workers. This economy can create new growth through economic operations which employ the use of new technology and knowledge that create new careers and learning opportunities. All of this happens regardless of the physical place and introduces the home as a viable workplace.

Another question comes to mind: both the fourth industrial revolution and globalisation affect the possibility of formulating a new policy view of the home (Zamagni, 2018). That said, the home is not immune as it becomes the new workplace, serving up productivity and subject to limitations, from negative views that home-based work impinges directly on family relations and child development more than centralised work settings. Nor should there be a perception of a zero-sum game. Past empirical studies have linked the inability to balance work and life, which suggested that adverse economic environments induce a more zero-sum game construal of success (Hutchinson, 2018). As workforce and workplace change, our received wisdoms about desirable outcomes need reappraisal. Research that is anecdotal and contemporary aids our understanding of the continuous process of renegotiation in the relationships of markets and society.

The incorporation of Maslow's Hierarchy of Needs

In order to better understand how WAH influences the economic dynamics of the job market, Maslow's Hierarchy of Needs is being applied as a framework for analysis. According to this theory, practices and strategies are based on motivations, which is important for understanding how to interact and engage with employees (De Vito et al., 2018). This is in regard to their performance, commitment, and satisfaction regarding their profession. Scholars believed that creating a motivational environment is crucial in workplace spaces, especially for those that don't compensate employees with high wages. Employee perceptions about their work, in addition to their satisfaction regarding their profession, helps to explain the motivations which lead them to take on specific jobs. It is widely believed that motivation focuses on persistence, direction, and intensity (De Vito et al., 2018). This refers to the strength of decision-making, the duration of time that is required to commit to that decision, and also the direction an individual takes. This concerns how an individual works for a company, and also how decisions are made as they continue to complete projects and tasks. How an employee decides to take on a new technology or client can also be seen within this lens.

The theory of Maslow has stated that individuals will satisfy basic needs before they are able to achieve higher-level desires. For example, the most basic needs are made up of physiological needs, which are on the bottom of this hierarchy (De Vito et al., 2018). This is regarded as necessary support to families and individuals. The next level is safety and security, which means that an individual has the ability to work in a safe, comfortable environment. Without this need being met, the individual will not be able to focus on higher goals. The need for safety may not be as important as physiological needs, or perhaps it is more important, as it depends on the individual. Next is the desire to belong, which means that employees may desire to be a part of a team or may need co-workers to support them. This means that these individuals may desire additional interaction, or communication, to feel as though they are part of a "whole." The next tier is the desire for self-esteem. This means that employees want to feel rewarded – to reveal their value proposition. At the very top of the hierarchy is self-actualisation. In this way, employees are able to provide for others. They have the ability to demonstrate subject-matter expertise. This can satisfy not only their own needs, but also the needs of other employees. These are all thought to depend on motivational forces which are based on career progression. The goal is to observe how WAH employees decide to take on jobs, their strategy for productivity, and other motivations which allow researchers to visualise how these individuals set goals. This allows the study of human motivations in regard to greater life satisfaction and achievement (Johnson et al., 2018).

Future implications

The changing face of today and future economic markets for jobs will be greatly influenced by technology and will drive entirely new expectations regarding wages and benefits. Due to evolving market drivers, WAH has exploded exponentially and should be viewed as transactional, and in broader terms than economic arrangements. Businesses can now outsource their work to on-demand workers independent of time or location of deliverable resources. This literature review informs that the integration between home and professional work will lead to considerations of what is changeable and inexorable in the future of home-based work and move beyond the occasional journalism onto sustained analysis and research.

Wages and benefits

Working conditions and wages are widely unstudied in the WAH sector, which means that the outcome of outsourcing and contracting self-employed individuals can change over time. This can create new gaps in wages and create wage inequality, as some companies may reduce the number of wages paid to these employees. Companies may shift the economic risk to workers by reducing compensation, as some workers may not understand how highly valued their talent is or what they are worth being compensated (Bernhardt et al., 2016). Additionally, the difference in contracting decisions can often create far different labour market outcomes (Bernhardt et al., 2016). While technological expertise can command higher wages, some roles may involve functions which are more supplemental than necessarily deliverable of services or products.

While some wage structures may work to the detriment of the independent employee, this enhances the level of global competition. The deregulation of labour markets and capital can shift the power from labour to capital (Bernhardt et al., 2016). However, individuals can choose how they market and appeal to employees. Some employees may only take specific wages and will be sure they have the talent to match the demand, while others will opt for the less obligatory jobs which carry lower wages and rewards.

There is not enough literature to cover how well wages are structured across occupations, industries, or business fields. Additionally, how this affects workers is still not widely understood. The addition of new information and technologies also helps to create lower costs, as the processing and effort required for work becomes more automated with time (Bernhardt et al., 2016). This can reduce the amount that individuals are paid concerning their level of production overall. However, this can be seen as an advantage. If technology is involved, organisations can better monitor and analyse the work that is completed, giving them improved control over activities. At the same time, those working from home are better positioned to control their "billable time." For this reason, there is some appeal to the influence of technology. Some wages increase due to cost-competition. For example, there may be a higher incentive to outsource due to the cost of a required service (Bernhardt et al., 2016). There are some reductions in product market regulations regarding the level of cost competition, which also enhance the level of trade liberalisation internationally. However, it can also be an enabler for deregulation across many sectors.

The deregulation of service industries can greatly harm independent workers, as they are no longer protected by unions. Typically, the deregulation of service industries often led to de-unionisation, where there was greater competition from non-union employees. This leads to an overall decrease in union power and protection of employee rights. Ultimately, this can result in a decrease in wages. In this economy, employees are not expected to appear for work regularly (De Stefano, 2015). Most of these employees are independent contractors, and receive no additional benefits beyond a wage, for example, health care or pension plans (Brookings, 2018). This means that there are challenges to family and home quality of life, as there is no job security, no paid holidays, no maternity leave, and there are no unemployment benefits. Without the labour protection, there is a risk to financial and economic stability in the family.

Technology enablers

Technology has boosted economic growth for freelancers overall. Additionally, it works alongside the demand for contingent workers (Tzeng, 2016). Technological change has also prompted a shift in attitude towards the hiring of on-demand employees. The online platform provides new economic trends, where mobile applications, online software, and other new tools help connect employees to supply and demand labour. Technology has made hiring WAH employees more convenient and more trustworthy. Standardised profiles have become common (i.e., LinkedIn), as well as ways to measure labour performance (website portfolios, testimonials, recommendations). There are ways to provide transparency and trust, where payments can be made through vehicles that provide encrypted transactions. PayPal, Dwolla, and many other new payment platforms has paved the way for all self-employed individuals.

Additional technologies include project management software, which helps to keep teams organised and more collaborative (Johns and Gratton, 2013). For managers who are working remotely, they have the ability to identify what tasks need to be completed, and the status of current tasks that are underway. This allows managers to be in constant communication with remote workers who can update and submit tasks to project management systems. These same management systems are helpful in optimising on-demand workers' output. Other systems, such as voice over internet protocol (VOIP) technology, also provides additional tools for virtual work. Individuals can perform phone calls through automated systems without the use of their personal phones or are able to forward calls to their phone with an anonymous phone number. Due to this, many individuals can be employed in a more professional and systematic way. A variety of other tools help keep self-employed individuals more organised, such as electronic calendars and schedulers, and browser tab software which help improve overall workflow. For the financial aspect of self-employed individuals, the use of accounting software and previously mentioned encrypted and secured payment systems provides accuracy and trust.

The use of technology doesn't come without its pitfalls. Many of the required technology should include security systems (antivirus scanners for malware), an additional cost factor to the business. For this reason, the inclusion of IT security is paramount must be factored into any cost centre metrics. The introduction of technology also creates new avenues for competitions, as some individuals may act as a single provider of services and expertise, as opposed to a major conglomerate, and outperform others based on rapid delivery and turn-around. Many small enterprise providers are, in fact, home-based entrepreneurs.

Conclusion

This chapter attempts to acknowledge a new reality of work, blending home and family, which has tended to be understated in its economic role. It proposes a new narrative, in which major changes should be understood, in essence, as disruptive challenges to established hierarchies. The new and extraordinary appearance of WAH individuals is revolutionising the way careers are approached. Not only does it restructure gender roles, it provides a new talented workforce that is not only adaptable to the changing economy, but also the technologies that acts as an enabler. Due to this adaptive workforce, employers have responded by providing new avenues for work. This includes less of the traditional full-time hourly wages, but increases flexible temp-work and contractual and pay-per-performance models where individuals can take up limited-scope projects. With so many new avenues for work, most individuals can overcome the economic pitfalls of an unstable job market, especially where the traditional long-term job opportunity no longer exists. Because of the oscillating economy, many companies have mandated workforce reductions, prompting downsizing of their opportunities.

Despite these setbacks, individuals are taking advantage of WAH – the new geography of work – where they can not only gain new talents in jobs they would not previously had access to had they been in a full-time work opportunity, but also managing their own contracts and work opportunities in ways conducive to work-life balance and the home as an economic actor. Many issues come with the WAH economy. It presents another form of job insecurity, such as the lack of worker protection, the potential for a company to release an employee at any time, as well as the ability of a company to provide low wages which may not fully compensate their employees for their talents. Employment relations continue to erode. However, because the WAH is now a global workforce, this forces senior leaders to link their companies' business and talent priorities. Employers will need to better understand the independent workforce and what motivates the people who participate in it (McKinsey Global Institute, October 2016). Those that present a high value with their talents will work at higher-paid roles, but must demonstrate greater flexibility, entertain more opportunities and optimise in favour of the home environment. Low-wage, commoditised work, may not carry the same quality, and could present limited options for work-life balance.

Technology has become a major component of these interactions. Technology automates, streamlines, and makes WAH work more trackable, traceable, and shareable. Technology will drive WAH behaviours as well as provide opportunities that optimise the home. However, it is also a challenge to the confident assumptions some commentators in work-life balance make that there is something inherently benign in technological disruption of hierarchical order. Consideration needs to be given to the experiences in the home employing work-life balance to identify means in which the economic energies transmitted can be agents of change to home as an economic unit aligned with the on-demand economy.

References

Berg, J., 2015. Income security in the on-demand economy: Findings and policy lessons from a survey of crowdworkers. *Comparative Labor Law & Policy Journal*, *37*, p. 543.

Bernhardt, A., Batt, R., Houseman, S. and Appelbaum, E., 2016. *Domestic Outsourcing in the US: A Research Agenda to Assess Trends and Effects on Job Quality*. Washington DC: US Department of Labor. https://www.dol.gov/sites/dolgov/files/OASP/legacy/files/Future_of_work_research_agenda_to_assess_trends_and_effects_on_job_quality.pdf.

Brookings, 2018, March. *Rethinking Worker Benefits for an Economy in Flux*. Available at: www.brookings.edu/blog/the-avenue/2018/03/29/rethinking-worker-benefits-for-an-economy-in-flux/ (Accessed: 8 July 2018).

Cappelli, P. and Keller, J.R., 2013. Classifying work in the new economy. *Academy of Management Review*, *38*(4), pp. 575–596.

De Hauw, S. and Greenhaus, J., 2015. 15 Building a sustainable career: The role of work – home balance in career decision making. *Handbook of Research on Sustainable Careers*, p. 223.

De Stefano, V., 2015. The rise of the just-in-time workforce: On-demand work, crowdwork, and labor protection in the gig-economy. *Comparative Labor Law & Policy Journal*, *37*, p. 471.

De Vito, L., Brown, A., Bannister, B., Cianci, M. and Mujtaba, B.G., 2018. Employee motivation based on the hierarchy of needs, expectancy and the two-factor theories applied with higher education employees. *IJAMEE*, *3*(1), pp. 20–32.

Greenhaus, J.H. and Kossek, E.E., 2014. The contemporary career: A work – home perspective. *Annual Review of Organizational Psychology and Organizational Behavior*, *1*(1), pp. 361–388.

Hutchinson, D., 2018. Work-Life balance in the workplace. In C. Aquino & R. Robertson (eds.), *Diversity and Inclusion in the Global Workplace*. Cham: Palgrave Macmillan.

Johns, T. and Gratton, L., 2013. The third wave of virtual work. *Harvard Business Review, 91*(1), pp. 66–73.

Johnson, J., Irizarry, M., Nguyen, N. and Maloney, P., 2018. Part 1: Foundational Theories of Human Motivation. In *Motivation 101: A Guide for Public Servants, 1*. https://stars.library.ucf.edu/motivationforpublicservants/1

Kumar, P.M. and Aithal, P.S., 2016. Working from Home-A Transition in the Concept of Workplace. *International Journal of Current Research and Modern Education, 1*(1), pp. 244–249.

Mas, A. and Pallais, A., 2017. Valuing alternative work arrangements. *American Economic Review, 107*(12), pp. 3722–3759.

Maslow, A.H. (1943). A theory of human motivation". *Psychological Review*. 50(4), pp. 370–396.

McKinsey Global Institute, 2016, October. *Independent Work: Choice, Necessity, and the Gig Economy*. Available at: www.mckinsey.com/global-themes/employment-and-growth/independent-work-choice-necessity-and-the-gig-economy (Accessed: 7 July 2017).

Osnowitz, D., 2010. *Freelancing Expertise: Contract Professionals in the New Economy*. Ithaca, NY: Cornell University Press.

Pew Research Center Social & Demographic Trends, 2013, March. *Modern Parenthood Roles of Moms and Dads Converge as They Balance Work and Family*. Available at: www.pewsocialtrends.org/2013/03/14/modern-parenthood-roles-of-moms-and-dads-converge-as-they-balance-work-and-family/ (Accessed: 7 August 2018).

Sappin, E., 2016. 7 Ways entrepreneurs drive economic development. *Entrepreneur*. Available at: www.entrepreneur.com/article/283616 (Accessed: 10 July 2018).

Sung, T.K., 2015. The creative economy in global competition. *Technological Forecasting and Social Change, 96*, pp. 89–91.

Tzeng, J., 2016. *Wages Rates, Types of Work, and Reputation on Online Platforms*. (Doctoral dissertation, New York University, Stern School of Business, New York).

Vanderkam, L., 2017. The productivity Boom we're missing–leveraging the working capacity of stay-at-home moms would be a big economic win. *City Journal the Shape of Work to Come*. Available at: www.city-journal.org/html/productivity-boom-were-missing-15259.html (Accessed: 7 July 2018).

Zamagni, S., 2018. The family and economic theorizing, Part IV, chapter 6. In A. Argandoña (ed.), *The Home: Multidisciplinary Reflections*. Cheltenham, UK: Edward Elgar Publishing.

Chapter 12

Caring for the home in Iberoamerica

A cross-country comparison

Sandra Idrovo Carlier, Belén Mesurado, and Patricia Debeljuh

Introduction

Communities around the world face conflicting forces that affect how work and home life interact. New work dynamics as well as new care needs influence how individuals perceive domestic chores (Freedman et al., 2014) and the developing and performing of the different home-making skills. However, when looking at the caring of the home we need to bear in mind that, as Argandoña (2018) suggests, from the multiple concepts of the home three internal common elements can be identified: "the person, the inner community or family, and a shared living space with an intention of continuity." And, as he continues, "there is also a fourth external element that cannot be excluded: the external social and material environment" (p. 11). Thus, how caring for the home is perceived differs along the lifespan (Leopold and Skopek, 2015) and is affected in turn by the perception and beliefs that communities hold in regards to those tasks and skills (Blair-Loy et al., 2015; Domínguez-Folgueras et al., 2016; Kossek, 2015).

Homes cannot be looked at in isolation; they exist within a society. In the same way, what caring for the home means cannot be explained in a vacuum. The meanings ascribed to the care needs fulfilled within the home, and the way they are fulfilled, are mediated by institutions and organisations (markets, churches, governments, companies); how they have developed historically; and governed by normative frameworks (laws, regulations, social and ethical norms, customs) (Argandoña, 2018). These elements interact and influence individual perceptions of how important or valuable the activities performed within the home or outside of it are.

Based in this reality, the Home Renaissance Foundation (UK), supported by the Walmart Centre for Work Family Balance (CONFyE, IAE Business School, Argentina) and the Culture, Work and Care Centre (CTC, INALDE Business School, Colombia), developed the Global Home Index (GHI), a worldwide research project aimed at determining how the work that is required to create a home is valued and experienced in different countries. For this specific study, we will only use data from the first part of the GHI and only from Iberoamerican countries. This research looks at how housework is perceived at the individual level: a) its importance; b) its dedication; and c) how it helps develop skills in different Iberoamerican countries. And, it especially looks at how national (HDI) and cultural (Global Gender Gap Index GGI) context is related to that perception. The research includes the following countries: Argentina, Colombia, Chile, Brazil, Peru, Ecuador, Uruguay, Mexico, Guatemala, El Salvador, and Spain. Results show certain general homogeneity among countries in their perception, but with some statistically significant differences among some of them and when gender is considered. In general, data confirms a devaluating perspective of care work (England, 2005) even though its importance to the public good is somehow asserted.

This chapter is arranged as follows: first, a review of the literature regarding care and the relation of care with elements at the cultural and social level. It also includes a look at the theories in relation to Latin and Iberoamerican cultural similarities and differences. Second, there is an explanation of the present study: its objectives, sample, and the methods used. The third part offers the results, and the final section presents a discussion of the findings and points towards future research venues.

Review of literature

The ever-constant technological advances bring about cultural and sociological changes that directly affect how we experience our lives: at home and at work. As new work dynamics appear, new ways of taking care of our personal and family needs develop. The second half of the twentieth century saw a very important increase of women participating in the labour force (Becker, 1985; Cotter et al., 2008). Such an increase in terms of paid labour caused the unpaid care of the home that women were doing before to become a "problem." Household members need to eat, get their laundry done, clean up their living quarters (occasionally, at least); children and infirmed adults require special attention, too. These needs do not disappear; what becomes scarce are the persons performing the work to fulfil those care needs and when and how to do it.

Care work refers to the provision of any face-to-face or hands-on service that develops the human capabilities of the recipient (England et al., 2002). These human capabilities refer to

> health, skills, or proclivities that are useful to oneself or others. These include physical and mental health, physical skills, cognitive skills, and emotional skills, such as self-discipline, empathy, and care.
>
> (p. 455)

Care work can be paid or unpaid. Unpaid care work usually takes place at home and is performed by family members or friends. The most time-intensive example of unpaid care work is parenting. Academic interest in care started with gerontologists and child development scholars who focus on the recipients of care. Later, and lead by feminist scholars, interest shifted towards the nature of the work, those who performed care work, and its relationship to gender and social inequality. More recent academic work has centred on the neoliberal move of care to the market and commoditised care into the family; the cultural and economic undervaluation of care labour; the structural positioning of care workers (according to gender, ethnic, nationality, and skills) within local and global labour markets; and the transnationalisation of care work (Huang, 2017).

England's review of care work theories (2005) highlights five theoretical frameworks developed to conceptualise care work. The "devaluation perspective" argues that care work is badly rewarded because care is associated with women, and often women of colour. The "public good" framework points out that care work provides benefits far beyond those to the direct recipient and suggests that the low pay of care work is a special case of the failure of markets to reward public goods. The "prisoner of love" theory argues that the intrinsic caring motives of care workers allow employers to more easily get away with paying care workers less. The "commodification of emotion" framework focuses on emotional harm to workers when they have to sell services that use an intimate part of themselves. Finally, the "love and money" perspective argues against dichotomous views in which markets are seen as antithetical to true care. Considering the scope and objectives of this research, we are especially interested in two of these frameworks: the devaluation perspective and the public good theory.

Devaluation of care work

This perspective argues that cultural biases limit wages and state support for care work because of its association with women (England, 2005). The supporters of this perspective hold that cultural ideas deprecate women and thus, by cognitive association, devalue work typically done by women. This rationale would explain why predominantly female occupations pay less than male-dominated fields, affecting both men and females in those occupations, but since there are more women working there, this heavily influences the gender pay gap (Cohen and Huffman, 2003).

Some argue that female-dominated jobs involving care are especially devalued because "care is the quintessentially female-identified activity" (Cancian and Oliker, 2000; England et al., 2002; Levanon et al., 2009). Moreover, as Green and Lawson (2011) underline, care work enters the commoditisation game with a handicap: its association with women and domesticity. Because there is the cultural assumption that, for example, caring for the home and household members is somehow work deemed "natural" for women to perform. Data from around the world confirm that women perform more unpaid care work than men, but in developed countries the number of hours women spend in unpaid care work has decreased drastically, although it still surpasses that of men (EUROSTAT, 2010). England (2010) argues that other signs that the devaluation of care work is due to its association with female work still prevails is that the number of males entering female-dominated professions and fields is smaller than the number of women entering male-dominated realms. The economic incentives for them to undertake work in women's professions simply do not exist. However, it is not just the lack of economic incentives that keep men from crossing the line into women's jobs; there is also the cultural backlash and disapproval they receive when daring to trespass gender boundaries.

It is not surprising then that society would perceive professional success as more important than caring for the home; because it would be success in a male-dominated realm with the economic benefits to prove it. Staying at home and caring for the needs of the family would be looked at as somewhat below that of professional success outside the home.

Care work within the public good framework

Scholars argue that paid and unpaid care work have more indirect social benefits than other types of work. This means that there is a high number of people who cannot be excluded from the indirect benefits that paid and unpaid care work produce, thus turning care work in a public good. Coleman (1993) argues that society has an interest in how well parents do the job of parenting, because that job can turn into net benefit or drag on society. Folbre (1994, 2001) also asserts that having and rearing children benefits people in society other than the children themselves. England (2005) poses that "at issue is not only how care imbues cognitive skills that increase earnings, but more broadly that receiving care also helps recipients develop skills, values, and habits that benefit themselves and others" (p. 385). "Benefits," continues England (2005), "to all the indirect recipients accrue because care workers help develop the capabilities of direct beneficiaries, and these beneficiaries spread them through social interaction" (p. 386). Within this perspective, the importance of caring for the home grows since this work would help develop human capabilities that in turn will aid in the growth of those around: not only parenting, but also all the housework that living entails.

However, unpaid care work is time and energy consuming. Therefore, with the main care provider now working outside the home but still performing most of the care work inside the home, women face a heavy burden. Studies of allocation of time show that working hours for women including paid and unpaid work have increased. This increase in turn has implications for personal health and the development of human capabilities. They are also relevant to subjective assessments of wellbeing such as the level of stress or feeling of being rushed (Ferrant et al., 2014; McDonald et al., 2005). As Folbre (2006) suggests, the allocation of women's time "affects their ability to develop their own capabilities – and that of their children. It also affects their relative standard of living, as measured by national income statistics" (p. 185). It is not only time allocation that is at stake in unpaid care work; energy to perform those tasks is also required. Becker (1985) indicates that household activities are high energy consuming, therefore affecting the amount of energy that women have left to allocate to other activities. The same restraints affect men who want to dedicate time to household work. Folbre (2006) states the dichotomy:

> Care imposes costs in the form of financial obligations, lost opportunities and foregone wages- but it also generates intrinsic rewards, stronger family and social ties, and high-quality services for the dependents.
>
> (p. 184)

However, as it has been mentioned before, national context macro elements such as labour market characteristics, culture and history, care provision, and gender ideology influence individual perceptions of unpaid care work. Thus, a look at the cultural and social traits of Latin America and of unpaid care work in the region is needed.

Latin America: Between similarities and differences

Researchers from different fields suggest that there are common contextual features that have shaped the development of Latin America. To begin with, a common history: since colonial times through independence, Latin American countries assumed the institutions of their colonisers, Spain and Portugal (Coatsworth, 2008; Ratliff, 2006). The common history also provided similar language and religious background (Catholicism). The latter being more spread out than the former (Brazil's language is Portuguese). This common history also served as an argument for modern regionalisms in the continent. As Riggirozzi (Red Latinoamericana de Política Comercial, LATN, 2010) points out, "a perceived sense of common legacy together with a realpolitik calculus of cooperation against imperialist external rule, political and economic, have been drivers of different regional arrangements and integration projects" (p. 5).

Along the same line, different authors have underlined other contextual elements that characterise the 20 distinct Latin American countries and identify them as belonging to one region and differentiating from other emerging economies (Grugel et al., 2008). These elements are related to similar political and economic organisations: almost all of them are liberal/electoral democracies and have pursued a dependent capitalist model of economic development (Nicholls-Nixon et al., 2011); and similar cultural views that focus on the individual and the family (Vassolo et al., 2011) to the extent of transforming it in a way of managing businesses and organisational structure called paternalism (Elvira and Davila, 2005) and prioritise the past and the present over the future. They also share similar social problems, such as political instability, corruption, work informality, poverty, and social distance that affect the way they harmonise their work duties and their lives at home.

All these similarities notwithstanding, there are several differences in how the Latin America countries face their problems and organise their family, social, and professional lives (Ruiz-Gutierrez et al., 2012; Susaeta et al., 2013). But most important is how not all of the citizens of Latin American countries identify with the Latin American label. This is the case of Brazilians. Onuki et al. (2016), in a study using data from *The Americas and the World* project in order to establish whether Latin Americans share a common regional identity, found that the majority of Brazilians do not identify themselves as Latin Americans. This result, according to the same authors, corroborates that "the self-identification of Brazilians diverges from those of their Latin American counterparts, which confirms Bethell's thesis of 'Brazilian exceptionalism'[1]" (p. 437).

Unpaid care work in Latin America

Once the general features of the Latin American landscape have been described, it is timely to look at the organisation of care. In this area, Latin American countries face similar challenges as those mentioned before for developed economies. However, some characteristics are peculiar to the region and are worth considering. According to Rodriguez (2012), the high level of labour informality makes organising care through legislation or by offering care services at the workplace almost impossible and of little impact.

Latin American countries offer very few state care provisions. While paid maternity and paternity leaves are present, maternity leave being longer than paternity, for those enrolled in formal work, there is hardly any other provision that considers the care that takes place at home (Vega and Gutierrez-Rodriguez, 2014). Thus, as Rodriguez (2012) indicates, the high level of informality nullifies the potential impact of supporting legislation or state provisions. Although through following the trends in developing countries, a certain kind of marketisation of care has taken place. Marketisation of care may be defined as "the increase of private providers within the publicly funded services as well as the increase of privately purchased help" (Szebehely and Trydegård, 2012: 307). In Latin America, such publicly funded services are very few, so for-profit actors offer their services, benefiting those that can afford their fees, not necessarily those who need those services. Again, within the family, women are the ones that shoulder the effort. Outside family, charity institutions become the main care providers, especially for older people that have no one or nowhere to turn to.

Another important trait affecting Latin American countries is the relevance of paid domestic care. With some variations among the different countries, nearly 20% of the economically active female population is occupied in this sector and they are employed by middle- and high-class homes to take care of their care work at home (Rodriguez, 2012). Legislation that protects these workers, mostly indigenous and African American women, is recently growing in the different Latin American countries (Vega and Gutierrez-Rodriguez, 2014), pushed by workers' organisations trying to implement the ILO 189 convention about domestic workers. These characteristics should help us interpret the data obtained in our research.

The present study

This study is exploratory and descriptive. It looks at how housework is perceived at the individual level: a) its importance; b) its dedication; and c) how it helps develop skills in different Iberoamerican countries. The research includes the following countries: Argentina, Colombia, Chile, Brazil, Peru, Ecuador, Uruguay, Mexico, Guatemala, El Salvador, and Spain. It also looks at how national (Human Development Index HDI) and cultural (Global Gender Gap Index GGI) context is related to that perception. The objectives are:

1 To identify society's perception of professional success compared with successful homemaking across ten Latin American countries and Spain and divided by sex.
2 To analyse the level of importance attributed to household tasks across ten Latin American countries and Spain and divided by sex.
3 To determine if men and women across ten Latin American countries and Spain perceive performing homemaking tasks as helping them develop skills.
4 To assess if men and women across ten Latin American countries and Spain perceive that work commitments lead them to neglect time dedicated to home and family life.
5 To analyse how many hours men and women across ten Latin American and Spain spend on household tasks per week.
6 To study if there are differences in the previous variables in countries with different levels of Global Gender Gap Index (GGI) and Human Development Index (HDI).

Sample: A total number of 2,750 of adults from ten different Latin American countries and Spain participated in this study (Argentina, Brazil, Chile, Colombia, Ecuador, El Salvador, Guatemala, Mexico, Peru, and Uruguay). Table 12.1 shows the characteristics of the different samples. Data was collected through an online questionnaire designed for this purpose (the GHI). To carry out the global survey, several partners (research centres, universities, colleges, NGOs related to the subject, etc.) were involved with the dissemination of this initiative. Answers were collected through a specially designed web page, available in seven languages: Spanish, Italian, English, German, French, Portuguese, and Hungarian.

Measurement

1 *General Perceptions in Relation to Household Tasks*. We designed an ad hoc questionnaire for this research that includes five questions regarding the individual perception of household tasks (See Annex 1). The scale includes five possible answers scored from 1 to 5 points (1 = I do not agree at all and 5 = I completely agree).

Table 12.1 Descriptive statistics for the samples

Country	*n*	*Age Average*	*Females (%)*	*Number of children*
Argentina	250	42.7	50%	3.28
Brazil	250	41.5	68%	1.86
Chile	250	42.1	58%	2.90
Colombia	250	42.3	50%	1.86
Ecuador	250	41.05	50%	1.84
El Salvador	250	41.6	63%	2.23
Guatemala	250	41.02	70%	2.23
Mexico	250	38.58	60%	1.56
Peru	250	41.51	63%	2.01
Spain	250	42.8	62%	2.58
Uruguay	250	38.1	50%	2.20

2 *Global Gender Gap Index (GGI)*. Through the Global Gender Gap Report (2016), the World Economic Forum quantifies the magnitude of gender disparities and tracks their progress over time, with a specific focus on the relative gaps between women and men across four key areas: health, education, economy, and politics. The GGI has three defining features. First, it focuses on measuring gaps rather than levels. Second, it captures gaps in outcome variables rather than gaps in input variables. Third, it ranks countries according to gender equality rather than women's empowerment.

3 *Human Development Index (HDI)*. The composite Human Development Index (HDI) integrates three basic dimensions of human development. Life expectancy at birth reflects the ability to lead a long and healthy life. Mean years of schooling and expected years of schooling reflect the ability to acquire knowledge. And gross national income per capita reflects the ability to achieve a decent standard of living. To measure human development more comprehensively, the Human Development Report also presents four other composite indices. The Inequality-adjusted HDI discounts the HDI according to the extent of inequality. The Gender Development Index compares female and male HDI values. The Gender Inequality Index highlights women's empowerment. In addition, the Multidimensional Poverty Index measures non-income dimensions of poverty.

Data analysis

Descriptive analyses of the variables under study were carried out. Five factorial Analysis of Variance (ANOVA) were performed in order to study the differences in: 1) Society´s perception of professional success compared to successful homemaking, 2) Level of importance attributed to household tasks, 3) Individual perception of homemaking helping to develop skills, 4) Individuals neglecting house work, and 5) Number of hours spent on household tasks across ten Latin American countries and Spain by sex. In these analyses, country and sex variables were used as independent variables. Finally, to study objective 6, two one-way ANOVA were performed in order to study if there are differences in the dependents variables in each country with different levels of Global Gender Gap Index (GGI) and Human Development Index (HDI). In these analyses, GGI and HDI were used as independent variables.

Results

The first objective of our work was to identify whether men and women across ten Latin American countries and Spain perceive that society values more professional success than successful homemaking. This study was undertaken using a factorial ANOVA, country, and sex variables were used as independent variables. The results indicate that there are no statistical differences between countries. All the participants from different countries perceive that society values more professional success than successful homemaking [F (10, 2728) = 2.29; p =. 06]. However, there are statistically significant differences between sex [F (1, 2728) = 10.62; $p \leq$ 01] and interaction between country by sex [F (10, 2728) = 3.97; $p \leq$ 05]. Argentinean and Chilean men perceive that society gives more importance to professional success than to successful homemaking than women from those countries [Argentina = t (248) = 3.52; $p \leq$ 001; Chile = t (248) = 4.28; $p \leq$ 001]. Moreover, Mexican women perceive that society gives more importance to professional success than to successful homemaking than Mexican men do [t (248) = -3.45; $\leq$ 001]. See Table 12.2.

The second objective was to analyse the level of importance attributed to household tasks across ten Latin American countries and Spain. We found statistically

Table 12.2 Mean comparisons

	Soc Imp		*Ind Imp*		*Skills Dev*		*Neglect*		*Ded hrs/w*	
Country	*M*	*F*	*M*	*F*	*M*	*F*	*M*	*F*	*M*	*F*
Spain	4,41	4,2	4,08	4,08	4,55	4,4	3,6	3,52	12,15	17,55
Argentina	4,36	3,87	4,31	4,47	4,5	4,61	3,57	3,13	16,31	22,82
Brazil	4,31	4,2	4,74	4,32	4,8	4,7	3,68	3,88	13,42	19,49
Chile	4,36	3,65	4,36	4,29	4,61	4,5	3,67	3,55	12,73	20,52
Colombia	4,13	4,07	4,13	4,35	4,5	4,6	3,78	3,77	15,24	19,86
Ecuador	3,97	3,97	4,2	4,18	4,5	4,5	3,7	3,52	11,75	17,55
El Salvador	4,11	4	4,2	4,53	4,6	4,7	3,52	3,52	14,17	18,47
Guatemala	4,14	4	4,33	4,18	4,7	4,6	3,61	3,59	9,64	18,94
Mexico	3,95	4,41	4,02	4,16	4,4	4,5	3,58	3,64	8,56	14,78
Peru	4,21	4,11	4,15	4,21	4,6	4,5	3,57	3,47	14,22	20,82
Uruguay	4,12	4,05	4,3	4,28	4,5	4,42	3,5	3,43	15,63	20,64

significant differences across countries [$F(10, 2728) = 8.25$; $p \leq 001$]. We also found statistically significant differences between sex [$F(1, 2728) = 3.27$; $p \leq 05$] and interaction between country by sex [$F(10, 2728) = 1.98$; $p \leq 05$]. Brazilian participants attributed more importance to household tasks than Colombian (Scheffe = .35, p ≤ 001), Ecuadorian (Scheffe = .40, p ≤ 001), Mexican (Scheffe = .49, p ≤ 001), Peruvian (Scheffe = .40, p ≤ 001), and Spanish (Scheffe = .50, p ≤ 001) participants. Moreover, the Salvadorian participants reported giving more importance to household tasks than Spanish participants did (Scheffe = .33, p < .05). There are no differences between other countries. Concerning differences between sex, Brazilian men attributed more importance to household tasks than women [$t(248) = 2.57$; $p \leq 01$], while Colombian and Salvadorian women attributed more importance to household tasks than men [Colombia = $t(248) = -1.99$; $p \leq 05$ and Salvador = $t(248) = -3.46$; $p \leq 001$]. See Table 12.2.

The third objective was to determine if men and women across ten Latin American countries and Spain perceive performing homemaking tasks as helping them develop skills. We found statistically significant differences across countries [$F(10, 2728) = 4.33$; $p \leq 001$], but there are no differences between sex and the interaction between country and sex. The post hoc analyses have shown that Brazilian participants reported perceiving that performing homemaking tasks helps them develop skills more than Uruguayans (Scheffe = .27, p ≤ 05) and Spanish (Scheffe = .27, p ≤ 05) participants. There are no differences between other countries. See Table 12.2.

The fourth objective was to assess if men and women across ten Latin American countries and Spain perceive that work commitments lead them to neglect time dedicated to home and family life. The results indicate that there are statistically significant differences between countries [$F(10, 2728) = 3.77$; $p \leq .001$] and sex [$F(1, 2728) = 3.24$; $p \leq .05$]. Brazilian participants reported a higher level of perception of work commitments leading them to neglect time dedicated to home and family than Argentineans (Scheffe = .47, p ≤ 05). Moreover, Colombian participants reported a higher level of perception of work commitments lead them to neglect time dedicated to home and family than Argentineans (Scheffe = .42, p ≤ 05). There are no differences between other countries. The results indicated that there are statistically significant differences between sexes in only one country. The Argentinean men perceive that work commitments lead them to neglect time dedicated to home and family life more than women [$t(248) = 3.35$; $p \leq 001$]. See Table 12.2.

The fifth objective was to analyse the differences in hours spent on household tasks per week across ten Latin American countries and Spain. The results indicated that there are statistically significant differences between countries [F (10, 2728) = 4.56; p ≤ 001] and sex [F (1, 2728) = 98.23; p ≤ 001]. Argentinean participants reported more hours doing household tasks per week than Mexican participants (Scheffe = 7.25, p ≤ 01). There are no differences between other countries. Concerning division by sex, results indicate that women from all countries spend more time on household tasks per week than men in all countries [Argentina = t (248) = -2.95; $p \leq 01$; Brazil = t (248) = 2.32; $p \leq 05$; Chile = t (248) = 3.92; $p \leq 001$; Colombia = t (248) = -2.05; $p \leq 05$; Ecuador = t (248) = -2.82; $p \leq 01$; Salvador = t (248) = -2.08; $p \leq 05$; Guatemala = t (248) = -4.16; $p \leq 001$; Mexico = t (248) = -4.79; $p \leq 001$; Peru = t (248) = -2.99; $p \leq 01$; Spain = t (248) = -3.34; $p \leq 001$; and Uruguay = t (248) = -2.76; $p \leq 01$]. See Table 12.2.

Finally, the sixth objective was to determine if there were differences in *General Perceptions in Relation to Household Tasks* between countries with different levels of Human Development Index (HDI). Using the Human Development Index (HDI), we established three groups: countries with medium human development (El Salvador and Guatemala), countries with high Human Development (Brazil, Colombia, Ecuador, Mexico, Peru, and Uruguay) and countries with Very High Human Development (Spain, Argentina, and Chile). Then, we studied the differences of the five items that include *General Perceptions in Relation to Household Tasks* between the three groups of countries with different levels of human development. This study was undertaken using a one-way Analysis of Variance (ANOVA), and each item of *General Perceptions in Relation to Household Tasks* were used as a dependent variable and the *Human Development Index* was used as independent variable. The results show no statistically significant differences among the countries.

Then, we studied if there are differences in *General Perceptions in Relation to Household Tasks* between countries with different levels of *Global Gender Gap Index (GGI)*. Using the *Global Gender Gap Index (GGI),* we established two groups: countries with level 3 (Brazil, Peru, Uruguay, and Guatemala) and countries with level 4 (Spain, Argentina, Chile, Colombia, Ecuador, El Salvador, and Mexico). Then we studied the differences of the five items that include *General Perceptions in Relation to Household Tasks* between the two groups of countries with different level of *Global Gender Gap Index*. The results show no statistically significant differences.

Discussion and future research

Results offer a somewhat homogeneous view of the ten Latin American countries and Spain, as far as how their perception of caring for the home goes. They all agree that society holds professional success in higher regard than success at homemaking. In this sense, the data falls along the arguments of the devaluation of care theory: care work is not as valued as other activities, or at least that is how Latin Americans and Spaniards think society perceives taking care of the home. When comparing among countries and looking at possible differences between men and women, men from Argentina and Chile stand out as considering significantly more than women in their countries that society values professional success more than successfully caring for the home. As a contrast, women from Mexico are the ones distinguishing themselves from men about that question. Interestingly enough, the three countries rank at the same level in the GGI, raising the question of identifying other elements that might be influencing the difference in perceptions. For example, and in line with Szebehely's view of marketisation and care work, a deeper look at state care policies and how they impact this perception seems in order. That there is no significant difference between Spain and the Latin American countries is surprising, when considering the level of economic development; but unsurprising when considering the common culture characterised by familyism and paternalism (Molyneux, 2006).

When focusing on how important household tasks are for Latin Americans, Brazilian participants stand out from the rest: they attributed more importance to household tasks than participants from almost all other countries. And when separating men from women, Brazilian men again distance themselves from women in their country: they significantly surpassed women when considering how important household tasks are for them. Again, more Brazilians reported perceiving that performing homemaking tasks helps them develop skills. High levels of agreement in both issues make sense: household tasks are important because they help develop skills. These results somehow feed Brazil's exceptionalism theory: they are not like all the other Latin American countries.

However, the fact that there are no significant differences among men and women in any country when asked if they think that performing household tasks help them develop other skills upholds the idea that caring for the home indirectly benefits others and not only the ones receiving care. In this case, it can be argued that care enhances the skills of the care provider as well as the direct recipient, strengthening the view of care as a public good that needs to be taken into account when designing social policies.

When it comes down to work and home competing for time, Colombians and Brazilians reported higher levels of perceiving that work commitments lead them to neglect time for their family and home, and there are no significant differences among men and women of those countries. But there is a difference in Argentina: significantly more men than women in that country perceive that they neglect their family and home because of work responsibilities. As pointed out when describing Latin American social and cultural context, family is important for them, thus, it is not surprising that they feel that they are losing the challenge of harmonising work and family. One would have also expected that precisely due to the importance of family and the role that women play in caring for the home, there would have been differences between men and women in other countries as well.

Men and women from Argentina are the ones spending more hours caring for the home than men and women from any other country. And, as in the rest of the world, in Latin America and Spain women from all the countries spend significantly more time on household tasks than men. This result contributes to the theory of devaluation of care work precisely because it is performed in great part by women. Once again, women's monopoly on caring for the home, wanted or forced, imposes a heavy burden upon their shoulders. Because in all the countries in the study, women make up half of the working population (on average) and end up working outside and in their homes with the consequences that hard daily routines bring about. Within this scenario, it is important to carefully think about state care provisions that might seem to aid in solving one problem but end up creating several others. For example, an extension in paid maternity leave might seem to alleviate childcare and ensure the mother's job; but at the same time, this extension might exacerbate discrimination against women in the job market. Leaves that are intended to secure quality care for the child in his/her firsts months cannot jeopardise women's job opportunities, especially when the number of homes where the woman is the main provider, or the only provider, is almost a third. A gender-neutral leave might have better effects since it would also include men in care duties.

Finally, neither level of HDI nor GGI seem to be related to any of the results. Somehow this result suggests that maybe common history and cultures of Latin American and Spain exert more influence in the development of perceptions than the level of human development reached or how narrow the gender gap is in these countries. One other future research venue could include looking at how younger Latin Americans and Spaniards (20–30 years old) perceive caring for the home. Since our sample media age ranges from 38–42.8, their vision might differ from that of younger generations. At the same time, caring for the elders is fast becoming a problem, since as part of the extended family in Latin America, they perform care duties that freed time for other members to work. Therefore, a look centring on the ageing population caring for the home would be of great help in Iberoamerican countries.

References

Argandoña, A. (2018) The Home: Multidisciplinary Reflections. In A. Argandoña (ed.), *The Home. Multidisciplinary Reflections*. Cheltenham, Edward Elgar, pp. 8–31.

Becker, G. (1985) Human Capital, Effort, and the Sexual Division of Labor. *Journal of Labor Economics*, 3 (1), Part 2: Trends in Women's Work, Education, and Family Building (January, 1985), S33–S58.

Bethell, L. (2010) Brazil and "Latin America". *Journal of Latin American Studies*, 42 (3), 457–485.

Blair-Loy, M., Hochschild, A., Pugh, A., Williams, J., & Hartmann, H. (2015) Stability and Transformation in Gender, Work, and Family: Insights from the Second Shift for the Next Quarter Century. *Community, Work, Family*, 435–454. [Online] Available from doi :10.1080/13668803.2015.1080664 [Accessed 20 December 2017].

Cancian, F. M., & Oliker, S. J. (2000) *Caring and Gender*. Thousand Oaks, CA, Pine Forge.

Coatsworth, J. H. (2008) Inequality, Institutions and Economic Growth in Latin America. *Journal of Latin American Studies*, 40, 545–569. [Online] Available from doi:10.1017/S0022216X08004689 [Accessed 14 January 2018].

Cohen, P., & Huffman, M. L. (2003) Occupational Segregation and the Devaluation of Women's Work Across US Labor Markets. *Social Forces*, 81 (3), 881–908.

Coleman, J. S. (1993) The Rational Reconstruction of Society. *American Sociological Review*, 58, 1–15.

Cotter, D. A., Joan, M., Hermsen, J. M., & England, P. (2008) Moms and Jobs: Trends in Mothers' Employment and which Mothers Stay Home. In S. Coontz, M. Parson, & G. Raley (eds.), *American Families: A Multicultural Reader*, 2nd ed. New York, Routledge, pp. 379–86.

Domínguez-Folgueras, M., Jurado-Guerrero, T., Botía-Morillas, C., & Amigot-Leache, P. (2016) "The House Belongs to Both": Undoing the Gendered Division of Housework. *Community, Work & Family*. [Online] Available from doi:10.1080/13668803.2016.1192525 [Accessed 10 January 2017].

Elvira, M., & Davila, A. (eds.). (2005) *Managing Human Resources in Latin America*. London, Routledge.

England, P. (2005) Emerging Theories of Care Work. *Annual Review of Sociology*, 31, 381–399. [Online] Available from doi:10.1146/annurev.soc.31.041304.122317 [Accessed 12 June 2016].

England, P. (2010) The Gender Revolution: Uneven and Stalled. *Gender & Society*, 24 (2), 149–166.

England, P., Budig, M., & Folbre, N. (2002) Wages of Virtue: The Relative Pay of Care Work. *Social Problems*, 49 (4), 455–473.

EUROSTAT. (2010) *Time Spent in Unpaid Forms of Work (as Main or Secondary Activity) by Sex and by Form of Work*. [Online] Available from http://ec.europa.eu/eurostat/web/products-datasets/-/tus_00npaywork [Accessed 15 February 2017].

Ferrant, G., Pesando, L. M., & Nowacka, K. (2014, December) *Unpaid Care Work: The Missing Link in the Analysis of Gender Gaps in Labour Outcomes*. Paris: OECD Development Centre.

Folbre, N. (1994) Children as Public Goods. *American Economic Review*, 84, 86–90.

Folbre, N. (2001) *The Invisible Heart: Economics and Family Values*. New York, New Press.

Folbre, N. (2006) Measuring Care: Gender, Empowerment, and the Care Economy. *Journal of Human Development*, 7 (2), 183–199.

Freedman, V. A., Cornman, J. C., & Carr, D. (2014) Is Spousal Caregiving Associated with Enhanced Well-Being? New Evidence from the Panel Study of Income Dynamics. *Journals of Gerontology*, Series B: Psychological Sciences and Social Sciences. [Online] Available from doi:10.1093/geronb/gbu004 [Accessed 12 June 2016].

Gender Gap Index (2016) *The Global Gender Gap Report 2016*. [Online] Available from http://reports.weforum.org/global-gender-gap-report-2016/ [Accessed 14 May 2017].

Green, M., & Lawson, V. (2011) Recentring Care: Interrogating the Commodification of Care. *Social & Cultural Geography*, 12 (6), 639–654.

Grugel, J., Riggirozzi, P., & Thirkell-White, B. (2008) Beyond the Washington Consensus? Asia and Latin America in Search of More Autonomous Development. *International Affairs*, 84, 499–517.

Huang, S. (2017) Care Work. In D. Richardson, N. Castree, M. F. Goodchild, A. Kobayashi, W. Liu, & R. A. Marston (eds.), *The International Encyclopedia of Geography*. John Wiley & Sons, Ltd. [Online] Available from doi:10.1002/9781118786352.wbieg0127 [Accessed 20 December 2017].

Kossek, E. (2015) Capturing Social and Cultural Influences: Relating Individual Work-Life Experiences to Context. *Community, Work and Family*, 371–376. [Online] Available from dx.doi.org/10.1080/13668803.2015.1081506 [Accessed 12 June 2016].

Leopold, T., & Skopek, J. (2015) Convergence or Continuity? The Gender Gap in Household Labor After Retirement. *Journal of Marriage and Family*, 77, 819–832.
Levanon, A., England, P., & Allison, P. (2009) Occupational Feminization and Pay: Assessing Causal Dynamics Using 1950–2000 Census Data. *Social Forces*, 88, 865–892.
McDonald, M., Phipps, S., & Lethbridge, L. (2005) Taking its Toll: The Influence of Paid and Unpaid Work on Women's Well-Being. *Feminist Economics*, 11 (1), 63–94.
Molyneux, M. (2006) Mothers at the Service of the New Poverty Agenda: Progresa/Oportunidades, Mexico's Conditional Transfer Programme. *Social Policy & Administration*, 40 (4), 425–449.
Nicholls-Nixon, C. L., Davila Castilla, J. A., Sanchez Garcia, J., & Rivera Pesquera, M. (2011) Latin America Management Research: Review, Synthesis, and Extension. *Journal of Management*, 37 (4), 1178–1227.
Onuki, J., Mouron, F., & Urdinez, F. (2016) Latin American Perceptions of Regional Identity and Leadership in Comparative Perspective. *Contexto Internacional*, 38 (1), 433–465.
Ratliff, W. (2006) America's Fledgling, Fumbling Democracies. *Review of Policy Research*, 23, 295–309.
Red Latinoamericana de Política Comercial. (2010, April) Region, Regionness and Regionalism in Latin America: Towards a New Synthesis (Working Paper N° 130). Buenos Aires, Riggirozzi.
Rodriguez, C. (2012) Work-Family Balance Issues in Latin America: A Roadmap to National Care Systems. Paper prepared for the Expert Group Meeting on "Good Practices in Family Policy Making: Family Policy Development, Monitoring and Implementation: Lessons Learnt", organized by The UN Department of Economic and Social Affairs, New York, 15-17 May.
Ruiz-Gutierrez, J. A., Murphy Jr. E. F., Greenwood, R. A., Monserrat, S. I., Olivas-Luján, M. R., Madero, S., . . . Uy, O. A. (2012) Work, Family and Values in Four Latin-American Countries. *Management Research: The Journal of the Iberoamerican Academy of Management*, 10 (1), 29–42.
Szebehely, M., & Trydegård, G. (2012) Home Care for Older People in Sweden: A Universal Model in Transition, *Health and Social Care in the Community*, 20 (3), 300–309.
Susaeta, L., Pin, J. R., Idrovo, S., Espejo, A., Belizón, M., Gallifa, A. . . . Pedrozo, E. A. (2013) Generation or Culture? Work Attitude Drivers: An Analysis in Latin America and Iberian Countries. *Cross Cultural Management: An International Journal*, 20 (3), 321–360.
Vassolo, R., De Castro, J., & Gomez-Mejia, L. (2011) Managing in Latin America: Common Issues and a Research Agenda. *Academy of Management Perspectives*, 25 (4), 22–36.
Vega, C., & Gutierrez–Rodriguez, E. (2014) Nuevas aproximaciones a la organización social del cuidado. Debates Latinoamericanos. *Íconos. Revista de Ciencias Sociales*, 50, 9–26.

Annex I

General perceptions in relation to household tasks

Please read the following affirmations in detail and indicate your level of agreement, using a scale of 1–5, where:

1 = I do not agree at all, 2 = I agree very little, 3 = I agree somewhat, 4 = I quite agree, and 5 = I completely agree

1 Society values professional success more than taking care of household tasks.
2 For me it is important to take care of household tasks.
3 I think that living family life and participating in household tasks helps me to develop my skills for other areas of life (e.g., learning how to serve others, to be adaptable, to adapt to different circumstances and needs, etc.)
4 I think that my work commitments lead me to neglect time dedicated to home and family life.
5 How many hours do you spend on household tasks per week? State a number.

Note

1 Bethell emphasises the country's unique colonial heritage, intellectuals' long-held dismissal of Brazil as a Latin American country, and the reluctance of consecutive Brazilian military governments to assume a leadership position as factors that have historically negated a sense of regional belonging (Bethell, 2010: 481).

Chapter 13

Working from home

Is technology a help or a hindrance in achieving work/life harmonisation?

Kathleen Farrell

Introduction

It is widely believed that technological innovations in microelectronics and telecommunication "could shift literally millions of jobs out of the factories and offices into which the Second Wave (Industrial Revolution) swept them and right back to where they came from originally: the home" (Toffler, 1981: 204), cited by Shamir and Salomon (1985). This change is impacting work organisations, employees, systems of transportation, energy consumption, air pollution, and the labour market (Shamir and Salomon, 1985). Information technology constitutes a necessary element in the office environment and there has been a decline in the physical significance of the workplace (Nakrosiene et al., 2019).

Work and family could be said to be two of the most significant elements of human life (Toyin et al., 2016). Indeed, work/family balance is one of the most challenging issues facing families in the twenty-first century (Walker et al., 2008). Friedman (2014: 12) highlights that to be effective one needs "to know what matters." He recommends an exercise called "Four Circles" representing the four domains "work, home, community and self." This helps reflect on the "values, goals, interests, actions and results" cultivated in each area, and whether the latter are compatible or opposed to each other. When people engage in flexible working, the relationship between work and home needs to be redefined and changes made (Tietze and Musson (2003, 2005). In relation to the gendered division of labour, Sullivan and Lewis (2001: 123) showed that divisions can be emphasised more as "teleworking can simultaneously enhance work/life balance while perpetuating traditional work and family roles."

Referring to leaders, Groysberg and Abrahams (2014: 60) state that "They've discovered through hard experience that prospering in the senior ranks is a matter of carefully combining work and home so as not to lose themselves, their loved ones, or their foothold of success." Zamagni (2018: 134) refers to work/life harmony and points to the need to "provoke a radical rethinking of the organization of work in the modern-day firm."

Different perspectives on teleworking

Bloom (2014: 28–29) claims that critics assert that employees who are not office-based are actually not working. IBM and Yahoo, among others, have both reversed their work-from-home policy (Useem, 2017: 27). Where collaboration is needed, "communications technology offering the fastest, cheapest, and highest bandwidth connection is still the office" (Useem, 2017: 27). If it is personal productivity that is required or jobs necessitating dealing with customers, or no interaction at all, then it's better to let people work remotely (Useem, 2017). Otani (2015) argues for flexibility and cites Sheryl Sandberg, Facebook's Chief Operating Officer, as making the important distinction between seeming productive and being productive.

Timsal and Mustabsat (2016) in their abstract pose the question "why a perk or benefit is now being considered as an ethical issue." Establishments which support work from home claim that this latter opportunity results in greater productivity. In a study conducted by Tunyaplin et al. (1998: 183), the participants were asked if, given the opportunity, how they would divide their time between a home office and a remote job site, i.e., how many days per week would they work from home? Over 75% of respondents, regardless of where they currently work, suggested they would spend only two or three days per week in the home office.

Working from home and identity

According to the literature on working from home, the results indicate that the success or failure of working from home is very closely linked to homeworkers' identity. (Tietze and Musson, 2010). Working from home involves the challenge of dealing with different identities, i.e., being at home and at work (Tietze and Musson, 2005). Tietze and Musson (2010: 154) argue that

> the shift of paid work into the home requires changes not only in conduct and behaviour, but in the assumptions and values which underpin them i.e. it requires identity work to be done. Thus, from an organizational perspective the introduction of telework schemes should be viewed not purely as a technical rational project, but also as an emotive value-based enterprise which triggers "identity work" and which therefore can potentially realign the individual's commitment to the work organization.

An understanding of the different identities employees engage in is necessary to understand the relationship between home and work and the meanings people give to home, work, and self. A restructuring of space is called for in the home where work and other activities involves some reorganising of family relationships (Richardson and McKenna, 2013).

The home has different actors and entails juggling roles and responsibilities. Technology has two sides. On the one hand, there is the "always-on" work culture of being connected 24/7, where working from home augments work done for the employer. However, technology can enhance work/life harmony if appropriate boundaries are set. The purpose of this chapter is to address the following question: Working from home: Is technology a help or a hindrance in achieving work/life harmony?

Literature review

Definition of Teleworking:

> Telework occurs when Information Communication Technologies (ICT) enables work to be accomplished at a geographical distance from the location where the work results are needed, or would have been traditionally carried out in the past. Typically, telework takes place in the home.
>
> (Hynes, 2014: 281)

According to the Telecommuting Statistics for 2017, Global Workplace Analytics Research found that there are optimistic signs for teleworking, with half of the US workforce holding a job that is compatible with at least partial telework and approximately one quarter of the workforce teleworks at some frequency. A further 80–90% of the US workforce say that they would like to telework at least part-time. Two to three days weekly seems to be the optimum time that allows for a balance of concentrative work (at home) and collaborative work (in the office). Consequently, Fortune 1000 companies around the world are revamping their space around the fact that employees are already mobile. Repeated studies indicate that they are not at their desk 50–60% of the time.[1]

Teleworking in Great Britain: The Office for National Statistics (2014) found that in the UK, there were 4.2 million people working from home in the first quarter of 2014, which is 13.9% of the total workforce. Of those working from home, approximately 1.5 million (or 5% of the workforce) work within the home or its grounds, while the balance of 2.7 million persons (8.9% of the workforce) utilised their home as a base, but worked in various locations.[2] Later in 2016, The Office for National Statistics found that more than half of British workers are satisfied with the balance of work and leisure time, while more than a quarter are dissatisfied. Some employers reported that 97% of employees find work/life balance challenging.[3]

Marcos and Bertaloso (2018: 50, 53) state that "Caring by being, not by doing, is the core feature of the domestic environment." The home is a space for "caring for the human being." In society, providing care services is a significant element of social protection which aims to provide better quality of life together with educational and employment possibilities for EU citizens. The latter encompasses health care, childcare, and long-term care. This is a significant question as more women are in paid employment while at the same time they are assuming responsibility for care in the family as well as household tasks. In December 2015, the

European Parliament published a Report on Creating Labour Market Conditions Favourable to Work Life Balance and a Resolution adopted on a European Pillar of Social Rights (European Commission, 2017). These combined legislative and non-legislative measures aim to increase women's participation in the workforce and address gender pay gaps and pension gaps. Also, to give employees more opportunities to balance work and family, especially in the case of men. In addition, the policy seeks to support member states with work family policies and to eliminate disincentives to work for second earners. In the EU, it is mandatory to provide maternity and paternity leave. Ireland recently introduced ten days paternity leave when a child is born.[4]

According to Adema et al. (2016: 29), the United States provides basic support for children, fathers, and mothers in the form of unpaid parental leave, child-related tax breaks, and limited public childcare. In contrast, the other member states of the Organisation for Economic Co-operation and Development (OECD) empower families through paid parental leave and comprehensive investments in infants and children.

Care and dependency: Davis and Lastra (2018: 144, 156) state that "care and dignity in old age are fundamental challenges for the future of our society." Pensions are not only important from the perspective of financial sustainability, but especially "for ensuring that the care and dignity of the elderly is maintained within the context of the home." According to Ulmanen and Szebehely (2015), family care has increased in all social strata with help being given by both daughters and sons. Family care was found to be more prevalent among older people with a lower level of education, whereas privately purchased services were more a feature of those with higher education.

Marketisation of care work: Du Roit and Van Bochove (2017: 76,77) claim long-term care (LTC) in European countries has undergone two forms of marketisation in the recent past. First, policies have explicitly fostered the outsourcing of professional services to private providers and the creation of (quasi) markets for social services. Second, often supported by cash-for-care benefits, people in need of care and their families have started purchasing LTC directly from individual workers. In both forms of marketisation, migrant care work plays a critical role.

According to Anderson and Hughes (2010: 381), women's experience of care work is conditioned by their employment status. For example, self-employed versus employee and the nature of care provided (direct or indirect). In their study, they conducted interviews among a group of Canadian women engaged in providing direct care (for example, childcare) and indirect care (for example, cleaning). It was found that the latter experienced great physical and emotional demand in their work. In comparison with childcare providers, cleaners reported more satisfaction with their income and financial responsibility. Also, the authors highlight the issue of independent contractors in care work and efforts to improve the economic security and status of care work.

Kittay (2011), referring to the most significant theories of justice, states personal dignity is closely related to independence. Human beings undergo periods of dependency in their lives. Rather than perceive assistance as a limitation, Kittay (2011) asks that the aforementioned be regarded as a resource at the basis of a vision of society that is able to account for inevitable dependency relationships between "unequals." The latter guarantees a fulfilled life for both the carer and the cared for. Also, Kittay (1999) researches the importance of dependency, work, and care. She engages in a study of John Rawl's liberal theory and examples of public policy in the US. The author seeks to show that both theory and policy fail women when they miss the critical relationship between dependence and issues of justice. Kittay (1999) underlines that for a truly inclusive feminism, it is necessary to take human dependency and its consequences into account.

Teleworking and theoretical framework: According to Nakrosiene et al. (2019: 88), citing Bailey and Kurland (2002: 394), there is a complete dearth of organisational theories in telework research which has been emphasised as the main obstacle to "identifying and explaining what happens when people telework." In order to theoretically categorise factors related to telework as potential job resources or demands affecting telework outcomes, similar to Nakrosiene et al. (2019: 88–92), the author used the job demands-resource theory (Demerouti et al., 2001). The model consists of job demands, namely physical workload, time pressure, recipient contact, physical environment, shift work, and job resources consisting of feedback, rewards, job control, participation, job security, and supervisor support (Demerouti et al., 2001, p. 502). Higher job demands have an adverse effect on health and increasing resources lead to higher levels of performance (Parker et al., 2017).

Job demands

Physical workload: Technology has had a significant impact on work, making work from home and other locations possible (Grant et al., 2013). Work has turned into an "unbounded activity" to be carried out "anytime and anywhere" (Kurland and Bailyn, 1999). According to Toffler (1980: 204–217), the present forms of flexibility have the capacity to convert the pre-industrial cottage into a post-industrial electronic cottage, where people can achieve a balance between work and home. "The supposed reason for introducing technology to the workplace is to shorten the time to do certain tasks and free up the worker's time for other projects. But that hasn't really happened. Technology has just changed the way we work. Modern work is much more frenzied, with a constant flood of information and endless interruptions from phone calls, email, and text" (Killeen, 2018: 8, 9). It is often challenging for employees to achieve a work/home balance (Kreiner et al., 2009; Mayo et al., 2011). Health issues and family difficulties can result from conflict between work and home (Grant-Vallone and Ensher, 2011). For employers, the consequences of work-home demands can manifest itself in higher levels of employee turnover, absenteeism, and less productivity (Allard et al., 2011, Ford et al., 2007).

Ojala et al. (2014) highlight that while home working can be portrayed as a great advantage for work/home balance, there is contradictory research about whether working from home strengthens or weakens work/family harmony. When work and home activities take place in the same physical space, physical, temporal, and psychological boundaries between work and home can become blurred. There is some research which indicates that teleworkers work longer hours (Harker and MacDonnell, 2012).

Time pressure: The advent of technology with its potential to turn the pre-industrial cottage into a post-industrial electronic cottage cradles a new system of production where individual agents are enabled to achieve a precious balance between the demands of work and home (Toffler, 1980: 204–217). Domestic relationships are affected and work values such as control are introduced into the home (Brocklehurst, 2001; Hochschild, 1997).

Recipient contact: According to NYTimes.com (2013) and Bayt.com (2015), the following are disadvantages of working from home:

- The difficulty in separating work from home.
- The difficulty in separating home from work.
- Self-imposed pressure of working endlessly.
- The feeling of being alienated from a company's major decisions and sometimes promotions.

In addition to work infringing on the physical space of home, work also impacts on the emotional and psychological space of home (Baines and Gelder, 2003). There are mixed results regarding the benefits of teleworking. According to Hartig et al. (2007), remote e-workers may experience an overlap between work and home which consequently lessens the restorative benefits of home.

Conversely the negative effects include:

- Work intensification with access to technology 24/7 leading to long hours, with little respite from work.
- Sitting behaviours many increase with the temptation to work for longer hours at the computer, thus causing physical problems.

Physical environment: Tietze and Musson (2010) warn of values of industrial production invading one's personal life. In their study involving three case studies, all of the protagonists had to find practical solutions to working from home such as the setting up of routines and tasks for carrying out home tasks as well as work tasks. In the case of Tom (case study), his identities were challenged both as a father and a manager. In Deirdre's case, her identity becomes more forged in the domestic environment, where she develops new routines and the professional practices which had been her main priority have now become less important. While Deirdre does not leave aside her identity from the world of work, she "discovers" new aspects of "who she is" or "who she might become." In her case, we see changing identities where the domestic element of Deirdre's sense of self come to the fore (Tietze and Musson, 2010: 153). Carrying out paid work from home offers not just the possibility of work/home balance, but there are questions of identity "which are central to understanding the mutually, constitutive relationship between domestic and professional spheres of life" (Tietze and Musson, 2010: 154).

Job resources: Space is perceived as fluid and in it actors carry out a performance by means of life's experiences and the significance they give these experiences (Berger and Luckmann, 1967). Richardson and McKenna (2013: 734) argue work and home have never been entirely separate spaces. The aforementioned authors perceive space as a "constructed rather than a fixed entity," in particular referring to "the processes of social action and interaction undertaken in relation to the connection between a space designated as *home* and a space identified as *work*" (Richardson and McKenna, 2013: 726). Flexible workers constantly engage in the reorganisation of spaces of work and home "to meet their practical, psychological and structural needs." "What was previously done at work is now done in the home: what was done outside the workplace (socialising) is now a main reason for going there." Associations are reconstituted by actors trying "to keep ties in place" through ways of ordering time priorities, etc. Flexible workers change their spaces and lives responding to "demands that surround them" (Goffman, 1971: 116).

Rewards

Some of the benefits for employees are:

- A flexible environment in which you get to decide your own working hours (in agreement with your employer).
- Fewer distractions and stress.
- Proximity to home and family members.
- Reduced travelling time.
- Better health and better work/life balance.
- Greater productivity and creativity (Timsal and Mustabsat, 2016).

Furthermore, Kossek et al. (2006), in a study of teleworking professionals, found that greater autonomy through teleworking led to less frequent occurrence of depression in women. Kossek et al. (2006) were of the view that teleworking may provide women with more flexibility to manage their work, resulting in greater levels of wellbeing as a consequence of being present in both work and family lives. Richardson and McKenna (2013: 732) found that working from home created "emotional distance" from colleagues. Those who engaged in flexible working gave more care to creating and maintaining relationships than when they worked in the office. Engaging in "high-quality" social relations with colleagues was a priority for all working flexibly. People wanted to stay visible in order to achieve career goals and performance goals.

Teleworking helps to recruit and retain talented workers by providing people with the ability to reduce commuting time and fit other activities around their work tasks, thus contributing to a diverse workforce (Beauregard et al., 2013). According to Grant et al. (2013: 532), the positive aspects of remote working can be summarised as:

- Increased productivity
- The ability to work flexibly and from different locations, within the temporal restrictions of office-based hours
- In some cases, reduced stress levels and greater wellbeing

Working from home requires personal control over working hours, the organisation of the home space, as well as negotiations among family members over the distribution of time and space (Felstead et al., 2005). Research shows that employers who have introduced flexible work have:

- Environmental benefits
- Improvements in employee morale
- Increased productivity
- Lower employee turnover
- Lower absenteeism

(Thomson, 2008; Lapierre et al., 2008; Poelmans et al., 2005)

Wheatley (2012) found that, in the case of women, remote working can result in saved time, but this time is not always spent on leisure activities but instead is spent on housework or paid work.

Job control

The challenge is the traditional management mindset which is control focused, believing employees have to be in view for productivity reasons. The office setting offers opportunities for collaboration which is important for effectiveness. It is claimed that working from home reduces work output and quality of work. Google, Yahoo, and Hewlett Packard have tried to reduce work from home (Pathak et al., 2015: 12). A full 76% of respondents to a recent FlexJobs survey said that when people need to get important work done, they avoid the office. A home office was a more popular choice than a coffee shop, library, or conventional office outside of normal work hours. Some 75% of employees claim that they are more productive at home due to fewer interruptions from colleagues and less distractions. A majority of employees prefer to work from home as a result of freedom from office politics and reduced stress from commuting (Grevstad, 2016). A study conducted by Lourenco and Lourenco (2016) demonstrated that women working in a cooperative exercised self-management in relation to flexible working hours.

The women were allowed to organise their workday with full control over their working time, although they still followed the terms of their collective contract (Lourenco and Lourenco, 2016: 580).

Teleworking challenges boundary management because the usual physical and time-based boundaries of the office space are absent. A study of a large public sector organisation in the UK shows how their long-standing teleworking programme results in above-average productivity for teleworkers compared to their office counterparts. Forty in-depth interviews were carried out with occasional teleworkers, partial teleworkers (20–50% of teleworkers) and full teleworkers who work the majority of the time away from the office. The interviews yielded evidence that teleworkers employ physical, time-based, behavioural, and communicative strategies for managing boundaries between work and home. In relation to physical activities, it was found that some employees had an office space in their home while others create separate space for work activities and for relaxation. In relation to time-based activities, although most people worked beyond the contracted time, many had strategies in place, e.g., to walk the dogs at 5 pm, children returning from school. Commitments to other people appear to produce stronger boundaries than being accountable only to oneself. The behavioural strategies employed relate mainly to information technology, such as switching the phone off when business time finishes, logging off computer systems, and shutting down the laptop, thus removing the temptation to check messages. Communicative strategies included getting family members to knock before entering the work space. According to Kreiner (2006), boundary management is a question of individual preferences, but the ability to manage preference can result in reduced work/life conflict and stress, as well as higher job satisfaction. Research shows that the danger lies in work spilling over into home time.

Kreiner et al. (2009) propose four divisions to manage boundaries between work and home, namely: physical, behavioural, home-based, and communicative tactics. Behavioural tactics are social practices that are used to decrease work/home conflicts (Kreiner et al., 2009). In a study conducted by Von Borell de Araujo et al. (2015: 570–576) applying the boundary tactics of Kreiner et al. (2009), three types of behavioural tactics were found: using other people who filter undesired demands from work and home; using technology, such as use of two cell phones; and setting priorities in advance, e.g., involving others in which items to filter and which to allow pass the boundary.

Temporal tactics involve managing work home time, and some mothers were found to change routines and block off time to attend to work or family issues, finding respite such as taking a break and synchronising tasks. Physical tactics include manipulating physical boundaries, e.g., turning off cell phone; manipulating physical distance between domains, e.g., some mothers chose to live close to work while others chose to live far away; and managing physical objects, e.g., choosing not to do anything related to work after 5 pm. Communicative tactics involve setting expectations, e.g., not working late and renegotiating expectations when an unexpected problem arises and confronting violations, e.g., if the boss calls on Sunday (Von Borell de Araujo et al., 2015: 570–576).

Gorham (2006) calls for women to exercise management skills in the home such as delegation of responsibilities, efficient use of time and resources, and coordination of activities. According to Mellner et al. (2016), employees now have more work flexibility and are more adept at organising their work in time and space, i.e., boundaryless work. The authors highlight the need to manage boundaries between work and personal life effectively, so as to renew one's energies and get adequate sleep. In a study carried out among Swedish professional workers (N=3,846), the results showed that working boundlessly in time, i.e., spread out over the whole day and week, was directly linked to long weekly work hours and a lack of psychological detachment. In contrast, working boundlessly in space, i.e., at various locations, was inversely associated with weekly work hours and had no association with psychological detachment.

Participation: Richardson and McKenna (2013) found that flexible workers developed customised rules to enable interactions with work colleagues and members of family which, in the majority of cases, led to better results. Even though teleworkers can generally develop strategies that align boundaries to their preferences for segmentation or integration, employees with greater job autonomy and control are better able to do so (Basile and Beauregard, 2016). The limitation to the study conducted by the aforementioned authors is that it lacks generalizability to teleworkers in organisations with "always-on" cultures who may experience greater pressure to allow work to permeate the home boundary (Basile and Beauregard, 2016). Hayman (2010), in a study of 336 employees, found that flex-time was more helpful in decreasing role overload and work/life balance issues than teleworking.

Job security: Castellano (2015) referred to a survey by Dell and Intel which showed that 52% of people think that employees working from home are just as, or more, productive than those in the office. However, some people are of the opinion that a disadvantage of remote working is that it results in less promotion opportunities for employees. According to the aforementioned survey, nearly a quarter of employees think remote work limits their career growth.

Supervisor support: Women are often being told that they must choose between the domains of work and family (Bailyn and Fletcher, 2003) and they can be under pressure to manage the demands of work and family without any help (Lourenco and Lourenco, 2016). Self-employment or business ownership has been proposed as a way for women to balance family and work responsibilities (Daniel, 2004; Walker and Webster, 2006). Strategies to be used by HR to regulate the interaction between work and home include:

- Building autonomy into teleworkers jobs
- Greater control over their work schedules
- Empowering employees to create or maintain boundaries that fit their personal preferences for integration or segmentation of work and home activities

A "good fit" will help organisations benefit from increased productivity and an increase in staff retention (Harker and MacDonnell, 2012).

Implications for society: There is a need for employer guidelines for working virtually, as well as infrastructure to support virtual work. Technology has many benefits if used appropriately, but the caveat is that it can lead to working 24/7. Before embarking on telework practices, it is necessary to

> fully understand the environmental and social consequences and impacts of working from home for individuals, organizations and the environment. . . . It is only then that a true assessment of the practical benefits of the practice of working from home can be made and we can decide if indeed it is a goal worth pursuing.
>
> (Hynes, 2014: 596)

Remote working and more flexible technology may have helped to improve job effectiveness, flexibility, and to some extent wellbeing, however, the more negative issues also need to be explored in more detail (Grant et al., 2013: 532).

Implications for policy: The digital revolution is creating new working models. There are increased opportunities for working from home as well as from any location, thus enhancing flexible work and work-home harmony. Zamagni (2018: 135) has highlighted how many work/life harmonisation policies are aiming to help women adapt to the working cycle and to increase family income as well as women's participation in the labour market. However, he draws attention to the fact that if the latter policies are "pursued to the detriment of intra-family and inter-family relations, then the net, long-term result will inevitably be a negative one." In Europe, there are variations in uptake of teleworking, but there is a lack of clarity as to why this is so. There is a need for substantial, in-depth empirical research in this particular area to identify the key indicators and conditions that permit the practice to flourish or fail (Hynes, 2014: 596). A greater insight into the latter will assist policymakers going forward. HR needs to be aligned to the company's overall strategy. For companies seeking radical innovation requiring a lot of collaboration, it may be beneficial to be office-based. However, for most companies pursuing incremental innovation, working from home contributes to keeping real estate and operational costs low. Furthermore, offering employees flexibility increases motivation and reduces turnover, thus increasing profitability (Pathak et al., 2015: 12). The aforementioned authors recommend that HR managers need to contribute at two levels:

1. At the level of setting a clear, coherent and logical work-from-home policy that is aligned with the company's strategy.
2. In ensuring that operational decisions are without favouritism and prejudice and align to the best interests of the employees and the company (Pathak et al., 2015: 14). HR has an important role to play to ensure teleworking is a

good experience for employees and staff need to be prepared to work in the home environment (Basile and Beauregard, 2016).

Implications for practice: In terms of working from home, it is important to consider the nature of the work involved. Some activities call for more collaboration, where the office offers a beneficial environment for this, while many other tasks can be done from home. Home is needed to recover one's energies and to renew oneself, thus contributing to health and wellbeing. Managing one's home life effectively is linked to effectiveness and job satisfaction in one's work role. The home plays a very crucial role in society from the perspective of a healthy home life being essential for a healthy work-life and a healthy society. Millennials make up the largest part of the US workforce and they aspire to more flexible work and better work/life harmony than previous generations. Isolation can be a challenge for those working from home. Argandona (2018: 11) states that the concept of the home focuses on three internal elements: the person, the inner community or family, and shared living space with an intention of continuity. But there is also a fourth external element which cannot be excluded: the external social and material environment. These elements work together; the person is at the centre, but the unifying concept is the home. It is important to find meaning in work and to replenish resources through physical, spiritual, social, and community renewal.

Notes

1 http://globalworkplaceanalytics.com/telecommuting-statist
2 http://webarchive.nationalarchives.gov.uk/20160105210705/www.ons.gov.uk/ons/rel/lmac/characteristics-of-home-workers/2014/sty-home-workers.html
3 www.theguardian.com/money/2016/jan/02/work-life-balance-flexible-working-can-make-you-ill-experts-say
Role of public policy and professional care work
4 www.eurofound.europa.eu/topic/care
https://eur-lex.europa.eu/legal-content/EN/TXT/?qid=1494930128433&uri=CELEX:52017DC0252

References

Adema, W., Clarke, C. and Frey, V. (2016). Paid Parental Leave and other Supports for Parents with Young Children: The United States in International Comparison, Organization for Economic Co-operation and Development, Paris, France, *International Social Security Review*, 69, pp. 29–51.

Allard, K., Haas, L. and Hwang, C.P. (2011). Family-supportive Organizational Culture and Father's Experiences of Work-family Conflict in Sweden, *Gender, Work & Organization*, 18(2), pp. 141–157.

Anderson, N. and Hughes, K.D. (2010). The Business of Caring: Women's Self-Employment and the Marketization of Care, *Gender Work and Organization*, 17(4), pp. 381–405.

Argandona, A. (2018). The Home: Multidisciplinary Reflections. In A. Argandona (Ed.), *The Home: Multidisciplinary Reflections*, Edward Elgar Publishing Limited, Cheltenham, UK.

Bailey, D.E. and Kurland, N.B. (2002). A Review of Telework Research: Findings, New Directions and Lessons for the Study of Modern Work, *Journal of Organizational Behavior*, 23(4), pp. 383–400.

Bailyn, L. and Fletcher, J.K. (2003). *The Equity Imperative: Reaching Effectiveness through the Dual Agenda*, CGO Insight No. 18, Center for Gender in Organizations, Boston, MA.

Baines, S. and Gelder, U. (2003). What is Family Friendly about the Workplace in the Home? The Case of Self-employed Parents and their Children, *New Technology, Work and Employment*, 18(3), pp. 223–234.

Basile, K.A. and Beauregard, T.A. (2016). Strategies for Effective Telework: How Effective Employees Manage Work/Home Boundaries, *Strategic Human Resource Review*, 15(3).

Bayt com (2015). Bayt: The Advantages and Disadvantages of Working from Home, www.bayt.com/en/career-article-1601/, accessed 30/8/17.

Beauregard, T.A., Basil, K.A. and Canonico, E. (2013) *Home is Where the Work is: A New Study of Home Working in Acas and Beyond*, Acas Research Paper, Ref 10/13, Acas, London.

Berger, P. and Luckmann, T. (1967) *The Social Construction of Reality: A Treatise in the Sociology of Knowledge*. Garden City, NY: Doubleday.

Bloom, N. (2014). To Raise Productivity, Let more Employees Work from Home, *Harvard Business Review*, 92(1/2), pp. 28–29.

Brocklehurst, M. (2001). Power Identity and New Technology Homework: Implications for "New Forms" of Organising, *Organization Studies*, 22(3), pp. 445–66.

Castellano, S. (2015, April). The Productivity Debate, *Association for Talent Development*, TD.

Daniel, T.A. (2004). The Exodus of Women from the Corporate Workplace to Self-owned Businesses, *Employment Relations Today*, 30(4), pp. 55–61.

Davis, E.P. and Lastra, R.M. (2018). Pension Provision, Lifetime Financial Sustainability, Care and Dignity in Old Age: Legal and Economic Issues. In A. Argandona (Ed.), *The Home Multidisciplinary Reflections*. Edward Elgar Publishing Limited, UK.

Demerouti, E., Bakker, A.B., Nachreiner, F. and Schaufeli, W.B. (2001). The Job-Demands Resource Model of Burnout, *Journal of Applied Psychology*, 86(3), pp. 499–512.

Du Roit, B. and Van Bochove, M. (2017). Migrant Care Work going Dutch? The Emergence of a Live-in Migrant Care Market and the Restructuring of the Dutch Long-term Care System, *Social Policy & Administration*, 51(1), pp. 76–94.

European Commission (2017). Communication from the Commission to the European Parliament, the Council, the European Economic and Social Committee and the Committee of the Regions an Initiative to Support Work-Life Balance for Working Parents and Carers, Brussels 26/4/17, 252 final, https://eur-lex.europa.eu/legal-content/EN/TXT/?qid=1494930128433&uri=CELEX:52017DC025, accessed 7/7/19.

Felstead, A., Jewson, N. and Walters, S. (2005). *Changing Places of Work*. Palgrave Macmillan, Basingstoke.

Ford, M., Heinen, B. and Langkamer, K. (2007). Work and Family Satisfaction and Conflict: A Meta-analysis of Cross-domain Relations, *Journal of Applied Psychology*, 92(1), pp. 57–80.

Friedman, S.D. (2014). Work+Home+Community+Self Skills for Integrating Every Part of Your Life, *Harvard Business Review*, 92((9), pp. 111–114.

Goffman, E. (1971). *The Presentation of Self in Everyday Life*. London, Penguin.

Gorham, A. (2006). Managing to Work: Why Mothers Need to Apply Workplace Skills in the Home, *Women in Management Review*, 3(4), pp. 191–196.

Grant, C.A., Wallace, L.M. and Spurgeon, P.C. (2013). An Exploration of the Psychological Factors Affecting Remote e-worker's Job Effectiveness, Well-being and Work-life Balance, *Employee Relations*, 35(5), pp. 527–546, https://doi.org/10.1108/ER-08-2012-0059

Grant-Vallone, E.J. and Ensher, E.A. (2011). An Examination of Work and Personal Life Conflict, Organizational Support, and Employee Health Among International Expatriates, *International Journal of Intercultural Relations*, 25(3), pp. 261–278.

Grevstad, E. (2016, January). *PC Magazine Digital Edition.*

Groysberg, B. and Abrahams, R. (2014). Manage Your Work, Manage Your Life, *Harvard Business Review*, 92(3), pp. 58–66.

Harker, M.B. and MacDonnell, R. (2012). Is Telework Effective for Organizations? A Meta- analysis of Empirical Research on Perceptions of Telework and Organizational Outcomes, *Management Research Review*, 35(7), pp. 602–616.

Hartig, T., Kylin, C. and Johansson, G. (2007). The Telework Tradeoff: Stress Mitigation vs Constrained Restoration, *Applied Psychology: An International Review*, 56(2), pp. 231–253.

Hayman, J. (2010). Flexible Work Schedules and Employee Well-being, *New Zealand Journal of Employment Relations*, 35(2), pp. 76–87.

Hochschild, A. (1997.) *The Time Bind. When Work Becomes Home and Home Becomes Work*. Metropolitan Books, New York, NY.

Hynes, M. (2014). Telework isn't Working: A Policy Review, *The Economic and Social Review*, 45(4), pp. 579–602.

Killeen, R. (2018). Workaholism in the Digital Age, *Sunday Business Post*, August 12.

Kittay, E.F. (1999). *Love's Labour: Essays on Women, Equality and Dependence*. Routledge, New York.

Kittay, E.F. (2011). The Ethics of Care, Dependence and Disability, *Ratio Juris*, 24(1), pp. 49–58.

Kossek, E.E., Lautsch, B.A. and Eaton, S.C. (2006). Telecommuting, Control, and Boundary Management: Correlates of Policy Use and Practice, Job Control, and Work-family Effectiveness, *Journal of Vocational Behavior*, 68(2), pp. 347–367.

Kreiner, G.E. (2006). Consequences of Work-home Segmentation or Integration: A Person-environment Fit Perspective, *Journal of Organizational Behavior*, 27(4), pp. 485–507.

Kreiner, G.E., Hollensbe, E.C. and Sheep, M.L. (2009). Balancing Borders and Bridges: Negotiating the Work /home Interface Via Boundary Work Tactics, *Academy of Management Journal*, 52(4), pp. 704–730.

Kurland, N. and Bailyn, L. (1999). Telework, The Advantages and Challenges of Working Here, There, Anywhere and Anytime, *Organisational Dynamics*, 28(2), pp. 53–68.

Lapierre, L.M., Spector, P.E., Allen, T.D., Poelmans, S., Cooper, C.L., O'Driscoll, M.P., Sanchez, J.I., Brough, P. and Kinnunen, U. (2008). Family-supportive Organization Perceptions, Multiple Dimensions of Work – family Conflict, and Employee Satisfaction: A Test of Model Across Five Samples, *Journal of Vocational Behavior*, 73(1), pp. 92–106.

Lourenco, M.L. and Lourenco, E.N. (2016). Women Workers, Social Sustainability and Working Time: A Study in a Cooperative Guided by the Principles of Economic Solidarity, *Social Responsibility Journal*, 12(3), pp. 571–583.

Marcos, A. and Bertaloso, M. (2018). What is a Home? On the Intrinsic Nature of a Home. In A. Argandona (Ed.), *The Home: Multidisciplinary Reflections*. Edward Elgar Publishing Limited, Cheltenham, UK.

Mayo, M., Pastor, J.C., Cooper, C. and Sanz-Vergel, A.I. (2011). Achieving Work-family Balance Among Spanish Managers and their Spouses: A Demands-control Perspective, *The International Journal of Human Resource Management*, 22(2), pp. 331–350.

Mellner, C., Kecklund, C., Kompier, M., Sariaslan, A. and Aronsson, G. (2016). Boundaryless Work, Psychological Detachment and Sleep: Does Working Anytime-anywhere "Equal Employees are "always on "? In Jan De Leeds (Ed.), *New Ways of Working Practices (Advanced series on management, Vol 16)*. Emerald Group Publishing Ltd, pp. 29–47.

Nakrosiene, A., Buciuniene, L. and Gostautaite, B. (2019). Working from Home: Characteristics and Outcomes of Telework, *International Journal of Manpower*, 4091, pp. 87–101.

NY Times.com (2013). NY Times Sunday Review editorial: Location, Location, Location, *NY Times.com*, March 3, accessed 25/8/17.

Office for National Statistics (2016). Work/life Balance: Flexible Working can Make You Ill Experts Say, www.theguardian.com/money/2016/jan/02/work-life-balance-flexible-working-can-make-you-ill-experts-say, accessed 29/8/17.

Office for National Statistics (2014). http://webarchive.nationalarchives.gov.uk/20160105210705/www.ons.gov.uk/ons/rel/lmac/characteristics-of-home-workers/2014/sty-home-workers.html, accessed 29/8/17.

Ojala, S, Natti, J. and Anttila, T. (2014). Informal Overtime at Work instead of Telework: Increase in Negative Work-family Interface, *International Journal of Sociology and Social Policy*, 34, 1(2), pp. 69–87.

Otani, A. (2015). Bloomberg Business: "Richard Branson: Marissa Mayer's Yahoo Work Policy is on the Wrong Side of History". https://www.bloomberg.com/news/articles/2015-04-24/richard-branson-marissa-mayer-s-yahoo-work-policy-is-on-the-wrong-side-of-history.

Parker, S.K., Morgeson, F.P. and Johns, G. (2017). One Hundred Years of Work Design Research: Looking back and Looking Forward, *Journal of Applied Psychology*, 102(3), pp. 403–420.

Pathak, A.A., Bathini, D.R. and Kandathil, G.M. (2015). The Ban on Working from Home Makes Sense for Yahoo. It needs the Innovation and Speed of Delivery that Come from Office-based Employees, *Human Resource Management International Digest*, 23(3), pp. 12–14.

Poelmans, S.A.Y., O'Driscoll, M. and Beham, B. (2005). A Review of International Research in the Field of Work and Family. In S.A.Y. Poelmans (Ed.), *Work and Family: An International Research Perspective*. Erlbaum, Mahwah, NJ, pp. 3–46.

Richardson, J. and McKenna, S. (2013). Reordering Spatial and Social Relations: A Case Study of Professional and Managerial Flexworkers, *British Journal of Management*, 25(4), pp. 724–736.

Shamir, B. and Salomon, I. (1985). Work-at-Home and the Quality of Working Life, *Academy of Management Review*, 10(3), pp. 455–464.

Sullivan, C. and Lewis, S. (2001). Home-based Telework, Gender and the Synchronization of Work and Family: Perspectives of Teleworkers and their Co-residents, *Gender Work and Organization*, 8(2), pp. 123–145.

Thomson, P. (2008). The Business Benefits of Flexible Working, *Strategic HR Review*, 7(2), pp. 17–22, https://doi.org/10.1108/14754390810853129.

Tietze, S. and Musson, G. (2010). Identity, Identity Work and the Experience of Working from Home, *Journal of Management Development*, 29(2), pp. 148–156.

Tietze, S. and Musson, G. (2005). Recasting the Home-work Relationship: A Case of Mutual Adjustment? *Organization Studies*, 26(9), pp. 1331–1352.

Tietze, S. and Musson, G. (2003). The Times and Temporalities of Home-based Telework, *Personnel Review*, 32(4), pp. 438–455.

Timsal, A. and Mustabsat, A. (2016). Flexibility or Ethical Dilemma: An Overview of the Work from Home Policies in Modern Organizations around the World, *Human Resource Management International Digest*, 24(7), pp. 12–15.

Toffler, A. (1980). *The Third Wave*. Pan Books, London.

Toffler, A. (1981). *The Third Wave*. Bantam, New York.

Toyin, Ajibade Adisa, Gbolahan, Gbadamosi and Ellis, L.C. Osabutey (2016). Work-family Balance: A Case Analysis of Coping Strategies Adopted by Nigerian and British Working Mothers, *Gender in Management: An International Journal*, 31(7), pp. 414–433, https://doi.org/10.1108/GM-01-2016-0010.

Tunyaplin, S., Lunce, S. and Maniam, B. (1998). The New Generation Office Environment; The Home Office, *Industrial Management and Data Systems*, 98(4), pp. 178–183.

Ulmanen, P. and Szebehely, M. (2015). From the State to the Family or to the Market? Consequences of Reduced Eldercare in Sweden, *Journal of Social Welfare*, 24(1), pp. 81–92.

Useem, J. (2017). When Working from Home Doesn't Work, *The Atlantic*, November.

Von Borell de Araujo, B.F. and Tureta, C.A. (2015). How do Working Mothers Negotiate the Work/home Interface, *Journal of Managerial Psychology*, 30(5), pp. 565–581. www.eurofound.europa.eu/topic/care accessed 7/7/19.

Walker, E.A. and Webster, B. (2006). Management Competencies of Women Business Owners, *International Entrepreneurship and Management Journal*, 2(4), pp. 429–529.

Walker, E., Wang, C. and Redmond, J. (2008). Women and Work-life Balance: Is Home-based Business Ownership the Solution? *Equal Opportunities International*, 27(3), pp. 258–275, https://doi.org/10.1108/02610150810860084.

Wheatley, D. (2012). Good to be Home? Time Use and Satisfaction Levels among Home-based Teleworkers, *New Technology, Work & Employment*, 27(3), pp. 224–241.

Telecommuting Statistics (2017). Global Workplace Analytics Research, http://globalworkplaceanalytics.com/telecommuting-statistics, accessed 28/8/17.

Zamagni, S. (2018). The Family and Economic Theorizing. In A. Argandona (Ed.), *The Home Multidisciplinary Reflections*. Edward Elgar Publishing Limited, Cheltenham, UK.

Chapter 14

Singapore

Developing life skills and changing mindsets about and through work in the home

Audrey Tan

Introduction

Singapore is an overachiever on the economic world stage with a heavy reliance on a generally untrained migrant domestic workforce and a culture where quantifiable markers such as income, job status, and material success have become hallmarks of achievement. It is easy to see that the work of the home, which attracts no remuneration, little acknowledgement, has no easily quantifiable societal contributions, and is so easily delegated away, would see an undermining of its value and dignity. Singaporeans value the family with 90% of respondents reporting that they had close-knit families (Matthews, 2015). However, with Singaporeans working the longest hours in the world (Evans, 2016), the percentage of foreign domestic help in Singapore is on the rise (Au-Yong, 2016). The work that goes into creating and maintaining the nurturing environment of the family can often be viewed by time-poor adults in a reductive way as a series of household chores delegable away to paid domestic help, so that family members are "spared" the chores so as to be able to perform "more important" tasks. This ignores the complexity of facets of care involved in creating the home environment, which includes managerial decisions that go into creating the kind of home environment which cannot be delegated to a third party, the caregiving elements of the different members of the family that forge relationships, and the life skills and character-building opportunities for children who contribute in helping out in the home. We wanted to address this reductive attitude towards the work of the home by a structured programme in Singapore which could address the true value of this work and how through it, the home can play a crucial role in developing character strengths and value systems in children.

The Homskil Initiative

Homskil began as a business partnership with the purpose of raising awareness and recognition of the value of the work of the home and its contribution to individuals, families, and society. We believed in the need to contribute to a paradigm shift in Singapore that would reclaim the often-lost significance and dignity of the work of the home in the family, and would give recognition to its pivotal contributing role of fostering healthy, happy families and impact the shaping of society and culture. In particular, we wanted to create a platform in Singapore that would allow us to address the inequity of value placed on the work in the home, and the eroding of the transmission of practical life skills and values to the young due to the particular stresses of Singaporean society and culture.

The context of this initiative lies in the characteristics of Singaporean society, which is meritocracy-driven, where one's worth and social status are often linked to one's positioning within the paid job market. As a tiny nation with no natural resources, Singapore stands as a rather remarkable overachiever on the world stage, rising from a third-world economy to first-world affluence in a single generation (OECD, 2010). Its greatest resource has been its highly educated workforce. In a recent report released by the Ministry of Manpower, Singaporeans clocked the most number of working hours in the world (Ministry of Manpower, 2017). Singaporean children are classified from the early age of nine according to academic performance and, despite Singapore being declared by the OECD as having the best schooling system in the world, in 2015, parents were placed in the position of spending on private tuition because of the perception that their children could not remain competitive without it, with 70% of primary school-aged children and 60% of secondary school-aged children in private schools (SPH Publishing, 2016). This setting lends itself to the creation of a pressure cooker environment that begins in the school room in the primary school years and carries over into the adult work environment. It also shapes societal and family demographics, with the proportion of women who stayed childless almost tripling between 1994 and 2014 (Department of Statistics, Singapore, 2016). Analysts cite a variety of reasons, including a decoupling of marriage and children, women focussing on careers and leaving them too late to have children, and changing norms and values regarding family and children (Tan, 2015).

It is easy to understand why work, like that in the home, which is unremunerated, is deemed inferior to work that is done outside the home and which is remunerated. Attempts have been made to quantify the value of this work. In economic terms, the value of the work of the home is called household production and attempts have been made to give it a value relative to a nation's gross domestic product or GDP. In Singapore, household production was cited as 5.4% of Singapore's GDP in 1986, rising to 8.5% in 2005, and then falling to 2.51% in 2015. In absolute terms though, this was worth a value of more than $48.5 billion (Quah, 2018). Quah, however, makes the point that

> The adequacy of the gross national product as a measure of economic growth and performance has always been questioned, with one of its main criticisms being that it understates economic welfare through the omission of non-market productive activity, of which household work forms a large portion.

Added to the difficulty in quantifying the value of domestic work is the added historical perspective in Singapore of a long association of work in the home being delegated to paid domestic help from overseas, with the first domestic workers being poorly educated women from China in the 19th and early 20th centuries, to the present foreign domestic workforce from the neighbouring countries of Philippines, Indonesia, and Myanmar. Its low job status in Singapore is reflected in the scarcity of local Singaporeans performing paid domestic work, and Singapore's heavy reliance on foreign domestic help to this day. Foreign domestic helpers are a large part of the Singapore home scene for many households, constituting about 18% of the total foreign workforce in Singapore (Ministry of Manpower, 2018), and the delegation of the work of the home to domestic helpers, many of whom come from poor neighbouring countries and who come with minimal school education and limited training, further reinforces the perception that it is work of little importance and of much menial standing since it can be delegated away to anyone with little to no training.

In this context of the stresses placed on academic excellence from youth, the material and social rewards of investing one's energies in the paid workforce, the historical cultural perception of the menial nature of housework, and the difficulty in accurately quantifying the value of the work done in the home, it is little wonder that in Singapore, there is a mindset that fails to acknowledge and to reward the intrinsic and contributive power that the work that goes into creating the home environment has on the formation of individuals, family, and society.

Through the Homskil initiative, we wanted to change this mindset and we felt that this could only be done through a programme that was able to address not just "the how" but "the why" as well. In other words, a programme that was able to not only impart practical skills on how to create, run, and manage a home efficiently and professionally, but also convince individuals who went through the course of why such work, which creates a person-centred home environment, is crucial to the wellbeing of individuals and the family. It was clear that providing just the "how" was not sufficient – the surfeit of do-it-yourself and "how-to" websites on any topic one wanted to research had been around for years without making much of an impression on the current culture existing in Singapore.

The Kenvale home management program

In 2015, Homskil, after some preliminary research of the market, decided to establish a collaboration with Kenvale College of Hospitality, Cookery and Events (KC) in Sydney, Australia, for the use of its home management content for a number of reasons. Firstly, the Kenvale course offered a cohesive programme that addressed all the major aspects of creating and managing a home. Secondly, Homskil was attracted by the fundamental ethos of KC, which was *"that those providing this care are not just undertaking a series of material tasks, which may seem insurmountable at times. Rather, they are affirming human dignity, humanising society and shaping culture"* (Kenvale College of Hospitality, Cookery and Events, n.d.). This resonated well with the mission and vision of Homskil. Thirdly, Homskil was attracted by the philosophical and anthropological elements of managing a home that KC offered in its teaching approach, as we consider these elements as key to effecting the paradigmatic change of attitudes in Singapore needed to value and dignify the work in the home. Fourthly, because of its modular format, there was scope for flexibility, as we had to take into consideration the different audience profiles which we hoped in time to target, and the variation in terms of their availability and interest. And lastly and very importantly, KC was amenable to customisation of its content to a local context. This was a crucial element, as the original material from KC was targeted at a Westernised audience and would have failed to resonate clearly in the Asian setting of homes in Singapore without some modification. The collaboration was later formalised in October 2015 and the first module of the Kenvale Home Management Course in Singapore was begun in March 2016.

Market survey

In 2015, our first step to determine to determine demand involved doing a market survey of a hundred women. An online survey was conducted involving ten key questions which addressed demographics, their motivation for doing such a course, and their preferences with regards to the format and content. The sample size was 100 women with their age distribution reflected in Figure 14.1, with the majority (72%) falling in the 35–50 age group.

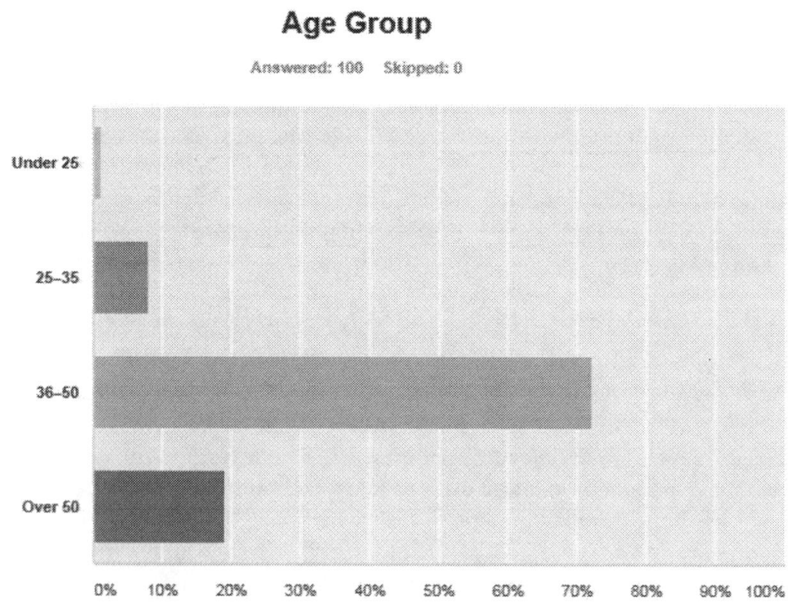

Figure 14.1 Age grouping of respondents

When we analysed their family situation, only 10% of our respondents were unmarried. Of the married women, 62% of them had one to three children, reflecting the overall demographics of families in Singapore where the average household size is 3.35 (Department of Statistics, Singapore, 2017). Only 7% were childless. In terms of employment status, the majority of our respondents (39.8%) were women with full-time home duties (which we will term full-time homemakers), with the next biggest category (34.69%) being in full-time employment, and the remaining categories (less than three days of employment per week, and three or more days of employment per week) being evenly split (12.24% and 13.28%, respectively) (Figure 14.2).

When asked about their primary incentive for doing a course in home management, the overwhelming majority indicated it was for practicalities – equal numbers were motivated by the desire to "run my home more effectively" and "learn new skills and ways of doing things" (42% and 43% respectively). Six percent of respondents indicated that the offering of the diploma was an important element – with 3% motivated by the qualification from completing the course, and another 3% were interestingly looking at starting their own home management consulting business (Figure 14.3). Of the six participants who had indicated reasons other than those listed in the questionnaire, four of them had either no intention of doing the course or had responded out of curiosity. Of the remaining two, one had

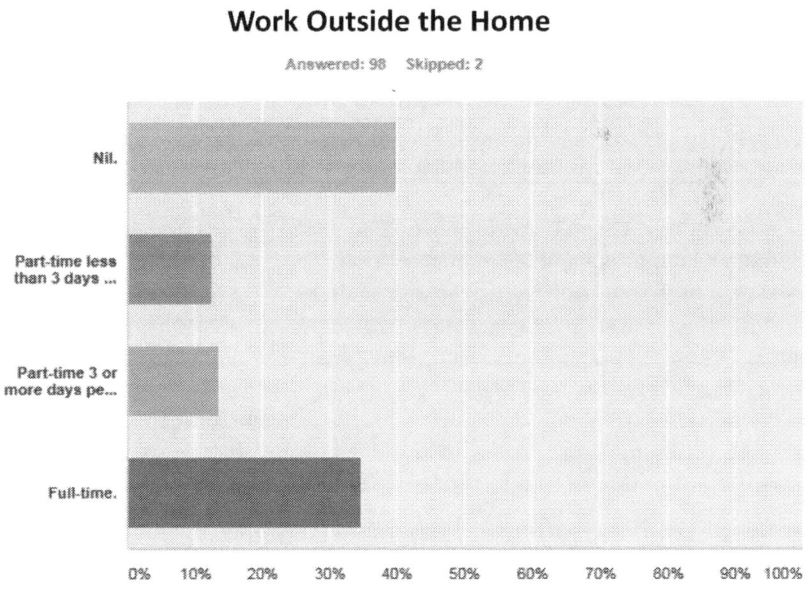

Figure 14.2 Employment status

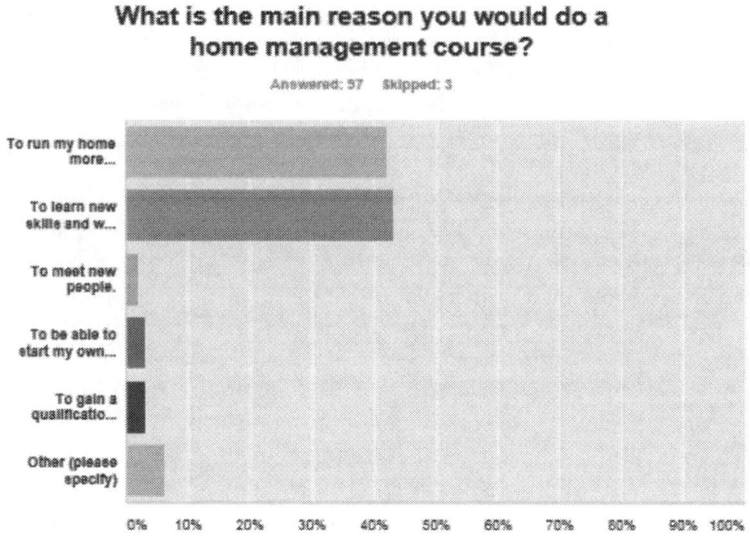

Figure 14.3 Motivation for doing a home management course

indicated she would do it to better help other parents and the other that it was a combination of factors rather than a single factor which would motivate her to do such a course.

We then addressed the issue of affordability by asking participants their responses to a \$65 charge for a session that was half a day in duration, with modules varying in length from three to ten sessions. Their responses were as follows (Figure 14.4):

The majority of respondents (almost 45%) found the proposed cost expensive, with a smaller number (32%) indicating it was reasonable or cheap. When we asked about preferred frequency of sessions, almost 80% were in favour of weekly or fortnightly sessions (41% and 38% respectively), with only 15% favouring monthly sessions, and 5% indicating they wanted options different from those made available on the survey. Reflecting the employment distribution of our participants of which two out of three either were full-time homemakers or in part-time work (cf Figure 14.2), unsurprisingly, more than half of them responded to the question of preferred timing for the course as weekday sessions, either in the morning or afternoon, with the remaining third indicating that afterhours sessions (either weekday nights or on a Saturday) would be better suited (Figure 14.5).

We then got participants to rank the seven modules in order of preference, from the most preferred to the least (Figure 14.6).

When we considered the top three preferences of respondents, the modules, in decreasing order of popularity, were time management, speed cleaning and home

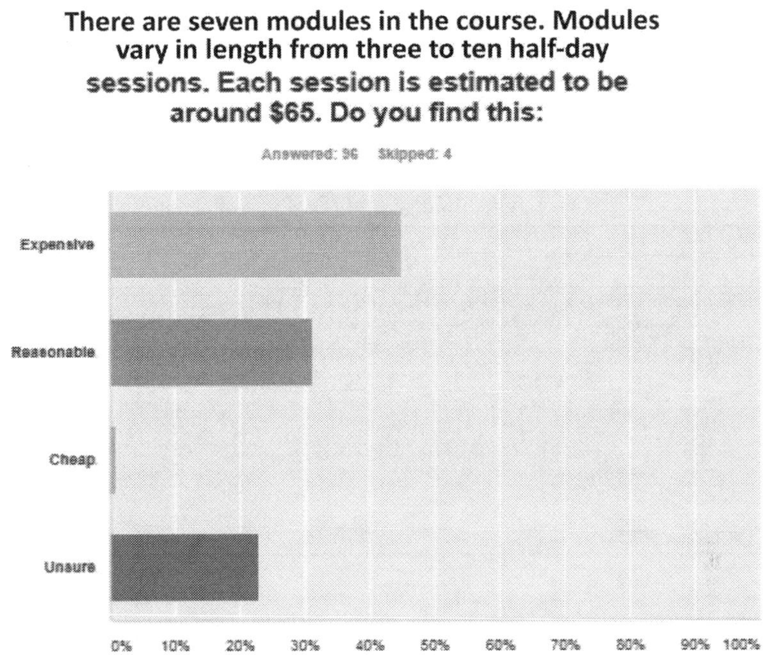

Figure 14.4 Pricing of modules

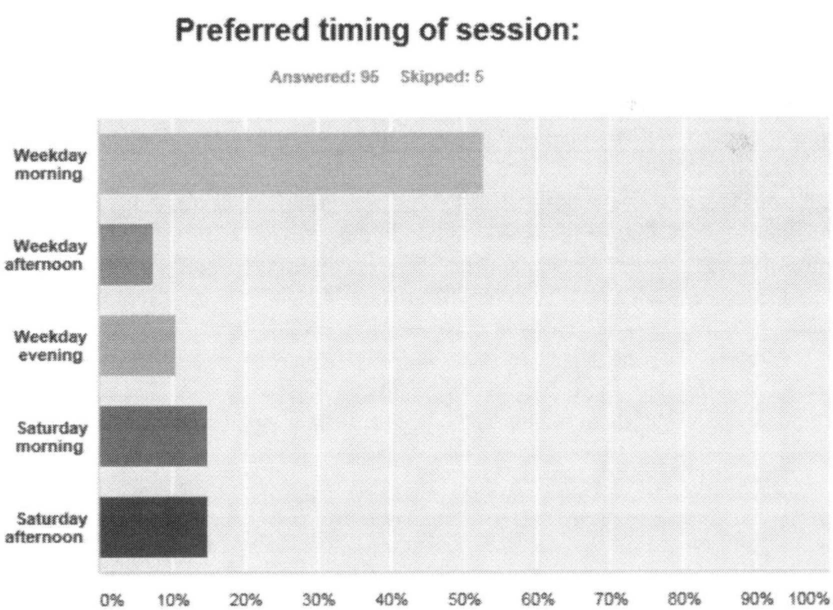

Figure 14.5 Preferred timing of sessions

There are seven modules. Please RANK each module according to your interest from first (most preferred) to seventh (least preferred) choice.

Answered: 90 Skipped: 10

	1st Choice	2nd Choice	3rd Choice	4th Choice	5th Choice	6th Choice	7th Choice	Total
Time Management	48.24% 41	8.24% 7	7.06% 6	4.71% 4	3.53% 3	18.82% 16	9.41% 8	85
Textile Technology & Science	2.35% 2	3.53% 3	15.29% 13	4.71% 4	17.65% 15	20.00% 17	36.47% 31	85
Speed Cleaning & Home Care	11.90% 10	22.62% 19	20.24% 17	21.43% 18	11.90% 10	8.33% 7	3.57% 3	84
Kitchen Theory & Practical	13.95% 12	20.93% 18	17.44% 15	24.42% 21	12.79% 11	5.81% 5	4.65% 4	86
Art, Beauty & Tradition	3.49% 3	12.79% 11	12.79% 11	24.42% 21	15.12% 13	15.12% 13	16.28% 14	86
Dining & Entertainment	8.33% 7	9.52% 8	15.48% 13	13.10% 11	23.81% 20	15.48% 13	14.29% 12	84
Finances	15.91% 14	21.59% 19	12.50% 11	6.82% 6	12.50% 11	15.91% 14	14.77% 13	88

Figure 14.6 Module preferences

care, and finances. Time management was the clear first choice for almost one in two of the participants, reflecting a general perception of a strong need for personal improvement in this area. The survey was completed with a question about their interest in signing up for a home management course (Figure 14.7). Almost two out of the three participants indicated a positive response, with another two out of three within this positive response group (42%) indicating that they would only do so if they were allowed to do selected modules.

From the small market survey and informal focus groups, we drew some conclusions. Firstly, while acknowledging that the work in the home is not the sole purview of women, in the initial phases of the programme, and especially for the first run of the course material, we would limit our target market to women. This was in light of findings in the 2013 report by the Ministry of Social and Family Development that the traditional gender roles within families prevailed with married working women carrying the brunt of caregiving and housework (MSF, 2013). Within this target market, we had identified three broad subgroups with different needs – full or almost full-time homemakers, working women with

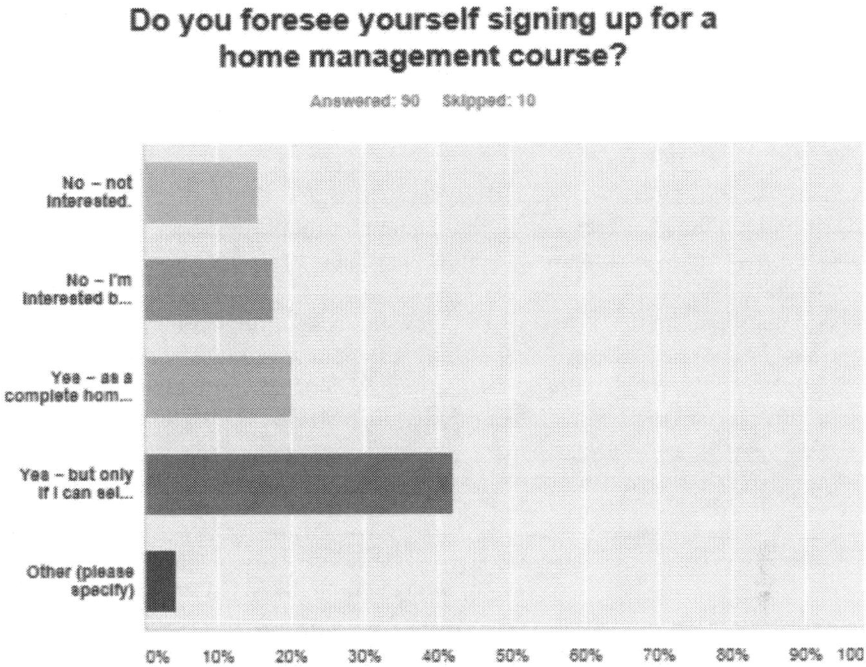

Figure 14.7 Interest in signing up for a home management course

established households, and young working women. Secondly, pricing had to be adjusted to suit market demands, but we would retain the fees structure of charging by the number of sessions per module. And lastly, that we would have to customise the material to a variable extent depending on the module.

The course

Having determined that there was a demand for such a course, we proceeded to establish steps to define our target audience, train a core team to run the programme, review and customise material from Kenvale, and consolidate a timeline for the key preparatory stages for launching the programme. The material that Kenvale had provided to us had been directed primarily at full-time homemakers, and as this subgroup of women had comprised 40% of our respondents and was our initial target market, this in theory made for less initial customisation of the material. Once we had identified the key individuals for the core team, an instructor from Kenvale (CP) flew to Singapore for two days of intensive training. This was a key element in the building stages of the course in Singapore because we needed the coordinators who would be in charge of the modules to be able to impart this convincingly through the different components of their modules, as well as to be able to align learning outcomes with teaching methods, delivery, and assessments such that these would be directed towards the defined graduate attributes of the Kenvale course (professionalism, identity, time management, communication, and lifelong learning). The programme's focus on the dual components of motivation and skills to address the importance of the work of the home in relation to the totality of the human person made it a course different from anything else that was offered on the market and which we felt positioned it well in that market. There were no other competitor programmes that offered a cohesive syllabus with emphasis on understanding the value of the work involved in managing a home.

Each coordinator was tasked with reviewing existing material from Kenvale, aligning the assessments and material with the subject outcomes that she had defined during the coordinator workshop with CP, decide on which elements of the module needed to be amended or omitted to the local context, and, lastly, what teaching approaches would be used.

A timeline was created in preparation for the launching of the programme:

6 months before commencement	Stage 1 (first year) teaching schedule, pricing and marketing schedule, coordinators confirmed
3 months before commencement	Website functional
2 months before commencement	Venue confirmation; marketing begins
1 month before commencement	Guest speakers, confirmed; subject outline completed
3 months before end of Stage 1	Planning for the Stage 2 begins with training of new coordinators for Stage 2 of the programme (the remaining 4 modules)

An important aspect of the programme was the integration of the student's home environment into the teaching, such that it was not just about learning theory but about students consolidating what they had learnt in the classroom and applying the knowledge to their own circumstances in the home. For example, in time management, students worked at creating their own planners based on their unique family and work circumstances. A significant component of the course was structured around helping the students better engage the family in acts of service within the home and to learn to be responsible for duties allocated to them. This was seen as a vital element in the skills of a good home manager – the ability to manage the different members of the family and to form them with good habits (virtues) and life skills. This was, once again, challenging the existing mindset of many Singaporean households where a child is often excused from all contribution to the family and chores outside of the school, and whose only responsibility was to excel at work. An example of involving the family were discussions centred around strategies to engage children to participate in household tasks and assuming responsibility for age-appropriate tasks.

The course in Singapore in its first run was structured around half day (3-hour) sessions from 9:30 am to 12:30 pm on Fridays for the duration of the module, with a short 15-minute break halfway through the session. Teaching was in blocks, which meant that modules ran successively rather than simultaneously. A two-week break ensued before the next module commenced. Students would be given the subject outline at the beginning of each module, which would include learning outcomes for the module, requirements for completing the module successfully, instructions regarding the module's assessment(s), and the marking matrix for the assessment(s).

Instructions were generally given early on in the module for assessments so that students had sufficient time to complete each assessment. Assessments were a core element in the structure of the course and were tailored specifically around the graduate attributes and the subject learning objectives. They were a key element in placing the students in situations which required them to live the graduate attributes and had to be quantifiable (assessable). For example, in time management, one of the assessments was structured around a planner that the student had to devise of a real working month in which she would demonstrate her ability to strategise, prioritise, and plan goals.

The methods of teaching depended on the content of the modules and included face-to-face lectures, small group work, practical demonstrations, interactive discussions, working with apps in the classroom, students demonstrating skills covered in the session through assessments, reflections, and student participation in accomplishing specific tasks.

Discussion

The fundamental purpose of beginning a home management course in Singapore was to strengthen individuals, families, and ultimately contribute to shaping society and culture. We saw the course as a means of addressing the reductive mindset in Singapore where the work in the home, because of a long history of paid, relatively cheap, and minimally qualified domestic help, and because of its own inherent nature (unpaid, unacknowledged, and with no formal channels of training to be officially recognised as a profession) has been seen to be menial, ideally delegated to others, and inferior to most other forms of work. The course was also seen to be able to offer a different paradigm for the primary role of children in the family in Singapore, which is currently largely driven by the pressured academic environment and the need to invest inordinate amounts of time to excel, or in some cases, just to keep abreast. Children, to the detriment of being formed holistically, are largely excused in such an environment from any role of service or responsibility in the family beyond studying to succeed. There is therefore a reductionist vision of a successful young adult, resulting in generations of young people who may academically excel, but who lack practical life skills and have missed opportunities to develop character strengths and virtues directed towards serving others.

Table 14.1 Summary of the Singapore home management course

Modules	*Time Management*	*Home Finance*	*Home Care & Maintenance*	*Textile Science*	*Beauty, Design, and Traditions*	*Kitchen Essentials*	*Dining and Entertainment*
No of participants	20	10	15	18	12	14	Pending
No of sessions (3 hrs)	4	3	5	5	4	8	3
No of assessments	2	1	2	2	2	3	2
No. of guest lecturers	2	4	5	4	4	9	3
Anthropology topic embedded	Femininity and identity (Class I and II) Social impact of the family	A brief examination of the philosophy of work	Service as a manifestation of humanity	Anthropological considerations of the work of the home (transcendence of the work of the home)	– Beauty of the person (visible and interior) – Beauty in nature and created things – Appreciating beauty	Professionalism and its role in the work of the home	The importance of family seen through relationships and family traditions
Venue type	Seminar room	Seminar room	Seminar room, car, home setting for assessments	Seminar room	Seminar room, home setting	Seminar room, demo kitchen	Home setting/ studio

The premise was that addressing this reductionist view of the work of the home could be achieved through offering a cohesive and professional approach to this work, which would raise awareness about the intrinsic dignity and value of this work, and its potential contributive effect within and beyond the boundaries of the home. We hoped to achieve this paradigm shift through a step-wise journey with the students who completed the course, firstly making them aware of the fruits of the work in the home done well; secondly giving them the skills to accomplish change within their own homes; thirdly helping them formulate for themselves ways to get their family members on board, and making it a joint family project; and, finally, being convinced of the value of what they do in the home because they are able to see for themselves the changes wrought in their homes and family by the effort they had put into the course.

The plethora of existing "do-it-yourself" and "how-to resources" freely available online and in short courses available in Singapore proved that just addressing the acquisition of knowledge and skills of performing tasks around the home alone would not be adequate in helping individuals develop a deeper understanding of the home environment, its impact on family, its contribution to society, and therefore its innate and deep value to individuals, family, and society. We needed to lead students to reflect on the deeper meaning and motivations for doing the work of the home well, and the derivation of its value and dignity. Hence, throughout the course, there were specific sessions which looked at the anthropology of the human person, work, and the home. Discussions and workshops were incorporated into all the modules to invite students to re-examine what home meant to them, and why the way they performed the work they did in the home mattered to them, their family, and to society.

Our premise that anthropology would be the component that would be most crucial in changing existing mindsets regarding the home was borne out by feedback which we gathered at the end of each module. There was a marked difference in the responses of students who only completed one or two modules, and therefore only small segments of anthropology, compared with those who completed the entire course of all seven modules and who would therefore have been exposed to the entire syllabus of anthropology. The students who had only completed one to two modules showed the least transformative effect in terms of their views regarding the work of the home, persisting with an acquisition mentality of specific skills. This was in contrast with the students who had completed the entire course. In a feedback interview, for example, in which the question was asked, "Has any of the content from the course made a difference to the way you manage aspects of your home?", one of them was able to list three broad areas where the course has made the most impact – making home management a family project, spending prudently, and introducing "Family Traditions" in the family as an on-going process as the children grow older. When asked about the contribution of the anthropological elements in the program, she responded:

> For the first time in my life, I was introduced to the "revolutionary" idea that homemaking is not only a profession like any other profession, with best

> practice methods, skill sets, and standards of excellence, but also an art where beauty and relationships are cultivated. It was a real eye opener. It helped me realize and understand my role in the home better.

With one out of five households in Singapore with live-in domestic help, an important component integrated into the programme was material adapted for the different nuanced needs of such households. This included fair management and appropriate delegation of duties to paid help, the importance of employers knowing how to perform the tasks of the home so that they can be better managers of their own homes, even if they don't, on a day-to-day basis, perform these tasks themselves, and the benefits and ways of involvement of family members through delegation of jobs in the home despite the presence of home help.

Taking into account the fast-paced lifestyle, time-poor facet, and the mentality of sparing children from all demands beyond academic of Singaporeans, course content was modified to include time-saving elements such as speed cleaning, managing time better, strategies of delegating tasks to family members, and communication skills. Through our feedback process, we were able to gather positive anecdotal evidence that transformative changes were possible even within a relatively short time frame with families being able to improve on the quality of family meals, family routines created which involved children helping out, and implementing new family traditions to strengthen ties, to name a few.

We judged the qualitative success of the course by whether our students were beginning to demonstrate the graduate attributes of the course as the course progressed. We found consistently, and consistent with anecdotal feedback from the Sydney programme, that those students who had persevered with completing all the modules successfully were able to demonstrate the most progress in their skill set and their understanding of the nature and potential of the work they do in the home and with their families. We did a feedback interview with these students and include quotes from them under the different graduate attributes.

A. Professionalism

When framed in the context of a question, "How has [the course] changed your perception of the work that is done in the home," some of our students replied:

> *Never knew there was so much work involved and needed so much brain power. Day-to-day operational leadership is required for the work done in the home.*
>
> *(EN)*

> *being a full-time homemaker was the last thing on my mind . . . I did not view being a homemaker as a profession as there is no pay cheque attached to the*

work, no professional body in this area with standards, professional exams unlike being a lawyer or an accountant. I thought homemaking was simply doing house chores which to me could be easily outsourced to a domestic helper. . . [The course] helped me appreciate the depth and richness of this profession called homemaking, and its pivotal role in the overall wellbeing of the family. I learnt that homemaking is a service to my family, not demeaning at all but a great tool to bring peace, order, joy, bonding in the family, as well as train the children with life skills, virtues formation, which are not taught anywhere but at home.

(CW)

B. Time management

Time management, as we saw with its popularity with our respondents in our market survey, was an issue which many struggled with. Some replies from our respondents:

I'm now in the habit of planning monthly, weekly and daily, it comes easily to my mind what is the goal to be achieved. I try to stop some time during the day to see what do [sic]I do, why and how. It helps me to think that I'm more in power [sic] with my life.

(PT)

[The calendar app taught in the time management module] made a big difference in allowing me to self-manage and plan ahead.

(CdC)

I manage my time by planning ahead. One of the things I wanted to do was to spend more time with my parents. I never found the time to do that. Through the time management module, I now go to my parents' place every Tuesdays and Fridays' and talk to them. No one is going to put a dollar value to this but its priceless to me.

(EN)

C. Identity

Identifying themselves as individuals who, through their work in the home, make valuable contributions to their family and society was problematic for most of the women beginning the course. Most admitted to describing themselves as "just housewives" or "just homemakers," even if they had been successful corporate managers, accountants, and other forms of professionals in their previous lives, who had made a conscious choice to devote more time to their families and had given up all or partly their paid professions.

From the small cohort of students who had completed all the modules to date:

> *I never saw myself as a homemaker, never thought I would enjoy being one or would have the ability to be a good one. . . . After stopping work outside, I was concerned about how my peers, friends and family would view me, "just a homemaker", the loss of a monthly income and financial independence, whether I would be bored. The fact is, I now feel so complete, so true to myself as a mother and as a woman, happy, thankful and fulfilled being a "professional homemaker", and not "just a homemaker". There is never a boring moment as there is so much to do, so much to learn and I am very happy being myself, for taking that leap of faith and choosing a path that unfortunately, is not so highly regarded or appreciated in this very competitive, grade-focused and materialistic society. I feel I can catch up on work outside if I really needed to, but I won't be able to catch up on my children's growing up years. I feel this is the time to be there for them, to see them grow from toddlers to teenagers, and it's now or never. In fact, I think if there is any job that is most important right now for me, it is taking care of my home. It is the job that I think I feel the proudest of right now compared to all my previous jobs. Seeing the joy and smiles of my family everyday, brings me the greatest joy which no amount of money can satisfy.*
>
> *(CW)*

> *I used to think I should provide for my children. [Homemaking] is so much more than putting a roof over their heads.*
>
> *(EN)*

> *I understand myself now as a key player in the family who is there for them.*
> *(CdC)*

D. Communication

A key goal was that the women became aware that managing their homes meant not just that they themselves could master the tasks around the home, but that they could transform the work of the home into a joint family project, involving the various members of the family in appropriate ways. Strategies were taught in various areas to include family members including the planning of household tasks, menu planning, and cultivating family traditions.

> *I find for major changes, holding a "family meeting" first, helps to communicate effectively to everyone about the changes that we would like to implement. E.g for the laundry workflow improvements we had a family meeting (including the helper) with a demonstration regarding how each of us was to sort their personal clothes before placing them in the laundry net (emptying*

the pockets, fastening the zip, turning all clothes inside out, sort by colour etc). At first, the boys were not consistent and their clothes were left unsorted for a few weeks. They would claim they were too busy with schoolwork. So, I calmly communicated to them that clothes that were not sorted would remain unwashed. This got them to try harder and make the effort to sort their clothes more consistently. For smaller things, such as handling knives to cut herbs or grater to grate carrots or cheese, it works just by demonstrating to them. My sons appreciate the fact that I don't talk down to them for their lack of experience or get annoyed easily or impatient as I used to in the past.

(CW)

Yes, I can work more effectively as a team leader and a team member of the family. The modules suggest to discuss with your family some tasks that could be implemented at home. This enabled the family to work as a team. Also, as a team leader, I need to organise the team and their contributions at home.

(PT)

E. Life-long learner

In this particular graduate attribute, a life-long learner was deemed to be qualitatively marked by developing problem-solving abilities, critical and creative thinking, a love and enjoyment of ideas, discoveries, and learning, and an ability to recognise and respond to the physical and psychological needs of one's self and others in the home.

The course has certainly broadened my mind. It has helped me to look at the work of the home more objectively, yet fulfilling. I now view each task as a project to be managed with systematic steps from beginning to end. E.g. applying the 3-step method for my monthly planner, the weekly menu planning requires many skills knowledge of nutrition, budget, consideration of taste and preferences of each member of the family, creativity (in terms of colour, texture), variety, introducing new dishes, sourcing of ingredients while staying within a budget, family holiday planning for our last June family holidays in Penang which worked out very well.

(CW)

My daughter is convinced the only reason why my head is so heavy is because it's full of ideas. Also, she is convinced there is no problem that I cannot solve. It is through good time management that I find out the issues that my kids face in school and the problems that my husband deals with at work. I calmly listen to them, give them my undivided attention and empathized [sic] them. Time management is an under-rated topic. Through good time management am I able to be the pillar of strength for my family.

(EN)

F. Impacting the family and the impacts on the family

Although "impacting the family" was not a specific graduate attribute, it was a desired outcome and it was useful to reflect on the success of it through notable impacts on the family.

> *I now include the rest of the family, delegate tasks, schedule "family meetings", to discuss and agree on action plans where everyone is involved. With more hands, the work is lighter, done much faster, less overwhelming for me, and the family gets to spend time together. Investing time to train my sons (10 & 13) is worth it, as they are now able to do many chores around the house, are involved in the running of the home, are more responsible and independent . . . . As a person, I have become more peaceful, calmer and confident as a Home Manager. The home has less clutter, is neat, feels more spacious and there is order in the different workflows. This sense of peace has had ripple effects to those around me, namely, my husband, children and the helper. There are more smiling faces, joy in the house. My sons told me that they have noticed that I do not raise my voice so often, while my husband noticed that I look happier, that our helper of ten years, looks happier too and more peaceful in the way she does her work. Our family has grown closer too . . . It is a place where we are all happy to come back to every day and even after a long holiday overseas, there is nothing like home.*
>
> *(CW)*

> *My family is eating better. More "real food" and less hormone injected meats. We eat as a family on the dining table and not feed the kids in front of the TV.*
>
> *I also changed the telco for a better rate and cancelled the club membership that I had for many years and hardly used.*
>
> *I am less stressed now, more in control. I realise this impacts everyone – when I am less stressed. I have learnt to delegate jobs to the older kids which previously I had not thought them capable of. But you know, they are!*
>
> *One of the most useful things I implement now is the family meetings which we have once a month. This is where the whole family comes together and we plan what we want to do over the next few weeks and we talk about what is working and what is not.*
>
> *(CdC)*

The course in Singapore is a work in progress. This first run of modules has been a much-needed pilot programme in which material has been trialled, feedback and suggestions garnered, and reflection by the coordinators and teachers collated.

In conclusion, beginning a home management course to try and change mindsets about the value and dignity of the work of the home was always an ambitious project. Its beginnings in Singapore are humble, a mere ripple in a big pond of indifference and ignorance regarding the intrinsic nature of the work in the home and its vast potential to be transformative. The amount of work that is needed with, at this stage, little remuneration, is intensive, especially in its first run through of customised material, but for those of us who have retained faith in the programme, it is because the vision of this course makes it worthwhile: that when the work of the home is done well, firstly, it is a living example of service for others and all that is accomplished through putting the good of others first, and is a much more resonant testimony to teaching the next generation about service than any lecture or other medium of communication. Secondly, by understanding the deeper motivations of the work in the home, this work becomes elevated into an act of love that cumulatively transforms a series of house chores and a living space into a home that nurtures, supports, and strengthens the family. And lastly, our faith in the programme is linked to its capacity to assist women (and later we hope men), through the work in the home, to form and educate the next generation in the important virtues and life skills, lessons which are learnt best in the cradle of the family, the home, and the bedrock of society. We believe that just as the work of the home, when done well, improves society and culture through the flow-down effect of well-formed and happy individuals, nurtured at home, going out into the world and creating their own ripple effect in all the myriad walks of life they thread, similarly, this programme will continue to make incremental steps towards changing society for the better if it continues to pass on to others the vision and the capability of working well within the home and through this work, enriching the lives of all within the family, and ultimately society. To end on the words of Carmen Pavia, who has played such a pivotal role in creating this programme:

> It is through service that we learn to recognise humanity in loved ones and strangers alike. Service becomes a bridge; joining our internal family to our external family, broadening our concept of self to become externally facing, further emphasising the virtue of service; to cease only serving our own cause and to adopt as our own, through service, the cause of humanity.
>
> (Pavia, 2014)

References

Au-Yong, R., 2016. *The Straits Times*. [Online] Available at: https://www.straitstimes.com/singapore/more-maids-foreign-family-members-of-citizens-in-singapore [Accessed 12 August 2018].

Department of Statistics, Singapore, 2016. Population Trends 2015. [Online] Available at: www.singstat.gov.sg/publications/publications-and-papers/population-and-population-structure/population-trends [Accessed 26 August 2017].

Department of Statistics, Singapore, 2017. Department of Statistics, Singapore. [Online] Available at: www.singstat.gov.sg/statistics/latest-data#22 [Accessed 9 September 2017].

Evans, A., 2016. *Press Release | Singapore's work-life balance improving – Increased flexibility is having a positive impact while overtime is highly productive*, Singapore: Morgan McKinley.

Kenvale College of Hospitality, Cookery and Events, n.d. Home Management. [Online] Available at: http://kenvale.edu.au/students/courses/home-management/.

Matthews, M., 2015. *The changing Singapore family*, Singapore: Institute of Policy Studies.

Ministry of Manpower, 2017. Summary Table: Hours Worked. [Online] Available at: http://stats.mom.gov.sg/Pages/Hours-Worked-Summary-Table.aspx [Accessed 23 August 2017].

Ministry of Manpower, 2018. *Foreign workforce numbers*. [Online] Available at: https://www.mom.gov.sg/documents-and-publications/foreign-workforce-numbers [Accessed 12 August 2018].

MSF, 2013. *Family and work*, Singapore: Ministry of Social and Family Development.

OECD, 2010. *Singapore: Rapid improvement followed by strong performance*, Paris: OECD.

OECD, 2016. Singapore Tops Latest OECD PISA Global Education Survey. [Online] Available at: www.oecd.org/pisa/ [Accessed 26 September 2017].

Pavia, C., 2014. Protecting the family: Building the home. *AD 2000*, 27. https://www.ad2000.com.au/protecting_the_family_building_the_home_february_2014.html.

Quah, E., 2018. *The Value of Unpaid Housework*. [Online] Available at: https://www.straitstimes.com/opinion/the-value-of-unpaid-housework [Accessed 12 August 2018].

SPH Publishing, 2016. 7 in 10 Parents Send their Children for Tuition: ST Poll. [Online] Available at: www.straitstimes.com/singapore/education/7-in-10-parents-send-their-children-for-tuition-st-poll [Accessed 26 September 2017].

Tan, T., 2015. More Women in Singapore are Staying Childless. [Online] Available at: www.straitstimes.com/singapore/more-women-are-staying-childless.

Index

Note: Italicized page numbers indicate a figure on the corresponding page. Page numbers in bold indicate a table on the corresponding page.

Made in the USA
Las Vegas, NV
19 September 2026

79b6db07-a3a4-4331-b8e3-ccb7beb61c6bR01